MW00810641

'It is a book that any future leader of Pakistan ought to have by their bedside, simply because it is the sum of all that has gone before.'
—*Mehr F. Husain*, author and columnist in *Dawn*, Karachi

'If there is a template of how not to rule Pakistan, Tilak Devasher's latest book would offer him [Imran Khan] a useful guide.'
—*C. P. Bhambhri*, author and scholar in *Business Standard*

'Tilak Devasher's second book, *Pakistan At the Helm*, is as good a read, and as instructive, as his first—*Pakistan: Courting the Abyss*.... This book will give pleasure and insights to all kinds of readers.'
—*Ambassador Vivek Katju*, former secretary, Ministry of External Affairs in The Wire

'The book is a series of speed biographies of each of Pakistan's leaders, from M.A. Jinnah to Pervez Musharraf and Nawaz Sharif and everyone in between, told through such entertaining nuggets about them.'
—*Nirupama Subramanian*, resident editor, *The Indian Express*

'[This] is an utterly compelling book that takes the reader down the tumultuous, often hilarious and ultimately tragic life and times of the diverse men and woman who have ruled Pakistan since 1947 ... a joy to read...'
—*Indranil Banerjie*, security and political risk consultant in *The Asian Age*

Praise for Pakistan: *Courting the Abyss*

'… easily the best book on Pakistan.'
—*Khaled Ahmed*, consulting editor, *Newsweek* Pakistan

'This book explains how and why Pakistan often finds itself on the brink. Devasher writes with empathy and his book is full of facts that cannot be ignored by Pakistanis or the rest of the world.'
—*Husain Haqqani*, author and former Pakistan ambassador to the US

'[Devasher] unpacks Pakistan with an empathy and familiarity that many Indian authors on the subject have so far failed to bring.'
—*Suhasini Haider*, diplomatic affairs editor, *The Hindu*

'There is no hostility in Devasher's must-read book for those who objectively wish to understand both the long-term challenges of Pakistan as well as the way forward.'
—*Aparna Pande*, director, India Initiative, Hudson Institute

'Devasher's book is one of the very few books written with great depth of information and analysis … a must-read for anyone who wants to understand Pakistan.'
—*Satish Kumar*, director, Foundation for National Security Research, former professor of diplomacy, JNU

'… there are few books by Indian authors that have sought to interpret the prodigal neighbour in a holistic, informed and empathetic manner. Tilak Devasher is the exception to this norm'
—*C. Uday Bhaskar*, director, Society for Policy Studies, New Delhi

'For any study of Pakistan and for anyone formulating India's policy with respect to Pakistan, this book is a must-read.'
—*Lt Gen. J.S. Bajwa*, in *Indian Defence Review*

PAKISTAN
THE BALOCHISTAN
CONUNDRUM

TILAK DEVASHER

ICWA

HarperCollins *Publishers* India

First published in India in 2019 by
HarperCollins *Publishers* India

Building 10, Tower A, 4th Floor, DLF Cyber City, Phase II,
Gurugram Haryana- 122002, India

www.harpercollins.co.in

This book is published in association with the Indian Council of World Affairs
(ICWA), Sapru House, Barakhamba Road, New Delhi 110001

2 4 6 8 10 9 7 5 3 1

P-ISBN: 978-93-5357-070-5
E-ISBN: 978-93-5357-071-2

Typeset in 10.5/14.2 Berling LT Std at
Manipal Digital Systems, Manipal

Printed and bound at
MicroPrints India, New Delhi

To

THE BALOCH

Who deserve better

Mujhe jang-e-azaadi ka maza maloom hai,
Balochon per zulm ki intheha maloom hai,
Mujhe zindagi bhar Pakistan mein jeenay ki dua na do,
Mujhe Pakistan me in saath saal jeenay ki saza maloom hai.
—Habib Jalib

(Rough translation)
I know the pleasure of the war of independence;
I know the heights of oppression inflicted on the Baloch;
Don't pray that I should live my entire life in Pakistan;
I know the punishment of living in Pakistan for sixty years.

Contents

IV: CHINESE GAMBIT

V: RELENTLESS PERSECUTION

VI: ENDURING INSURRECTION

Balochistan at a Glance

Overview:

The largest province of Pakistan created in July 1970.

Area:

3,47,190 sq. km; 44 per cent of land area of Pakistan.

Population:

Pakistan 2017: 207.685 million; 1998: 132.352 million. Growth: 2.4 per cent.
Balochistan 2017: 12.335 million; 1998: 6.567 million. Growth: 3.37 per cent.
Overall, 5.94 per cent of Pakistan's population in 2017 as compared to 4.96 per cent in 1998.

Male: 6.4 million; Female: 5.8 million.
Population Density: 19 per sq. km
Literacy Rate: Pakistan: 58.92 per cent; Balochistan: 43.58 per cent

The Division-wise area/population[1]:

Division	Area (sq. km)	Population (1998)	Districts
Quetta	64,310	1,699,957	Quetta, Pishin, Qila Abdullah, Chagai, Nushki.
Zhob	46,200	1,003,851	Zhob, Musakhail, Qila Saifullah, Loralai, Barkhan, Sherani.
Kalat	140,612	1,457,722	Kalat, Mastung, Khuzdar, Kharan, Washuk, Awaran, Lasbela.
Sibi	270,55	4,94,894	Sibi, Ziarat, Dera Bugti, Kohlu, Harnai
Nasirabad	16,946	1,076,708	Nasirabad, Jaffarabad, Jhal Magsi Kachi.
Makran	52,067	832,753	Kech, Panjgur, Gwadar

Social Indicators[2]

Indicators	Balochistan	Pakistan
Female Literacy	15%	33%
Primary School Enrolment	49%	68.3%
Female Participation	21%	49.2%
Access to Sanitation	7%	18%
Infant Mortality Rate (per 000'LB)	108	100
Village Electrification	25%	75%
Access to Safe Drinking Water	20%	86%

List of maps and tables

Maps

Tables

xiv

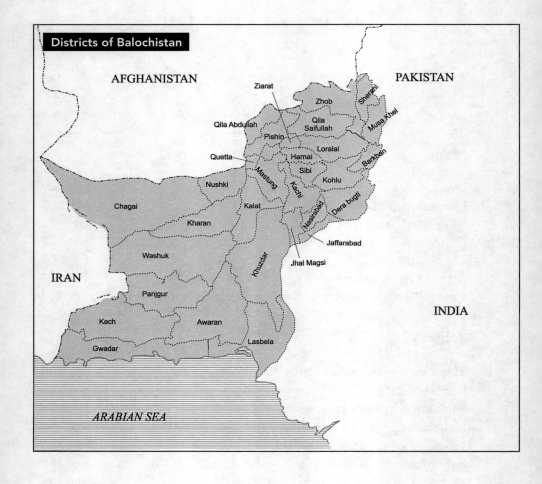

Districts of Balochistan

Preface

WHILE RESEARCHING FOR MY FIRST book, *Pakistan: Courting the Abyss*, I came across two laments about Balochistan that moved me deeply. The first was the anguished cry of a father at the 'enforced disappearance', i.e., extra-judicial abduction, of his son:

> I am tired of speaking, of crying, of telling our story again and again. If only suicide was not prohibited by religion, I would have killed myself. The court has been hearing our case for years but my son is still not with me.[1]

The second was the lament of a young student:

> What concerns me most is a word. It is a simple word that is not heard on the lips of people in most parts of the world, but for me it is a word that desperately needs to be heard more often. Whenever I do hear this word, or say it myself, it stirs emotions that I cannot explain. I cannot do justice to the memories they evoke.

> That word is *Balochistan*.

> We pleaded and knocked on every door there is in the name of justice. Yet, no one heard us. What have we received from the people of Pakistan except neglect and torment?[2]

The pain and pathos in these two laments motivated me to study Balochistan in all its dimensions and to try and lift the veil of secrecy that Pakistan has imposed on the province. The result is this book.

Balochistan is a complex province with two main ethnic groups—the Baloch and Pashtuns. The book is focused on the Baloch and touches on the Pashtuns only in passing.

The words 'Baloch' and 'Balochistan' have been spelt in several ways over the years—Baloch, Baluch, Belooch, Biloch, etc. In this book, the words used are 'Baloch' and 'Balochistan' after the 1990 provincial government decree that the official English spelling was to be 'Baloch'. The plural of Baloch is also Baloch. The language is spelled as Balochi.

A word about statistics. Unfortunately, no two sets of statistics on the same issue match. Hence, I have tried to use the best available and, at places, have also given variations to enable the reader to make an informed judgement.

At the time of writing, the detailed results of the 2017 census have not been published. Hence, where available, the provisional census figures have been used. In other cases, figures from the 1998 census have been used.

———•———

I would like to thank the Indian Council of World Affairs (ICWA) for commissioning this book. My special thanks to Ambassador Nalin Suri, the former Director General of ICWA, for encouraging and supporting me in the writing of the book.

My thanks to my wife and children for being pillars of strength in all my writing endeavours. My thanks also to my editors Udayan Mitra and Antony Thomas at HarperCollins India for all their effort in bringing out this book.

Despite the support, all the shortcomings and errors in this book are mine.

Introduction

Life is still in the grip of chilling poverty and deprivation. The first crescent is yet to be visible and children are yet to learn to pick flowers. Flowers may lose fragrance but at least not lose petals.
Balochistan is distinct from rest of Pakistan not only geographically but also in its sufferings and the treatment meted out to it ...
No one wants to be aware of suffocation of people in Balochistan ...
This is the fateful hour for Balochistan ...
The discontent due to hatred and alienation and lack of voice in own affairs nurtured miseries and expropriation. Mistrust and hatred spreads and grows in evil soil of poverty and strife. These reach their full growth when the hope of a people for a better life is dead. The hope should be kept alive. Investment is needed for happiness and living of people struggling against overwhelming odds since long.
No remorse can mend a heart deprived of love. The truth exists, and ultimately comes out.

THE ABOVE WORDS ARE NOT written by a Baloch separatist or a journalist sympathetic to Baloch national aspirations or even by a human rights activist recounting the tragedy that Balochistan faces due to the suppression of its people by the Pakistani state. These words, surprisingly, are part of the Executive Summary of the White Paper for the Budget 2015-16 prepared by the Finance Department of the Government of Balochistan.[1]

These words poignantly encapsulate the tragedy of Balochistan and articulate Pakistan's enduring Balochistan conundrum. The fact that the provincial government of Balochistan (2013–18), in which the then ruling party at the federal level—the Pakistan Muslim League-Nawaz (PML-N)—was a coalition partner, was moved to express such sentiments in the budget documents shows how widespread the disaffection with Pakistan is in Balochistan.

Balochistan presents a mosaic of conflicts and fault lines with multiple layers of violence. These range from those between the Baloch nationalists and the state; inter- and intra-tribal feuds and clashes to ethnic divisions, sectarian clashes and terror strikes. During the last decade, the most ominous development has been the sickening frequency with which people have gone missing and how their tortured bodies have started turning up after some time. This is proof that the constitutional right to life and freedom from arbitrary detention are violated with impunity. These multiple conflicts have facilitated criminal elements and groups to mushroom in the province.

As a result, kidnapping for ransom has become part of the prevalent terror. Add to this the smuggling of drugs and weapons from Afghanistan—via the porous border and through the coastal region of Balochistan—as well as human trafficking,[2] and the complex nature of the province can well be understood. Not surprisingly, Balochistan, even seventy years after the creation of Pakistan, has been described as 'an edgy place',[3] 'a boiling cauldron of ethnic, sectarian, secessionist and militant violence, threatening to boil over at any time.'[4] The Human Rights Commission of Pakistan (HRCP) likened the situation in the province to 'an active volcano that may erupt anytime with dire consequences. The situation is alarming and worsening by the day.'[5]

The moot question is, why is Balochistan a lingering problem, a festering sore for Pakistan? The short answer is that, of the various conflicts, the most enduring and bitter one has been between the Baloch nationalists and the state, which has been continuing in some form or the other ever since the forced accession of the princely state of Kalat (as most of Balochistan was then called) to Pakistan in 1948. The Pakistan state has accentuated the conflict by treating the province as a colony, to be used to extract its resources without ploughing much back to improve the living conditions of the local people.

In its essentials, this conflict is between two mutually opposing narratives: that of the Pakistan state and that of the Baloch nationalists. The state narrative has its roots in the movement that led to the creation of Pakistan. Mohammad Ali Jinnah's (henceforth Jinnah) argument for Pakistan was built on the ideological edifice of Islam providing the glue for a nation. In his presidential address to the open session of the Muslim League in Lahore on 22 March 1940, Jinnah said: 'The Mussalmans are not a minority. The Mussalmans are a nation by any definition ... and they must have their homelands, their territory, and their state.'[6]

Such an argument, however, was contrary to what Islam preached, as had been pointed out by Maulana Abul Kalam Azad, a senior leader of the Congress party, in an interview: 'It [Pakistan] is being demanded in the name of Islam.... Division of territories on the basis of religion is a contraption devised by Muslim League. They can pursue it as their political agenda, but it finds no sanction in Islam or Quran.... Strictly speaking, Muslims in India are not one community; they are divided among many well-entrenched sects. You can unite them by arousing their anti-Hindu sentiment but you cannot unite them in the name of Islam. To them Islam means undiluted loyalty to their own sect.'[7] Not surprisingly, Islamic scholars like Maulana Abul A'la Maududi, the founder of the Jamaat-e-Islami (JI), opposed the creation of Pakistan since it was claimed in the name of Islam.

In the Muslim majority provinces of the north-west and east of India, Islam was not the salient identity. Hence, Jinnah's vision that Islam would provide the glue for the divergent nationalities that came to constitute Pakistan came a cropper. Here, with the population being overwhelmingly Muslim, Islam was never in danger. Such a slogan made political sense in the Muslim minority provinces like the United Provinces (UP) and the Central Provinces (CP) where there was resentment among the Muslim elite at having lost power to the British, and the fear of being swamped by the numerically larger Hindu population under a representative government. Islam had become the salient identity for the minority population in these provinces. By trying to transfer the fears of the Muslims in the minority provinces on to the Muslim majority provinces, where the Baloch (together with Bengali, Pashtun, Punjabi and Sindhi) ethnic identity was the salient one, Pakistan started on shaky foundations.

Additionally, during the Pakistan Movement, Jinnah had argued strongly for a weak Centre and strong provinces. His break with Jawaharlal Nehru was precisely on this point, since the Indian National Congress under the leadership Nehru wanted a strong Centre. In fact, greater autonomy for the provinces was part of Jinnah's famous fourteen-point demands of 1929. This, however, was a tactic to ensure the support of the Muslim majority provinces where the Muslim League was weak or non-existent. After Pakistan was created, Jinnah changed tracks overnight and ensured that Pakistan became a unitary state even though the 23 March 1940 Lahore Resolution had originally talked of 'constituent units' that would be 'autonomous and sovereign'. Thus, the Baloch, together with the Sindhis and Pashtuns, were not allowed autonomy or delegated the powers to govern themselves—a promise that Jinnah had made in the run up to the creation of Pakistan.

Just as Jinnah dismissed provincial autonomy after Pakistan was created, so too did his successors, civilian and military. Since 1947, the effort of every government, especially of the military, has been to trample on provincial rights and autonomy and to impose the Central government's authority in Pakistan in the quest of creating a 'strong and unified' Pakistan. It has been argued that the highly centralized state of Pakistan and its unwillingness to allow regional autonomy has been one of the key factors that led to the nationalist forces repeatedly launching a guerrilla war against the state.[8] Gen. Zia-ul-Haq, for example, said that he would 'ideally like to break up the existing provinces and replace them with fifty-three smaller provinces, erasing ethnic identities from the map of Pakistan altogether.'[9]

Instead of understanding the real reasons for the secession of East Pakistan to form Bangladesh in 1971, the catastrophe reinforced the feeling that provincialism and provincial autonomy would lead to further dismemberment of the state. Hence, any form of provincial rights or nationalist movements was anathema and the military was used to crush such movements. As history shows, identity issues, problems of nationalism and ethic aspirations are rarely resolved with military force alone. In 1974, Zulfikar Ali Bhutto held that regionalism or provincialism, connoting the pre-eminence of narrow, parochial loyalties, vis-à-vis the nation-state of Pakistan, would lead to catastrophe.[10] In 1977, President Zia expressed similar sentiments when he met the Baloch leaders in jail. During the meeting, Zia told them that 'we are all Muslims, and we should not say that we are Baloch or Pashtuns'. The Baloch leader Mir Ghaus Bakhsh Bizenjo replied that 'we are Baloch and Pashtuns and we will never make a viable Pakistan except on that foundation'.[11]

The efforts to create a centralized state included policies like 'One Unit', 'Basic Democracies', merging the Pashtun areas (the old British Balochistan plus some Baloch areas) into Balochistan in 1970, etc. Implemented in 1955, the 'One Unit', for example, created a single provincial entity that subsumed all the provinces of West Pakistan as a counter to East Pakistan, which was numerically superior to other Pakistani provinces.

While One Unit failed to establish a Pakistani identity amongst its disparate minorities; it had the effect of further alienating the smaller ethnic groups. In reality, the efforts at creating a centralized state have had the opposite effect of heightening alienation among Baloch nationalists and fuelling the national movement. As Selig Harrison, an authority on Baloch nationalism, notes: 'Dominated by Punjabi military and bureaucratic elites, a succession of authoritarian Pakistani regimes has identified their interests with the preservation of a unitary state and have thus resisted pressures for democratic government that have been linked, inseparably, with demands for provincial self-rule.'[12] In the process, Pakistan lost East Pakistan that became Bangladesh. In Balochistan, Bhutto dismissed the government of Sardar Attaullah Mengal in 1973 precisely because it was articulating provincial rights. Thus, the Baloch demand for provincial rights was consistently denied by the state of Pakistan.

Two reasons account for the failure to forge a common national identity using Islam and centralization. One, none of the provinces that became West Pakistan were in the forefront of the Pakistan Movement and neither did the Muslim League have a significant presence here. In fact, there was no Muslim League presence in the Baloch areas and no Baloch attended the 1940 Lahore session of the Muslim league.[13] Two, centralization could not replace the centuries-old ethno-nationalism of the people of the various provinces of Pakistan. All the provinces had separate histories, cultures, languages, etc. Islam in the area was a common bond but given the overwhelming majority of Muslims, it was not the only important identity. Not surprisingly, the creation of a state based primarily on an Islamic identity led to a host of issues, especially when faced with a people like the Baloch whose tribal traditions were of a more secular nature. As Abdul Hayee Baloch, a Baloch political leader, put it: 'The establishment has never accepted the fact that Pakistan is a multi-nation country. Pakistan came into existence in 1947, but Balochs, Pathans, Sindhis, Punjabis and Seraikis have been here for centuries. They have their own cultures and languages.'[14]

Such feelings required deft and sophisticated handling, traits that the leaders of Pakistan severely lacked and continue to lack. Even though East Pakistan broke away to become Bangladesh precisely because for the people of East Pakistan, language was more important a marker of identity than religion, Pakistan continues to persist with an Islam-based centralization policy. For the Baloch, their national identity emphasizes their centuries-old culture and their specific territorial presence rather than Islam—at least not the kind being propagated in Pakistan. The Baloch were, thus, at cross-purposes with the very idea of an Islam-based Pakistan. The Pakistan state failed to understand this in 1947 and it has consistently failed to understand this till now.

———•———

The Baloch narrative hinges on the indelible historical memories of being independent and the injustices the people feel that they have undergone since they were forced to accede to Pakistan. Earlier, in the nineteenth century during British rule, decisions of the boundary commissions had altered the historic boundaries of the state between the British Empire, Persia and Afghanistan.[15] Despite this, there was a rump Baloch nation represented by the princely state of Kalat that declared independence in August 1947 after the British left the subcontinent. Many Baloch believed and continue to believe that the forced accession of the Kalat state to Pakistan in March 1948 snuffed out their identity. The basic Baloch position is that the Khanate of Kalat was never a part of India. The British violated solemn treaty arrangements by treating it as an Indian state just prior to their departure and Pakistan was guilty of forcing its accession. This is an issue that resonates even today and is perhaps the single, most important, reason why the Baloch have not reconciled to being part of Pakistan.

Post accession, the alienation of the Baloch was aggravated due to the treatment meted out to them that has resulted in systematic economic exploitation and discrimination. This was coupled with the perception that their Baloch identity was being further sacrificed at the altar of a common Pakistani identity. The feeling has grown that the federal government, dominated by Punjab, was discriminating against them and was 'colonizing' their province by exploiting their vast natural resources. This feeling of alienation has been further stoked by recent developments: the continuing military operations in the province with its offshoots of enforced disappearances and kill-and-dump policies; the exclusion of the Baloch in decisions pertaining to mega projects like the China–Pakistan Economic Corridor (CPEC) and development of the Gwadar port; the fear of being turned into a minority in their own province and so on.

As a result, when the Baloch compares himself with his counterparts in other provinces, especially Punjab, he asks, rightly, what has he gained from being a part of Pakistan? What Prince Abdul Karim wrote in 1948 from exile in Afghanistan to his brother the Khan of Kalat, Mir Ahmad Yar Khan, seems as if it could have been written in 2019: '... the Pakistan people are not only more aggressive than the British, but they are also in the habit of biting off their own friends... From whatever angle we look at the present government of Pakistan, we will see nothing but Punjabi fascism. The people have no say in it. It is the Army and arms that rule... There is no place for any other community in this government, be it the Baluch, the Sindhis, the Afghans or the Bengalis ... total Punjabi Fascism rules supreme everywhere.'[16] Six decades later, Nawab Khair Bakhsh Marri was to echo similar sentiments when he said in an interview: 'We cannot live with the Punjabis. There is no room for compromise in my book. We have to get rid of them.'[17]

All this has bred a feeling that Balochistan is not an equal partner in Pakistan. Way back in 2003, a team of the Human Rights Commission of Pakistan, '... noticed discontent almost everywhere in Balochistan because of the widely shared perception of the people's exclusion from public affairs. They felt deprived and ignored.'[18] In 2009, the HRCP reported that a section of the Baloch had concluded that they were being viewed as enemies of the state: 'They feel abandoned by the people as well as political forces in the rest of the country.

There is a sense of isolation, rejection and dejection.'[19] It cautioned that the '… sense of deprivation and suppression is deep rooted in Baloch nationalist identity; the establishment's failure to negotiate and compensate further isolates a population that has long put up with armed and aggressive tactics to curb the struggle for their rights'. For the Baloch, this, together with socio-economic disparities and lack of provincial autonomy, has made the conflict essentially one over identity—to preserve their culture, language and ultimately all that it means to be a Baloch.[20]

The mega projects being implemented with the assistance of China (Gwadar port and the CPEC) have exacerbated Baloch grievances. With China investing upwards of $60 billion in various projects and the port of Gwadar in Balochistan being the outlet, the strategic importance of Balochistan has increased phenomenally. This, in turn, has changed the dynamics between Islamabad and Quetta. It is this changed dynamics that has increased the ferocity of the crackdown on the Baloch while they apprehend becoming a minority in their own land.

The Baloch are not per se opposed to such massive projects like the development of Gwadar as a major port. What they object to is that they have not been consulted; and they believe, based on earlier such projects, that jobs and benefits would go to the dominant Punjabis. Already, there has been an influx of workers from outside the province into Gwadar and they have been buying up local land. The Baloch see this as clinching evidence of outsiders, especially the Punjabis, getting rich at their expense.

———◆———

Balochistan also suffers from many missed opportunities on the one hand and outright deceptions on the other. In 1950 and again in 1960, Sardar Abdul Karim and Sardar Nauroz Khan respectively were duped into giving up arms and surrendering to the government on solemn promises, sworn on the Koran, of safe passage. Instead, they were tried in military courts. While both got long prison sentences, the son and six other companions of Nauroz Khan were hanged. In 1973, Zulfikar Ali Bhutto promised provincial autonomy as a quid pro quo for Baloch support for a consensus constitution. But having got that, he dismissed the government of Sardar Attaullah Mengal in Balochistan that led to a four-year insurgency. In 2000, negotiations began with a reluctant Marri scion Hyrbyair Marri in London but his demands were dismissed. In 2001, Musharraf called off talks with Akbar Bugti at the last minute just as the latter was about to board a special plane that had been sent for him. In 2005, the recommendation of a multi-party parliamentary committee on Balochistan was shelved. The then US ambassador Ryan Crocker told the chairman of the committee, Mushahid Hussain, 'Senator, had your report been implemented, the situation in Balochistan would have been restored to normalcy.'[21]

Balochistan's share of the national GDP had dropped from 4.9 per cent in the mid-1970s to less than 3 per cent in 2000. The province has the highest infant and maternal mortality rates, the highest poverty rate and the lowest literacy rate in Pakistan. Within Balochistan, 'an average Baloch is twice as poor as an average Punjabi, Pashtun, or Hazara resident of the province.' Even in Quetta, the capital, only a third of the households are connected to the government water supply system and receive water for about one or two hours a day.[22]

Summing up the feeling of relative deprivation, *Jabal*, the official organ of the Baloch People's Liberation Front, had stated way back in July 1977: 'In Islamabad's calculations, Balochistan is a vast estate for plunder, an arid desert floating on oil and minerals. A large part of their political strategy is dictated by the desire to extract this treasure for the benefit of the Pakistani bureaucratic bourgeoisie and foreign imperialist interests.... The Pakistani oligarchy needs Balochistan's oil and minerals to overcome the severe economic crisis gripping the whole country.'[23] The situation is no different four decades later.

————•————

The federal government has often tried to co-opt the Baloch with developmental projects, but none of them have achieved any measure of success. The reason for this was well articulated by Nawab Khair Bakhsh Marri. According to him, the Baloch wanted 'to modernize and to develop in ways and at a speed that we think makes sense under our conditions... But they [Punjabis] don't want us to carry out modernization under our own control. They want to modernize us in their own way, without listening to us.' Most of the roads built in Balochistan, he declared, were 'not for our benefit but to make it easier for the military to control us and for the Punjabis to rob us. The issue is not whether to develop, but whether to develop with or without autonomy. Exploitation has now adopted the name of development.'[24]

As Baloch journalist Malik Siraj Akbar puts it, 'development' itself has different meanings for the Baloch and the federal government. For the Baloch, development is linked with the creation of employment opportunities and consequent improvement in their standard of living. For Pakistan, development means obtaining Balochistan's mineral wealth and expediting the development of the Gwadar port and the CPEC.[25] If the only way to do this is to consolidate its military presence and cause demographic imbalance vis-à-vis the Baloch people, then so be it. What Pakistani leadership has not appreciated is that by depriving the Baloch of the fruits of their resources, the long-term success of either development or of foreign investment would be doubtful.

The Central government argues that a few 'miscreants', i.e., a small number of tribal sardars, are creating trouble, are misleading the Baloch in order to maintain their privileges and grip on power and derailing the Central government's effort to modernize and develop Balochistan. What the government has not been able to explain convincingly is why have so many Baloch, especially in the non-tribal areas like the Makran coast, taken up arms against the Central government, if it is only the sardars fighting for their privileges. Clearly, the message of the tribal chiefs resonates with the Baloch population motivating them to pick up arms, while the message of the Central government does not. The government does not seem to have understood that the people treated social and political issues separately. They opposed the domination of the sardars but supported the same sardars in political matters. That was why they blamed Islamabad and not the sardars for their deprivation.[26]

In reality, the situation is not due to a few 'miscreants' but is a complex combination of political memories of past injustices, betrayals inflicted on the Baloch, the economic neglect of the province and exploitation of its resources by Punjabi 'colonialists' for their own benefit, and now the fear of being converted into a minority due to the development of the Gwadar port and CPEC. The conflict is thus centred on a deep-seated belief among many Baloch that they should be masters of their own destiny. The Punjabi-dominated federal government, however, disputes such assertions. As Selig Harrison puts it: 'To the Punjabis, who make up 58 per cent of the population, it is unthinkable that a Baloch minority of less than 4 per cent [6 per cent now] should have special claims to Baluchistan, which represents 42 per cent [44 per cent actually] of the land area of the country.'[27] Consequently, positions have hardened on both sides.

The federal government did take several initiatives from 2008 onwards to structurally address issues of marginalization of Balochistan. These included the Eighteenth Amendment to the Constitution, the seventh National Finance Commission (NFC) Award, the *Aghaz-e-Haqooq* Balochistan package, the *Pur Aman* Balochistan package (details in the chapter on state response), and so on. These, on paper, granted financial, political and administrative autonomy to Balochistan and other provinces. However, the government has not been able to reap the fruits of these initiatives, and unrest and insurgency in Balochistan has continued. To believe that such 'packages' would win over the Baloch—with ongoing enforced disappearances and extra-judicial killings of Baloch political workers by the security forces—was naive.

———•———

What do the Baloch want? At one end of the spectrum are separatists like Brahamdagh Bugti, grandson of the slain Baloch leader Akbar Bugti, who says that the Baloch tribesmen are fighting not only to demonstrate their displeasure but to make it abundantly clear to the Central government that they 'should leave our homeland'.[28] Today, such an assertion carries more weight than at any other time. Though the four previous insurgencies in 1948, 1958, 1962 and 1973–77 were confined to tribal pockets, they transformed the Baloch tribal society into a nascent nation. The current insurgency has crossed the tribal barrier. It has now acquired grass-root support and acquired a momentum of its own that has enabled it to survive over the last decade and a half.

At the other end of the spectrum are Baloch politicians who are opposed to violence and separation from Pakistan. They would be

happy with greater provincial autonomy and control over their affairs—
economic, political, social and cultural. They too articulate resentment
at the way Balochistan has been exploited.

————◦————

The violence and brutality of the state has escalated to a higher level
ever since the outbreak of the current phase of insurgency that began
in the first decade of this millennium. This is evident in the increased
targeting of middle-class activists who have come to form the backbone
of the movement. A large number of them have been subjected to
'enforced disappearance' or have gone 'missing', only to turn up later
as bodies riddled with bullets and bearing torture marks. The issue of
enforced disappearance is clearly the most horrifying aspect of the
situation in Balochistan. Thousands of Baloch political activists have
gone missing, while hundreds of them have been killed and dumped
across Balochistan in kill-and-dump operations. The Supreme Court of
Pakistan is on record that intelligence agencies and security forces have
been involved in these extra-judicial arrests and killings. However, the
judiciary has not been able to implement remedial action.

In addition to the above complexities, Sunni extremists, led by the
Lashkar-e-Jhangvi (LeJ), have been on a killing spree, targeting hundreds
of Shia Muslims, most of whom ethnic Hazaras. It is widely believed
that the LeJ is covertly supported by elements within the Pakistani
security establishment.

The conflict between the Baloch armed groups and the state has
also led to the former killing unarmed Punjabi civilians—university
professors, schoolteachers, journalists and labourers—as a part of their
'revenge strategy' against the government. As a result of these attacks,
thousands of Punjabis, locally known as 'settlers', have fled Balochistan.

An added complexity is the presence of the Afghan Taliban and their
'Quetta shura' in the Pashtun areas of the province. It is important
to distinguish between them and the Baloch. The Baloch are fighting
for their rights and even survival, which is quite distinct from the
Taliban who are seeking to claw back into power in Afghanistan. The
Taliban want to establish an Islamic caliphate in Afghanistan and are

being backed by Pakistan. The Baloch ethnic insurgency focused in the Baloch areas is, on the contrary, a secular fight against the Pakistan state.

A marked feature of the situation in Balochistan is the persistent lack of information about developments there. There is very little reporting about Balochistan in the media in Pakistan except when there is a violent incident there. The situation is, however, changing gradually. Balochistan and the conflict that continues within it has now started making the news indirectly, thanks to the focus on Gwadar and CPEC–related discussions of security requirements.

The US and other Western powers have remained largely mute spectators despite the appeals of the Baloch to pressurize Pakistan to stop its brutal repression in the province. Such a stand has been largely dictated by their dependence on Pakistan for cooperation in the fight against the al-Qaeda and Taliban in Afghanistan. Till the 1970s, US attitude towards and knowledge about Balochistan was best represented by a remark of Henry Kissinger, then a Harvard professor. On a visit to Pakistan in 1962, when asked to comment on the insurgency in the province, he remarked, 'I wouldn't recognize the Balochistan problem if it hit me in the face.'[29]

Things began to change after the Soviet invasion of Afghanistan in 1979 when Balochistan became a major conduit for the supply of weapons to the Afghan mujahideen. There was renewed interest in the region in the wake of the 9/11 terrorist strike in the United States when President Pervez Musharraf provided access to several key installations, including the airfields in Pasni and Dalbadin, from where US forces supported their operations in Afghanistan. Even so, the US policy towards Balochistan, insofar it has one, is dictated by its overall approach towards Pakistan.

———•———

The book begins by discussing the land and people of Balochistan, about their composition and disposition within the province. It elucidates the geography, demography and the strategic importance of the province. The fact that Balochistan covers almost half of the land area of Pakistan while accounting for just about 6 per cent of the country's population is a stark reminder that more attention needs to be given to its geographical and demographic peculiarities to understand the province's economic and social development. The main resource of the province is its geography and strategic location but its Achilles heel is the skewed land to population ratio.

The next section (II) studies the historical development of Balochistan, especially during the British rule and the partition of the subcontinent. This is of critical importance since the root cause of Baloch alienation is the questionable legitimacy of the accession of the Baloch state of Kalat to Pakistan. Most Baloch believe that the Khan of Kalat was not only forced to sign the Instrument of Accession but that it was an illegal accession. The two Houses of the Baloch legislature had been empowered to decide the issue of accession and the Khan could not have done so on his own. There is also an element of 'stab in the back' since it was Jinnah who, as the Khan's lawyer, had argued the case for Kalat's independence with the British. Once the British left and after he became Governor-General of Pakistan, Jinnah forced the accession of Kalat to Pakistan, betraying the trust reposed in him.

Section III focuses on the roots of Baloch alienation with special emphasis on the political and administrative marginalization, economic exploitation of the resources of Balochistan over the decades and the consequent deprivation of the people. Citing statistics, this section compares Balochistan with the other provinces of Pakistan to understand why the alienation among the Baloch is so deep-rooted and persistent. In fact, the socio-economic indicators of Balochistan are alarming. It is a province that suffers from an acute water shortage; 70 per cent of the people live in poverty; about 1.8 million children are out of school and more than 5,000 public schools consist of a single room; the maternal death rate stands at 758 out of every 100,000; and almost 15 per cent of the people of Balochistan suffer from Hepatitis B or C. Add to this, poor governance, massive corruption, nepotism, mismanagement of resources and unemployment, and the potent, dangerous mix can well be imagined.

The next section discusses in detail the development of the Gwadar port and the CPEC that has been billed as a game-changer for Pakistan. Will it be a game-changer for Balochistan too? If so, why are the Baloch so opposed to it? The Baloch cite the fact that natural gas was discovered at Sui in Balochistan in the 1950s, yet major parts of the province are still deprived of its benefits. Not surprisingly, there is the cynical belief that the province will not get its fair share of the benefits of the development of the Gwadar port or of the economic corridor.

Section V looks at the serious human rights violations in Balochistan, especially by the state in trying to deal with the insurgency. Kept under wraps for long, the true situation of the human rights violations is gradually beginning to see the light of day. An important element of such violations is the crackdown on the media to keep a lid on the happenings in Balochistan and to ensure that only the state's narrative prevails.

The last section looks at the current insurgency in Balochistan with focus on the separatist challenge that Pakistan faces and the response by the Pakistani state, especially the army, to this challenge. This would include the various stratagems adopted by the state to thwart the insurgency and whether and to what extent they have been successful.

Finally, the conclusion will touch upon what the future holds for Balochistan and Pakistan. Is the situation irretrievable? How plausible is Balochistan breaking away from Pakistan, a la Bangladesh?

Pakistan's conundrum is that Balochistan is too large and too strategically important a province to loosen its grip. Yet, the policies adopted for the last seven decades have done everything to keep the province alienated rather than bring it into the mainstream.

Will the next seven decades be any different?

I

AN ANCIENT CIVILIZATION

1

The Land

BALOCHISTAN IS AN ANCIENT LAND with the history of its people shrouded in mystery and debate. Its geographical location had given it a distinct position as a bridge between the Indian and the Mesopotamian civilizations. Archaeological discoveries at Mehergarh in Balochistan make it among the earliest civilizations in the world; the Kech civilization in central Makran dates back to 4000 BC, the buried city near Zahidan, the provincial capital in western Balochistan, now in Iran, dates back to 3000 BC.[1] According to the *Imperial Gazetteer*: 'All tradition asserts that the former rulers of Kalat were Hindus, Sewa by name. It is not improbable that they were connected with the Rai dynasty of Sindh, whose genealogical table includes two rulers named Shiras.[2] Kalat was, in fact, once called Kalat-e-Sewa (Sewa's Fort), after Sewa, a legendary Hindu hero of the Brahvi-speaking people.

Arguably, the earliest account of Balochistan was written by Lucius Flavius Arrianus (Arrian) whose *Anabasis of Alexander* described Alexander's campaigns and his epic march through the deserts of Balochistan and the Makran coast on his way back to Greece. During the retreat in 325 BC, he was greatly harried by the Baloch. His biographer wrote, 'I had never seen the Great Alexander so sad and dejected—filled with sorrow and uncertainty.... The outcome [of fighting with the Baloch] was disastrous for Alexander's army and against himself.' Alexander, in fact, had almost perished during the campaign that took the lives of almost three quarters of his army.

3

Historians claim that Alexander had not experienced anything as terrible in his travels before and had come the nearest to defeat in Balochistan's almost impenetrable deserts and rugged terrain.[3] It is here that a soldier brought Alexander a helmet filled with water when there was none for miles. Instead of quenching his thirst, he spilled the water on the burning sands to assure his soldiers that he would not drink if they could not.[4]

According to the *Imperial Gazetteer*: 'When the site of the present arsenal at Quetta was being prepared, a statuette of Hercules was discovered. Mounds opened at Nal and Mamatawa in the Jhalawan country have yielded interesting finds of pottery. That found at the former place possesses striking resemblances to pottery of the eighth century BC found in Cyprus and Phoenicia and of Mycenaean technique. At Chhalgari in Kachhi are indications of interesting Buddhist remains. Such finds of coins as have been made from time to time render it clear that all sorts of traders, from ancient times to the present, have left traces of themselves along the routes leading from Persia to India.'[5]

Greek historian Herodotus had divided Balochistan into three distinct parts—Aracosia: Kandhar and Quetta region; Drangiana: Helmand, Sistan and Chagai; and Gedrosia: Makran coast.[6]

Centuries later, the Baloch fought and harried the British during the Raj. Rudyard Kipling wrote here. Prior to the partition of India, the distinguished faculty members and graduates of the Staff College in Quetta included Field Marshals Bernard Law Montgomery, Sir Claude Auckinleck, Lord Slim of Burma, S.H.F.J. Manekshaw, K.M. Kariappa and Muhammad Ayub Khan, and Generals Lord Ismay and Sir Douglas Gracey.[7]

————•————

Located on the south-eastern Iranian plateau, with an approximately 600,000 sq. km area, rich in diversity, Balochistan is larger in size than France (551,500 sq. km).[8] In terms of geography, it has more in common with the Iranian plateau than with the Indian subcontinent. Edward Wakefield, a British political officer who travelled in Balochistan, made the following observations about the climate and geography of

Balochistan: 'From our carriage windows ... I looked out on a new world, a world that had nothing in common with the India we had known before. Here were rugged, barren, sun-browned mountains, cleft by deep ravines and gorges. Forbidding of aspect in the full light of day, the hills were now, in the first light of dawn, clothed with a gentle effulgence that made them seem welcoming and friendly. The air, too, was different from that of India, but of the Central Asian plateau. Simply to breathe such air in such surroundings was exhilarating.'[9]

In 1946, M.A. Jinnah, the legal advisor of the Khan of Kalat, submitted a Memorandum to the Cabinet Mission that, inter alia, demanded the separation of Balochistan from British India on geographical grounds: 'Geographically, Kalat does not fall within the territorial limits of India. On the north, it is separated from India by the massive barrier of the southern buttresses of the Sulaiman Mountains. On the south, there is the long extension from Kalat of the inconceivably wild highland country, which faces the desert of Sindh, the foot of which forms the Indian frontier. This, the land of the Baluch, and the flat wall of its frontier limestone barrier is one of the most remarkable features in the configuration of the whole line of the Indian borderlands.'[10]

However, as has been well put: 'The force of historical experience has defied the logic of geography, and the political history of the area has been linked with powers that were centred in the Indo-Gangetic plains of the Indian subcontinent.'[11]

Balochistan is divided into four major physical areas: the Upper Highlands, the Lower Highlands, the Plains and the Deserts. The Upper Highlands, known as Khorasan, rise as high as 3,700 metres (m), with valley floors about 1,500 m above sea level. The Upper Highlands fall mainly in districts Zhob, Qila Saifullah, Pishin, Quetta, Ziarat and Kalat. It comprises a number of ranges such as Sulaiman, Tobak Kakari, Murdar, Zarghoon, Takatu and Chiltan ranges. The Lower Highlands are bracketed by three mountain ranges: the Mekran, Kharan, and Chaghi. They have an altitude ranging from 600 m to 1,200 m (1,970 ft to 3,940 ft). They are located in south-eastern Balochistan. There is a relatively small area of Plains as compared to Balochistan's total land area. These are the Plains of Kachi, Lasbela and that of river Dasht. The Kachi plains, situated to the south of Sibi extend into Nasirabad division. Then there is the southern part of Dera Bugti district, and narrow plain area along the Makran coast stretching from Kachi to the Iranian border. The Deserts make up the north-west portion of the region mostly in Kharan and Chaghi districts. They are marked by their unique mixture of sand and black gravel.[12]

Sir Thomas Holdich, the British geographer and traveller, described Balochistan as a 'brazen coast, washed by a molten sea'. The *Imperial Gazetteer* gives a succinct summary: 'Rugged, barren, sunburnt mountains, rent by huge chasms and gorges, alternate with arid deserts and stony plains.... This is redeemed in places by level valleys of considerable size, in which irrigation enables much cultivation to be carried on.'[13]

The distinguishing feature of the white clay mountains of the Makran coast is that, instead of stone, they are made up of limestone or conglomerate and look like a wall. In the words of Holdich, these mountains appear: 'Gigantic cap-crowned pillars and pedestals [that] are balanced in fantastic array ... successive strata so well-defined that it possesses all the appearance of massive masonry construction ... standing stiff, jagged, naked and uncompromising, like the parallel walls of some gigantic system of defences and varying in height above the plain from 5,000 feet to 50 feet'.[14]

More recently, in 2009, Robert Kaplan wrote:

> To travel the Makran coast is to experience the windy, liberating flatness of Yemen and Oman and their soaring, saw tooth ramparts the color of sandpaper, rising sheer off a desert floor pockmarked with thorn-bushes. Here, along a coast so empty that you can almost hear the echoing camel hooves of Alexander's army, you lose yourself in geology. An exploding sea bangs against a knife-carved apricot moonscape of high sand dunes, which, in turn, gives way to crumbly badlands. Farther inland, every sandstone and limestone escarpment is the color of bone. Winds and seismic and tectonic disruptions have left their mark in tortuous folds and uplifts, deep gashes, and conical incrustations that hark back far before the age of human folly.[15]

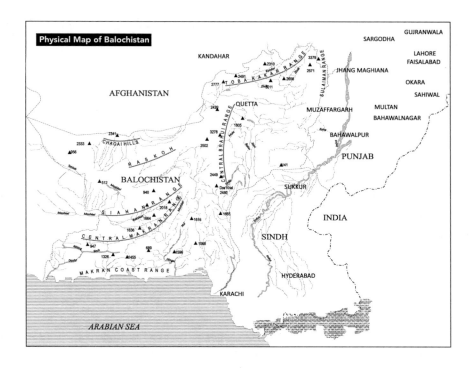

Ecological factors have contributed to the division of agricultural centres and pasture lands. This, in turn, has impacted the development of the tribal economy and institutions. Describing the Baloch economy in the early 1980s, Selig Harrison wrote: 'Instead of relying solely on either nomadic pastoralism or on settled agriculture, most Baloch practise a mixture of the two in order to survive.'[16] This is also borne out by a Brahvi saying: 'God is God, but a sheep is a different thing.'[17]

Balochistan has two raised plains or plateaus. One is in Kalat and the other is the Quetta Valley. Kalat is a quadrangular plateau, measuring about 480 km (300 miles) by 480 km (300 miles) where the ancient capital city of Kalat is situated at a height of over 1,800 m (6,000 ft). Kalat straddles the mountain area of Sarawan in the north and the searing desert of Jhalawan to the south. Quetta lies at a height of 1,675 m (5,500 ft). Originally, it was called Shal. The British made it the capital of the province on 21 February 1877.

Makran is unlike the rest of Balochistan. Nearly 95 per cent of its population is concentrated on less than 5 per cent of the land in contrast to the isolated tribal pockets in the rest of Balochistan. Its main port is Gwadar. It was at one time owned by Oman having been gifted by the then Khan of Kalat in the eighteenth century. Gwadar was sold back to Pakistan for about $3 million in 1958. 'The sales agreement gave the sultan recruiting rights, and large numbers of Makranis serve in Oman's Army and Navy', writes Mary Anne Weaver. According to her, residents of Gwadar retain dual nationality with Oman and every year a large number of Makranis go and work in the Gulf.[18]

Balochistan has been described as 'a brooding and melancholy place',[19] arid, rugged and harsh. A British explorer wrote thus in the nineteenth century of the desolation of Balochistan:

> The coast-line of Baluchistan is six hundred miles long. On it there is one tree, a sickly, stunted-looking thing, near the telegraph station of Gwadar, which serves as a landmark to native craft and a standing joke to the English sailor. Planted some years since by a European, it has lived doggedly on, to the surprise of all, in this arid soil. The Tree of Baluchistan is as well known to the mariner in the Persian Gulf as Regent Circus or the Marble Arch to the London cabman. With this solitary exception, not a trace of vegetation exists along the sea-board from Persian to Indian frontier. Occasionally, at long intervals, a mud hut is seen, just showing that the country is inhabited, and that is all. The steep, rocky cliffs, with their sharp, spire-like summits rising almost perpendicularly out of the blue sea, are typical of the desert wastes inland.[20]

As is to be expected, such a vast area has extraordinary climatic variations. In the northern and interior highlands, the temperature often drops to 40 degrees Fahrenheit in winter, though the summer is temperate. In contrast, temperatures soar between 100 and 130 degrees Fahrenheit in the summer in the coastal region though the winter is more favourable. Balochistan does not normally receive more than 5 to 12 inches of rain per annum despite being in the direction of the south-west monsoon.[21] This is due to the low altitude of the Makran ranges. The infrequent rains occur mostly in winter though in the Lower

Highlands and in areas closer to the Arabian Sea, rain falls in summer. As a result, only about 7 per cent of the area is arable.

In 1839, another British officer, John Jacob, serving with General Keane's forces marching to Afghanistan, wrote of the climate in these words:

> From April to October the heat in this part of the world is more deadly than the sword of a human enemy and scarcely an escort at this time marched through the country without losing many men for this cause alone ... the place is remarkable for its dust storms of almost incredible violence and density. They occur frequently at all seasons of the year, sometimes changing the light of midday to an intensity of darkness to which no ordinary night ever approaches, and this darkness in severe storms lasts occasionally for one, two or more hours. These dust storms on both sides of the desert are sometimes accompanied by blasts of the simoon, a poisonous wind which is equally destructive to vegetables and animal life.[22]

A Baloch proverb describes the heat of the plains in summer: 'O God, when thou hadst created Sibi and Dadhar, what object was there in conceiving hell?'[23]

The harshness of nature probably explains why, although many of the great civilizations—Greek, Arab, Hindu, Turkish, Persian—have sent conquerors through the area, there are few surviving traces of their passage.[24] Neither of them succeeded to assimilate Balochistan into their empires.

A relatively recent phenomenon of concern is a surge in the sea level. Reports indicate that the sea is intruding inland and encroaching upon properties and farmland. Over the last few decades, millions of hectares of land have been lost due to this phenomenon. The most affected areas along the Makran coast include Dam Bander, Pasni, Sub Bander, Pashukan and Jiwani. The coastal erosion has been exacerbated by the destuction of mangrove forests, already under pressure from the fuel wood and timber mafia, in Balochistan. From 1990 to 2015, the Food and Agriculture Organisation's Global Forest Resources

Assessment 2015 report discovered, Pakistan experienced its highest rates of deforestation at 2.1 per cent on an average, which also includes the felling of mangrove forests.[25]

———◆———

The Baloch culture owes much to the geography of the country: its rugged mountains and arid expanses of semi-desert wasteland has expectedly bred a distinct and self-reliant people who are used to hardship. Equally, their tribal structure and social mores replicate the harsh environment in which they live. As has been well put, 'The specificity of Balochistan geography and geopolitics has affected and shaped the character of the Baloch, their vision of the world and the way they have continued to reproduce and reinterpret their cultural elements and traditions.'[26] One example of the toughness of the people is described by Sylvia Matheson thus: 'Only an exceptionally hardy people could have campaigned as the Bugtis did at that time, marching as much as sixty miles without a halt, raiding a camp or a military post, then retreating all through the intense heat of the day, the entire time without water or rest.'[27]

It is this inhospitable terrain and climatic conditions that have been the greatest assets of the Baloch against invading armies despite being numerically smaller and has protected them from most outside influences. However, these same geographical conditions made communication difficult and led to isolation and divided the Baloch among themselves into competing tribes.[28] It also prevented the growth of a centralized government at Kalat that could control the vast areas over a sustained period of time. It was largely due to this lack of communications that the Khan of Kalat was unable to rally the Baloch tribes against the British in 1839.[29]

To further their imperial interests, the British built railways and roads in strategic areas connecting Balochistan to British India, Iran and Afghanistan. In the beginning of the twentieth century, the total length of the railway was about 650 km. The opening of the Nushki Railway, completed in 1905, increased the total to about 775 km. The total length of roads and paths in 1903, was about 1,800 km.[30] During the First and Second World Wars, new roads were built for military supply into Iran and the Middle East. Significantly, the early Baloch nationalists were aware of the importance of the communication system in the development of nationalism. Thus, the Baloch national conferences held in 1932 and 1933 demanded the construction of new roads and the opening of post offices.[31] Despite this, when the British left the subcontinent in 1947, the vast province had only a limited communication system primarily for the use of the military.

Poor communication and transport infrastructure continued to exacerbate the backwardness of the province. While the province has the largest road network in the country of 22,000 km of 'metal and shingle' road (40 per cent of the total in the country) most of it is in a dilapidated condition due to poor maintenance.[32]

Creation of the Province

A variety of views has been put forward regarding the national and ethnic borders of Balochistan. The *Encyclopaedia of Islam* says: 'The exact boundaries of Balochistan are undetermined. In general, it occupies the south-eastern part of the Iranian plateau from the Kirman desert east of Bam and Bashagird to the western borders of Sindh and the Punjab.'[33] *Encyclopaedia Britannica* defines the borders as stretching '... from the Gomal river in the north-east to the Arabian Sea in the South and from the borders of Iran and Afghanistan in the west and north-west to the Sulaiman mountains and Kirthar Hills in the east, including the region of south-eastern Iran.'[34] Lord Curzon had defined Balochistan as 'the country between the Helmand and the Arabian Sea and between Kirman and Sind.'[35]

Perhaps the most striking definition was that given by Mir Nasir Khan II, Khan of Kalat (1840–75). When asked about the borders of Balochistan by the British and Afghan envoys at his court, he stated, 'My ancestor and namesake Nasir Khan Nuri had already replied in geographical terms to a similar question long ago; and I repeat: all those regions where the Baloch are settled are a part and parcel of our State.'[36]

Prior to the arrival of the British, Balochistan was divided into four princely states or regions. They were (1) Kalat (2) Lasbela (3) Makran (4) Kharan. All of them were under the Khan of Kalat when the incumbent was strong enough to assert his control. The present-day province of Balochistan came into existence in July 1970. An understanding of how its borders evolved during the British period and after the creation of Pakistan is crucial because often people get confused about the large Pashtun population in Balochistan and try and link the Pashtun Taliban to the Baloch.

As Olaf Caroe, the British governor of the North-West Frontier Province (NWFP) put it, Balochistan is a misnomer: 'The valley of Shal [Quetta], about seventy miles north of Kalat and situated at 5,500 feet [1,675 m] above sea level at the head of the Bolan Pass, is exactly on the line of ethnic division. In the centre of it is the town of Quetta. All the country to the north is a part of the Pathan belt and inhabited by Pathan tribes of which the Tarins, Achakzais, Kakars and Panris are the most important. To the south of Quetta all the people are Brahvis and Baloch.'[37]

The British intervention in Balochistan—a process that would forever change its destiny—began due to the compulsions of the Great Game. The advance of the Tsarist empire into Central Asia made the British apprehensive about the safety of their Indian empire. To forestall the Russian advance towards India, the British used Afghanistan as a buffer between the two empires. For this, it became necessary to control parts of Balochistan bordering Afghanistan so as to secure lines of communication and transportation through the Bolan Pass to Chaman and beyond. The effort to ensure that Afghanistan remained a buffer led to the First Afghan War (1838–42) that proved to be a disaster for the British. The one important lesson they learnt from the movement of the 'Army of the Indus'—the name of the British Indian force that invaded Afghanistan in 1839—was that to keep the passage through the Bolan Pass to southern Afghanistan open and safe, they had to establish some sort of control over the adjoining areas of Balochistan.

Following the Second Afghan War (1878–79) and the Treaty of Gandamak (1879), the British annexed large parts of Pashtun territories north of the Bolan Pass that were grouped into a chief commissioner's province called British Balochistan even though they were predominantly Pashtun areas. To further stall the potential Russian advance towards India, the British demarcated their border with Iran and Afghanistan giving away large parts of the princely state of Kalat to these two countries. This was an imperial tactic to befriend these rulers to pre-empt their joining the Russians. Under the final outcome of the boundary settlements imposed on the Baloch: (i) Seistan and Western Makran, Sarhad, etc., became part of Iran; (ii) Outer Seistan and Registan came under the control of Afghanistan; and (iii) Jacobabad, Derajat and Sibi were included in British India. In return, the Khanate of Balochistan was recognized as an independent state with the status of a protectorate.[38]

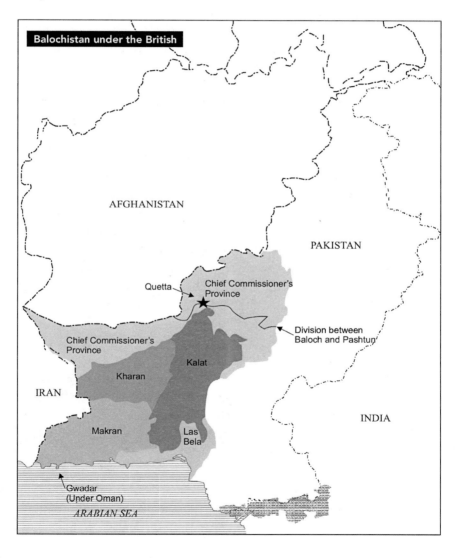

Balochistan under the British

Thus, under the British, Balochistan had two main administrative units—the Kalat state (75 per cent of the area and the three constituent states of Las Bella, Kharan and Makran), and areas under the British. The latter consisted of British Balochistan; areas leased by the British from Kalat and the Marri and Bugti tribal areas. A succinct picture of Balochistan during British rule is described in the 1911 *Britannica*:

[Balochistan] is divided into two main divisions, British Baluchistan, which is a portion of British India under the chief commissioner, and the foreign territories under the administration or superintendence of the same officer as agent to the governor-general [AGG]. The former portion, with an area of 9,403 sq. km, consists principally of tracts ceded to the British government by Afghanistan under the Treaty of Gandamak (1879), and formally declared to be part of British India in 1887. The second class comprises three subdivisions, namely areas directly administered, native states and tribal areas. The directly administered districts include areas acquired in various ways. Some portions are held on lease from the Khan of Kalat; while others are tribal areas in which it has been decided for various reasons that revenue shall be taken. They include the whole of the Zhob and Chagai political agencies, the eastern portion of the Quetta tahsil and other tracts, among which may be mentioned the Bolan Pass, comprising 36,401 sq. km in all. The whole of the northern boundary, with the north-eastern corner and the railway which traverses Baluchistan through Quetta up to New Chaman on the Afghan-Baluch frontier, is therefore in one form or other under direct British control. The remainder of the territory (79,382 sq. km) belongs to the native states of Kalat (including Makran and Kharan) and Lasbela. Tribal areas, in the possession of the Marri and Bugti tribes, cover 7,129 sq. km.[39]

Thus, it was the fear of Russian advance towards India that was the pivot for the Great Game in the nineteenth century and later, it was the Soviet quest for a warm-water port through Afghanistan and Balochistan that led to the renewed Great Game in the twentieth.

Pakistan inherited Britain's apprehensions of Russian/Soviet control of
the Baloch coast that could fundamentally change the military equation
in the region, quite apart from giving Moscow a powerful new launch
pad for influence in the 'wells of power' of the Middle East.

As Mary Anne Weaver writes, the British made the Quetta
cantonment their base as also circuit houses near the frontier. However,
they administered little else in Balochistan. The nawabs and sardars,
who had been bolstered with the support of the Raj, had total
command over their lands. 'Quetta was a tiny outpost that the British
had transformed into this Victorian sector of cricket fields, sprawling
bungalows, and street lanterns that once burned coconut oil. Quetta
was, after Aldershot, the largest garrison-station in the empire, and there
was also the Staff College—one of only two in the entire empire.'[40]

Quetta became the headquarters of the fourth division of the
Western Command. In 1903, the troops consisted of three mountain
batteries, two companies of garrison artillery, two British infantry
regiments, three 'native' cavalry regiments, six 'native' infantry
regiments and one company of sappers and miners. The total strength
of troops on 1 June 1903 was 9,771—2,650 British and 7,121 'native'.
The greater part of the garrison was quartered at Quetta and in a
number of outposts; the remainder was distributed at Loralai, Fort
Sandeman and Chaman, each of these stations being garrisoned by
'native' infantry and cavalry.[41]

After the forced accession of Kalat to Pakistan in 1948, the Balochistan
States Union (BSU) was established in 1951-52, wherein Lasbela,
Makran and Kharan were merged into Kalat. These four territories
would share a common executive, legislature and judiciary under the
common constitution of Pakistan, with the prime minister a nominee
of the Pakistan government. Later, the Khan and others were made to
sign 'The Balochistan States Union Merger Agreement' that abrogated
all previous agreements and treaties between the state of Kalat and
Pakistan. The four states were dissolved and their rulers pensioned off,
with substantial hikes in the amount of their privy purses, and the area
constituted as Kalat Division. Later, Kalat Division became part of the
then West Pakistan under the One Unit Scheme in 1955 while British
Balochistan along with the tribal agencies became part of West Pakistan
as the Quetta Division in the same year. With the abolition of the One

Unit plan on 1 July 1970, the combined divisions of Quetta and Kalat came together as the newly created province of Balochistan.

A and B Areas

Balochistan is divided into two areas for purposes of policing—category 'A' and category 'B'. The category 'A' areas consists mainly of towns and cities and remains under a regular police force. In 2006, as the Human Rights Commission of Pakistan noted, there were eighty-nine police stations and the sanctioned strength of the police was 19,145.[42]

The 'B' area (almost 95 per cent of Balochistan) is under the control of the levies[43] who in 2006 maintained 286 police stations and employed 13,357 personnel. By 2018, the strength of the levies went up to 23,132.[44] The local sardars and civil bureaucracy dominated the levy system. The recruitment of levies was not based on merit but on the recommendation of the 'local influentials'.[45] Several political and economic interests had developed around this system.

Under President Musharraf, in order to cut the sardars down to size, all 'B' areas in the province were converted into 'A' areas and police empowered to maintain law and order across the province. Billions of rupees were committed to streamlining the conversion but it remained controversial. Many Baloch parliamentarians expressed apprehensions about rising unemployment among those who were relieved from the levy force. They were, however, assured that the levies would be trained and inducted into the police force.[46]

After the Eighteenth Constitutional Amendment (2010) when powers were devolved to the provinces, the Balochistan cabinet overturned the decision taken under Musharraf to merge the two areas. Accordingly, the police force was withdrawn from 'B' areas and the levy force revived there. Now, levies operate in 'B' areas of the province and the police in the 'A' areas as earlier.[47]

Strategic Importance

Balochistan's strategic importance invited the attention of the British but worked to its detriment. Under Pakistan too, it is Balochistan's strategic and geographic importance that has again attracted attention. Once again, it is working to its disadvantage.

With almost 44 per cent of Pakistan's landmass, Balochistan is perhaps Pakistan's most strategically located province. In the north, the districts of Chagai, Quetta and Zhob make up the border with Afghanistan. On the west, the districts of Makran, Kharan and western Chagai make up another border with Iran. In the east are the Pakistan provinces of Sindh, Punjab and part of Khyber Pakhtunkhwa (KPK). In addition, its 760-km coastline is almost two-thirds of Pakistan coastline with an approximately 180,000 sq. km exclusive economic zone that is largely untapped.

Balochistan sits astride the Straits of Hormuz, one of the choke points of the Indian Ocean that provides access to oil tankers bound for the West, China and Japan. Nearly 40 per cent of the world's oil supplies pass through the Straits of Hormuz. It is in every country's interest to ensure that the shipping lines of the Persian Gulf remain open and are secured. Balochistan's geographical proximity to the oil and gas deposits of Central Asian regions adds to its strategic importance.[48] It provides the closest access point to landlocked Afghanistan, the Central Asian states and the Xinjiang province of China to the Arabian Sea and the Indian Ocean.

Three of Pakistan's naval bases are located on the Baloch coast— Ormara, Pasni and Gwadar. In addition to providing Pakistan with a deep-water port and the potential for millions in revenue, Gwadar provides Pakistan with strategic depth. This is something that the main naval base at Karachi does not. In fact, Karachi had been blockaded and attacked by India in the past. Chagai in Balochistan is home to Pakistan's nuclear testing sites. Additionally, Balochistan's immense area allows Pakistan the flexibility to scatter its nuclear arsenal and thus protect it from potential attacks.

The proximity of the main opium producing centres in Afghanistan— the provinces of Helmand, Kandahar and Zabul—to Balochistan and the Chaman crossing makes it crucial for smuggling narcotics out of the country, as noted in the Introduction.

Balochistan is also the place where 'the cornerstone of Pakistan's foreign policy', namely the endangered Houbara bustard is allowed to be slaughtered by Arab sheikhs, especially in the districts of Turbat, Loralai, Muskhel, Chagai and Jhal Magsi. In a review petition filed before the Supreme Court of Pakistan seeking to reverse its 19 August 2015 ban on hunting the Houbara bustard, the government of Pakistan stated that inviting Arab dignitaries to hunt the bird in Pakistan was a 'cornerstone of foreign policy';[49] and the ban on falconry hunting of Houbara bustard could further affect the already weakened relations with the Arab states. The clinching argument made by a former law minister of Pakistan as well as chairman of the Senate, Farooq H. Naek, before the Supreme Court was that hunting of the Houbara was intolerable and excruciating for India. It was India's agenda to seek a ban on Houbara bustard hunting as foreign dignitaries were investing in Pakistan, and India did not want to see Pakistan develop.[50] Faced with such 'weighty' arguments that the Houbara was the 'cornerstone of Pakistan's foreign policy' and the supposed involvement of India, the Supreme Court on 22 January 2016 relented and lifted the ban on hunting the endangered bird, thus restoring Balochistan's strategic importance!

———◆———

Strategic location apart, Balochistan's supposed treasure of minerals and energy resources is one of the major factors behind the turmoil in the province. According to a famous Baloch proverb, 'A Baloch may be born without socks on his feet, but when he grows up every step he takes is on gold.'[51] Balochistan is reputed to have vast mineral and energy resources—36 per cent of Pakistan's total current natural gas production, as also reserves of coal, gold, copper, silver, platinum, aluminum and uranium. Reko Diq, Saindak, Sui[52] and Chamalang produce a wealth of resources like copper, gold, natural gas, coal and other minerals. Reko Diq is a copper and gold mine in Chagai district with an estimated mineral resource of at least 54 billion pounds of copper and 41 million ounces of gold.[53] The Saindak mine is estimated to have copper ore reserves of 412 million tonnes containing on average 0.5 gram of gold per tonne and 1.5 grams of silver per tonne. According to official estimates, the project has the capacity to produce 15,800 tonnes of blister copper annually, containing 1.5 tonnes of gold and 2.8 tonnes of silver.[54] Chamalang coal mines, spread over an area of 1,300 sq. km, are located in Loralai, Kohlu and Barkhan. A total of 500 million tonnes of coal deposits have been confirmed worth over Rs 2,000 billion.[55]

Balochistan's location, adjoining Afghanistan, made it important to the US in the 'War on Terror' for carrying out operations against the Taliban after 9/11. Airfields in Pasni, Dalbadin and Shamsi in Balochistan were used extensively since 2001 to provide logistical support for special forces and intelligence operations. At Shamsi, CIA operatives launched drones that attacked the Taliban in Afghanistan and in the tribal belt. In addition, it has often been speculated that the US presence in Balochistan could also be due to its potential for operations against Iran's nuclear programme. In fact, in 2006, investigative reporter Seymour Hersh had even written that US special forces had been implanted into Iran from secret bases in Balochistan.[56]

Following the US campaign against the Taliban that began in November 2001, Balochistan became a significant exit route for al-Qaeda and Taliban fighters seeking safe havens in Pakistan. When the US and International Security Assistance Force (ISAF) troops were at their peak in Afghanistan, Balochistan was also a critical link in the supply route from Karachi to Afghanistan via the Chaman border crossing.

Decades ago, Selig Harrison had written, 'If it were not for the strategic location of Balochistan and the rich potential of oil, uranium and other resources, it would be difficult to imagine anyone fighting over this bleak, desolate and forbidding land.'[57] Since he wrote, Balochistan has become key to the energy security of Pakistan. The rising requirement for energy resources has resulted in increasing the economic and strategic salience of the province. It is this assured access to natural gas resources that is the prism through which Pakistan looks at Balochistan.

As Robert G. Wirsing puts it, '… assured access to hydrocarbon or other energy resources, including both oil and natural gas, has in recent decades assumed a far greater importance than hitherto as a driver of Pakistan's security policy, both domestic and external.'[58] Energy security is now a foremost national priority. Resultantly, Balochistan's economic and strategic importance has been enhanced exponentially making it crucial for Pakistan to deal with the growing separatism in the country.[59]

Notwithstanding future discoveries of oil, presently it is Balochistan's natural gas that is of critical significance for Pakistan's energy profile. Wirsing adduces three reasons for this: (i) natural gas makes up about 50 per cent of Pakistan's total energy consumption and is by far the principal energy source. 'This makes Pakistan's economy one of the world's most natural gas dependent'; (ii) of Pakistan's proven natural gas reserves—in 2006 estimated at 28 trillion cubic feet (tcf)—as much as 19 trillion tcf (68 per cent) were located in Balochistan; (iii) Balochistan produces between 36 and 45 per cent of Pakistan's natural gas, but consumes only 17 per cent of it.[60]

The Sui gas fields in Dera Bugti district of Balochistan contributes the largest share of gas. This is also the stronghold of the Bugti tribe that has been in an adversarial relationship with the state since the early years of this millennium. It was consequently among the areas most seriously impacted by militancy leading to disruptions of gas supplies. As Wirsing notes, since the state-owned Sui Southern Gas Company alone, for example, has a 27,000-km pipeline distribution network across Sindh and Balochistan, the scale of the problem of monitoring and policing the pipelines can well be imagined.[61]

This, according to him, has a threefold impact on the situation in Balochistan. First, it puts Balochistan and Baloch nationalism on a much higher priority for the Central government, reinforcing its policy of zero tolerance and ruthless crushing of the insurgency. Second, it provides added incentives to the Baloch insurgents to reclaim control of Balochistan by a higher level of insurgent activity. Finally, by harnessing Balochistan's potential for an important corridor for energy trafficking in the region, it provides major opportunities and incentives for addressing Baloch nationalist demands in a positive and peaceful manner.[62] The moot point, of course, is whether the government and especially the army will do so.

There are three proposals of energy trafficking, two on an east–west axis and one on a north–south axis. The first is a 2,700-km (1,678-mile) Iran-Pakistan-India (IPI) pipeline, with a capacity to transport 2.8 billion cubic feet (bcf) of gas daily from Iran's huge offshore South Pars field to terminals in Pakistan and India. Second is the 1,680-km (1,044-mile) Turkmenistan-Afghanistan-Pakistan-India (TAPI) pipeline, with the capacity to transport up to 3.2 bcf daily from Turkmenistan to markets in Afghanistan, Pakistan and India. Both would have to pass through Balochistan.[63]

The IPI pipeline has been a non-starter given the problems between India and Pakistan and between Pakistan and Iran. In February 2018, Iran threatened to move the International Court of Justice (ICJ) against Pakistan for unilaterally shelving the IP gas pipeline project invoking the penalty clause of the 2009 Gas Sales Purchase Agreement (GSPA). Under the penalty clause, Pakistan was bound to pay a penalty of $1 million per day from 1 January 2015 if it failed to take gas from Iran. Iran has asked for payment of over $1.2 billion that is almost equal to the cost of the project. According to media reports in June 2016, Pakistan had shelved the IPI gas line project and now Iran has presented the bill for doing so.[64]

The TAPI pipeline was inaugurated on 23 February 2018 with leaders of the four countries attending its groundbreaking ceremony in Serhetabat followed by another in Herat. The pipeline costing $8 billion is expected to be completed within two years to begin pumping 32 billion cubic metres (bcm) of natural gas annually from Turkmenistan's giant Galkynysh gas field through Afghanistan and Pakistan into India. For the present, even the Taliban have vowed to protect the pipeline.[65]

The third is the China–Pakistan Economic Corridor (CPEC) on a north–south axis consisting of port, road and rail infrastructural networks billed as part of China's 'One Belt One Road' (OBOR) or Belt and Road initiative (BRI) initiative. It seeks to connect Gwadar in Balochistan with Kashgar in China's Xinjiang province. This too will have to pass through Balochistan. The development of the Gwadar port and the CPEC has further heightened Balochistan's strategic significance. The port and corridor could potentially transform Pakistan into an economic hub. CPEC is on its way to be operationalized, further underlining the strategic importance of Balochistan.

These developments have resulted in the efforts of the Central government to forcefully exert its authority in the province leading to an adverse reaction from the Baloch nationalists. The development of Gwadar port is likely to lead to an influx of non-Baloch and this has raised fears among the Baloch of their being converted into a minority in their own land. Along with other historical and economic factors, the Baloch nationalists have come to view the mega project as an attempt to subjugate them and exploit their resources for the benefit of Punjab. This has provoked a violent backlash from Baloch militants, leading to a harsh reaction from the Pakistan Army. The tit-for-tat cycle seems to have developed a momentum of its own with more and more Baloch getting disillusioned with the state.

2

The People

BALOCHISTAN IS A MULTI-ETHNIC PROVINCE consisting of the Baloch concentrated mostly in the south and south-west, the Brahvi, an ethnic group of Dravidian origin based in central Balochistan, and Pashtuns in the north. In the 1901 census, the British showed the Baloch and the Brahvi as separate ethnic groups. According to it, the Baloch were less numerous than both Brahvis and Pashtuns. The exact numbers were: Baloch, 80,000; Brahvis, 300,000; and Pashtuns, 200,000. The census figures further stated that the number of Baloch staying outside Balochistan in Sindh and Punjab were 950,000.[1]

According to the 1998 census, the province hosted about 5 per cent of Pakistan's population. Of this, ethnic Baloch (including the Bravhis) formed 54.7 per cent and Pashtuns 29.6 per cent of the population, with the rest divided between Punjabis, Hazaras and others. In other words, ethnic Baloch formed only about 3.5 per cent of the total population of Pakistan while the province formed almost 44 per cent of the area of Pakistan. This unique demographic-cum-territorial configuration necessitates that for any development effort to be successful, there has to be a much higher per-capita expenditure as compared to other provinces. Historically, this need was not recognized at the national level until the seventh National Finance Commission (NFC) Award in 2009.

The Baloch are spread around the province in 22,000 settlements that range from the capital city of Quetta to a sprinkling of small hamlets having less than 500 houses.[2] Over two-thirds of its inhabitants reside in rural areas whereas half of its urban population is concentrated in

Quetta, Khuzdar, Turbat, Hub and Chaman. The rural areas primarily consist of scattered settlements of sparse populations. The average population density of the province is nineteen persons per square kilometre and varies greatly across districts.[3] A large number of Baloch reside outside the province, especially in Karachi. It is believed that the Baloch population in Karachi could well exceed that in Balochistan itself.

Who Are the Baloch?

The exact meaning and origin of the term 'Baloch' is somewhat cloudy. According to the *Imperial Gazetteer*, the word Baloch means wanderer or nomad.[4] This view was also propounded by G.P. Tate, the then assistant superintendent, Survey of India, who held that the name has historically meant 'nomads'.[5] It would, therefore, be a synonym for 'bedouin'.[6] Another view is that the word 'Baloch' is the corrupted form of Melukhkha, Meluccha or Mleccha, which was the designation of the modern eastern Makran during the third and second millennia BC, according to Mesopotamian texts.[7] Munir Ahmad Gichki, a professor of history at Balochistan University, however, relates it to 'Gedrosia' or 'Bedrozia', the name of the Baloch country in the time of Alexander the Great (356–23 BC).[8] Muhammad Sardar Khan theorized that the term Baloch is a derivative of Belus, the title of Babylonian or Chaldian kings. Nimrud, the son of Kush or Cush or Kooth, was called Nimrud the Belus.[9] The followers of Nimrud were known as Belusis. Among the Arabs, Belusis were pronounced Balos.[10] Thus, the word Baloch has come from Belusis or Balos, Sardar Khan argues.

Taj Mohammad Breseeg, a Baloch historian, quotes the Kurdish scholar Mohammad Amin Seraji who believes that the term 'Baloch' is the corrupted form of the term Baroch or Baroz. Arguing on the origin and the meaning of the term, Seraji says, the Baroz has a common meaning both in Kurdish and Balochi, which means the land of the rising sun (ba-roch or 'towards sun'). Located at the eastern-most corner of the Median Empire, the country probably got the designation 'Baroch or Baroz' during the Median or early Achaemenid era, believes Seraji. According to him, there are several tribes living in Eastern Kurdistan, who are called Barozi (because of their eastward location in the region).[11]

Etymology apart, there are two competing theories on the historical origin of the Baloch: the first states that the Baloch are a native people who have been described as the Oritans, the Jatts, the Medes, etc., in ancient records; the second states that the Baloch migrated into the area from Syria some 2,000 years ago.[12] The dispute is likely to keep historians busy for a long time.

What is interesting about the debate is that it was joined by Muhammad Ali Jinnah who presented 'The Memorandum of the Government of Kalat' to the British Cabinet Mission in 1946. In it, an Arab origin for the Baloch was claimed. Thus, in para six, the Memo states:

> In the first place, ethnographically, the people of Kalat and of the territories under its suzerainty, have no affinities with the people of India. The Ruling Family of Kalat is of Arab origin, and not, as usually stated, of Brahuic extraction. They belong to the Ahmadzai branch of the Mirwari clan, which originally emigrated from Iran to the Kolwa Valley of Makran. Apart from the Brahvis, all the important and influential tribes are also of non-Indian origin. The Marri and Bugti tribes, who occupy the most southern buttresses of the Sulaiman Mountains, are Rind Baluchis, almost certainly of Arab extraction. They came to Sindh either with the Arab conquerors, or after them, and remained mixed up with the original Hindu inhabitants.[13]

In short, the history of the origin of the Baloch people is shrouded in controversy primarily due to the absence of authentic, documented source material. Not surprisingly, Mir Ahmed Yar Khan Baloch, the Khan of Kalat wrote: 'Authorities on the subject have not been able to state anything authentic about the exact origins of the Baloches.'[14]

Whether an indigenous people or a migratory one, the Baloch have lived in the area of Balochistan since at least the start of the Christian era. The central marker that unites the Baloch community is a more or less well-articulated conception of all Baloch as descended from a common ancestor, thus constituting a 'qaum' (nation). The Baloch claim to descend from a single ancestor, Amir Hamza, the uncle of Prophet Muhammad, and can prove it to their full satisfaction with genealogical tables, ballads and traditions.[15] The same is true of the Brahvis, who also claim to descend from a single ancestor, Braho or Ibrahim, from Allepo.[16]

Based on the study of the different views on the origin of the Baloch, Inayatullah Baloch concludes that 'It would be true to say that the present-day Baloch are perhaps not a single race, but are a people of different origins, whose language belongs to the Iranian family of languages.' According to him, the Baloch are mixed with Arabs in the south, Indians in the east, Turkmen and other Altaic groups in the north-west and in the coastal area a mixture of Iranian, Assyrian and Negro stock.[17]

In 1890, Sir Edward Oliver, a British colonial officer who had served in Balochistan, described Baloch tribesman as 'essentially a nomad—good looking, frank, with well-cut features, black and well-oiled flowing hair and beard, attired in a smock frock, that is theoretically white, but never is washed save on the rare occasions when he goes to durbar.'[18]

This is how Sylvia Matheson described a Baloch: 'Just twenty-one years old, Sardar Akbar Shahbaz Khan Bugti, Tumandar of the warrior Bugti tribe ... was a sight to gladden the eyes of any romantically-inclined girl. He was well over six feet tall, with a magnificent head of thick, shining, black, curly hair and beard to match, lively intelligent eyes, a humorous mouth (what could be seen of it under the superb, curling moustache and beard), and fine, clean-cut features. Almost impossibly good-looking in fact.[19]

Baloch Ethnic Grouping

The Baloch are divided into seventeen groups and some 400 subgroupings.[20] Of the seventeen, the two major groups are the 'Eastern', or Sulaiman Baloch, who are the larger of the two groups and 'Western', or Makran Baloch, who have traditionally been viewed as the 'original nucleus' of the Baloch people.

The Sulaiman Baloch include the tribes of Bugtis, Buzdars, Dombkis, Kaheris, Khetrans, Magsis, Marris, Mugheris, Rinds and Umranis while the Makran are made up of the Buledi, Dashtis, Gichkis, Kandais, Rais, Rakhshanis, Rinds, Sangus and Sanjranis. Traditionally, the Rinds have been regarded as being on top of the pecking order, though it is the Bugtis and the Marris who have become dominant in modern Baloch politics and been at the centre of the recent unrest. The Marris, who control almost 9,000 sq. km of land and are Balochistan's largest tribe (they number 134,000), consider themselves Balochistan's master tribe.[21]

Among the Brahvis, who are found in the central mountain region south of Quetta, there are three subdivisions: the Brahvi nucleus, the Jhalawan Brahvis and the Sarawan Brahvis. The Brahvi nucleus tribes include the Ahmadzai, Bangulzai, Bizenjo, Gurguari, Iltazai, Kalandari, Kambrani, Mengal, Mirwari, Raisani, Rodeni and Sumalari. The Ahmadzais occupy the top of the social hierarchy among Brahvi, and is the tribe of the Khan of Kalat, though a Jhalawan tribe, the Mengals, have become a powerful player in Balochistan politics.[22] Most of these tribes are bilingual and are quite fluent both in the Balochi and Brahvi languages.

According to the *Encyclopaedia Britannica*, there is a nucleus of eight Brahvi tribes to which other people have been affiliated so that the number of tribes has swelled to twenty-nine. Mir Ahmed Yar Khan, the Khan of Kalat, calls the Baloch and the Brahvis two groups of the same people. The 'group which was originally called "Ibrahimi Baluches" is now pronounced as "Brahvi Baluches"'.[23]

Tribal System

Despite the tough geography, difficulties in communication as well as differences in language and dialect among the various Baloch groups, a specific tribal, political, social and economic organization developed over the centuries. The tribal system, in fact, is the very basis of Baloch society and culture and has shaped the general structure of Baloch life and institutions. Tribal loyalties based on common descent continue to dominate the Baloch society to a large extent. The allegiance of most of the Baloch has been to their extended families, clans and tribes. According to Sherbaz Khan Mazari, a Baloch politician, 'In a tribal culture, lineage counts for everything, and one's roots are inextricably linked with the present. Heritage invariably, and often invisibly, shapes and forms the contours of one's life.'[24]

According to Taj Mohammad Breseeg, tribal ties, however, are of little significance in Makran (both Pakistani and Iranian Balochistan) in southern Balochistan. Neither can the Kacchi plains in the east nor Lasbela in the southernmost part of Balochistan be characterized as tribal. In contrast, tribal social structure is important in Dera Bugti, Kohlu and Barkan, in Kalat and Khuzdar districts in central Pakistani Balochistan, northern Iranian Balochistan, Sarhadd, southern Afghanistan, Nimruz, and even to some extent in the rural areas of Sindh and Punjab.[25]

The traditional tribal society has created hurdles in the development of Baloch nationalism since loyalties of tribal members extend to individual tribes rather than national entities or a political ideology. An individual's identity is based on his belonging to a tribe and not the nation. The failure of different tribes to unite in the cause of Baloch nationalism has been due to this strong element of tribal loyalties. As a result, a unified nationalist movement could not take shape in the run-up to the creation of Pakistan in 1947 and the forced accession of the province. Some Baloch leaders did try to articulate a sense of common ethnic identity but it was the endeavour of only a few and failed to catch the imagination of most of the Baloch.

In recent years, a new non-tribal leadership has emerged from among the Baloch. This cuts across different regions and socio-economic classes. These nationalists are toeing a separate line and urging the sardars to leave their individual goals and champion the nationalist causes. As has been well put: 'The process of horizontalization of the Balochi society and polity may have just begun. The Balochi nationalists may have embarked upon a long journey ahead.'[26]

Given these constraints, the current rise of a non-tribal or pan-tribal nationalist movement is a very significant development. The dilemma for the nationalists is that tribal support remains an important element for the success of a national movement, which also makes them susceptible to tribal rivalries.[27]

Tribal Rivalries

Balochistan has a history of intertribal feuds that have given birth to long-lasting wars between the tribes. A critical feud was Nawab Bugti's fight with another Bugti sub-tribe, the Kalpars. As a result, Amir Hamza Bugti, the son of the Kalpar Wadera, was assassinated. The Kalpars took revenge by assassinating Nawab Bugti's, youngest son. In the ensuing skirmishes, thousands of Kalpars had to flee the Bugti area with government support. Such was the animosity that even a lawyer from Lahore, who was defending the Kalpars accused of killing the Nawab's son, was gunned down in Quetta in June 1995. Other tribal rivalries include: Bugti vs Ahmedans; Bugtis vs Mazaris; Bugtis vs Raisanis; Gazinis vs Bijranis; Marris vs Loonis; and Rind vs Raisani.[28]

Sardari System

At the core of the Baloch tribal structure is the sardari system. According to Taj Mohammad Breseeg, 'The sardari system appears to have had its origins in the Mughal period of Indian history, but it is believed to have assumed its present shape rather late, during the period of British colonial rule.'[29] Under the centuries-old system, tribesmen pledged their allegiance to sardars, or tribal chiefs, in exchange for social justice and the maintenance of the 'integrity of tribe'.[30] The sardars, in turn, pledged their loyalty to the Khan at Kalat and defended the Khan's khanate against any outside attack or provided the Khan with material and moral help during his campaigns. It was a well-federated system operating through tribal loyalty and patronage. According to Martin Axmann, '… the sardari system represented the keystone of British indirect rule in Balochistan. Without sardari collaboration British control of the region would have been impossible.'[31]

Unlike the egalitarianism of the Pashtun tribal organization, the Baloch sardari system was hereditary and the sardar or tribal chief exercised absolute and unquestioned control over his fellow tribesmen. He functioned as chief executive, legislator and judge. The sardar even controlled the social life of his subjects; and consequently, out of fear or reverence, the Baloch gave unswerving loyalty to him. The sardar's extraordinary authority within this structure probably stemmed from the essentially military character of early Baloch tribal society.[32]

From the sardar, power flowed downward to waderas, the section chiefs, and beyond them to the subordinate clan and sub-clan leaders of the lesser tribal units. Thus, for the tribesmen, the concepts of the nation state and obedience to the Central governments under which they lived have had little meaning. Ordinary Baloch were resigned to the rule by the sardars and were characterized by the British as 'slaves of the sardars'.[33] It is a land that is ruled so autocratically by its nawabs that, in the words of the historian Charles Chenevix Trench, 'An oath of innocence taken with one's hand on the Nawab's head was always accepted.'[34]

The 'jirga' or tribal gathering is and remains an integral part of the tribal structure. Under the British, Sir Robert Sandeman introduced a new kind of jirga, the 'Shahi Jirga' (Grand Council or the council of the main tribal sardars) for the area under their control—British Balochistan. In this jirga, only sardars and aristocrats could be members. The Shahi Jirga was held at Quetta, Sibi and Fort Munro once or twice a year. The new jirga could impose taxes on property and labour; only the Political Agent could review the decisions of the jirga. As described by Janmahmad, 'The Shahi Jirga was a shrewd mechanism of indirect rule with powers vested in a few carefully selected tribal elders loyal to the British and ready to act against their own people.'[35]

In 1968, under the Ayub Khan government's, Criminal Law (Special Provisions) Ordinance, 1968, the jirga system was legally recognised in 'B' area. All disputes would be settled through jirgas.[36]

The sardari system was outlawed on 8 April 1976, by prime minister Zulfikar Ali Bhutto. This was an attempt to reduce the power of the various tribal chiefs so as to enable the forcible incorporation of the various tribes into the mainstream of Pakistan's political, economic and social life. However, though weakened, the system continued to exist in Balochistan. Bhutto, moreover, did not repeal the 1968 Jirga Ordinance that was applicable in the 'B' areas that constituted 95 per cent of Balochistan. It was only in 1990 that the Balochistan High Court struck down the Ordinance of 1968, thereby abolishing the justice system administered through jirga.[37]

Interestingly, while the sardars are blamed for the continuation of the system, the reality is somewhat different. In June 1972, the Leader of the House, Sardar Attaullah Mengal, moved a resolution in the Balochistan Assembly demanding that the federal government abolish the sardari, the jirga and the tribal system since the provincial assembly did not have the authority to do so. The federal government took no action in this regard and about eight months later, on 14 February 1973, the National Awami Party government (which was responsible for presenting the resolution in the assembly) was overthrown and a military operation was launched in Balochistan.

The resolution moved by Attaullah Mengal read: 'Now that the Tribal System has lost its advantages keeping it instated is going to act as a hurdle in the development of the people of these tribes.' Speaking during the debate, Gul Khan Nasir, the nationalist poet, said, 'Mr. Speaker! as long as this institution remains (even as a vestige) it will keep our nation divided into various tribes and sub-tribes which will render it impossible for us to achieve economic progress.'[38]

Ironically, the policy of the federal government to deny the essentials of provincial autonomy has strengthened the tribal system. The sardars continue to influence the justice system and the working of the police. The sardari system will not disappear unless the grievances related to provincial rights are removed. So long as this does not happen the people will continue to bear the load of archaic social structures despite their manifest unhappiness with them.[39]

Cultural Values

The collective character of the Baloch is manifested in what is called 'Balochmayar' (the Baloch code of honour). It is this that distinguishes them from others and thus forms an important feature of the Baloch identity.[40] The honour code is not only strongly held but it has given the Baloch a consciousness that is above tribal, political and geographical boundaries. A Baloch would be willing to sacrifice his all—including his life—to protect it. Henry Pottinger, a nineteenth-century British officer who had extensively travelled in the area, thus described the Baloch adherence to their code of honour: 'When they once offer, or promise to afford protection to a person who may require or solicit it, they will die before they fail in their trust.'[41].

One example of this relates to the Mughal emperor Humayun. In 1543, Humayun, who had been exiled, was forlornly wandering towards Kandahar with his pitiful troops. He entered the territory of the Magsis and set up camp in the chief's village. The Magsi sardar was absent at that time. By the next morning, Humayun and his men realized that they were prisoners as the tribesmen refused to let them leave until their chief's return. Late that night, the chief returned and met with Humayun. He showed him the farman that he had received from Humayun's brothers, Mirza Kamran, ruler of Kandahar and Mirza Askari, requesting him to imprison the ousted emperor and deliver him to them in return for a generous reward. The Magsi chief admitted to Humayun that he had planned to attack him and his party with the intention of capturing him. But now that Humayun had chosen to camp at his home village, he was no longer an enemy but had become, by Baloch tradition, his honoured guest. Humayun's sister writes in *Humayun-Nama* that the Magsi sardar told Humayun '… now I will sacrifice my life and the lives of my family, I have five or six sons, for your Majesty's head, or rather for one hair of it. Go where you wish. God protect you.' If the Magsi chief had not been loyal to the Baloch code, the history of Mughal India might have been dramatically altered.[42]

The key elements of the common code of honour are valuing loyalty, blood vengeance, believing in 'an eye for an eye and a life for a life' and adhering to the simple rule that 'he shall take who has the power, and he shall keep who can,'[43] protection of those seeking refuge, hospitality to guests, death to both parties in adultery, and women's right to petition for peace and the pardon of offence.[44] Inayatullah Baloch quotes a Baloch 'Battal' or proverb on the Baloch concept of revenge: 'The Baloch's revenge for blood remains as young for two hundred years, as a deer of two years.'[45]

The customary Baloch approach towards women is one of great respect. Even in anger, a man was not supposed to lay a hand on a woman. Any act of molestation is considered a heinous crime, the punishment of which was death. This explains the fierce Baloch reaction at the rape of Dr Shazia Khalid in 2005 that aggravated the current Baloch insurgency (details in the chapter on Insurgency). Tribal blood feuds were often resolved with women going bareheaded to the family of their rivals and pleading for resolution. As per Baloch custom, a man cannot refuse a request made by a bareheaded woman. Once the request for reconciliation was met, the patriarch of the rival faction had to 'restore' the woman's dignity by placing a sari or dupatta over her head before she was returned to her family.[46]

The British were all praise for the courage and chivalry of their Bugti opponents. As Edward Oliver wrote in 1890, 'War is looked upon as the first business of a gentleman, and every Balochi is a gentleman'. However, frustrated by the continuous attacks and raids on their cantonments, on 6 August 1846, the British declared the Bugti tribe outlaws and put a price of ten rupees (about fifteen shillings—quite a large sum at that time) on every man's head, dead or alive.[47]

Baloch–Pashtun Divide

Though there are other ethnic groups present in the province such as Hazaras, Sindhis and Punjabis, the two dominant ethnic groups in

Balochistan are the Baloch and the Pashtuns. In the northern districts of the province, the primary ethnic identity is that of the Pashtuns—the same ethnic group across the border in Afghanistan and KPK including the now defunct Federally Administered Tribal Areas (FATA). It is believed that the term Pashtun or Pathan is derived from the Sanskrit word 'Pratishthan', which means people who are established and command respect in society.

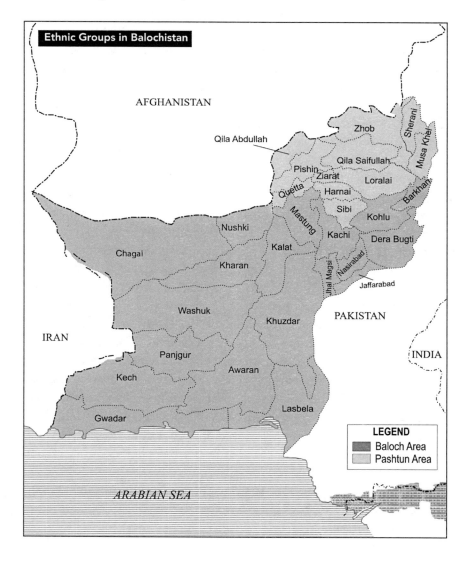

The predominant Pashtun tribes in Balochistan include Kakar, Ghilzai Tareen, Mandokhel, Sherani, Luni, Kasi and Achakzai. Even though the figures are contested, Pashtuns form the second-largest ethnic group in Balochistan, ranging from 29 per cent as per the 1998 census to 50 per cent as claimed by Pashtun nationalists. Quetta, the capital, has a multiethnic population while one ethnic group or the other inhabits other parts of the province. Even in Quetta, different ethnic groups live in separate areas.

There is a historical background to the Baloch–Pashtun divide in Balochistan. Britain's strategic interest of keeping Afghanistan as a buffer against Russian expansion dictated that they develop road and rail links in the northern parts of Balochistan. The infrastructure links developed during the British time enabled the Pashtun-inhabited areas to achieve greater economic progress than the Baloch areas within the province.

The warped economic development during the colonial era was reinforced after the creation of Pakistan when little attention was paid to the province. The situation was further complicated because of the continuous influx of refugees from Afghanistan, first due to the Soviet invasion of Afghanistan in 1979 and later during the Taliban rule. This has been facilitated due to the porous border between Balochistan and Afghanistan. The southern Afghan city of Kandahar, a stronghold of the Taliban, is just 120 km from the Pakistani border city of Chaman.

For example, the population of the area shot up from just over 85,000 in 1941 to over four million by 1981. As per Balochistan government figures, the province hosts around 784,000 Afghans of which 337,045 are registered Afghan migrants while the rest are illegal migrants living in the province.[48] The refugee influx provoked Baloch apprehension that the demographic balance in the province was getting altered. As a counter, the Pashtun leadership in Balochistan has argued that the Afghans have merely moved around within their own 'watan' or homeland. They have not settled in the Baloch areas so the Baloch should not have a problem.

The presence of the Taliban, and Quetta becoming their de facto capital in Pakistan, brought an extra presence of the army and paramilitary troops in the province. This has raised further concerns among the Baloch for whom the additional presence of security forces is problematic due to the Punjabi-dominated Pakistan Army's history of repression.

In the run-up to the creation of the province in 1970, the Pashtun nationalists, led by Samad Khan Achakzai, wanted the merger of the Pashtun territories (largely consisting of the former British Balochistan) with the then North-West Frontier Province (now Khyber-Pakhtunkhwa) to create a united Pashtun province. The Pakistan Muslim League, Balochistan chapter, led by Qazi Isa and Nawab Jogezai, wanted the restoration of the former British Balochistan and the Kalat state as separate provinces. The National Awami Party favoured merging the two units into a single province.[49] In the event in July 1970, the boundaries of contemporary Balochistan were announced that merged the erstwhile Kalat Division and Quetta Division into one province.

Samad Khan's son, Mehmood Khan Achakzai, formed the Pashtunkhwa Milli Awami Party (PkMAP) in 1989 to articulate the viewpoint of the Pashtuns of Balochistan. He agrees with the Baloch that 'Pakistan is a Punjabi empire subjugating other nationalities'. However, the PkMAP believes that it has three options: (1) Balochistan should be declared a two-nation province (Baloch and Pashtun), with equal representation and rights for both; (2) a new province for the Pashtuns of Balochistan should be created; or (3) Pashtun areas of Balochistan should be made part of the NWFP (now Khyber Pakhtunkhwa—KPK).

But the Pashtun–Baloch political differences have seldom escalated into conflict and they have coexisted for years, mainly because the two ethnic groups live in different areas. There is very little intermix of population, except in Quetta, Sibi and parts of Loralai. Moreover, the nationalists among both the ethnic groups have a common dislike for Punjabi exploitation, a shared history of cooperation and engagement with left-wing politics.

The one issue that could have created tensions was the census. Last held in 1998, the census could not be held till 2017 due to 'security concerns'. At the time of writing, the detailed results of the 2017 census have not been made available. For the Baloch, the holding of the census in the presence of Afghan refugees was problematic. For the Pashtun nationalists, the possibility of local Pashtuns being ignored in the name of Afghan refugees was an issue of concern. Consequently, the census could have been a tense time for Baloch–Pashtun relations. However, the provisional results of the census show that the Baloch continue to retain their majority in the province and hence the protests have been muted.

3

Religion

Islam

ISLAM CAME TO BALOCHISTAN VIA Mohammad bin Qasim's invasion of Sindh in AD 711 and by the ninth century, the population had been converted. Before converting to Islam, the Baloch were believed to be Mazdaki and Zoroastrian.[1] The remnants of a few Zoroastrian traditions are still evident among some Baloch tribes. While the bulk of the Baloch are Hanafi Sunnis, there is a sizeable Shia Hazara community, primarily in Quetta, who had migrated to the area from Bamiyan in Afghanistan to escape the brutal persecution of Abdur Rahman in the late nineteenth century. There is also a significant Zikri population in Makran.

The intermix of religions is primarily due to the Baloch having shunned religious extremism or sectarianism. Consequently, Hindus, Shias and Zikris have till recently lived in harmony and without prejudice, fear or hatred. Intermarriage between the Sunni-Baloch and the Zikri-Baloch, despite their different religious beliefs, do take place. It is common to find among the Baloch that one brother is a Zikri while the other is a Sunni.[2]

Religion has not played an important role in the daily life of the Baloch who have been averse to mixing religion with politics.[3] As E. Oliver pointed out, the Baloch '... has less of God in his head, and less of the devil in his nature' and prefers to have his prayers said for him.[4] In another instance, in the late nineteenth century, when British authorities asked Baloch and Pashtuns how their civil cases should be decided, the Baloch replied: 'Rawaj' (Baloch customary law); the Pashtun answered: 'Sharia' (Islamic law).[5]

The Baloch approach to religion is also demonstrated by this interesting story: 'Once, a Baloch was asked why he did not keep the fast of Ramzan. Replied the Baloch that he was excused as his chief was keeping it for him. "What are you doing?" he asked a practising Muslim about his evening prayers. He was answered: "Praying in the fear of God." Rejoined the Baloch: "Come along to my hills where we don't fear anybody."'[6]

Thus, historically speaking, the Baloch always have had a more secular and pluralistic view on religion than their neighbours. As has been well put: 'It is not by chance that the Baloch enjoy the unenviable reputation of being "bad Muslims".'[7] Even in traditional Baloch society, the mullah was looked upon as a functional figure rather than a revered one.[8] While they accept Islam as an important facet of their life conditioning their existence, they do not see it as the most important part of their identity and have not accepted the ascendancy of religion over sociocultural values. As observed by Nina Swidler, '... religion does not distinguish Baloch identity'.[9] So far, they have been largely impervious to the persistent efforts at Islamization. They have also not allowed Islamists of any variety to gain traction in their area even though references to the Quetta shura of the Taliban can confuse many. As such, the view that the Baloch nationalist sentiments are being overridden by Islamist politics is perhaps incorrect.

However, this could be changing due to the continued support of radicalization and encouragement of terrorist groups like the Lashkar-e-Taiba (LeT) and the sectarian terrorist group the Lashkar-e-Jhangvi (LeJ) by the Pakistan state. Thus, Wahabism that was alien to Balochistan has made an entry and is impacting an increasing number of people.

It was Gen. Zia-ul-Haq who sowed the seeds of extremism in Balochistan. Zia had a twofold objective in his Islamization policies. One, he wanted to use it as a weapon against the Baloch insurgency that had ended in 1977. As a result, there was an influx of 'tablighi' activities and a mushroom growth of madrassas. According to a recent report, 85,000 students were studying in 1,095 madrassas across Balochistan.[10] Second, in order to prevent another Bangladesh, Zia also saw Islam as an effective unifying force that would subsume the Baloch ethnic identity into a larger Islamic identity.[11] As a result of Islamization, radicalization has increased in the once secular province. There has also been a corresponding rise in the activities of sectarian groups with a phenomenal increase in the number of sectarian killings, especially of the Shia Hazaras in Quetta carried out by the LeJ.

Under Gen. Musharraf, further encouragement was given to the setting up of madrassas in order to access Baloch areas that were stubbornly opposed to the mullahs. These efforts were at the expense of secular education. The budget of the ministry of religious affairs of the province was much higher than that of the ministry of education.

Politically too, the growing presence of the clergy was in evidence as a result of the manipulated elections of 2002 under President Musharraf. This allowed the coalition of religious parties called the Muttahida Majlis-i-Amal (MMA), led by Maulana Fazlur Rehman's Jamiat Ulema-i-Islam (JUI-F), to join the provincial government in October 2002. A spin-off for Musharraf was that he could frighten the West into supporting him by citing the coming into power of the MMA and potential growth of fundamentalism. By a sleight of hand, he was able to confuse the Pashtun-dominated areas of northern Balochistan with the Baloch territories in the south. As the International Crisis Group (ICG) puts it, '… reliance on the Pashtun religious parties to counter the Baloch opposition has strengthened Islamist forces at the cost of the moderate Baloch'. It noted that 'The international community, particularly the US and its Western allies, seemed to ignore the domestic and regional implications of the Balochistan conflict, instead placing their faith in a military government that is targeting the anti-Taliban Baloch and Pashtuns and rewarding pro-Taliban Pashtun parties.'[12]

What the Pakistan leadership under Musharraf did not realize was that in an attempt to curb Baloch nationalism, they unleashed the genie of radicalization and sectarianism in a hitherto secular province through the increase in the number of Deobandi madrassas. In the process, in the long term, sectarianism was reinforced in Pakistan.

Growth of Sectarianism

Sectarian militancy and violence in Balochistan—part of the wider sectarian conflict in Pakistan—has risen exponentially over the last decade. Although sectarianism is not indigenous to Balochistan, according to one study, sectarianism is growing in all the Baloch districts and especially in the districts of Mastung and Lasbela. The prime targets of sectarian violence in Balochistan has been the Shia community, particularly the Shia Hazaras, at the hands of the LeJ which is an anti-Shia, anti-Iran terrorist group.[13] Some Brahvis have reportedly joined the sectarian groups and are being used to target the Shia Hazaras and the Baloch nationalists.

As noted by Ali Dayan Hasan, '… there has also been a complex and contradictory but close historical relationship between the state and the LeJ both in Balochistan and beyond.'[14] Several strands testify to this official backing: their ability to hold public rallies despite being banned;[15] sectarian attacks taking place in areas with a strong Frontier Corps (FC) presence;[16] taking off passengers from buses, identifying Shias and then killing them, all of which takes time. As has been well put, 'Sectarian violence has increased because of a clear expansion of operational spaces for violent sectarian groups to function within. Methods used in the recent sectarian incidents show that the groups operate with confidence and without fear of being caught.'[17] Such ease of operations would be possible only when the terrorists know that '… the police and the courts don't have the capacity to investigate, prosecute and convict sectarian killers'.[18] Clearly, therefore, sectarian groups are deliberately being allowed to function by the state.

Over the years, Mastung has emerged as the main centre of sectarian militancy. Perhaps the largest Sipah-i-Sahaba seminary outside southern Punjab is in Mastung, in the heart of the territory controlled by the Raisani tribe. This serves as one of the bastions of religious extremism in the province. Mastung was once a strong centre of Baloch separatists but is being taken over by sectarian groups. The killing of twelve Islamic State (IS)/Daesh terrorists by security forces in Mastung in 2017 is evidence of this development. Mastung is also a strategic point for targeting convoys of Shia pilgrims going to Iran.[19] The trail of most of the attacks on Hazara Shias in Quetta, which have claimed hundreds of innocent lives over the last decade, leads to this district. Despite several LeJ terrorists being killed in a crackdown by security agencies, the surge in violence indicates that sectarian networks are still capable of launching high-profile terrorist attacks. Meanwhile, Pakistani sectarian militants have also found sanctuaries in Afghanistan, allowing them to move about freely on both sides of the border and making it much harder for Pakistani law enforcement agencies to track them down even if they had the will.

There is also a more sinister design behind the Islamization process. According to Naseer Dashti, the distinct secular identity of the Baloch is part and parcel of their nationalist aspirations. Dilution of the secular identity would adversely impact their political resistance to the efforts of the Pakistan state to ram a Pakistani identity. This would be just the first step in the Baloch acceptance of the exploitation of their resources at the altar of 'Muslim brotherhood'.[20]

The Human Rights Commission of Pakistan also noted that unlike in the past, '… religious fanaticism was not merely being exported to the province from elsewhere, it was now being bred in Balochistan. A growing network of madrassas had contributed to aggravation of inter-sect tensions. There were fears that the security forces were patronizing militants and Quetta was being turned into a haven for militants.'[21] As a result, in the past decade or so, the advent of extremist militants had led to unprecedented sectarian bloodshed in Balochistan. In trying to pit religious extremism against Baloch nationalism, the state could be making a huge mistake. The transnational agendas of the extremist groups could pose an even bigger threat to the state.[22]

While evidence on the ground is thin, the government has been trying to show a linkage between the Baloch groups and the Lashkar-e-Jhangvi. For example, the then interior minister Rehman Malik declared in the Senate that the two groups 'had been related to each other for five years'.[23]

Overall, though some Baloch have been used for sectarian killings, so far Baloch nationalism has proved to be stronger and Islamization policies have not really succeeded where ethnic Baloch have been predominant. Yet, Islamization continues to be a significant element of Islamabad's strategy. The intention of the state in the Pashtun and the Baloch areas is clearly to use Islam to curb both Pashtun and Baloch nationalism.

Daesh and Tehreek-e-Taliban Pakistan (TTP)

The Balochistan government has frequently claimed that the Daesh did not operate within the province and debunked claims by the group. However, the violent activities of the Daesh have been gradually increasing. It carried out a suicide blast prior to the July 2018 general elections during a large political rally in Mastung on 13 July 2018 killing more than 130 people. Among the martyred were the younger brother of former Balochistan chief minister Aslam Raisani and Balochistan Awami Party (BAP) candidate Nawabzada Siraj Raisani.[24] The Mastung massacre negated the claim of the army that the backbone of terrorism had been broken. Prior to this attack, Daesh had claimed responsibility of a devastating attack against lawyers in Quetta in August 2016 and a shrine in Kuzdar in November 2016.

While both the Daesh and TTP have a covert presence in Quetta, elsewhere in Balochistan their operations differ based on ethnic identities. Thus, the Daesh is believed to largely exist in the Baloch-dominated districts of Mastung and Kalat while the TTP networks appear to be concentrated in the Pashtun-majority districts of Chaman, Qila Abdullah, Pishin, Zhob and Qila Saifullah. The terrorist roots of the two groups also differ: the Daesh terrorists are largely drawn from militant sectarian groups, notably the Lashkar-e-Jhangvi and splinter groups violently focused on minority Muslim sects since the 1990s. The TTP, on the other hand, is comprised of runaway militants from the tribal areas, whose aim is to target security personnel and political figures.[25] However, these are not water-tight compartments and there is overlapping. Thus, the Lashkar-e-Jhangvi has also established nexus with the Jaesh-e-Islam and Tehreek-e-Taliban Pakistan.

Zikris

The term Zikri is derived from the Arabic word Zikr (remembering and recitation). The origin of the Zikri sect and their belief system is not well documented because almost all their religious and historical records were obliterated due to oppression during the rule of Mir Nasir Khan in the eighteenth century. Whatever information available is from the few preserved religious works, oral traditions and the writings of non-Zikris.[26]

The Zikris are the followers of Syed Muhammad Jaunpuri, who is considered to be the Mahdi. According to Ibn Khaldun, the renowned Arab sociologist-historian, 'It has been well-known (and generally accepted) by Muslims in every epoch, that at the end of time a man from the family (of the Prophet) will without fail make his appearance, one who will strengthen the religion and make justice prevail.'[27] According to Inayatullah Baloch, '... though neither the Koran nor hadith supports this popular Muslim belief, nevertheless, the concept of the Mahdi remains part of Muslim traditions, though Shias and Sunnis differ in their formulation of it. In fact, there is a long list of individuals in Muslim history who have claimed to be the promised Mahdi.'[28]

Syed Muhammad was born in Jaunpur, UP, India in 1443 and was a great Sunni scholar. He claimed to be the last Mahdi and either he or one of his disciples founded the Zikri sect. Zikri scholars claim that the Mahdi lived in Makran where he spent most of his time in zikr at the Koh-e-Murad.[29]

According to Inayatullah Baloch, the principal tenets of the Zikri doctrine are; (i) while the Prophet preached the doctrine of the Koran in its literal sense, it remained for the Mahdi to further elucidate its meaning; Syed Muhammad Mahdi was in fact the interpreter (Sahib-e-tawil) of the Koran; (ii) Prophet Mohammad is the last prophet and Syed Muhammad is the last Mahdi; (iii) the Kalima to be modified with a new Kalima, 'There is no god but Allah. Muhammad Mahdi is his messenger'; (iv) instead of namaz (prayer), people should recite Zikr (a formula of repeating the various names of Allah); and (v) the fast of Ramazan should be replaced with a monthly seven-day fast. Thus, Zikri doctrine deviates from orthodox Muslim belief but Zikris consider themselves to be true Muslims.[30]

The city of Turbat in Kech, Makran, is the Zikri holy city where they have built the Koh-e-Murad. According to the Zikris, this is a shrine but some orthodox Muslims charge that the Zikris consider it to be a Kaaba, akin to the one in Mecca. The places of worship of the Zikris, both temporary and permanent, are known as zikarana or zikrkhanah.[31] Not surprisingly, the Zikris attach religious significance to sites in Balochistan for which they have developed a special veneration. Their rites of worship are mostly conducted in Balochi. Consequently, Zikri poets and religious scholars have enriched Balochi literature.[32] For them, Balochistan, especially Turbat, is the 'Gul-e-Zamin' (flower of the earth). This patriotic attitude on the part of the Zikri Baloch is held by many to be the forerunner of modern Baloch nationalism.[33]

In the past, the Zikris had faced persecution under Mir Nasir Khan in the eighteenth century. In modern times, such persecution was very evident under the Zia-ul-Haq dictatorship. In 1978, several religious-political parties organized the Tehrik-e-Nabuat (movement for the finality of the prophethood) in Balochistan and launched an aggressive campaign against the Zikris. Over the decades, as religious extremists established themselves in Balochistan, persecution has only increased. For example, in 2014, at least six Zikris were massacred in Awaran, and slogans have appeared in the province warning the Zikris to 'convert' or die, signed off by an outfit calling itself Lashkar-i-Khorasan.[34]

The Zikris largely inhabit Makran, Lasbela and Karachi. In fact, Makran's population is composed of two Muslim sects—the Namazis (Sunnis) and the Zikris. Prior to 1947, it was estimated that Zikris formed about half the population of Makran. Some have estimated that in the 1990s, the Zikri population in Makran had declined to one-third or one-fourth of the total. According to Inayatullah Baloch, the principal Baloch subgroups belonging to the Zikri sect are the Sajdis, the Sangurs, the Rais, the Darzadas, the Meds and the Koh-Baloch. In addition, some followers of the Zikri faith are also found among the Baloch nomads in the Khuzdar and Kharan regions of eastern Balochistan.[35]

The Baloch Students Organization (BSO)[36] has been in the forefront of defending the religious rights of the Zikris. It has organized political rallies to mobilize popular support against sectarianism in and around Makran. They have also highlighted Baloch cultural principles as Balochness (Balochiat) and the Baloch code of honour (Balochmayar) that demands that Baloch defend religious minorities and weak groups. They have also published and distributed pamphlets underlining the Zikri fervour for Balochistan. Thus, despite hurdles created by fundamentalists and at times the state, the BSO has won the support of the majority of Makran's Sunni Baloch in defence of the religious rights of the Zikris.[37]

Hazaras

Hazaras are Shia Muslims[38] who had migrated from Afghanistan after being persecuted in the Hazarajat area of Afghanistan during the late nineteenth century and later in the 1990s. The nearly half a million

Hazaras are mainly confined to Quetta, where they are dispersed around two main areas of the city: Hazara Town and Mehrabad and with the second biggest concentration in Mach. In Quetta, they are among the most developed communities, being educated, hard-working and with impressive women's literacy figures. The Hazara women work in hospitals, schools and universities.

The killing of the Hazaras has been both systematic and sustained. According to the Human Rights Commission of Pakistan, 'The targeting of the Shia Hazaras of Balochistan is one of the most violent and persistent persecution of any community in Pakistan on account of religious beliefs.'[39] Not surprisingly, many have termed it ethnic cleansing while the BBC in 2013 had termed Quetta 'hell on earth'. Since 2002, close to 3,000 Shias have been killed, most of them belonging to the Hazara community.[40] It has forced many Hazara youth to flee the recurring violence by any means possible. A popular saying in Quetta is that a Hazara is born in Afghanistan, grows up in Pakistan and is buried in Iran.[41]

The following features of the situation are worth noting. First, targeted attacks on the Hazara have continued despite the deployment of a large number of security personnel. Second, the attacks themselves are coordinated and not random. This would indicate availability of sufficient advance information. Third, almost every family in the community has lost a relative in these attacks and there does not appear to be an end to the targeting. Fourth, despite Balochistan crawling with all shades of intelligence agencies, the roots of terrorism targeting the community have not been traced. All this raises questions about the failure and inability of the state to protect half a million people in Quetta.[42] As the *Dawn* put it, 'Clearly either the state is complicit or its security policies are flawed.'[43]

The Hazaras are easily identified and targeted due to their distinctive facial features. As a result of the targeted killings, Hazara women have started wearing purdah in order to hide their distinct features, something they had not done earlier. The men have taken to wearing sunglasses to prevent identification.[44]

Not surprisingly, the Hazara community feels under siege. Its leaders told a HRCP delegation in 2009 that '... security agencies and the government bore ethnic and sectarian biases against them and were protecting and patronizing the perpetrators of the crimes against them'. Expanding on this theme, they accused the police of not taking sectarian killings and crimes against the Hazara community seriously: no effort was ever made by the government to conduct an impartial inquiry into serious charges; the findings of the tribunals set up to probe the loss of lives in 2004 and 2008 had not been made public till then; no government or public official had ever condemned their targeted killing nor had come to offer condolences or any compensation to the victims' families. The HRCP's conclusion was that the community had lost trust in the provincial government's ability to book the perpetrators of the murders.[45]

Sectarian considerations apart, the HRCP further noted the relative prosperity of the Hazara community due to the substantial remittances received from expatriates. This also accounted for the increasing crimes against the community. 'It seemed a campaign had been launched to terrorize the community so that they left Quetta by selling their businesses and property at throwaway prices. Pamphlets had been left at their homes telling them to sell their houses and leave.'[46]

A HRCP mission that met the representatives of the Hazara community in June 2011 found that there was no change in the targeting. They accused the banned groups Sipah-e-Sahaba Pakistan and Lashkar-e-Jhangvi for such terrorist acts. More than eighty Hazaras had been killed in the 3 September 2010 attack on an Al-Quds Day procession in Quetta that had been allowed by the local administration.[47] A Hazara community leader described one such terrorist attack to the HRCP delegation in 2012. According to him, in 2011, a bus full of pilgrims left Quetta for Iran. After crossing seven security check posts and 200 metres short of another check post, the bus was stopped in Mastung by armed men. Twenty-four Hazara men and boys were lined up and executed. It took five minutes to kill them all. Women and children were made to watch. This, according to him, did not happen even in Rwanda. Despite meeting everyone in the hierarchy from police officers to the president and prime minister, nothing changed. The political parties just joined the community for fateha and left. The inescapable conclusion was that the state was getting them killed.[48]

One other consequence of the killings is the impact it has had on the education of the next generation of Hazaras. Some years ago, there were around 250 Hazara students in the Balochistan University in Quetta. By 2013, there were only two or three left. The majority of the Hazara students in the university used to be girls because boys were usually sent to big cities outside Balochistan for education. Currently, there are no Hazara girls in the Balochistan University. All of the eleven Hazara faculty members have left the university. In view of the fear, there was a trend among the members of the community to seek asylum in Australia and other countries. Many ran considerable risks and travelled illegally by sea in rickety boats to get there. Despite the dangers, around 6,000 Hazaras had left for Australia.[49]

Hindus

Hindus have enjoyed a lot of goodwill in traditional Baloch society. They were, in fact, very prominent in the economic life of the province. Historically, a local Hindu invariably headed the finance ministry in Kalat. There were also examples of Hindus serving as governor of a province. When the British laid siege to Kalat in 1839, Finance Minister Dewan Bucha Mull, a Hindu, died defending Kalat. During the communal carnage of the Partition in 1947, it was only in Balochistan that the Hindu community was untouched and continued to live in peace. Under Kalat's constitution promulgated by the Khan in 1947, five Hindus were elected to the fifty-two-member Lower House—Dar-ul-Awan.[50]

In 2003, a HRCP team commented about the tradition of tolerance, noting that the Hindu minority displayed no visible feelings of insecurity. Forced conversions were not an issue. The Hindus considered themselves to be a part of the Baloch struggle for their rights.[51] There was a sea change by 2009 when another HRCP team reported that the Hindus seemed to be the worst affected by the actions of both the state and the militants. Hindus were worried about dwindling employment opportunities, kidnapping for ransom and forced conversion of Hindu girls to Islam. For example, in 2009, more than 1,000 Hindus lived in the town of Kalat. They told the HRCP that they no longer felt safe in Kalat's exclusive Hindu Mohallah.

There was a lot of pressure on the community to move out and settle in a new locality but they were afraid to do so out of fear for their security. Hindus complained that they could not go out of town even in daytime for reasons of security; they had failed to get an appointment with the Balochistan chief minister and the governor to convey their concerns; for the last five years, the district minority committee had not met, indicating the government's indifference to their problems. The police rarely took notice of crimes against them; Hindu traders had to pay extortion money amid threats of their shops being bombed unless they made the payment. In short, they felt like second-class citizens. The community was afraid that the tradition of tolerance that was once the hallmark of Baloch society was coming to an end.[52]

Although conversion of Hindu girls through marriages was not as widely reported in Balochistan as in Sindh, a few cases of conversion had taken place. In Quetta, some cases were reported in which young Hindu girls were first lured into a relationship and then converted to Islam.[53]

There was no improvement in the situation in 2011 when local elders of the Hindu community shared with the HRCP mission their concerns about targeting of members of their community amid increasing lawlessness in Balochistan. A social activist from the Hindu community drew the mission's attention to growing discrimination against minorities in Balochistan in the last few years. He said more than thirty persons from the Hindu community had been kidnapped for ransom. Those who tried to resist kidnapping attempts were killed. He said that members of the Hindu community were migrating to other countries but that was possible only for the affluent ones.

Education of the girl child in the minority communities had been seriously impacted as parents feared that they would be kidnapped and forcibly converted to Islam. He cited the conversion and marriage of one such girl, Sapna Kumari, where the Mullah who had kidnapped and forced her to embrace Islam threatened to murder her three brothers and father if she testified in court that she had been converted and married against her will. Kumari was a minor but the court ordered her to go with her 'husband'. He said that personnel of the intelligence agencies also targeted members of the Hindu community and inquired about their relatives in India and elsewhere.[54]

One of the reasons for targeting the Hindu population was their economic prosperity on account of their prominence in trade. They were, therefore, regularly kidnapped for ransom. The Hindu community in Quetta claimed that the house of every single member of their community had been robbed at least once. Their children were not safe and they were living in constant fear. As a result, systematic migration had taken place from areas with substantial concentration of Hindu population. For example, Mastung district had a Hindu population of at least 600 individuals a few years earlier. No more than forty remained in 2013. In fact, by 2013, 40 per cent of the minority population had left the province due to rising intimidation, forced conversions, violence and intolerance.[55]

4

Language

BALOCHISTAN IS A MULTILINGUAL PROVINCE. Though Balochi/ Brahvi and Pashto are the dominant languages, Urdu, Punjabi, Seraiki and Sindhi are also spoken in certain areas.

Population by mother tongue in percentage terms as per the 2017 census and its comparison with the 1998 census is as follows:

Year/ Language	Urdu	Punjabi	Sindhi	Pashto	Balochi	Seraiki	Others
1998	0.97	2.52	5.58	29.64	54.76	2.42	4.11
2017	0.81	1.13	4.56	35.34	52.61	2.65	2.90

Language distribution as per districts in percentage terms in the 1981 census was as follows[1]:

	Balochi	Brahvi	Pashto	Sindhi	Punjabi	Seraiki	Urdu
Panjgur	99.41						
Turbat	99.66						
Gwadar	98.5						
Kohlu	96.24						
Kharan	69.85	29.39					
Chagai	57.08	34.80					
Nasirabad	41.73	17.1		26.1		12.57	
Dera Bugti	Data	Not	Available				
Kalat	6.71	87.2					

Khuzdar	33.80	62.08					
Zhob			98.09				
Loralai			98.09				
Pishin			97.55				
Sibi	15.09		49.77	20.12			
Quetta		17.13	36.47		18.85		11

Two distinct linguistic streams make up the Baloch—Balochi and Brahvi. Balochi is believed to have originated in a lost language linked with the Parthian or Medean civilizations that flourished in the Caspian and adjacent areas in the pre-Christian era.[2] According to Selig Harrison, while Balochi 'is classified as a member of the western group of the Iranian branch of the Indo-European language family, consisting of Persian, Pashto, Balochi and Kurdish, Balochi is a separate language and is closely related only to one of the members of the Iranian group, Kurdish'. Though it has borrowed from Persian, Sindhi, Arabic and other languages, it has preserved distinctive features of its own.[3]

According to Inayatullah Baloch, prior to the nineteenth century, Balochi was an unwritten language, used in conversation in the Baloch court. The official written language was Persian. It was British linguists and historians who introduced Balochi in the Roman script. In the late nineteenth century, the Naksh or Arabic script became popular.[4]

Balochi can be divided into two major dialect groups, namely Eastern Balochi and Western Balochi. Eastern Balochi is spoken mainly in the north-eastern areas of Balochistan and in neighbouring areas of the provinces of Punjab and Sindh. Western Balochi is spoken in the western and southern areas of Balochistan as well as in Karachi and other parts of Sindh, the Gulf States, Iran, Afghanistan and Turkmenistan.[5]

According to European scholars, 'Brahvi reveals a clear and unmistakable resemblance to the Dravidian languages of southern India', especially Tamil. The Brahvi are perhaps the only Dravidian survivors in northern India, after the Aryan invasion. Arguing on linguistic basis, Muhammad Sardar Khan believes that the Brahvis are of Dravidian origin. However, he accepts that most of the Brahvi population, as estimated by him in 1958 'less than quarter of a million', was racially Baloch.[6] Noted commentator Mohan Guruswamy writes that he '... ran into a bunch of school kids from Kalat at the National

Museum in Karachi and they were amused that I knew that *uru* meant village, *arisi* meant rice and *tanni* meant water even to me from distant southern India.'[7] Interestingly, *Eelam* (which means 'independence' in Tamil) was the name of a Brahvi-Urdu weekly that started publication in 1960 and had exhorted the government to promote both Brahvi and Balochi.

Multilingualism is common among the Baloch and Brahvi. Thus, Tariq Rahman notes, 'The Balochi and Brahvi languages are symbols of the Baloch identity, which is a necessary part of Baloch nationalism.'[8] Selig Harrison adds, 'Despite the isolation of the scattered pastoral communities in Balochistan, the Balochi language and a relatively homogeneous Baloch literary tradition and value system have provided a unifying common denominator for the seventeen major Baloch tribal groupings scattered over the 207,000-square mile area.'[9]

Baloch–Brahvi Differences

An effort has been made to create divisions in the Baloch national movement by projecting Brahvi as a separate ethnic/linguistic group. Pakistani governments, as the British before them, classified the Brahvi as a separate ethnic group in order to weaken Baloch nationalism.[10] As Nina Swidler, an anthropologist who studied the Brahvis, notes, 'Baloch scholars accept past ethnic and tribal divisions, but are reluctant to do so in the present. They point to the cultural similarities between Baloch and Brahvi that far outweigh their differences, and suspect the government of fanning ethnic differences to undermine a national identity.'[11] She did not discover much difference between the Baloch and the Brahvis, apart from the language. Selig Harrison writes, 'In terms of vocabulary ... Brahvi is merely a variant of Balochi.'[12]

Another interesting element, which strengthens the cause of Baloch nationalism is the bilingualism of the Brahvis.[13] The majority of the Brahvis regard Balochi as their second language. Prominent Brahvi families, like the royal family of Kalat and the Bizenjo family, speak Balochi as their first language. Moreover, almost all the Brahvi tribes in Iranian Balochistan speak only Balochi.[14] It is interesting to note that many founders and prominent members of the Baloch national movement, like Mir Abdul Aziz Kurd, Mir Ghaus Bakhsh Bizenjo and Agha Abdul Karim, are of Brahvi origin.

Both Balochi and Brahvi-speaking intellectuals and politicians emphasize unity and similarities rather than the differences while articulating and promoting Baloch nationalism. Both Baloch and Brahvi intellectuals cite *Koord Gal Namik*, a book written in 1659 by Akhund Saleh Mohammad, a minister in the court of Mir Ahmed Khan I, the Khan of Kalat, as proof that they are one people. The book asserts that the Baloch are Kurds and that the Brahvis, called Brakhuis, are one of the tribes of the Kurds.[15] What this shows is the desire as far back as the seventeenth century to emphasize the commonalities between the Brahvi and Baloch tribes. Clearly, it is in the interests of both Baloch and Brahvi speakers to be treated as one people. Hence, Baloch nationalists—both Baloch and Brahvi—reject the idea of there being antagonism in the Brahvi and Baloch language movements.

Over time, the Baloch language and culture have come to resonate throughout most of the province so that most of the population can be characterized as Baloch. 'See to our graveyards', Dawood Khan Ahmadzai, son of the last Khan of Kalat, Mir Ahmad Yar Khan, pointed out, 'our forefathers are engraved in their gravestones as the Baloch.' He continued, 'We follow the same customs from the cradle to the grave.'[16]

An interesting example of the Brahvi regarding themselves as part and parcel of the Baloch nation relates to the Khan of Kalat. In 1932, the British External and Political Department prepared a draft speech for the Khan and sent it to him for his approval. The Khan objected to the words 'Brahvi–Baloch' and demanded the removal of the word 'Brahvi' on the plea that Brahvi are Baloch and not a separate group.[17] In 1947, the government of Kalat wrote to the British government that Brahvis are racially and culturally Baloch.[18] In his address to the Baloch nation on 15 August 1947, the day of Independence, Khan Ahmad Yar Khan declared: 'I am proud to address you in Balochi today. Insha Allah, whenever I will address you in future, it will be in Balochi because it is the language of the Baloch nation.'[19]

Given the attempts of the state to fan the Baloch–Brahvi differences, Baloch nationalists do not give primacy to identifying language as the only criterion for nationality. They see such attempts as a conspiracy of the anti-Baloch forces, i.e., government of Pakistan or foreign scholars. Since the Brahvis see themselves as Baloch, the supposed element of tension between Brahvi and non-Brahvi Baloch intellectuals is not really relevant. Baloch identity is defined more by a certain cultural similarity, a way of life, rather than giving primacy to language alone. Though language has been an important marker of identity, it has been less important as a symbol of Baloch nationalism than similar movements among the speakers of Bengali, Sindhi, Pashto, Seraiki and Punjabi.

Growth of the Baloch Language Movement

There were two trends that sowed the seeds of the language movement as well as Baloch nationalism. The first was the accounts of European writers and travellers in the nineteenth and early twentieth centuries which, according to Taj Mohammad Breseeg, enthused Baloch consciousness of modern Baloch nationalism. Such works would include Lt. Henry Pottinger's *Travels in Beloochistan and Sinde* (1816) that gave a detailed account of the geography, history and politics (1809-10) of Balochistan. This was followed by the four-volume work of Charles Masson (1842); A.W. Hughes's (1877) work on Baloch history, geography, topography and ethnology that included a comprehensive map of Balochistan for the first time; the works of Longworth Dames (1904) and (1907), and other British officials and scholars who prepared the Provincial Series of the Imperial Gazetteer of India (1908), that included the Balochistan District Gazetteer. Thus, by the early twentieth century, writes Taj Mohammad Breseeg, '… the western methodology for the conceptualization of the Baloch nation was established.'[20]

The second trend was the growth of the anti-British intellectual movement started in the 1880s in Balochistan, called the 'Darkhani movement'. It was inspired and pioneered by Maulana Mohammad Fazil of Darkhan (now called Fazilabad). The Maulana called a gathering of the Ulema in 1883, where it was decided to translate religious books in Persian or Arabic into Balochi and Brahvi to effectively counter missionary propaganda.[21] This literary movement produced a fairly large number of books up to the end of the nineteenth century that were published from the Maktaba-e Darkhani (the Darkhani school).[22]

The British replaced Persian as the official language with Urdu and English. The deliberate introduction of an Indian language, Urdu, to replace Persian was done to isolate Balochistan from the Iranian Balochistan.[23] Pakistan has followed the example of the British. In its attempt to forge a common identity and snuff out provincial sentiments, Pakistan has not allowed Balochi to be the language of instructions in schools even at primary level. In fact, a unique feature of Balochistan is that in the University of Balochistan in Quetta, Balochi language is taught at the master's level but not in the primary schools or in basic educational institutions.

In 1990, the Balochistan Assembly passed a bill called the The Balochistan Mother Tongue Use Bill, No. 6 of 1990 that sought to make Balochi, Brahvi and Pashto compulsory medium of instruction at the primary level in rural schools. However, on 8 November 1992, during the chief ministership of Taj Mohammad Jamali who headed the Pakistan Muslim League (Nawaz) (PML-N) government, a cabinet decision was taken to discontinue the experiment. The textbooks board was asked not to produce any more books nor were teachers imparted any further training. Most writers called this decision a conspiracy of the Punjabi bureaucracy that did not favour the development of a Baloch identity.[24]

Despite these constraints, Balochi language has been an important unifying factor among the Baloch. It has made an important contribution in making the people conscious of their separate identity. As Brian Spooner wrote, 'Baloch identity in Balochistan has been closely tied to the use of the Balochi language in inter-tribal relations.'[25] At the same time, the Baloch nationalists realize that their language requires standardization and modernization as well as the creation of new terms to express modern knowledge.

In 1927, the Baloch nationalists, Abdul Aziz Kurd and Master Pir Bakhsh, also known as Nasim Talwi, together started publishing a newspaper called *Balochistan* in Delhi.[26] By the 1930s, the first modern Baloch political groups were organized and newspapers began to appear. Abdul Aziz Kurd's Ajnuman-e-Balochistan (Organisation for the Unity of Balochistan) published *Al-Baloch*, a weekly from Karachi, which demanded an independent state comprising the Kalat State, British Balochistan, Dera Ghazi Khan and Iranian Balochistan. From the inception of the Baloch literary movement, themes of nationalism and ethnic identity were popular and many Baloch writers were involved in nationalist political struggles.[27] Their concerns were secular: identity, freedom, control over resources, jobs, power and so on, and were expressed in the idiom of political debate.

Role of Electronic and Social Media

The growth of the electronic and especially social media has been embraced by the Baloch to maintain contact with the Baloch diaspora. According to Taj Mohammad Breseeg, the Baloch have established online magazines, newsgroups, human rights organizations, student groups, academic organizations and book publishers for a trans-national community. Some of these informative and insightful English media include: Balochistan TV, balochwarna news, radiobalochi.org, balochvoice.com, balochunity.org, balochinews.com, zrombesh.org, baloch2000.org, etc. Based out of the country, they have significantly contributed to the development of the Baloch identity.[28]

The social media, especially Facebook, has brought about a silent revolution to change the way Balochi language is written. The script in which Balochi is written is Arabic. The move to change the script to Roman, according to Táj Balóc (formerly Taj Baloch), was because, 'The Arabic script is a major factor in the underdevelopment of the Balochi language. Native Balochi speakers can easily read Urdu, also written in the Arabic script, but they find it hard to read their own language in the same script. The reason is that Balochi is a vowel-sensitive language and the Arabic script supports only consonant-sensitive languages.'[29]

As a result, many times the Arabic script confuses the Baloch in writing. For example, three different words for three different things— lion, milk, poetry—have three unique vowel sounds in Balochi. But when they are written in the Arabic script, they look the same. In the Arabic script, vowels are usually dropped. Only in religious texts, consonants are regularly accompanied by vowels in order to avoid any rare confusion. 'Also, there are only six vowels in Arabic. Balochi has ten. How do you write the additional Balochi vowels in this script?' Táj Balóc asks.[30]

The strongest argument against changing the script is of course religious. The very first drafts of written Balochi, which came from

British officers during the colonial rule, were written in Roman. But later, the Arabic script was chosen for religious reasons, as an overwhelming majority of the Baloch followed Islam. But, argues Balóc, 'Turks are also Muslims. Does it affect their faith when they use the [Roman] script? It's a totally linguistic issue. Why make it religious?' Apparently, the man who standardized the current Arabic script for Balochi in the 1950s, Syed Hashmi, was convinced that Balochi was better off with the Roman script. However, he was forced to follow the Arabic script for religious reasons.[31]

There have been earlier efforts, too, to change the script from Arabic to Roman. In the 1970s, an influential group of Baloch writers, led by nationalist poet Gul Khan Nasir, then Balochistan's education minister, tried to change to Roman. However, the effort came to naught in the face of opposition, led by religious and literary figures that supported the Arabic script for religious reasons. Again, during the insurgency of the 1970s, some nationalists led by guerilla commander Abdul Nabi Bangulzai also tried to introduce the Roman script for Balochi in his guerilla camps. His intention was more nationalistic than linguistic since the Arabic script was seen as a tool of the occupying Pakistani state to keep the Baloch land with Pakistan in the name of Islam.[32]

What has changed since then is the access to the Internet that has provided the people with a virtual platform.

II

TIMES GONE BY

5

History till Partition

Early History: Jalal Khan/Mir Chakar Rind/Mir Nasir Khan

THE EARLY SIGNS OF BALOCH consolidation can be traced to the confederacy of forty-four tribes under Mir Jalal Khan in the twelfth century. Baloch writers have paid great tributes to Jalal Khan, who is regarded as the 'founding father of the Baloch nation' for forming the first Baloch confederacy in Balochistan.[1] In the fifteenth century, Mir Chakar Rind (1487–1511) established another confederacy of the Baloch tribes referred to by historians as the 'Rind–Lashari Union.[2] It was one of the largest Baloch tribal confederacies stretching from Kirman in the west to the Indus in the east, thus uniting for the first time large parts of the Baloch areas. Mir Chakar is best remembered for his successful invasion of Punjab, annexing Multan and other southern areas in the early part of the sixteenth century. Baloch nationalists describe Mir Chakar's rule as the Golden Age of the Baloch and regard him as the 'Great Baloch'.[3] He is seen as giving the scattered Baloch tribes a common identity and is considered 'like a pillar of strength for the Baloch race and author of Baloch code of honour and Balochi traditions'.[4]

Political unity was, however, ephemeral and dissipated after his death. In 1666, the Baloch tribes elected Mir Ahmad Khan as the Khan of Kalat establishing the first Kalat confederacy. Stretching from Kandahar in Afghanistan in the north to Bandar Abbas in Iran in the west and to Dera Ghazi Khan and Karachi in the east and south-east, this was bigger than Chakar Khan's confederation. It brought most of the Baloch areas under one rule.

Under Ahmad Khan's grandson, Mir Nasir Khan (ruled 1749–94), governance structures took shape. He set up a loose bureaucratic arrangement embracing most of Balochistan for the first time. He established a unified Baloch army of 25,000 men and 1,000 camels and organized the major Baloch tribes under an agreed military and administrative system.[5]

Kalat was divided into two units: a directly administered one consisting of the territory of Kalat plus annexed territory and conquered lands, and a second one consisting of two provinces, Sarawan lying to the north of Kalat under their hereditary chief, the Raisani Sardar, and Jhalawan lying to the south of Kalat under the Zehri Sardar. These were administered independently by sardars appointed by the Khan. Nasir Khan ruled through a council of sardars and the tribes adopted an agreed system of military organization and recruitment.

In 1765, Mir Nasir Khan had a narrow escape in a battle with the Sikhs. He had fallen off his horse and in the process, the turban he was wearing got loose. As a result, his long hair popped out from beneath his headwear. One Sikh soldier rushed towards him with his sword raised. However, another Sikh soldier halted his comrade's blow in the nick of time saying that the fallen man was a Khalsa (Sikh). The soldier had mistaken the turban-less Nasir Khan as a Sikh. By the time the soldiers became aware of their mistake, Nasir Khan was on his feet and was surrounded by Baloch soldiers and so escaped.

Mir Ahmed Yar Khan Baluch, *Inside Baluchistan: A Political Autobiography of His Highness Baiglar Baigi: Khan-E-Azam-XIII*, Karachi: Royal Book Company, 1975, pp. 86–87.

Situated at the tri-junction of Persia, Afghanistan and the Indian subcontinent, the state of Kalat was inevitably vulnerable to the influence of the more powerful kingdoms in the neighbourhood.[6] In the initial years of Nasir Khan's rule (1749–94), Kalat was a tributary of Afghanistan. This has prompted some Afghan nationalists to claim the inclusion of Balochistan in a 'Greater Afghanistan'. However, by 1758, Nasir Khan threw off subservience to the Afghans, fighting Ahmad Shah Durrani's forces to a standstill. Thereafter, Kalat continued to be a military ally of Afghanistan and was sovereign until the arrival of the British.[7]

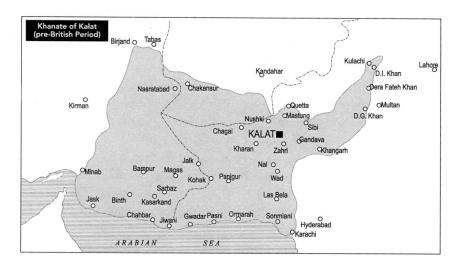

Nasir Khan's predecessors had paid tribute to Persia and Nasir Khan himself was installed in power due to the backing of Emperor Nadir Shah of Persia.[8] When Nadir Shah invaded India, Nasir Khan helped him with men and money. In return, Nadir Shah gave him the title of 'Baigler Baigi'—Prince of Princes—of all Balochistan.[9] After the assassination of Nadir Shah and the resultant confusion in Iran, Nasir Khan discarded the tributary status.

Since Balochistan was not a fertile area, the revenue that could be extracted was limited. Resultantly, both the Persian and Afghan empires were not involved in the day-to-day administration of the region. As Paul Titus puts it, 'Balochistan's distance from centres of power, its harsh, arid climate and its limited productivity have meant that the Baloch have generally been marginal to major events in the seats of imperial power.'[10] He adds that while Balochistan's historical marginality enabled the Baloch to preserve their autonomy, in the post-colonial era, they were incrementally assimilated into Pakistan. Such assimilation would paradoxically bring about an increased sense of marginalization because they were a small minority in the larger state.

Nasir Khan's empire and Baloch unity did not survive his death primarily because it was based on his personality rather than on an institutionalized structure.[11] Baloch nationalists nostalgically remember Nasir Khan's era as a glorious period in their history. It was his reign that brought the whole of Balochistan (including those regions which are now part of Iran and Afghanistan) under one state authority. This historical precedent for the concept of a unified Baloch political identity is still harked back till today.

From 1805 until the British intervention in 1839, the successors of Nasir Khan were nominally independent, largely due to the disinterest of the neighbouring rulers in the inhospitable terrain. However, soon thereafter, Balochistan would be transformed into an essential cog in the Great Game between Russia and Great Britain.

Mir Ghaus Bakhsh Bizenjo, former governor of Balochistan and a leading nationalist, argued in a 1978 interview with Selig Harrison that 'Just as it served the interests of the British to foster a unified Afghanistan as a buffer state so it was necessary, conversely, to divide the Baloch in order to make the frontiers of the Raj contiguous with Afghanistan and to assure unimpeded military dominance in the frontier region.' He contended that 'Nasir Khan's Kalat Confederacy might have emerged in a buffer state role instead if the Russians had swallowed up Afghanistan before Britain embarked on its "forward policy".'[12]

British Rule

The advance of Tsarist Russia into Central Asia led to British involvement in Balochistan to safeguard the Indian Empire. What concerned the British was that Afghan ruler Dost Mohammad Khan had refused to turn away Russian emissaries from Kabul. Thus, the British felt it necessary to intervene militarily in Afghanistan to ensure that Kabul kept the Russians out. The northern route to Kabul via Peshawar and the Khyber Pass was in Sikh hands. Though by then the Sikhs were allied with the British, Maharaja Ranjit Singh decided not to allow a large invading force to march through his territory. Hence, a southern route to Kabul had to be discovered. For this, a safe passage through the Bolan Pass to southern Afghanistan was imperative. This required control over the areas of Balochistan bordering Afghanistan. Thus began the process of British intervention that would adversely impact the destiny of Balochistan.

In 1838 the British signed a safe passage agreement with Mehrab Khan, the Khan of Kalat, who guaranteed the safety of the British army—the Army of the Indus—through his territory. However, the Baloch tribes did not honour this and harassed and plundered the British forces along the line of the march. This made the movement of the army through the Bolan Pass hazardous.

The British assumed bad faith on Mehrab Khan's part and claimed that the tribal attacks were a breach of treaty. When the Khan refused to surrender, the British decided to undertake a punitive expedition to Kalat town to exact retribution. General Wilshire was accordingly detached from the Army of the Indus with 1,050 men to assault Kalat. A gate was knocked in by the field-pieces and the town and citadel were stormed in a few minutes. About 400 Baloch were killed, among them Mehrab Khan himself, and 2,000 were taken prisoners. His son, Mir Nasir Khan II was later raised to the masnad by the tribesmen.

What was noteworthy about the British reaction to the rapid advance of the Tsarist Empire into Central Asia was that it led to the development of a unique concept of the definition of frontiers and the demarcation of borders. Sir Henry Rawlinson[13] and Sir Alfred Lyall,[14] in the face of the Russian advance, developed the notion of a 'Frontier of Separation' as opposed to a 'Frontier of Contact'. In contrast to a 'Frontier of Contact' in which the British and Russian empires would have a common border and be in direct conflict, the 'Frontier of Separation' would provide a buffer between the two empires. For Rawlinson, due to the simultaneous expansion of the British and Russian empires, contact between them had to be avoided. This could be done 'by narrow strip of territory, a few hundred miles across' intervening between their political frontiers—in effect, the creation of some form of protectorates to act as buffers.[15] For Sir Alfred Lyall, '... the true frontier was not coterminous with the limits of territory actually administered by the Government of India. Beyond this were areas that the Government of India insisted were vital to its security, but where it did not attempt to exercise any administrative control.'[16]

The concept of the 'Frontier of Separation' required a distinction between the exercise of power within the boundaries of administration and within boundaries of influence. This led to a unique solution that was the threefold frontier. The first frontier was the outer limit of the directly administered territory of British India where full administrative control including British law and political systems were enforced. The second frontier was the area under 'indirect control' where British law and administration, including taxation, was not applied.[17] Responsibility for day-to-day administration in these areas was left to the tribal chiefs. The British exercised a veneer of control through the army. These 'un-administered areas', like the Indian princely states, had a certain degree of political autonomy but unlike them were not assimilated into mainstream Indian life. On the contrary, they maintained their separateness.[18] The third frontier was the outer limit of the British area of influence. It was beyond defined boundaries and formed the protectorate or buffer states against Russian influence. These independent states were tied to the Government of India through treaties.

Balochistan became part of this peculiar frontier structure of the Indian empire as the second frontier, the un-administered territory between the boundary of administration that defined Sindh and eventually the Durand Line—the delimited and demarcated boundary with Afghanistan.[19]

While the fear of Russian advance was real, it was yet distant. The more immediate threat was from the depredations of the mountain tribes. To deal with this, the British adopted two fundamentally conflicting approaches: 'Forward Policy' whose aim was to administer the area and its people, and a 'Close Border Policy' the objective of which was merely to monitor and manipulate the land and people.[20] The latter was based on formal treaty relations between the British Empire and the ruler of an independent territory. Such borders were considered a state boundary. District officers were not supposed to either cross the border without a military escort nor to extend the border.[21]

After the British military disaster during the First Afghan War (1838–42) and consequent upon their withdrawal from Afghanistan, the occupied districts were returned to the Khan of Kalat. The annexation of Sindh in 1842 and Punjab in 1849 enabled the British to consolidate the empire. For the next three decades, the British implemented the 'Close Border System' in which they increased their presence (especially military) in areas under their direct control and limited their actions in areas not yet pacified to punitive military expeditions against rebellious tribes.[22] To protect Sindh, the policy was to maintain the power of the Khan of Kalat over the mountain territories to the west. In return, the Khan would restrain the tribes from invading Sindh. Since this was not very successful, in 1854 under the governor-generalship of the Marquis of Dalhousie, General John Jacob, the political superintendent and commandant on the Sindh frontier, was deputed to arrange and conclude a treaty with the Kalat state then under Nasir Khan II.

According to the terms of the treaty, British political agents were deputed to Kalat during the next twenty years; the Khan received a yearly subsidy of 50,000 rupees; British expeditions passed through the Bolan Pass on their way to Kandahar and Afghanistan, but up to 1876, the country was considered independent. The central point of the policy was, as the Governor of Bombay noted in his Minute of 10 February 1871, 'The policy to be pursued [is] to acknowledge no authority but that of the Khan, to recognize the chiefs in no other capacity than his subjects, to abstain from interference …'[23] Interestingly, the Punjab government had a contrary view and proposed a more aggressive British role and argued that direct contact with the tribes was essential.[24]

The Close Border Policy, however, produced continual disorder. The sardars saw British policy as strengthening the power of the Khan at their expense since they did not have direct access to the British. The policy put the British in the position of supporting the Khan who was unable to keep the border raiders in check. Reports from agents and officials restated the familiar theme: the inability of the rulers to control their border people.[25] This led the British to implement a policy of collective responsibility, punishing entire tribes for individual crimes to pressurize them to discipline the tribesmen.

By the mid-1870s, the British had come to the conclusion that their Close Border Policy, and its notion that the 'trans-border tribes' could be controlled using 'subsidies, blockade, occasional manipulation of tribal affairs and, when absolutely necessary, punitive expeditions', had not produced the desired effect.[26] Hence, they moved towards the

'Forward Policy'. This task was entrusted to Captain Robert Sandeman, deputy commissioner of Dera Ghazi Khan (Punjab) (later knighted) who came to Balochistan in 1875. He is credited with the establishment and consolidation of British rule in Balochistan.

Sandeman was an assertive critic of the Close Border Policy, arguing that imperial interests were best served by dealing directly with the chiefs. In 1876, he negotiated a treaty with the Khan of Kalat that signalled the end of the Close Border Policy. The treaty supplemented the 1854 treaty. Under it, the British Government undertook to respect the independence of Kalat, but assumed responsibility for internal order.

The key change that Sandeman wrought was to ensure that it was the British who would give out the allowances to the sardars rather than routing them through the Khan. This gave the British power over individual sardars. The British also kept the power to approve their appointment and removal. Without the subsidy carrot and the removal stick, the Khan's power of control over the sardars was effectively blocked. Sandeman was very clear that, 'It is unfair to expect tribes or tribal chiefs to do your work and carry out your policy unless you make it worth their while; but when you have made it worth their while, when you have given them the "quid" be careful to exact the "quo".'[27]

Following the 1876 treaty, British troops were to be deployed in the Khanate; there were further agreements in connection with the construction of the Indo-European Telegraph, the cession of jurisdiction on the railways and in the Bolan Pass, and the permanent lease of Quetta, Nushki and Nasirabad. Thus, under the Forward Policy, the British presence in Balochistan steadily expanded. The success of Sandeman's approach was manifest during the Second Afghan War (1878–80), when Kalat remained allied with the British.

By the terms of the Treaty of Gandamak in 1879 with Amir Yaqub Khan of Afghanistan, Pishin, Sibi, Harani and Thal-Chotiali were ceded to the British Government. The Marri and Bugti tribal areas were also demarcated and set aside as 'tribal areas'. The rest of the territory was left under the de jure control of the Khan of Kalat; this was the Kalat state that formed the bulk of Balochistan. In the 1880s and 1890s further territories were added: Loralai, the Khetran country, now known as the

Barkhan tehsil and the Zhob valley where a headquarters was built at a place called Appozai, that came to be known as Fort Sandeman.[28]

The Sandeman system, as it came to be called, rested on the occupation of central points in Kalat and tribal territory in considerable force, linking them together by fair-weather roads and leaving the tribes to manage their own affairs according to their own customs and working through their chiefs and maliks. The maliks were required to enlist levies paid by government and though regarded as tribal servants, they were controlled by the district officers. Such a system, of course, involved the upholding of the authority of chiefs and maliks, if necessary by force, should their authority be challenged.[29]

Sandeman understood that the sardars were the best guarantors of peace in their area. So, he empowered the sardars with guns, money and horses and in return obtained their allegiance and their guarantee of maintaining local law and order. He found it easier and cheaper to control a handful of traditional chiefs rather than try to control the tribes directly. The sardari system was thus strengthened but made dependent on the British. Those who opposed British authority were labelled ruffians and scoundrels. Sandeman never hesitated in using brute physical force whenever he thought it was required.[30]

Given their strategic interests, the British developed only the infrastructure vital to the defence of Balochistan. In contrast, due to their economic and political interests in Punjab and Sindh, the infrastructure developed in these regions favoured agricultural growth and industrialization. Such a structurally imbalanced legacy would continue after Pakistan's creation. The post-colonial ruling elite did very little to undo the economic and political inequality among the different ethnic groups and regions. Power asymmetries among ethno-regional groups reinforced regional disparities and ensured that the distribution of resources remained biased in favour of Punjab.[31] This disparity and domination of Punjab would become a major conflict driver in Pakistan.

Division of Balochistan

An adjunct to the imperial design of keeping the Russians away from India was the parcelling out of Balochistan. The British ignored all evidence of certain areas falling under the jurisdiction or influence of the Khan of Kalat as also history, geography and culture. They gifted these areas away to either Persia (renamed Iran) or Afghanistan, in a bid to placate their rulers and befriend them in apprehension of an attack from Russia. This was the 'Great Game' of those times and the Baloch had to pay dearly for the selfish motives of the colonial rulers.[32]

The Goldsmid Line divided Balochistan into two parts, giving in 1871, roughly one-fourth of Balochistan to Persia in the far west; in the north, the Durand Line assigned a small strip to Afghanistan in 1894. More border adjustments between Balochistan and Persia took place in 1896 and once again in 1905. These awards, under the so-called Anglo-Persian Joint Boundary Commission, ceded more territory to Persia and permanently divided the Baloch tribes of Siestan and western Makran. Subsequently, after its accession to Pakistan, the Baloch majority district of Jacobabad were transferred to Sindh, and Dera Ghazi Khan to Punjab.[33] Thus, by 1905, the demarcation of the boundary between British India and Iran on the one hand and between British India and Afghanistan on the other had quite effectively and unalterably divided the Baloch among three states: British India, Afghanistan and Iran.

Rise of Baloch Identity and Nationalism

Baloch scholars believe that a distinctive Baloch culture, language and identity started emerging from the twelfth century onwards. According to Selig Harrison, the fiercely independent and proud Baloch were, for one, able to preserve their separate cultural identity despite continual pressures from the strong cultural influences of neighbouring Iran and Afghanistan. For another, the isolation of the various communities in Balochistan kept the Balochi language and value system insulated, which provided a unifying common denominator.[34] In modern times, several factors helped break down tribal barriers. These included: improved communications, development of rudimentary infrastructure and transportation, a nascent educated middle class and, most importantly, a common sense of abandonment, political marginalization, economic disparity compared with other provinces, a perception of Punjabi colonization, the overbearing domination of civil–military bureaucracy, and the growing fear of becoming a minority in their own land.

Baloch resistance to the British had continued throughout the nineteenth century. These were, however, acts of individual tribal chiefs who felt wronged by government actions. They could not assume a national struggle primarily due to lack of communication between the Baloch tribes, lack of a proper political organization to mobilize the masses, and an adversary that had far superior weapons and resources.[35]

————•————

If a date is to be given to the emergence of the Baloch nationalist movement, it would be 1929 when the Anjuman-e-Ittehad-e-Balochistan (Organisation for Unity of the Baloch), a clandestine organization, was set up in Mastung. Mir Muhammad Yusuf Ali Khan Magsi, the first president, and Abdul Aziz Kurd were the two principal leaders thrown up by this movement. The Anjuman marked the beginning of a secular, non-tribal nationalist movement as opposed to the tribal movements of the past. The bulk of its leadership and membership, notes Breseeg, were largely drawn from the urban bourgeoisie, educated youth and nationalist-minded members of the clergy and tribal aristocracy.[36]

In 1929 Magsi published an article, 'Faryad-e-Balochistan', (Cry of Balochistan), in the 17 November 1929 issue of the weekly *Hamdard*, Lahore. In the article, he appealed to the Baloch to organize themselves for the liberation and unity of Balochistan and demanded constitutional reforms. Magsi's article is perceived to be the first Baloch literary document in the cause of Baloch nationalism.[37]

The founding fathers of Baloch nationalism were influenced by the Young Turks, the Bolshevik Revolution and the nationalist movement in British India. The influence of these movements and their ideologies can be observed in the programme of the Anjuman and in the statements and writings of Magsi. To promote nationalism and patriotism, Magsi called for the Baloch people to work for the following principles and goals:[38]

(i)   The unification and independence of Balochistan;

(ii)   A democratic and socialist system guided by Islamic universalism;

(iii) The abolition of rule by tribal sardars (sardari nizam);

(iv)   Free and compulsory education for the Baloch people, and equality for Baloch women; and

(v)   The promotion Baloch culture.

Magsi believed that Baloch unity and the independence of Balochistan depended on socio-political changes in Baloch society. The Anjuman also opposed communalism and sectarianism, a policy that encouraged minorities such as the Zikris to support it.

The first successful nationalist campaign was launched in 1929 against state recruitment into the army that turned into an armed mutiny. The following year, in 1930, several underground political groups were formed and an anti-colonial 'Quit Balochistan' movement was launched. The announcement prompted the Kalat state to issue an arrest order against Magsi but he escaped to Jacobabad in the nick of time. From there he launched his nationalist agitation and financed the publication of Baloch nationalist newspapers from Karachi.

In December 1932 a three-day 'Balochistan and All-India Baloch Conference' was held at Jacobabad. The conference attracted prominent delegates from all over the region. The first conference was such a success that a second one was convened in Hyderabad, Sindh, at the end of December 1933. In 1934, though Magsi suggested an armed struggle for the liberation and unification of Balochistan, the leaders realized that this was a difficult task. They, therefore, supported the strengthening of the Kalat state's legal status as a sovereign state, hoping it would become the nucleus of a larger Balochistan state after the British left. They also wanted the introduction of an elected system instead of the sardari system.[39]

Following the death of Nawab Magsi in the 31 May 1935 Quetta earthquake, the Anjuman was renamed the 'Kalat State National Party' (KSNP) on 5 February 1937. The aim of the party was to establish constitutional rule in the Khanate and create an independent, united Balochistan after the departure of the British. The party agreed with the Khan that Kalat state, like Nepal, had direct treaty relationships with London.

The KSNP did not support the Muslim League that stood for an independent homeland for India's Muslims. In fact, with their secular, anti-imperialist and populist ideas, many of the KSNP leaders were closer to the Indian National Congress and especially to Maulana Abul Kalam Azad and other moderate Muslims, who supported a secular, federal, united India. The secularism of the Baloch together with the strong tribal bonds had ensured that in the 1940s the Islamic rhetoric of the Muslim League failed to make an impact on them.

As the British withdrawal from India started looming in the mid-1940s, a few Baloch leaders tried to generate a sense of common ethnic identity by calling for an independent Balochistan.[40] However, Baloch separatism was still the project of only a few and failed to become a cohesive grass-root-level ideological movement.[41]

6

Accession to Pakistan

Events Around Partition

AS THE SUN BEGAN TO set on the British Empire in India, several questions arose about the status of Kalat and its future, questions that continue to have a resonance even today. The key questions were: what would be the status of the princely state of Kalat on the lapse of British paramountcy; what would be the status of British Balochistan; how would the leased areas of Quetta, Nushki and Nasirabad be treated; would they be restored to the Khan; and what would be the future of the tribal areas in Balochistan?

Historically, the legal status of Kalat was different from that of other princely states in the subcontinent. According to Martin Axmann, 'The relations between the Government of India and the Khanate of Kalat were, theoretically and formally up to August 1947, based on the long-standing Treaty of 1876 which committed the British in Article 3 to recognize and respect Kalat's independence.' He also cites the First Administrative Report of the Balochistan Agency of 1886 that stated that in 1877, Khudadad Khan (Khan of Kalat) '... occupied a position of a Sovereign Prince entirely independent of the British Government with which he was connected only by his treaty engagements.'[1] Due to this position, the Khan did not join the Chamber of Princes in Delhi. He always maintained that Kalat was on a separate footing and not part of Britain's Indian empire. Likewise, while the 560-odd princely states in India were clubbed as category A under the political department, states like Kalat, together with Nepal, Bhutan and Sikkim were clubbed in category B under the External Affairs Department of the Government of India.

————•————

Despite all the evidence to the contrary, the Government of India Act of 1935 unilaterally included Kalat among the princely states of India and sanctioned its right to be represented in the Federal legislature. The Act also formally established the province of British Balochistan.[2]

In protest, the Khan issued several letters to the British government demanding the restoration of his powers that had been guaranteed under the Treaty of 1876. In one such letter in July 1938, the Khan demanded the framing of a fresh treaty that would put '… into effect in letter, in spirit and in practice, the Treaty of 1876, which safeguarded the interests of the two Governments' and the '… restrictions and conditions imposed, contrary to the terms of the Treaty of 1876 … may be withdrawn and rescinded and the independence of the Kalat government may be honoured scrupulously in accordance with the Treaty of 1876'.[3] However, all he got was a personal letter from the Crown Representative assuring him that such reaffirmation was unnecessary, and that the Viceroy recognized the Treaty of 1876 as fully valid in every respect, and that it would henceforth form the basis of the relations between the British Government and the Kalat state.[4]

The Khan had two memorandums formally submitted to the Cabinet Mission in March 1946 (prepared by Barristers Sir Sayyid Sultan Ahmad and Sirdar D.K. Sen but presented by M.A. Jinnah in May 1946). The first titled 'Memorandum of the Government of Kalat' dealt in detail with the claims of Kalat in respect of Lasbela and Kharan and the Marri and Bugti tribes.

The memo went to great pains to articulate why Kalat was not an Indian state. It argued that:

[O]n the transference of power in British India, the subsisting treaties between the Khan of Kalat and the British Government would come to an end, and whatever obligations have been imposed on the Khan by these treaties will ipso facto terminate. The consequence will be that the State of Kalat will become fully sovereign and independent in respect of both external and internal matters, and will be free to conclude treaties with any other Government or State. The Khan of Kalat and his people are most anxious that the completely independent status, which will emerge as a result of the transference of power in British India, should continue, and the State of Kalat should not be asked to come within the framework of the proposed Indian Union.[5]

As far as Lasbela and Kharan were concerned, the memo held that Lasbela was a district of Kalat State within the province of Jalawan while Kharan was a part of the territories of the Kalat State with its chief being one of the Sarawan sardars. Therefore, both were a part of the territories of Kalat.[6]

The second memo was titled 'Retrocession of Quetta, Nushki and Nasirabad' and concerned the return of these leased areas after the British departure. The memo stressed that although administration of these territories was vested in the British government and it was in actual possession of these areas, sovereignty of these areas remained with the Khanate of Kalat. Therefore, it was urged that before the British handed over power in India, they should formally declare that they relinquished or retroceded all their powers and authority in and over the niabats and districts of Quetta, Nushki and Nasirabad. This should be followed by the actual delivery of possession.[7]

As the Cabinet Mission could not find flaws with the legality of the demand, it left the issue unresolved.

As late as June 1947, Jinnah assured Kalat of the continuance and safeguard of its independent status. In a statement issued to the press on 18 June 1947 Jinnah said, '... I am of the firm opinion that the Memorandum of the Cabinet Mission of 12 May 1946 ... nowhere makes it obligatory upon them (Indian states) to merge themselves with any Legislative Assembly, be it Indian or Pakistani.' He added, 'It is my personal belief that if any State wants to remain aloof, it may do so without any pressure from any quarter, whether it be the British Parliament or any political organization in the country.'[8]

Thus, Kalat in 1947 was not really obliged to join either India or Pakistan. When it was decided to partition India, Mir Ahmad Khan, the Khan of Kalat, claimed with some justification that Kalat was never a part of India and made it clear that he sought independence.

At a round table conference held in Delhi on 4 August 1947 and attended by Lord Mountbatten, the Khan of Kalat, chief minister of Kalat and Jinnah, it was decided that 'Kalat State will be independent on 5 August 1947 enjoying the same status as it originally held in 1838 having friendly relations with its neighbours'.[9]

As a corollary to the round table conference, a standstill agreement between Kalat and Pakistan was signed on 4 August 1947 (publicly announced a week later on 11 August). Jinnah and Liaquat Ali signed on behalf of the future state of Pakistan and Sultan Ahmed on behalf of Khanate of Kalat. The operative portions of the communiqué dated 11 August 1947 are worth quoting from:

> As a result of a meeting held between a delegation from Kalat and officials of the Pakistan States Department, presided over by the Crown Representative, and a series of meetings between the Crown Representative, HH the Khan of Kalat, and Mr Jinnah, the following was the situation:
>
> The Government of Pakistan recognizes Kalat as an independent sovereign state, in treaty relations with British government, with a status different from that of Indian states.
>
> Legal opinion will be sought as to whether or not agreements of leases made between the British government and Kalat will be inherited by the Pakistan government.[10]

Separately, the British informed the rulers of Kharan and Lasbela that control of their regions had been transferred to Kalat state, and the Marri and Bugti tribal regions which were under British control were also returned into the Kalat fold, thereby bringing the whole of Balochistan under the suzerainty of the Khan of Kalat.[11]

Mountbatten did not sign the communiqué recognizing Kalat's independent status even though he was involved in its finalization. The minutes of his meeting with the Kalat delegation note that while the PM of Kalat had asked for a statement declaring the recognition by the Crown Representative of Kalat's independent status, 'the Viceroy replied that the advice which he had received on this point from the Political Adviser precluded this; in any case, a declaration by the Crown Representative would be of little value at the present time'.[12]

Some have, therefore, argued that though Kalat was recognized as independent, the fact that Mountbatten did not sign it made the declaration inoperative since it did not signal the recognition of the British government.[13] The contrary view is that since Pakistan, the successor state, had recognized Kalat's independence and Jinnah, its future Governor-General, had unequivocally signed it, did it really matter that Mountbatten himself had not signed the declaration? The Kalat delegation itself did not make much of Mountbatten's refusal to sign and thus signal the recognition of the British government. A plausible reason why Mountbatten did not sign the declaration and why Pakistan accepted Kalat's independence pertains to the importance of the leased areas of Quetta, Nushki and Nasirabad.

In a letter to Jinnah in July 1947, Barrister M. Ziauddin explained the importance of these areas: '... Balochistan as a province will in any case be a liability for Pakistan, but disintegrated and shorn of the Leased Areas it will become a millstone around its neck. At the present if Pakistan loses Quetta it loses one of the most important military stations, and the strategic routes to Persia and Afghanistan ... the potential mineral wealth of Balochistan exists in the tribal areas. Therefore, all the potential sources of Balochistan's wealth will also go out under the present scheme [of retrocession].'[14]

According to author Yaqoob Khan Bangash, Mountbatten was not keen for Kalat to gain control of the strategic Bolan Pass and Quetta.[15] Mountbatten wrote to the Secretary of State on 25 July 1947 (i.e., before the 4 August meeting):

> The Kalat States' representative claimed that they were an independent and sovereign state in treaty relations with the British Government. The Pakistan States Department readily agreed to this view since, in their opinion, the successor authorities in India would inherit any treaty obligations with foreign states on behalf of India, whereas of course the Indian Independence Bill renounces all treaties entered into with Indian states ... it looks as though if the Khan of Kalat insists

on his independent status it will cost him the leased territories including Quetta—a high price to pay for vanity.[16]

Not surprisingly, Sardar Abdul Rab Nishtar, Pakistan's states minister, explained to the Viceroy's secretary George Abel: 'The Pakistan Government would claim to succeed to the treaty obligations and rights of HM's Government. Otherwise, if Kalat claimed like Indian states to be independent, it would also claim retrocession of leased areas ...'[17] Thus, it was to Pakistan's advantage to accept Kalat's independence but decline to accept the retrocession of the leased areas in its negotiations with Kalat. It was obvious that Pakistan only recognized Kalat as a non-Indian state to prevent the retrocession of the leased areas. As Yakoob Bangash puts it, '[T]he Government of Pakistan had no qualms about recognising Kalat as independent since they were sure that neither Britain nor India would recognize it as a separate country and hence a mere communiqué recognizing Kalat's independence would do little harm.'[18]

The legal opinion of the British Foreign Office and the Political Department was that Pakistan only inherited the leases 'on the basis that Kalat state is an independent sovereign state in treaty relations with HMG;'[19] otherwise, the leases lapsed under the Indian Independence Act. The Khan tried in vain to argue that the leases were 'personal' to the British government and hence, with their departure, automatically lapsed. This was held to be untenable.

Thus, the Khan was faced with a double whammy: Mountbatten not signing the declaration and Pakistan signing it in bad faith only to get control of the leased areas. Once this was achieved, Pakistan would move to forcibly take over the rump Kalat state.

———•———

One of the problems that the Khan faced in the negotiations with Pakistan was that his prime minister Nawabzada Aslam Khan was also a member of the Pakistan civil service and perceived as 'Pakistan's man' in Kalat. As events showed, Aslam's loyalty towards Kalat was suspect and he was responsible for many problems relating to accession. For example, in early October 1947, he asked for 'instructions' from the Government of Pakistan. Aslam wrote to Foreign Secretary Ikramullah:

'... I would request that I very kindly be guided with such further instructions in this regard as you may deem fit to give ...'[20]

There is another interesting possibility of why Jinnah supported the idea of an independent Balochistan. According to the Khan of Kalat, Jinnah regarded Balochistan as his back-up plan in case the demand for Pakistan did not succeed. There was a secret plan with Jinnah and Choudhry Khaliquzzaman (a senior Muslim League leader) that in case the demand for the creation of Pakistan did not materialize, an independent, sovereign Balochistan would help Indian Muslims in their armed struggle for their homeland—Pakistan.[21]

Whatever the reason, based on the 4 August agreement, the Khan declared the independence of Kalat in a formal proclamation on 12 August 1947 effective from 15 August. The Kalat state flag was raised as prayers were read out for the Khan of Kalat. The Government of Kalat State Act 1947 was promulgated as the new constitution of Balochistan. He established two houses of parliament to ascertain the will of the people concerning the future of the state. Elections were held shortly and though held on a non-political basis, the Kalat State National Party candidates won thirty-nine out of fifty-two seats in the Dar-ul-Awam (Lower House of parliament). While not 'democratic' in the modern sense, the Dar-ul-Awam and Dar-ul-Umra (Upper House) were broadly representative of public opinion in the state.[22]

In October 1947 before the Khan went to Karachi to meet Jinnah, he, together with the prime minister and foreign minister, considered various options about the future of Kalat: merger with Iran or India or Afghanistan (all rejected on various grounds); becoming a British protectorate (rejected by the foreign minister), and finally a fifth option, that of independence, in which Kalat would maintain friendly relations with Pakistan and ensure sovereign equality.[23] The option of merger with Pakistan was not even considered.

The Dar-ul-Awam held a session in mid-December 1947 when the issue of accession was debated. Ghaus Bakhsh Bizenjo (later to be known as Baba-e-Balochistan) made his famous speech:

We can survive without Pakistan. We can remain without Pakistan. We can prosper outside Pakistan. But the question is what Pakistan would be without us ...? If Pakistan wants to treat us as a sovereign people we are ready to extend the hand of friendship and cooperation. If Pakistan does not agree to do so, flying in the face of democratic principles, such an attitude will be totally unacceptable to us, and if we are forced to accept this fate then every Baloch son will sacrifice his life in defence of his national freedom.

A resolution was passed demanding that 'relations with Pakistan should be established as between two sovereign states through a treaty based upon friendship and not by accession'.[24]

On 4 January 1948, the Dar-ul-Umra, the Upper House comprising sardars, discussed the question of merger with Pakistan and reiterated the independence and sovereignty of Kalat, rejecting accession to Pakistan.[25] It declared, 'This House is not willing to accept a merger with Pakistan which will endanger the separate existence of the Baloch nation.'

Indian Role

Controversy surrounds the role, if any, played by India in the developments leading up to Kalat's forced accession to Pakistan. The controversy circulates around reports that the Khan had sought to accede to India but was turned down.

After the signing of the 4 August 1947 standstill agreement between Kalat and Pakistan, Kalat drew the attention of New Delhi to it. This agreement, as noted earlier, had recognized the Khanate as an independent state. The Khanate invited India to enter into a similar agreement. Later, it also sent a request for permission to establish a trade agency in Delhi. However, the Indian government refused to consider these requests.[26]

These developments did not escape Pakistan. As early as November 1947, Pakistan's Foreign Secretary Ikramullah had spoken about 'rumours' that the Khan was negotiating with both India and Afghanistan.[27]

The Khan of Kalat in March 1946 had deputed Samad Khan—a member of the All India Congress Committee (AICC)—to plead Kalat's case with the Congress leadership. Jawaharlal Nehru, however, totally rejected the contention of Kalat being an independent state and stated that the Congress would not accept, on any account, attempts to bring about such a deal. Presumably, this was due to the Congress's antipathy to the princely states without, however, making a distinction between the state of affairs in Kalat and the other princely states. Nehru had noted in 1946: 'The fact that Kalat is a border state adds to its importance from our point of view as frontiers are always strategic areas. An independent India cannot permit foreign forces and foreign footholds such as Kalat might afford near its own territories.'[28]

Subsequently, Ghaus Bakhsh Bizenjo, president of the Kalat State National Party, went to Delhi and met Maulana Abul Kalam Azad, president of the Congress. Azad agreed with Bizenjo's contention that Balochistan had never been a part of India and had its own independent status governed by the Treaty of 1876. However, Azad argued that the Baloch would never be able to survive as a sovereign, independent state and would ask for British protection. If the British agreed and remained in Balochistan, the sovereignty of the subcontinent would become meaningless. Hence, though Azad admitted that the demands of the Baloch were genuine and that Balochistan had never been part of India, yet he could not help in maintaining Kalat's independence.[29]

An All India Radio (AIR) broadcast of 27 March 1948 reported a press conference in Delhi addressed by V.P. Menon. According to the report, V.P. Menon stated that the Khan of Kalat had been pressing for Kalat's accession to India instead of Pakistan and that India had not paid any attention to the suggestion and India had nothing to do with it. The Khan listened to the 9 p.m. AIR news and was extremely upset at the dismissive manner in which he had been treated. He is reported to have informed Jinnah to begin negotiations for Kalat's treaty relationship with Pakistan. Significantly, the minutes of a cabinet meeting held on 29 March 1948 as well as Prime Minister Nehru's reply to a question on 30 March 1948 in the Constituent Assembly stated that V.P. Menon had, in fact, made no such comments and that there was an error in reporting by AIR. Despite this attempt at damage control, the harm had already been done.[30] Quite possibly, pressing matters pertaining to Kashmir and Hyderabad occupied the attention of the Indian leadership who were thus unable to evaluate the strategic significance of a sovereign Balochistan. This also explains why India did not protest at the Pakistan Army's occupation of Kalat.

British Balochistan

According to the Indian Independence Act, the fate of British Balochistan and the Baloch tribal areas that included Marri, Bugti, Khetran and Baloch tribal areas of Dera Ghazi Khan was to be decided by a referendum. The referendum was, however, to be limited to the British-nominated council of tribal elders, the Shahi Jirga, and the Quetta municipality. It was decided to hold the Jirga on 30 June 1947 but it was deviously held a day earlier without informing all the members. Thus, only eight out of a total of fifty-five representatives (forty-three of the Shahi Jirga and twelve from the Quetta municipality) were present. According to Axmann, 'It is difficult to ascertain whether or not the Jirga did actually cast votes. Even today the validity of the referendum is contested, and the circumstances that led to its members voting in favour of Pakistan are controversial. Some Baloch scholars maintain that the Shahi Jirga did not vote at all, and claim that a conspiracy between the British and the supporters of the Muslim League against the Baloch and their demand for "national liberation" was contrived.'[31]

With this referendum as its basis, British Balochistan, including the leased and tribal areas that were constitutionally part of the Khanate, were quite controversially acceded to Pakistan on 15 August 1947.

Some Pakistan historians have tried to argue that the Khan's stand of resisting accession was flawed and point as evidence to the so-called referendum of the Shahi Jirga held in Quetta on 29 June 1947. However, the participants were those who had been appointed by the British and the Jirga's recommendation related only to British Balochistan.[32] It did not in any way compromise the Khan's sovereignty or suggested that he had acceded to Pakistan.

Accession of Kalat

To recap, by 1948 the Khan of Kalat had declared independence, both Houses of the Kalat parliament had endorsed this decision and rejected accession with Pakistan; the Muslim League had acknowledged the independence of Kalat as late as in August 1947. Despite all this, and despite the close personal relationship that Jinnah had with the Khan of Kalat and despite the Khan having made large financial contributions to the Muslim League, on 27 March 1948 the Pakistan Army invaded Kalat. The Khan surrendered and signed the instrument of accession. This was accepted by Pakistan on 30 March 1948. Thus ended the 227-day independence of the Kalat confederacy formed by Mir Ahmad Khan's ancestors almost 300 years ago. During its brief independence, Kalat had its own embassy in Karachi where its ambassador to Pakistan functioned and displayed the Kalat state flag.

What explains this sudden somersault? Why, after becoming Governor-General, did Jinnah begin to pressurize Kalat to accede to Pakistan?

The Khan had been in direct touch with Jinnah since 1936 when the Khan asked him to advise on constitutional matters concerning the Kalat state. The relationship was to continue till 1948 when Jinnah died.

In his memoirs, the Khan writes that he played host to Jinnah several times in Quetta, Mastung and Kalat. The Quaid and his sister used to be duly accorded a royal reception each time they came, including a 21-gun salute just as the viceroys of India used to be greeted. They were given an equally hearty send-off when they left. Great care was taken to provide them with the best of amenities during their stay.

The Khan further writes that after weighing Jinnah in gold, 'I had the personal satisfaction of presenting a necklace to Miss Fatima Jinnah, the sentimental value of which, needless to say, exceeded by far the paltry amount of Rs 1,00,000 which it really cost.'

The Khan also sent out his personal bodyguard to Bombay in 1943 for the Quaid's personal protection after an unsuccessful attack on Jinnah. He remained with him faithfully as his bodyguard right up to 7 August 1947.

Mir Ahmed Yar Khan Baluch, *Inside Baluchistan: A Political Autobiography of His Highness Baiglar Baigi: Khan-E-Azam-XIII*, Karachi: Royal Book Company 1975, pp. 136–38.

Documents available now show that it was British advice that greatly influenced Jinnah to force the accession of Kalat to Pakistan in 1948. Initially, the British policy was to respect the independence of Kalat under the 1876 treaty. Such a policy was predicated on using an independent Kalat as a base for their activities in the region. Maj. Gen. R.C. Money, in charge of strategic planning in India, had formulated a report in 1944 titled 'Post-War Reconstruction—Baluchistan' on the post-war scenario.[33] The report suggested that 'Baluchistan is the right place for a considerable imperial garrison after the war.' It added that after the transfer of power in British India, 'Baluchistan is the most suitable location for the British Garrison' on the ground that Baluchistan 'is not part of British India'. Secretary of State Leo Amery's appreciative letters to Money dated 18 November 1944 and to Lord Wavell, dated 23 November 1944 showed his agreement with Money about his defence scheme in which Baluchistan was regarded as a separate country like Afghanistan and Tibet.[34]

However, by 1947 the British felt that instead of locating a base in a weak Balochistan, such a base could be established in Pakistan that was more than willing to accommodate the British. Hence, it was in British interests to ensure that Balochistan was kept within Pakistan and did not become an independent entity.[35]

After the Second World War, Britain was concerned about the rise of the Soviet Union as a great power. Hence, Pakistan became of great importance for the defence of the Persian Gulf and the 'wells of power', i.e., oil. Given the anti-imperialist movement in Iran against the British-supported king Reza Shah, and an apparently pro-Soviet Union Afghanistan, Britain felt it necessary to strengthen Pakistan. Occupation of Balochistan by Pakistan was among the strategic moves in this respect, writes Axmann.[36]

Initially, there was some thinking about controlling the crescent of territory from the Gilgit agency to the deserts of Balochistan. Sir Olaf Caroe, the then governor of the NWFP, for example, had even suggested that a long strip from the Gilgit to Balochistan should be carved into a separate territory and administered directly by Britain. This idea was not accepted and instead Pakistan was chosen to be the bulwark for Western interests against the Soviet Union in southern

Asia.[37] A Pakistan without the state of Jammu and Kashmir (especially Gilgit–Baltistan) and Balochistan would not have served the purpose.

Narendra Singh Sarila in his book *The Shadow of the Great Game: The Untold Story of India's Partition* has quoted British documents to show how Pakistan was to become the lynchpin in British defence plans for the Middle East and the Indian Ocean area. 'A top secret British Chiefs of Staff report of 7 August 1947, stated: "The area of Pakistan [West Pakistan and the north-west of India] is strategically the most important in the continent of India and the majority of our strategic requirements could be met ... by an agreement with Pakistan alone. We do not therefore consider that failure to obtain an agreement with India would cause us to modify any of our requirements."'[38]

For this purpose, it was necessary that Pakistan was viable. Without Balochistan, it would have been difficult to give a proper geographical and strategic viability to Pakistan. Thus, the British changed tracks and worked out a strategy to ensure Balochistan's accession to Pakistan instead of becoming an independent entity. Accordingly, the British authorities pressed upon the Pakistani leaders to take practical steps for the incorporation of Kalat into the newly created state.[39]

Secretary of State Lord Listowell advised Mountbatten in September 1947 that because of its location, it would be too dangerous and risky to allow Kalat to be independent. An extract of a secret memorandum prepared by the British minister of state for commonwealth relations office on 12 September clearly indicates Britain's masterminding role in the events leading to the occupation of Kalat by Pakistan in 1948:

> Pakistan has entered into negotiations with Kalat on the basis of recognizing the state's claim to independence and of treating the previous agreements between the Crown and Kalat providing for the lease of Quetta and other areas, which would otherwise lapse under section 7(I) (6) of the Indian Independence Act, as international agreements untouched by the lapse of paramountcy. The Khan of Kalat, whose territory marches with Persia, is, of course, in no position to undertake the international responsibilities of an independent state, *and Lord Mountbatten, who, before the transfer of power, was warned of the dangers of such a development, doubtless passed on this warning to the Pakistan Government* [emphasis added]. The UK High Commissioner in

Pakistan is being informed of the position and asked to do what
he can to guide the Pakistan government away from making any
agreement with Kalat which would involve recognition of the
state as a separate international entity.[40]

Referring to a telegram of 17 October 1947 from Grafftey-Smith,
the British high commissioner in Karachi, the Political Department,
in a note on Pakistan–Kalat negotiations, held that Jinnah had second
thoughts regarding the recognition of Kalat as an independent
sovereign state, and was now desirous of obtaining its accession in the
same form as was accepted by other rulers who joined Pakistan. The
same note mentioned that an interesting situation was developing as
Pakistan might accept the accession of Kalat's two feudatories, Lasbela
and Kharan.[41]

Significantly therefore, *Mountbatten had been advised even before the
transfer of power of the danger of Kalat being independent.* This perhaps
explains why he did not sign the 4 August 1947 document. Likewise,
as early as October 1947, even before Jinnah had broached the issue of
Kalat's accession with the Khan, the British high commissioner reported
about Pakistan tempting Lasbela and Kharan to accede to Pakistan.

Given British prompting, it was not surprising that by October
1947 Jinnah had a change of heart on the recognition of Kalat as an
'Independent and a Sovereign State', and wanted the Khan to sign the
same form of instrument of accession as the other states, which had
joined Pakistan. Jinnah was, of course, aware of the sentiments in Kalat
since on 29 October 1947 Kalat's prime minister Aslam had informed
the Government of Pakistan that '… not only HH but the vast majority
of his people, including the sardars, also are totally against accession.'[42]
The Khan who could not have known about the British thinking and
intentions got the shock of his life when he visited Karachi, the capital
of the new state of Pakistan, in October 1947. He found Jinnah's tone
had mysteriously changed. He was no longer a friend nor Kalat's lawyer
but a hard-nosed Governor-General who demanded that the Khan
accede immediately to Pakistan. The British high commissioner had
clearly worked on Jinnah.

Bolstered by the resolutions of both the Houses rejecting accession
to Pakistan, the Khan dug in his heels. He expressed his reluctance
to abandon the nominally achieved independent status but was ready

to concede on defence, foreign affairs and communications. However, he was unwilling to sign either a treaty or an instrument, until and unless he had got a satisfactory agreement on the leased areas. As he prevaricated, the Government of Pakistan worked on the rulers of Lasbela and Kharan, who were feudatories of the Khan, and of Makran that was never more than a district of the state of Kalat.[43]

By February 1948, the discussions between Kalat and the Government of Pakistan were coming to a head. On 15 February 1948 Jinnah visited Sibi and addressed a Royal Durbar. The Khan failed to turn up for the final meeting with him, pleading illness. In his letter to Jinnah, he said that he had summoned both the Houses of the parliament, Dar-ul-Umra and Dar-ul-Awam, for their opinion about the future relations with Pakistan, and he would require two months to obtain their views. The Dar-ul-Awam of Kalat met on 21 February 1948 and decided not to accede but to negotiate a treaty to determine Kalat's future relations with Pakistan. The Upper House asked for three months for further consideration.

By now, relations between the Khan and Jinnah had deteriorated. On 18 March Pakistan announced accessions of Makran, Kharan and Lasbela to Pakistan.[44] This deprived Kalat of more than half its territory and its access to the sea. The following day the Khan of Kalat issued a statement refusing to believe that Pakistan as champion of Muslim rights in the world would infringe the rights of small Muslim neighbours, pointing out that Makran as a district of Kalat had no separate status and that the foreign policy of Lasbela and Kharan was placed under Kalat by the Standstill Agreement.

Time had, however, run out for the Khan. The plans for the invasion of Kalat were finalized on 22 March 1948 when Prime Minister Nawabzada Liaquat Ali Khan of Pakistan presided over a meeting of the three services chiefs to oversee the military invasion. Despite the Standstill Agreement, on 27 March 1948, Lt Col Gulzar of the 7th Baluch Regiment under GOC Maj. Gen. Mohammad Akbar Khan invaded the Khanate of Kalat. General Akbar escorted the Khan of Kalat to Karachi and forced him to sign the instrument of accession. Jinnah accepted the Instrument of Accession on 30 March 1948.

The Khan's signing of the Instrument was without obtaining formal sanction from the Baloch sardars and in opposition to the decision of the Baloch legislature (in October 1947 and January 1948). As the Khan wrote in his memoirs: 'Without obtaining the formal sanction from the tribal sardars, I signed the merger documents in my capacity as the Khan-e-Azam on 30 March 1948. I confess, I knew I was exceeding the scope of my mandate.'[45] The far-fetched justification he gave was:

> Had I not taken the immediate step of signing Kalat's merger, the position of Pakistan would definitely have gone worse. The British Agent to the Governor-General could have played havoc by leading Pakistan into a fratricide war against the Baloch. The army of Afghanistan could have easily entered into Balochistan. India, too, could have aggravated the situation by sending her naval warships to the Makran sea-coast obviously to help the Baloch, but in reality, this would have provided the best pretext for Russia to advance through Afghanistan and capture the ports on the Makran sea-coast![46]

Whatever the argument, the accession was regarded and continues to be regarded as 'illegal and oppressive' because it was only the two legislative chambers of Kalat that were authorized to decide the issue of accession. Both the chambers had clearly decided against accession. The Baloch have never gotten over their anger at the way the accession of Kalat was manipulated and they continue to treat the accession as invalid.

Martin Axmann has written probably the best epitaph for Kalat: 'The death of the state was the birth of the nation. The Baloch lost their 'national homeland' and turned into a marginal ethno-linguistic minority of Pakistan. This situational switching moulded the Baloch nation. It produced a conflict between the dominating national group of Punjabi-Pakistani and the dominated sub-national group of Baloch.'[47]

Pakistan had signed a Standstill Agreement with Kalat on 11 August 1947. It had signed a similar Standstill Agreement with the Maharaja of Kashmir in August 1947. Pakistan broke both these agreements. Its subsequent history would show similar disdain for international commitments.

7

Post-Accesssion Insurgencies

THE ONE COMMON THREAD THAT runs through the history of Balochistan since 1948 is the Baloch frequently breaking out in rebellion against the state. Every rebellion has lasted longer than the previous one, every rebellion has encompassed a wider geographical area than the previous one and every rebellion has involved more Baloch than the previous one. This must say something about the legitimacy of the Pakistan state in the eyes of the Baloch.

After forcing Kalat's accession, Pakistan restored the status quo ante in April 1948, that is, as had been the case in British times, a political agent, an officer subordinate to the Agent of the Governor General (AGG) in Quetta, was appointed to look after the administration of the state. The two legislative chambers were abolished, the cabinet dissolved and several cabinet ministers exiled or arrested in mid-April 1948. This put an end to the brief independence enjoyed by the Khanate after the British had left India.

1948 Insurgency

While the Khan acquiesced in the accession of Kalat, his brother Abdul Karim Khan declared a revolt and launched guerrilla operations against the Pakistan Army in Jhalawan district. Prior to the partition of the subcontinent, Abdul Karim had been the commandant of Kalat state's military and, during Kalat's short-lived independence, he held the post of governor of Makran. He proclaimed the independence of Kalat and issued a manifesto in the name of the Baloch National Liberation Committee rejecting the accession agreement signed by the Khan. With him were several leading figures in the Baloch nationalist movement, including Gul Khan Nasir and Muhammad Hussain Unka, along with several officers and some troops of the Kalat state army.[1]

Karim Khan hoped to obtain Afghan support since Afghanistan had objected to the inclusion of the Baloch and Pashtun areas in Pakistan and had even opposed the admission of Pakistan to the United Nations. While the Pakistani version is that Karim received substantial Afghan support, the Baloch nationalist version is that Afghanistan denied support since it favoured the inclusion of Balochistan in Afghanistan rather than as an independent country.[2]

Though not many new followers crossed over from Pakistan to join the rebels who had established a camp near the border, Abdul Karim managed to keep alive the flag of nationalist defiance until 1950. In late May 1950, the Khan, threatened with reprisals by the Pakistan Army, persuaded Karim Khan to surrender. According to Selig Harrison, Pakistani officers reportedly signed a safe-conduct agreement with Abdul Karim's representatives in the Harboi mountains and swore an oath on the Koran to uphold it. However, the agreement was dishonoured and the prince was ambushed and arrested along with 102 of his followers on their way to Kalat.[3] Karim and his followers were all sentenced to prison terms. Karim would spend several years in Pakistani prisons.

Karim Khan's was the first Baloch insurgency against Pakistan. Though militarily not very significant, it is important in Baloch history for two reasons. First, it established that the Baloch did not accept the forced accession of Kalat to Pakistan. Second, as Harrison notes, 'It led to the widespread Baloch belief that Pakistan had betrayed the safe-conduct agreement. The Baloch regard this as the first in a series of broken treaties that has cast an aura of distrust over relations with Islamabad.'[4] Karim Khan was to become the first modern rallying symbol for the Baloch liberation movement. Subsequent Baloch history would reinforce the impression of broken promises and repression by the government.

Developments in the 1950s

The 1950s saw the resurgence of nationalist aspirations in politics. Prince Abdul Karim was released in 1955. Soon after his release he again attracted the attention of the authorities by launching a new political party, Ustaman Gal, which had the stated goals of making Pakistan a people's republic, establishing a Baloch province and preserving the Balochi language and culture. The nucleus of the party were the members of the former Kalat State National Party (KSNP). In 1956 the Ustaman Gal joined the Pakistan National Party (PNP) to form the National Awami Party (NAP).

Meanwhile, on 14 October 1955, President Iskander Mirza officially terminated the Balochistan States Union (detailed earlier in the chapter on Land) and made it part of the 'One Unit' of West Pakistan. This was an attempt by Punjabi interests to combine the ethnically diverse provinces of West Pakistan, including Balochistan, into one administrative entity to counter the numerical, ethnic and linguistic challenges posed by an ethnically homogenous and numerically larger East Pakistan. In reality, it was a crude effort at establishing a national identity by trying to paper over ethnic and regional differences against the backdrop of rising discontent in Pakistan's eastern wing.

The impact of the ploy was, however, just the reverse. Instead of being suppressed, the ethno-national aspirations in West Pakistan were further strengthened. The ethnic minorities and the smaller provinces saw the 'One Unit' as posing a threat to their identity and autonomy, and galvanized concerns to protect their own identities. 'One Unit' thus became a unifying factor for the nationalist parties in the smaller provinces of West Pakistan.

1958 Insurgency

The Khan of Kalat could mobilize various tribal chieftains against the 'One Unit' scheme since it was perceived as concentrating excessive power in the federal government and circumscribing provincial autonomy. What upset the Baloch was the fact that 'One Unit' ensured that the establishment of Balochistan as a province with its own assembly even after a decade of accession, was forestalled. In October 1957 the Khan held a meeting of the important Baloch sardars in Karachi where the demand to end the 'One Unit' system was made. In a meeting with President Iskander Mirza in October 1957 they asked him to exempt Kalat from the scheme and to allot more government funds on developmental activities in Kalat. Though the 'One Unit' plan originally had little to do with the Baloch, its implementation ignited a Baloch uprising. As Nawab Khair Bakhsh Marri put it, 'Our people have slowly sensed that they [Pakistanis] would destroy our identity as a nation if we did not fight back.'[5]

When some Baloch sardars started non-cooperating with the government, it was alleged that the Khan had raised a parallel army to attack the Pakistan military. Ayub Khan, then commander-in-chief of the Pakistan Army, ordered it to march into Kalat on 6 October 1958, a day before Mirza imposed martial rule in Pakistan. The Khan of Kalat was arrested on 6 October 1958 on the charge of gathering 80,000 tribesmen 'to revolt against the government' and of secretly negotiating with Afghanistan for a full-scale Baloch rebellion. The only evidence was that his Afghan wife had gone to Kabul.[6]

The Khan denied these allegations. The general feeling was that President Iskander Mirza had encouraged the Khan to assert his autonomy in order to find a pretext to impose martial law.[7]

On 6 October 1958, a day before martial law was declared in Pakistan, the army besieged Kalat and sacked the palace. According to the Khan, his wife and children were locked up in a room. The royal treasury was placed under military control. The treasury was full of ancestral valuables and ancient coins and several other antiques. Things went on disappearing till everything was lost. 'The loot even bypassed the technique of the Tartars of the bygone days. Kalat was the worst sufferer, comparable to the destruction of Delhi or the sack of Baghdad in the past.'

Mir Ahmed Yar Khan Baluch, *Inside Baluchistan: A Political Autobiography of His Highness Baiglar Baigi: Khan-E-Azam-XIII*, Karachi: Royal Book Company 1975, p. 183.

These developments sparked the second insurgency in Balochistan, barely eleven years after the creation of Pakistan. Its leader was the eighty-year-old Nawab Nauroz Khan Zehri, the Sardar of the Zarakzai tribe of the Kalat region. Together with 500 armed men he launched an insurgency and put up a stiff resistance in the Mir Ghat mountains. The Jhalawan sardars loyal to the Khan also resisted the army's campaigns in Danshera and Wad. In the chain reaction of violence and counter-violence the government bombed villages suspected of harbouring guerrillas.

On 19 May 1959, Nauroz Khan along with his fighters surrendered near Anari Mountain after the authorities swore on the Koran the acceptance of their demands. According to Baloch nationalists, Nauroz Khan agreed to lay down his arms in return for the withdrawal of the 'One Unit' plan and the guarantee of safe conduct and amnesty for his men. Once again, the army dishonoured its solemn pledge on the Koran. Nauroz Khan and his companions were arrested, shifted to the Quetta cantonment, tried by a special military court and sentenced to death on 7 July 1960. The Nawab's eldest son Battay Khan Zarakzai along with six colleagues were hanged.[8] Nauroz Khan, due to his advanced age, and his minor son Mir Jalal Khan were imprisoned for life. The Nawab himself died in prison on 25 December 1965 becoming another martyr of the Baloch nationalist movement.

After they were hanged, the authorities sadistically requested the aged Nauroz Khan to identify the bodies. 'Is this one your son?' an army officer cold-heartedly asked the old warrior as he pointed to the body of the elderly warrior's son. Nauroz Khan stared at the soldier for a moment, then replied quietly, 'All these brave young men are my sons.' Then looking at the faces of his dead supporters, he noticed that the moustache of one of them had drooped in death. He went over to the body and tenderly curled the moustache upwards while gently admonishing, 'Even in death, my son, one should not allow the enemy to think, even for one moment, that you have despaired.'

Sherbaz Khan Mazari, *A Journey to Disillusionment*,
Karachi: OUP, 1999, pp. 84–85.

For the Baloch, Nawab Nauroz Khan and the seven martyrs form an important chapter in their struggle. On the one hand he came to symbolize the determination of the Baloch to not to bow to unjust and brutal assaults on their freedom and to resist, regardless of the price that must be paid for this honourable path. Emulating them is the dream. On the other hand the treatment meted out to him has reinforced the impression of the treachery of the Pakistani government.

The 1958 revolt was followed by the Pakistan Army setting up new garrisons at key points in the interior of Balochistan. Over the next decade Balochistan was treated like a colony rather than a part of the Pakistan state. Punjabis and other non-Baloch groups dominated the administration while the Baloch were kept out of governance.

1962 Insurgency

The immediate provocation for the third Baloch insurgency of 1962 was that the results of the elections held under Gen. Ayub Khan's 'Basic Democracies' were not honoured. Ayub was furious that several nationalists like Khair Baksh Marri and Attaullah Mengal had been elected. He dismissed them peremptorily and nominated sardars of his choice to head local government institutions. The plan backfired as Baloch tribesmen assassinated several of the nominated sardars and also began attacking the newly-established Pakistan military posts in Balochistan. In August 1962 Ayub Khan on a visit to Quetta publicly threatened the Baloch with '… complete extinction if they continued to oppose'.[9] Pervez Musharraf, another military dictator, would make a similar threat decades later that would fuel another insurgency.

The Baloch insurgencies of 1948 and 1958 had been impulsive and short lived. The credit for creating an organized and sustained armed struggle goes to Sher Mohammad Marri, respectfully called Babu (Uncle) by the Marris while the Punjabi media often called him General Sherov to imply he served Russian interests.[10] He realized the need of transforming the disorganized and sporadic struggle adopted so far into a classic guerrilla warfare. With the support of Khair Bakhsh Marri he established the first Parrari[11] camp in 1962 to challenge the Pakistan Army in an organized manner. By July 1963 a network of twenty-two base camps had been set up, each manned by about 200 full-time fighters. The base camps were located largely in the Mengal tribal areas of Jhalawan in the south and the Marri and Bugti areas in the north. The demands included the withdrawal of the Pakistan Army from Balochistan, the unification of all Baloch areas, provincial autonomy and the ending of the oppressive sardari system.[12] The Parrari movement later became the Baloch People's Liberation Front (BPLF).

The Parraris, using guerilla tactics, ambushed convoys, bombed trains and carried out other acts of violence. In retaliation, the army staged savage reprisals. For example, it bulldozed 13,000 acres of almond tress owned by Sher Mohammad and his relatives in the Marri area. However, Gen. Ayub Khan for all his bluster could not crush the Baloch. The fighting continued sporadically until 1969 when Gen. Yahya Khan, Ayub Khan's successor, got the Baloch to agree to a ceasefire, dismantled the 'One Unit' plan and created the four provinces of Punjab, Sindh, North-West Frontier and Balochistan. Yahya also ordered elections to the national and provincial assemblies in December 1970, the results of which led to the creation of Bangladesh and radically altered the geography of Pakistan.

Despite the ceasefire, the Parraris assumed that the renewal of hostilities with Islamabad, sooner or later, would be unavoidable. As such, the organizational infrastructure was kept intact, many cadres went underground and continued to train, garner equipment and organize resistance. The Parrari is significant not only because its military force would grow to over a thousand during the 1960s but also because it would be responsible for establishing parallel governments in many areas of Balochistan that built schools and provided medical services.[13]

Fanned by the waves of separatist propaganda that these developments inspired, the Baloch Student Organization (BSO) was formed in 1967. Efforts were made to homogenize the Baloch language and the Baloch press became more prominent than ever before. Nationalist publications such as the *Chingari* prospered and the Balochistan People's Liberation Front grew stronger. The Baloch no longer viewed themselves as a series of individual tribes; a cohesive ethnic identity was beginning to develop.

The 1973–77 Insurgency

The fourth insurgency broke out in 1973. It was provoked by Bhutto's dismissal of the ten-month-old Balochistan government led by Attaullah Mengal of the NAP on 12 February 1973. The dismissal was followed by the arrest of Baloch leaders Mengal, Ghaus Baksh Bizenjo, Khair Baksh Marri and others. The banning of the NAP and the way its leaders were treated reinforced the perceptions of the nationalists that they would not be able to secure their rights through democratic means alone. The dismissal of the Mengal government became another milestone in the history of Pakistan's betrayal of Balochistan.

Pakistan, and especially the army, was still recovering from the shock of the vivisection of the country in 1971 and was unwilling to countenance even legitimate nationalist demands. The fear was that Balochistan could well become another Bangladesh in the making and so it sought to crush any signs of ethno-nationalist demands.

The Mengal government had been sworn in on 1 May 1972 amid high hopes and expectations but from the first day encountered hurdles in its path. An immediate cause of friction between the Centre and the province was the desire on the part of the latter to empower the Pashtuns and the Baloch. It sought to do this by appointing them to key positions in the provincial administration, a move that the Centre viewed with suspicion. The provincial government also sought a greater share in the natural resources of the province. It accused the Centre of discrimination in the allocation of industries. The dehi muhafiz (rural police), established by the Mengal government in 1973, was viewed by Islamabad as a 'NAP army' though subsequently, the succeeding PPP government maintained this force, renaming it the Balochistan Reserve Force. Clearly, the Baloch leadership, like political leadership elsewhere, was keen to consolidate its political base. This, however, was disliked by the PPP–dominated Centre that had virtually no base in the province.

Matters were made worse by Bhutto's arrogance that could not stand the assertion of provincial rights by the nationalist government of Balochistan. Bhutto accused the provincial government of repeatedly exceeding its constitutional authority and entering into a conspiracy with foreign powers.

Two other events are noteworthy. The first was the bickering between the Baloch. Thus, Nawab Akbar Khan Bugti, who had developed differences with Governor Bizenjo, accused the NAP of hatching what became known as the 'London Plan' to separate Balochistan and the North-West Frontier Province from Pakistan. The charge of treason was raised against NAP leaders Attaullah Mengal and Pashtun leader

Wali Khan claiming that they had met with the then Bangladesh prime minister Mujibur Rahman to 'plan the disintegration of Pakistan ... into several autonomous states'.[14]

The second was the extraordinary discovery of a large cache of 300 Soviet-made sub-machine guns and 48,000 rounds of ammunition in the house of the Iraqi defence attaché in Islamabad. Though it was claimed that they were meant for Baloch leaders, it was subsequently revealed that the arms had actually been found in Karachi. They were meant for the Iranian Baloch in retaliation for Iran's support to Iraqi Kurds.[15]

Even without these two levers, there were several reports about PPP–led disruption of the provincial government. Provincial government employees who were mostly non-Baloch and who owed their allegiance to the Centre were 'instructed to put every possible obstruction' and they 'acted in complete disregard of their minister's instructions'. Furthermore, 'They were made to believe ... that the NAP ministries were only for a short period. Hence they should not ruin their future by becoming loyal to them.'[16]

Following the dismissal of the Mengal government, several Baloch militant organizations sprang up after April 1973 to ambush army convoys. The main force was the left-wing Balochistan People's Liberation Front (BPLF) led by Mir Hazar Khan Marri. It operated largely from the Marri territory and from sanctuaries in Afghanistan. Bhutto retaliated by sending the army into Balochistan. The armed struggle continued over the next four years with varying degrees of severity.

For many nationalists, Bugti's collaboration with the Central government and chronic factionalism among NAP leaders exemplified the destructive divisiveness of the tribal system. In the words of Shaista Khan Mengal, a nephew of Gul Khan Nasir and a leader in the insurgency, 'Imagine if the five Baloch leaders of the NAP had stayed together instead of each having his own political agenda. They could not make an effective organization. If five leaders can't stay together, how can a nation? I don't blame the Pakistan intelligence services for what happened. The fault is with our tribal customs and politics.'[17]

Selig Harrison describes the BPLF as '... an exotic amalgam of Baloch nationalists and independent Marxist–Leninist thought that rejected the primacy of either Moscow or Peking and had close ties with Nawab Khair Bakhsh Marri.'[18] The aims of the rebels were confined to immediate issues: the release of NAP leaders, restoration of their government and greater autonomy for Balochistan. There was no attempt to restructure Baloch society and neither was educating the populace a significant part of their strategy. Some sardars even opposed political education. A minority in the BPLF called for uniting all the Baloch in Iran, Pakistan and Afghanistan as Greater Balochistan.[19]

Overall, the nationalist leadership's reaction was impulsive and they lacked a political strategy. Hence, the insurgency started as a sporadic revolt, gained momentum when more and more tribes joined in, but had no clear goal to achieve.

During the four-year insurgency, the fighting was more widespread than it had been in the 1950s and 1960s. There were 178 major engagements and 167 lesser incidents between the Pakistan forces and Baloch militants. The Baloch militants adopted classic guerilla tactics avoiding direct confrontation, instead ambushing army convoys and harassing its supply lines. By July 1974 some of its successes included: cutting off most of the main roads into Balochistan; periodic disruption of the Sibi–Harnai rail link, thereby blocking coal shipments from the Baloch areas to the Punjab; and attacks on drilling and survey operations that hampered oil exploration activities.[20]

Gen. Tikka Khan led the military crackdown on the Baloch insurgency and came to be known by the moniker of 'Butcher of Balochistan'.[21] At the height of the war, Harrison notes that there were over 80,000 Pakistani troops in the province against 55,000 Baloch fighters. Unable to break the back of the insurgents, the military in 1974 brought in air power in the form of Mirage and F-86 fighters to bomb entire villages. The then Shah of Iran, apprehending trouble in Iranian Balochistan, supported the Pakistani forces in decimating the Baloch resistance. He provided US $200 million in aid and sent in thirty US Cobra Helicopters manned by Iranian pilots who pounded the Baloch pockets of resistance.[22]

Gen. Zia-ul-Haq, who ousted Bhutto in a coup in July 1977, ended the insurgency by entering into a negotiated settlement. By then, more than 5,000 Baloch fighters and at least 3,000 military personnel had been killed. Zia did not accede to any of the demands raised by the rebels, but ended military operations and withdrew troops; released thousands of Baloch leaders and activists; granted a general amnesty to all those who had taken up arms; remitted all sentences; returned properties that had been confiscated. Zia dropped the Hyderabad Conspiracy Case[23] against the Baloch leaders and sent Attaullah Mengal, a heart patient, to the UK for surgery at government expense. All this had a dramatic effect.[24]

As a result, Balochistan did not trouble Zia and remained peaceful for the next two-and-a-half decades. Most of the Baloch leaders left Pakistan and went into exile in Afghanistan, the UK and other places outside Pakistan. Several Baloch groups migrated to Afghanistan where they were permitted to set up camps by President Mohammed Daoud Khan.

Peace, however, was deceptive. The insurgency undoubtedly had ended but the Baloch conflict had not been resolved. The four-year-long insurgency had politicized the populace, aroused nationalist feelings, created more bitterness and hatred for Pakistan and above all instilled in the Baloch '... feelings of unprecedented resentment and widespread hunger for a chance to vindicate their martial honor'.[25] According to Selig Harrison, when the Baloch started the insurgency in 1973, they were not looking for independence but regional autonomy within a restructured constitutional framework. However, when the insurgency ended, separatist feeling had greatly increased due to the excessive use of superior firepower, especially air strikes against civilians, by the state. The 1973–77 insurgency, he wrote, aroused a degree of psychological alienation from Islamabad that was 'strikingly reminiscent of the angry climate that was developing in East Pakistan during the late 1960s.[26]

In the end nothing had really changed in Balochistan. For, as Mir Ghaus Bakhsh Bizenjo said in his statement to the Supreme Court of Pakistan:

> I must accept that by use of superior force, it is possible to maintain state borders, even gain new territories, hold colonies or slaves in chains for certain historical periods, but you cannot create brotherhood by means of bayonets, butchery, death and destruction. You cannot create a united nation by force. Nations

have risen and come into being in historical processes by feeling of common interests, by voluntary unions, by recognition of each other's rights, by respect and brotherly love for one another. Bayonet and bullets cannot give birth to a united nation, they can only damage that objective irreparably.[27]

The two important lessons the Baloch learnt from the insurgency was that they would have triumphed if they had better weaponry, and that their cause suffered from its disorganized character.[28] Other reasons for the collapse of the resistance was the extensive use of air power, the Iranian military involvement in the conflict, lack of external support and the antagonistic attitude of the Western powers towards the Baloch national struggle given that the 1970s saw the cold war at its peak. Any national liberation struggle was seen by Western powers as an extension of Soviet influence.[29]

Post-1970s

By the 1980s, the Baloch nationalist movement showed signs of decline. There were growing differences between personalities on strategies and goals. One major difference was that a group of Baloch leaders led by Ghaus Bakhsh Bizenjo favoured a political struggle while others led by Attaulah Mengal and Khair Bakhsh Marri supported insurgency. Mengal and Marri believed that Pakistani political process was not worth any effort and instead the Baloch should work openly for independence. Bizenjo, on the other hand, believed that conditions were unfavourable for independence and so the Baloch should fight for their rights within the political system. These differences were irreconcilable and the leaders went their own way.[30]

The differences between the Pashtun and Baloch leaders too widened as the Baloch leadership perceived the Pashtuns being favoured by the state. This led to a split in the NAP and the formation of a separate party, the Pakistan National Party (PNP) led by Bizenjo. Zia-ul-Haq exploited these differences and cultivated prominent Pashtuns to counter the influence of the Baloch sardars opposed to his policies. Influential tribal leaders like Prince Moinuddin Baloch (younger brother of the Khan of Kalat) were accommodated in the federal cabinet.[31]

In the 1980s and 1990s, Balochistan's stunted economic development continued. Additionally, the increased Pashtun migration into Balochistan during the Afghan war raised fears about the Baloch majority in the province. Politically, during the democratic interlude of the 1990s, Mengal and Bizenjo formed the Balochistan National Party (BNP) and Nawab Akbar Khan Bugti established Jamhoori Watan Party (JWP). They also entered into coalition governments. Musharraf's coup in 1999 and his electoral engineering of sidelining mainstream political parties and catapulting the religious group Mutahidda Majlis-i-Amal (MMA) in the 2002 elections was a major setback for Baloch nationalism. The political vacuum during the Musharraf years would set the stage for the next and fifth insurgency in Balochistan.[32]

III

THE ROOTS OF
ALIENATION

8

Political and Administrative Marginalization

THE ROOTS OF BALOCH ALIENATION are multidimensional. The major cause, of course, goes back to the forced accession of the princely state of Kalat that the Baloch did not accept and considered illegal in 1948. This issue continues to be disputed even now. The sense of alienation has been exacerbated several notches due to the feeling among many Baloch that since the creation of Pakistan, Balochistan has been increasingly 'colonized' by the ethnically dominant Punjabis who control the Central government.

A section of the Baloch nationalists believe that the centralizing nature of the Pakistani federation is such that smaller nationalities like the Baloch are not accommodated within the federation. One reason is that representation in elected bodies and state institutions as also distribution of resources (till recently) were based upon population. Balochistan, despite having 44 per cent of Pakistan's territory, has only 6 per cent of the country's total population. Thus, the province is not proportionately represented within the federation. Additionally, given its geostrategic importance, the nationalists maintain that the federation is only interested in harvesting the strategic and economic potential of the province without paying much attention to its numerically small population. The actions of successive governments have instilled the belief that the social and economic uplift of the Baloch is not the priority of the federation.[1]

The key elements in the political alienation are: lack of representation in politics, in the bureaucracy and in the armed forces; heavy military presence in the province; woeful condition of education; apathy of the rest of Pakistan at the plight of Balochistan; and the fear of becoming a minority in their own homeland.

Political Under-representation

Balochistan has been and continues to be grossly under-represented in state and Central government structures. In fact, in all the organs of the state, there are very few Baloch in the higher rungs of the Central and state governments, ministries or the armed forces of Pakistan. Not surprisingly, instead of identifying with the government, the people perceive the government and its organs as aliens lording over Baloch territory. Speaking from personal experience, Malik Siraj Akbar, a Baloch writer now based in the US who grew up in Balochistan during 1980s and '90s, recalls: 'We did not feel properly represented in any domain of life in Pakistan.'[2]

One study revealed that during the thirty-year period from 1947 to 1977, only four out of the 179 persons who were members of the Central cabinets were ethnic Baloch. Only one of them (Akbar Bugti) was a Central minister prior to the 1970s.[3]

Politically, till the 1990s, provincial governments with a semblance of Baloch representation were allowed to function for only three years in all. The first was the National Awami Party coalition in 1972-73 led by Sardar Attaullah Mengal that lasted about ten months before being dismissed by Z.A. Bhutto; second was the government of Nawab Akbar Bugti (1988–90) that was dismissed when Benazir Bhutto's first government was sacked; and the third was a coalition government headed by Akhtar Mengal in 1997-98, which could function for fifteen months. This had bred the belief that Baloch governments were not allowed to complete their terms by the Punjabi establishment.

It has been estimated that the average size of national constituencies in Punjab is 1,388 sq. km, in Khyber Pakhtunkhwa it is 2,129 sq. km, in Sindh 2,310 sq. km. The average constituency size of the three provinces is about 1,942 sq. km. By comparison, the average constituency size in Balochistan is 12.8 times higher, at 24,799 sq. km. Average constituency size in Balochistan is eighteen times larger than in Punjab while its population is less than the area in absolute numbers. The provincial assembly constituencies too are much larger in area than in the other provinces. Average provincial constituency size in Balochistan is 6,808 sq. km, compared to 691 sq. km in Punjab, 752 sq. km in KPK and 839 sq. km in Sindh.[4]

The absurdity of the electoral system in Balochistan can be gauged from a few examples of the newly-formed electoral constituencies after the provisional results of the 2017 census. Thus, NA-272 Gwadar-cum-Lasbela constituency comprises the entire 760-km-long coastline of Balochistan, starting from Karachi and going up to Iran. The mind boggles thinking how a candidate could possibly campaign or what distances a person would have to travel to cast his/her vote in the constituency. The geographical area of NA-270, encompassing four central Balochistan districts, Panjgur, Washuk, Kharan and Awaran, is a staggering 94,452 sq. km. To put this in perspective, it is bigger than the area of Khyber Pakhtunkhwa and is almost half the size of Punjab province. Legally, of course, the delimitation has been done as per the population but it does not account for the skewed land to population ratio of the province. Thus, while the population density in this constituency is eight persons per sq. km, in central Karachi the population density in constituencies NA 253–256 is 43,000. Is it possible that the population living in these areas can exercise their political rights with equal ease?[5]

Hence, in Balochistan's case, numerical equality of constituencies has resulted in marginalization and exclusion. In the former Federally Administered Tribal Areas (FATA) constituencies, the state had legally allowed the population to be half that of the national average to compensate for 'the representation deficit'. No such provision was ever made for Balochistan. Clearly, the electoral delimitation is not geared towards mainstreaming the Baloch. On the contrary, it would only strengthen the Baloch narrative of deprivation and increase their alienation.[6]

Bureaucratic Under-representation

In the bureaucracy, according to a study, of the 830 civil service posts in Balochistan, ethnic Baloch held only 181 in 1979. There was just one Baloch each holding the rank of secretary, director and deputy commissioner. As regards the police, all the high officials were non-Baloch and so were three-quarters of the police force. The status in judicial services was not very different.[7] During the beginning of the Bhutto period, it was estimated that out of approximately 40,000 civil employees in Balochistan, only about 2,000 were Baloch and most of them held inferior jobs.[8]

To correct the age-old imbalance in representation of the Baloch and to create in them a sense of participation in governance, the Zia-ul-Haq regime promised in 1980 to make their representation in the federal bureaucracy commensurate with their 3.9 per cent share of Pakistan's national population. Despite this, according to Baloch MP Abdul Rauf Mengal, as on March 2005, there were very few government servants from Balochistan in Islamabad and not a single Baloch in foreign missions abroad. According to a statement made by then Senator Hasil Bizenjo in the Senate on 29 April 2009, not even a single head of around sixty government organizations and institutions was from his province.[9] The government and its organs, therefore, continued to be perceived as outsiders ruling over the Baloch

Even today most officials working in senior positions in Balochistan, from chief secretary to inspector general of police as well as most of the government secretaries in Balochistan, come from Punjab or other provinces. The late Nawab Bugti used to often tell his visitors that if they visited the Balochistan secretariat and checked out the nameplates outside each office, they would find virtually no locals running provincial affairs. Moreover, in the central bureaucracy, despite the province-wise quota based on population, most of the positions have gone to non-Baloch under the 'domicile clause' of the quota system.[10] Resultantly, thousands of people are occupying government jobs either on bogus and doctored identity documents showing them as Baloch or are receiving salaries without doing any work.[11]

No less a person than the former chief minister of Balochistan Dr Abdul Malik told the senate standing committee on interprovincial coordination that lots of people were getting jobs in various federal departments and corporations on the Balochistan quota, on the basis of fake domicile certificates. This fake domicile certificate racket has been going on systematically and wilfully to deprive the Baloch people of progress on the economic ladder.[12] Senator Jehanzeb Jamaldini repeated the charge when he said, 'People of other provinces get domicile of Balochistan and get jobs on our quota. Officials of District Management Group (DMG), police and other departments, when temporarily posted in Balochistan, make Computerized National Identity Certificates (CNICs) and domiciles for their kids from the province and later get jobs on our quota.'[13]

For example, it was revealed in May 2016 by arrested employees of National Database and Registration Authority (NADRA) that corrupt officials had issued as many as 90,000 identity cards to foreigners in Qila Abdullah and other areas. The employees revealed that the officials had pocketed a bribe of somewhere between Rs 40,000 and Rs 100,000 per identity card.[14]

The provincial government had sent the data of 295,457 employees to NADRA for verification. During the process, the CNICs of 249,000 government employees were confirmed while those of 45,000 could not be. They had either fake or wrong ID card numbers. The CNICs of 28,367 were found to be fake, CNICs of 1,600 employees were found blocked,[15] 271 employees held more than one CNIC and occupied two government jobs simultaneously. It also found that forty-one employees were below eighteen years of age when appointed and were, therefore, ineligible for the posts they currently occupied; another 624 were found to be foreigners. Likewise, when the data of 46,932 pensioners in the province was passed through the same verification process, the identity of 12,341 of them could also not be validated.[16]

At the same time, the Senate Standing Committee on Cabinet Secretariat was informed that a large number of posts of Grade 18 and above were lying vacant in Balochistan for a long time. It was reported that officials were serving on only forty-two out of 103 posts of Grade 18, 19, 20 and 21 in the province. Only one appointment had been made out of five posts in Grade 21; five out of twenty-three in Grade 20; nineteen out of thirty-five in Grade 19; and seventeen out of forty posts were filled in Grade 18.[17] As a result, the Balochistan government had resorted to desperate measures like trying to fill 20,000 out of 35,000 vacancies in different provincial departments in ninety days.[18]

As per a recent study by noted economist Kaiser Bengali, there were fifty-three divisions in the federal administrative structure including eleven offices catering to the President House, Supreme

Court and others. He noted that of the total employees in the basic pay-scales (BPS) of 1–22, only 4.1 per cent were from Balochistan— one percentage point less than its population share. The provinces share in the higher posts BPS 17–22 was even lower at 3.9 per cent. The province's share in BPS 20–22 was a mere 2.1 per cent. According to him there were thirteen out of fifty-three divisions and offices, including the President's Secretariat, where there were no Balochistan-domiciled personnel in BPS 1–4; there were no Balochistan-domiciled officers in BPS 20 in thirty-one out of fifty-three; there was no Balochistan-domiciled officer in BPS 21 in forty-nine out of fifty-three and there were forty-seven out of fifty-three where there were no Balochistan-domiciled officers in BPS 22. In other words, there were only thirty-two Balochistan-domiciled officers out of a total of 1,525 officers in BPS 20–22. His conclusion is stark: 'The absence of Balochistan-domiciled officers in the top echelons of the civil service means that the province has little say in national level policymaking.'[19]

In September 2017, members of the treasury and opposition benches joined hands to criticize the federal government for not addressing the issue of denial of jobs and the discrimination against local youths in the foreign office, planning commission and other autonomous organizations. One member pointed out that officers of the Central Superior Services (CSS) from other provinces were given several facilities and perks on their appointments and postings in Balochistan. These included promotions to the next grades, one extra salary and four return air tickets, etc. However, officers from Balochistan were denied all these facilities when they were posted to other provinces. Former chief minister Dr Abdul Malik Baloch revealed that 110 autonomous corporations were working in the country but there was no representation from Balochistan in these institutions. He accused Islamabad of 'behaving like the East India Company'.[20]

According to the data made available to the National Assembly, more than 3,000 posts reserved as per the 6 per cent quota for the province under the *Aghaz-e-Haqooq-e-Balochistan* package (details mentioned in a later chapter) for those domiciled in Balochistan were vacant in fifty federal government ministries and departments. Moreover, Balochistan's quota for the top posts was close to non-existent as only six ministries had twelve posts allocated for the province in Grade 20, four had been sanctioned in Grade 21 while there was no quota for the province in Grade 22. Furthermore, no quota had been set aside for the province in Grades 20 to 22 in the rest of the twenty-four ministries. According to Mir Muhammad Yousaf Badini, a senator from Balochistan, the issue had been raised several times before the government and parliament but nobody took Balochistan seriously. Another senator from Balochistan, Daud Khan Achakzai, asked, 'If the quota is not fulfilled, how will the sense of deprivation be diminished?'[21] The disparity among provinces was also revealed when the Chief Justice of Pakistan Mian Saqib Nisar while hearing suo motu cases at the Quetta Registry pointed out the province was paying its doctors Rs 24,000 a month whereas a driver of the Supreme Court was being paid Rs 35,000.[22]

Under-representation in the Army

In the armed forces, the number of Baloch has been extremely small. Historically, there was always resistance to recruitment from Balochistan into the British Indian Army. This finally resulted in 1929 in an armed uprising in the Baloch regiment, which since 1929 did not have any Baloch in it.[23] Many years later, Baloch nationalists in Makran were to launch an agitation during the 1960s and 1970s against recruitment in the Oman Army.

An academic study revealed that from the areas that became Pakistan, British recruitment was 77 per cent from Punjab, 19.5 per cent from NWFP, 2.2 per cent from Sindh and 0.6 per cent from Balochistan.[24] In post-colonial Pakistan, the proportion did not change much. The ethnic group strength of Pakistan's military officer corps in the 1970s was approximately estimated as 70 per cent Punjabi, 15 per cent Pashtun, 10 per cent Mohajir and 5 per cent Baloch and Sindhi.[25] As regards higher military positions, it was maintained that until June 1959, out of twenty-four generals in the Pakistan Army, eleven were Punjabis and eleven Pathans.[26] Even later, there were hardly any Baloch in the top echelons of the armed forces.

According to former Baloch chief minister Attaullah Mengal, 'There are only a few hundred Baloch in the entire Pakistan Army. The famous

Baloch Regiment has no Baloch in it. The Kalat Scouts was a paramilitary force raised during the Ayub regime and had only two people from Kalat within its ranks. The same is the case with the Sibi Scouts created to police the Marri areas. It does not have a single Baloch in its ranks. The officers are from Punjab and soldiers from the Frontier.'[27]

According to another study, ex-servicemen from Balochistan for the period 1995–2003 numbered 3,753 men only while the numbers for Punjab and the NWFP for the same period were 1,335,339 and 229,856, respectively.[28] The quota for recruitment of soldiers from Balochistan and Sindh was raised to 15 per cent in 1991. Similarly, the height and educational standards were relaxed for them. Despite this, it was estimated that in December 1998 there was a shortfall of about 10,000 other ranks from Balochistan and interior Sindh.[29] Moreover, with the quota being on a provincial basis and based on ethnicity, it was assessed that the bulk of recruits to the army from Balochistan were Pashtuns rather than ethnic Baloch.

Could this situation be changing? According to the army chief Gen. Qamar Javed Bajwa, more than 25,000 Baloch students were receiving quality education at various Army and Frontier Corps-run schools and cadet colleges all over Pakistan: 'Nearly 20,000 sons of Balochistan are serving in the army, including over 600 as officers, while 232 cadets are undergoing training at the Pakistan Military Academy (PMA), Kakul,' he added. These numbers get even higher, Bajwa continued, when 'we take into account Baloch youth in Pakistan Air Force, Pakistan Navy' and other law-enforcement agencies. However, once again, he did not clarify if these were ethnic Baloch. The use of the term 'sons of Balochistan' obviously meant the whole of Balochistan.[30]

In 1997, Senator Kachkool Ali Baloch complained that despite having 750 km coast out of total 1,100 km in Pakistan, not a single seaman in the Navy belonged to Balochistan.[31]

Military Footprint

Balochistan has a heavy military footprint that is a hark back to its colonial past and its forced accession to Pakistan. Apart from the four existing cantonments at Quetta, Sibi, Loralai and Khuzdar, there are three naval bases, four missile testing sites, two nuclear development sites and fifty-nine paramilitary facilities. According to press reports, Sardar Akhtar Mengal stated that there are 35,000 Frontier Corps (FC), 12,000 Coast Guards, 1,150 levies, 6,000 Balochistan Reserve police, 2,000 marines and four army brigades deployed in Balochitan.[32] Today, provincial governments in Pakistan have no rights to levy either entertainment tax or property tax on the property located inside the cantonments, including private properties. The cantonments have become a sort of parallel government by themselves where the writ of the provincial government does not run.

The proliferation of cantonments is a sore point with the Baloch. They perceive these cantonments as usurpation of their traditional land by the army. According to a report, 'Over 500 acres of land was forcibly occupied in Sui', when citizens refused to sell their land; the same process is being repeated in Kohlu 'leading to similar resentment'.[33] Not surprisingly, in the Baloch perception, the cantonments are instruments of colonization and the security forces the colonizing forces. In addition, the Frontier Corps, a paramilitary force manned mostly by outsiders operating under the Central government, has by its conduct left no stone unturned to heighten the animosity of the Baloch. Over the years its check posts, numbering 493 in 2006, have become instruments of extortion, humiliation and intimidation.[34] As a result, Baloch leaders have been agitating vociferously in parliament and outside against the setting up of three new cantonments at Sui, Kohlu and Gwadar in the province.

The Human Rights Commission of Pakistan (HRCP) sent a mission to Balochistan in October 2003 that visited several towns, cities and villages in Balochistan to assess the situation. In its report, HRCP called for a revamping of the law and order machinery and making the intelligence agencies accountable, and warned of the dangers of militarization of the people. The mission noted: 'The dangers of militarization of the people cannot be exaggerated. Even a minimum degree of respect for the history of Balochistan demands that any extension of defence establishments in the province should be subject to double scrutiny and it should be undertaken only after convincing the people of its justification. The need to reduce the military's presence in jobs traditionally and rightly reserved for civilians is even greater in Balochistan than in other provinces.'[35]

Education

The educational system in Balochistan is dysfunctional. Figures, including for access to education, are appalling and far below those of other provinces. It is self-evident that no improvement in living standards and alleviation of poverty can be possible without improvement in educational levels and standards. In fact, high rates of illiteracy and low standards of educational progress are the root cause of the Baloch lagging behind other provinces.[36]

According to figures revealed by provincial ministers in 2017, one million to 1.1 million children were enrolled in government schools; around 350,000 children were studying in madrassas and 300,000 children were studying at private schools.[37] In 2009 the number of children studying in 1,095 madrassas was only 85,000. According to the adviser to the Balochistan chief minister on education, over 1.6 million children of school-going age were not in schools. However, according to a report released by the Academy for Educational Planning and Management (AEPAM), a federal government institution, more than 1.8 million children were out of school in Balochistan. Education Statistics 2014-15 launched in February 2016 by AEPAM estimated that 24.02 million children between the ages of five and sixteen were out of school in Pakistan. Balochistan had the highest percentage of out-of-school children at 70 per cent, followed by Sindh at 56 per cent and Punjab at 44 per cent, and Khyber Pakhtunkhwa with the lowest percentage of out-of-school children at 36 per cent.[38]

By the government's own admission, of the 22,000 plus settlements in the province, there were government-run schools (primary, secondary and high schools) in only about 12,500 of them.[39] The situation regarding girl's education is far worse since girls continue to suffer severe disadvantages and exclusion in Balochistan. A staggering 75 per cent of girls aged between five and sixteen are out of school compared to 65 per cent boys within the same age bracket in Balochistan, according to NGO Alif Ailan. There is one girls high school every 77 sq. km. Owing to scarcity of high schools for them, girls in the respective areas have little option but to give up their education after completing middle school.[40]

School dropouts is another major issue. Every year 130,000 students enrol in schools but only 61,000 appear in matriculation examinations, out of which only 30,000 are able to pass while the number of university pass-outs is 3,000.[41]

At an all-Pakistan level, eleven out of the sixteen districts in Pakistan with the worst net enrolment rate (NER) record were in Balochistan: none of the districts in the province lay in the highest quality of district education rankings. Of the thirty-two districts in Balochistan, twenty-three districts had an education score of less than 50 per cent.[42]

Another problem with education was the issue of ghost schools. Speaking in the Balochistan assembly, the former minister for education Abdul Rahim Ziaratwal revealed that there was no record of 15,000 teachers and there were 900 ghost schools with almost 300,000 registered students that were fake.[43] Yet, government records showed that funds were dispersed to those schools and teachers were receiving salaries every month.

Article 25A of the Constitution made education for children aged five to sixteen a part of Fundamental Rights. The challenge for Balochistan is to convert the net enrolment rates (NERs) of primary, middle and secondary enrolment from the current 56, 25 and 14 per cent respectively to 100 per cent.[44]

The Economic Survey of Pakistan 2011-2012 provides a comparative survey of literacy rates (10 years+) in Pakistan and the provinces:

	2008-09			2010-11		
	Male	Female	Total	Male	Female	Total
Pakistan	69	45	57	69	46	58
Punjab	69	50	59	70	51	60
Sindh	71	45	59	71	46	59
KPK	69	31	50	68	33	50
Balochistan	62	23	45	60	19	41

Higher Education

Another example is the shocking stepmotherly treatment meted out to Balochistan by the Higher Education Commission (HEC), the supreme regulatory body of higher education in Pakistan, and how Balochistan has been deprived of its due rights. According to the HEC's Annual Report 2012-13, the share of Balochistan in HEC scholarships and grants is not more than 3 per cent, which is half of Balochistan's constitutionally mandated quota of 6 per cent. Some of the details are as under:

- Balochistan received only thirty scholarships or 1 per cent of the total scholarships granted by the HEC for PhDs.
- Under the category of Foreign and Indigenous Scholarships, Balochistan and FATA combined got twelve out of 8,317 scholarships offered to university students, i.e., a joint share of 0.14 per cent.
- Under a programme that provides financial grants to scientific projects of university teachers to promote scientific research and innovation in higher education institutes, Balochistan only got 2.62 per cent of the grants for 2012-13.
- Only one out of 130 symposiums/training workshops/seminars and conferences to disseminate their scientific works was supported by the HEC in Balochistan while forty-six such events were sponsored by HEC in Islamabad alone.
- In 2012-13, Balochistan got only 4.09 per cent of Rs 12.014 billion development grants released by the HEC for establishment or expansion of universities.[45]

The National Research Programme for Universities (NRPU) is the highest awarded fund for research and capacity development for research and researchers of the HEC. It funds up to Rs 20 million for each project. In the three-year period 2015-16 to 2017-18, the HEC approved 2,109 projects. The province-wise distribution was more than 70 per cent to Punjab and the Federal area while Balochistan's share was less than 1 per cent and even a low of 0.4 per cent in 2015-16.[46]

Article 37(A) of Pakistan's Constitution enjoins the state to '... promote, with special care, the educational and economic interests of backward classes or areas.' The purpose clearly is that the backward areas of Pakistan, which includes Balochistan, should get more than their share till the time they reach the same level as other areas in terms of socio-economic development. The HEC has clearly been violating the Constitution by providing Balochistan with even less than its constitutionally mandated 6 per cent quota.[47]

The first university in Balochistan was set up in 1970. Almost fifty years later there are only five universities in Balochistan, and even these are not provided with the same opportunities in terms of receiving donor money, exchange programmes and other benefits of foreign aid, as universities in other provinces. This puts the students in Balochistan at a greater disadvantage, practically stunting the ability of the Baloch people to fully develop themselves, compete and work for their province.[48] There were a total of 3,200 students at Balochistan University. Of these, fewer than 500 were Baloch; of a total of 180 faculty members, only thirty were Baloch.[49]

Apathy of the Rest of Pakistan

The apathy of the rest of Pakistan to developments in Balochistan also contributes to the alienation of the Baloch. Addressing a seminar on 'Stability in Balochistan: Challenges and Possibilities' at the Punjab University, Lahore, the chief minister of Balochistan, Dr Abdul Malik Baloch, issued a timely warning that in order 'to resolve the issues of the province once and for all, we need to change the present mindset. Otherwise, no one would be able to control the next, sixth rebellion in the province.'[50]

Filmmaker Sharjil Baloch interviewed several people in Lahore about Balochistan. His questions mostly drew a blank. Lahoris were blissfully unaware of the developments in Balochistan and most could not name even a single city or town of the province. Commented Zohra Yusuf, '… the rest of the country is not losing any sleep over Balochistan.'[51]

In 2010, when the incidents of kill-and-dump[52] of abducted persons in Balochistan started to reach their peak, the BBC Urdu service carried out a survey in Lahore in which they asked people questions about the province. The absolute ignorance became a national joke for a few days.

Hashim bin Rashid, a lecturer in Lahore, writes that in 2015 he asked all his students, '"Who is Mama Qadeer?"[53] Not one of them had a clue. The only answer I got was, "The activist jailed in Gilgit-Baltistan." [That activist was Baba Jan.] Yes, they knew about the missing persons, but not much. The separatists were all foreign paid, which meant that the only way to deal with them is to crush them. Punjab remained aloof to the Mama Qadeer-led long march that ended in early 2014.'[54]

Hussain Nadeem, teaching at a top university in Pakistan in 2011, asked his students a simple question: name three cities in Balochistan. 'The struggle that students faced in naming cities other than Quetta and Gwadar exposed how depressingly little the highly educated lot of Pakistan knew about Balochistan. It also revealed how little the largest province of Pakistan mattered in national discourse, academia, and at the individual level.'[55]

In 2003, the HRCP noted '… discontent almost everywhere in Balochistan because of the widely shared perception of the people's exclusion from public affairs. They felt deprived and ignored. The political activists only articulated, often in bitter terms, the feelings of nearly all sections of the civil society.'[56] In 2009 it noted, 'In this crisis, a section of the people of Balochistan has been driven to the conclusion that they are being viewed as enemies of the state. They feel abandoned by the people as well as political forces in the rest of the country. There is a sense of isolation, rejection and dejection.' Further, 'The Baloch feel that security agencies treat them like enemies and as if they are not the citizens of Pakistan. It was a common complaint that the security personnel have adopted the same attitude and the same hatred towards the Baloch as they had for the Bengalis.'[57]

Another example of apathy is the appalling case of the description of Baloch as 'uncivilized people who remain busy in fighting and killing' and they are 'the people who lived in the desert and looting caravans' that came to light in a sociology textbook taught at intermediate level in Punjab. The book, written by Abdul Hamid Taga and Abdul Aziz Taga, was also one of the most highly recommended textbooks for the competitive Central Superior Services (CSS) exams.[58] What made matters worse was that the book had been in use for over two decades, colouring the minds of thousands of students during this period in the most dominant province of the country about the least developed province. Not a feather was ruffled, no controversy was generated and it was accepted as true.[59]

The government's apathy was also seen in the woefully inadequate relief efforts following the cyclone and floods in June–July 2007 that also ravaged Sindh. In July, the death toll was 180, climbing to 420 by

September. According to National Party (NP) leader Dr Abdul Hayee Baloch, 'This cyclone was several times more devastating than the earthquake of 2005 [in Pakistan-occupied Kashmir—POK], yet, it has received several times less attention from the government.' He lamented that the government was '… totally apathetic to the plight of the Baloch people'.[60] Describing Islamabad's response a month after the calamity as ineffective, insufficient and slow, the Rural Development Policy Institute (RDPI), using the National Disaster Management Authority's data, reported that only seven relief camps were set up in Balochistan in June and July compared to 108 in Sindh, though Balochistan was harder hit. Over 5,000 villages in Balochistan (and 1,400 in Sindh) were affected. Losses in Balochistan amounted to $417 million (Rs 24 billion). The agricultural sector was almost completely wiped out, with more than 320,000 hectares of crops and orchards destroyed; most people lost their livestock, while 5,000 km (worth $43 million or Rs 2.6 billion) of roads were washed away in the province.[61]

This state of affairs was confirmed by noted human rights activist I.A. Rehman who, speaking at a book release function in Karachi, stated: 'When a flood strikes Punjab, the roads get repaired quickly. I saw this myself that it took eleven years to repair a road after floods destroyed parts of Balochistan.' He added: 'When we would not assure them [the Baloch] that they are equally important as anyone in Lahore or Islamabad, then we can never prosper.'[62]

Census

Baloch nationalists had opposed a population census in the province for years, fearing that the millions of illegal Afghan refugees living there would get included. According to a rough estimate, over three million Afghan nationals had entered Balochistan since the Soviet invasion of Afghanistan in 1979. Though they lived largely in the seven Pashtun-dominated districts, the Baloch feared that their inclusion in the census would lead to Pashtun claims of equal or even majority population in Balochistan leading to the Baloch becoming a minority in their homeland.

The disquiet among the Baloch over the census was well articulated by the then federal minister for ports and shipping and president of the National Party, Senator Mir Hasil Khan Bizenjo, who said that if results of the census were not in favour of the interests of the Baloch people, they will not accept it. Former chief minister Dr Abdul Malik said that the Baloch people were facing two challenges: one was the CPEC and the other was the census. 'If the establishment converts the Baloch into minority, I and my party will not accept the census,' Dr Malik declared.[63]

At a gathering of Baloch political parties held in Quetta on 27 January 2017, serious concerns were expressed about the census, and in particular about its ramifications for the province. Three demands emerged from this gathering: that the census not be held until the repatriation of Afghan refugees; that it be delayed in areas where the Baloch had been internally displaced as a result of Baloch militancy; and that tribal elders be involved in conducting the census. The participation of tribal elders was felt to be a huge help since the province was a largely tribal society where people knew one another and were wary of outsiders.

Such fears were compounded by the confession and subsequent conviction of a number of senior National Database and Registration Authority officials on charges that they had issued thousands of Computerised National Identity Cards (CNICs) to illegal Afghan immigrants in exchange for bribes. This was especially so due to the sudden spike in population in Pashtun–dominated districts like Qila Abdullah, Qila Saifullah and Zhob—areas where the population has risen by more than 100 per cent.

The only party publicly backing the census and the issuing of national identity cards to Afghans was the Pashtunkhwa Milli Awami Party (PkMAP), led by Mehmood Khan Achakzai. Clearly, Achakzai's concern was for the vote bank they represented, one that was growing larger by the day.[64]

According to the preliminary results of the 2017 census, the total population of Balochistan had increased from 6.565 million in 1998, when the last census was held, to 12.335 million. The results revealed that the Baloch population had shrunk from 61 per cent to 55.6 per cent in the province in the twenty-one districts where the Baloch formed a majority, though the total number of Baloch all over Pakistan had increased from four million in 1998 to 6.86 million in

2017. According to the 2017 census data, the overall average growth of population in Balochistan was recorded at a much higher rate of 3.37 per cent compared to the national average of 2.4 per cent.

Sadique Baloch, chief editor of Quetta-based *Balochistan Express*, told *Dawn* that part of the reason for a decrease in the Baloch population of various districts was migration to other provinces and Afghanistan because of ongoing conflict in certain areas. He added that most of the Baloch residing in conflict-ridden areas had migrated to Punjab, Sindh and Quetta. The population of the districts where the Pashto-speaking population was in majority accounted for 26 per cent of the total Balochistan population. This was a slight fall from 26.6 per cent over a period of nineteen years. The Pashtun-majority districts are Qila Abdullah, Pishin, Harnai, Ziarat, Qila Saifullah, Loralai, Musakhel, Sherani and Zhob. The total number of people living in these districts was reported to be 3.2 million in 2017, which had gone up from 1.74 million reported in 1998.[65]

In Balochistan before the census began, it was believed that the results of the exercise in the province would lead to a hue and cry among the Baloch. However, they were not as irked as expected. For, in the lead-up to the census, the question on every Baloch tongue was: are we going to turn into a minority in our own province? Disaggregated results of the percentage of ethnic and minority groups in Balochistan are awaited, but the provisional results released made it very clear that the Baloch were still the majority group in the province.

9

Economic Exploitation

Economic Potential

THE ISSUE OF EXPLOITATION OF Balochistan's natural resources and inadequate allocation of funds for the province's development is a major component in the sense of alienation and resentment in Balochistan. This is largely because for Islamabad, the efforts to 'develop' Baluchistan focuses on 'things'—ports, roads, dams, etc., rather than on the people—while for the Baloch, ownership of these resources and their utilization for the people of the province are uppermost.

The economic potential of the province has been detailed in several reports. In 1944 Maj. Gen. R.C. Money, in charge of strategic planning in India, wrote a secret memorandum stating that Balochistan could be a viable state if its natural and agricultural resources were developed.[1] After the forced accession of the state of Kalat to Pakistan, the Central government planned to develop Balochistan to exploit its resources and settle the Muslim refugees from India. For this purpose, the Pakistan government approached the Water Development Division of Johnston International of Los Angeles to suggest a plan for the 'development of Baluchistan'. The US experts required certain data to enable them to suggest a development plan. The data was obtained from several government departments.[2] However, what was done subsequently is not known.

In 1952 Maneck B. Pathawala, the honorary adviser to the Ministry of Economic Affairs of Pakistan, published a monograph based on the material secured from government agencies to discuss the potentialities of Balochistan. His conclusions: 'The problem of Baluchistan thus resolves itself into: 1. Conserving water; 2. Conserving soil; 3. Promoting vegetation cover.' He highlighted the scope for resettlement and stabilization of population, especially refugees in this low-density zone of Pakistan; fruit cultivation; growing grass for grazing; sheep rearing; fishing; tourism—all of which were dependent on water.[3]

Half a century later, a World Bank report of 2008[4] about the potential and reality of Pakistan noted: 'Balochistan offers some of the best assets for development.' These included natural and locational resources; the largest land area of any province of Pakistan; vast rangeland for livestock; two-thirds of the national coastline, giving access to fishery resources; ideally situated for trade with Iran, Afghanistan, Central Asia and the Persian Gulf countries; abundance of natural gas that has been supplied to Pakistan's economic centres, supporting the country's industrialization; and large deposits of coal, copper, lead, gold and other minerals.

'And yet, Balochistan's economy has not done well', the report lamented. 'The province has Pakistan's most anaemic growth record, worst infrastructure, worst water crisis, and weakest fiscal base. The poor economic performance leads to poor living standards. Balochistan has the highest poverty—along with NWFP (now KPK), lowest social indicators, and, in parts of the province, the weakest state institutions.' Together with internal conflicts, these factors had given Balochistan '... a reputation of being a backward region, far distant from Pakistan's economic hubs, with a life burdened by the toils of the field and rangeland and tribal disputes rather than a hub of activity surrounding world-class mining explorations, modern trade links, sustainable agriculture and an empowered community.' The report added that the quality of employment was such that workers produced about one-quarter less than workers in NWFP and Punjab, and over one-third less than workers in Sindh. Employment-wise, less than one in five workers held a regular salaried job, of which the private sector supplied just one in four. Despite this, the report found that workers in Balochistan migrated less than other workers.

The report cautioned that the projected increase of Balochistan's population from 7.8 million in 2005 to 11.1 million in 2025 [In 2017 it had already reached more than 12 million.] posed major challenges for policymakers in terms of providing education and employment opportunities. As per demographic projections, the labour force could rise from 4.1 million in 2005 to 7.2 million in 2025. Based on the historic employment elasticity, this would require creating an additional 158,000 jobs annually which would, in turn, require an economic growth of at least 6.5 per cent.

According to the Balochistan government's White Paper on the Budget 2015-16, the main nodes of potential economic growth in Balochistan, within the context of Pakistan's national economy and the wider regional and global economy, were identified as: (a) mineral resources; (b) trade and transit routes; and (c) coastal development. It noted that Balochistan's strategic location had placed it at the crossroad of potential intra- and inter-regional trade.[5]

Despite the various reports identifying the economic potential of Balochistan, nothing much has been done to harness that potential.

Overview of Balochistan's Economy

According to the government's Budget White Paper 2015-16, 'for the last fifteen years, the overall share of Balochistan in the national Gross Domestic Product (GDP) has remained constant at 4 per cent'. The Budget White Papers of 2016-17 and 2017-18 show this share being doubled to 8 per cent of the national GDP without any explanatory note.[6] However, according to a recent study by noted economist Kaiser Bengali during the three decades period 1970s to 1990s, per capita growth was 0.3 per cent, implying zero growth and stagnancy. As a result, Balochistan's average share in national income dropped from 4.5 per cent in the 1970s to 4 per cent in the 1980s and 1990s, indicating marginalization. Post-2000, the situation did not improve either given that gross regional product (GRP—the provincial equivalent of GDP estimates for the country as a whole) growth in Balochistan over the decade 2000–11 was the lowest at 2.8 per cent—less than 60 per cent of the average combined GRP growth of the other three provinces.

'Balochistan is not only lagging behind other provinces, but falling further behind,' according to Bengali.[7]

Gross Regional Product by Province: Average Growth Rate- 2000-11[8]

Province	Overall
Punjab	4.5
Sindh	4.7
KPK	5.5
Balochistan	2.8

The reasons for persistent underdevelopment, notes Bengali, '… can be traced directly to gross federal underinvestment in basic infrastructure in the province'. According to him, underinvestment is indicated by the fact that the average federal Public Sector Development Plan (PSDP) allocation for development schemes in Balochistan over the period from 1989-90 to 2015-16 constituted less than 6 per cent of the total federal PSDP allocations and a mere 0.19 per cent of national GDP. These meagre shares were also overestimates given that actual releases were generally less than budgetary allocations.[9]

This 'underpins the fact that historically Balochistan's economy has largely underperformed compared to its potential. The underlying facts behind this weak economic performance of the province include volatile political and security environment, and structural bottlenecks.'[10]

Historically, Balochistan's economy has relied on the following sectors: agriculture, transport/storage and wholesale, and manufacturing. These three sectors contributed approximately 77 per cent to Balochistan's economy during FY 2005-06 to FY 2015-16.

Agriculture is the leading contributor to Balochistan's GDP. During the last decade, its average share in provincial GDP was recorded at 34 per cent. It is also one of the leading employment generating sectors, employing 60.65 per cent of the total labour force. The agriculture sector, however, has only been able to grow at 2.6 per cent during the last decade due to mismanagement of resources. The key challenges to the growth of this sector are water scarcity and lack of a value chain, which can enhance the value addition of this sector.[11]

In Balochistan, only 3.3 million acres are cultivated out of a total acreage of some 85 million. Of these, only some 80,000 acres are irrigated.[12] Tube wells are the largest source of irrigation in all the districts except Nasirabad, Jafarabad and Jhal Magsi (which are irrigated by canals). These tube wells have, however, had a negative impact on the water table, which in many parts of the province (like Quetta, Mastung and Qila Saifullah) is going down by over 1.5 metres per year.[13]

Transport, storage and wholesale have contributed 27 per cent to the provincial GDP on an average during the last decade and have grown by an average annual rate of 5.16 per cent. It is also the second largest employment generating sector in Balochistan's economy.[14]

Minerals are a source of significant wealth for Balochistan, but have not been fully exploited and contribute a negligible 3 per cent to the GDP (5 per cent according to the government). Balochistan has large reserves of natural gas and coal, but 40 per cent of the province's needs are still met using firewood and dung cakes. An estimated 2 million tonnes of wood is burnt each year. Gas consumption in the province is low due to the limited supply of piped natural gas and liquefied petroleum gas. Most of the 2 million tonnes of coal produced in the region is exported to other provinces.[15]

The quality of communication networks is also poor, offering scarce coverage. Road density in the province is half the national average: 0.16 and 0.32 respectively.[16] Balochistan has around 22,000 km of metalled and shingle roads, though a large part of the province is poorly connected. Inadequate infrastructure—limited road access and poor condition of the road networks—has constrained the Baloch from accessing markets, education and health facilities, and opportunities for livelihood.[17]

The government plans on constructing a $1.67-billion road network, which it says would link Balochistan to the rest of the country and make Gwadar port the hub of regional trade with China and Central Asia.[18] Baloch nationalists, however, believe this road-building project is aimed at easier extraction of Balochistan's natural resources and to enable the Pakistan Army and security agencies to expand their control over the province.[19] It is this distrust of the Centre that lies at the heart of Baloch opposition.

There is clearly a huge mismatch between Balochistan's potential and policies that have been followed by successive governments, both federal and provincial. In fact, based on the feedback received from the government and other stakeholders, the World Bank had identified the following key priorities for Balochistan:

(i)   Conservation and efficient use of water—storage dams, modern irrigation techniques and agriculture/farming practices, recharging of ground water, availability/quality of drinking water;
(ii)   Renewable energy—solar and wind power;
(iii)   Social sectors—education, skill development of local population, health and nutrition (particularly girls' education, mother and child healthcare);
(iv)   Connectivity and trade logistics—both interprovincial and trade outside Pakistan around mining, fisheries, fruits/agricultural produce;
(v)   Transparency, accountability and anti-corruption mechanisms;
(vi)   Natural resource management—livelihoods, community participation and benefit sharing around the local resources;
(vii)   Engagement of women and youth—as cross-cutting priority, and strategy to reduce risk of conflict in the province.[20]

Almost none of these priority sectors have been focused upon by either the provincial or federal government. It is hardly surprising, therefore, that Balochistan continues to languish at the bottom of every provincial comparison.

Issue of Natural Gas

The critical resource that is at the centre of Baloch estrangement is natural gas. Balochistan's natural gas production is critical to Pakistan's economy. Yet, the way the gas has been exploited actually violates constitutional provisions for the supply of gas. As per Article 158 of the Constitution of Pakistan: 'The Province in which a well head of natural gas is situated shall have precedence over other parts of Pakistan in meeting the requirements from that well head.'

Natural gas was discovered at Sui in Dera Bugti in 1952. For about a decade and a half thereafter, Balochistan was almost the sole provider of gas to the country. Its average share of gas output over the period

1955–69 stood at 91 per cent. However, with discoveries in other provinces, especially Sindh, Balochistan's share in total gas production has consistently declined to 21 per cent over the last decade (2005–14) and less than 20 per cent currently. Despite Balochistan's declining share in gas output, the absolute quantum of gas extraction at Sui continued to rise at an accelerated pace for nearly half a century from 1,535 mmcf (million metric cubic feet) in 1995 to peak production at 387,368 mmcf in 2001.[21]

However, the Baloch have failed to benefit from their gas deposits. No gas was supplied to Balochistan for nearly three decades till 1982 while the average rate of growth of extraction of gas from Balochistan during this period stood at 22 per cent per annum. Correspondingly, between 1983 and 2000, Balochistan's share in total national gas consumption remained a mere 2 per cent. Post-2000, Balochistan's share in total national gas consumption rose to over 7 per cent on account of the setting up of the 900 MW gas-fired Uch power plant at Dera Murad Jamali in Nasirabad district.[22] The town of Dera Bugti itself was supplied with gas only in the mid-1990s, forty years after gas was discovered in the district. While most of Punjab has access to it, even Balochistan's provincial capital Quetta was supplied natural gas only as late as 1980.[23] In May 2014, the Ministry of Petroleum and Natural Resources revealed in the Senate that out of the thirty-two district headquarters of Balochistan, only thirteen had natural gas facility and 59 per cent of the urban population in the province was deprived of it.[24] In comparative terms, almost 97 per cent of Punjab's urban population has access to gas. Thus, a large number of rural areas in Balochistan, including those near the gas fields did not have access to gas.

In 1995, Balochistan contributed nearly 56 per cent to Pakistan's total output of natural gas, but by 2007 its share had dropped to 22.7 per cent. That year it consumed only 5.81 per cent of the country's total output.[25] According to F. Grare, provincial consumption was only 17 per cent of its own production, with 83 per cent of its natural gas being supplied to the rest of the country for industrial and household use.[26]

The second issue is of royalty and specifically the quantum of royalty. In accordance with Rule 18 of Pakistan Petroleum (Production) Rules

1949, royalty on a gas field is calculated by using annual gas production and a fixed price for the well head. Balochistan receives a 12.5 per cent royalty from its natural gas revenues but that royalty is based on a well-head price that is far lower than that of other provinces.[27]

Thus, the injustice is not only in consumption but is also significant in the discriminatory well-head prices. Balochistan's average gas field well-head price per mmbtu (million metric British thermal units) was Rs 66.34, for Sindh Rs 142.57 and for Punjab it was Rs 162.93. The reason for this differentiated well-head price was because it was based on per capita provincial income in 1953. This had resulted in a well-head price in Balochistan that was much lower than in Sindh and Punjab, resulting in Balochistan receiving far less in royalties than the other two provinces. The well-head price of gas was enhanced to Rs 163.13 mmbtu only during the financial year 2009-10.[28]

Moreover, the 12.5 per cent royalty and gas development surcharge was made admissible only after 1991, thirty-nine long years after discovery of natural gas in Balochistan. Thus for decades, Balochistan lost out even on royalty.[29]

It is believed in Balochistan that the well-head price of Sui (which forms the basis for calculating royalty payable to the province) was kept low by the federal government to cross-subsidize higher-priced (at the well head) natural gas from other provinces (who correspondingly receive higher royalty amounts) at the expense of Balochistan.[30] In effect, Balochistan, the poorest province has been subsidizing the richer provinces. There is rising resentment in the province that even though its natural gas generates $1.4 billion annually in revenue, the government remits only $116 million in royalties to the province.[31]

According to Kaiser Bengali, the subsidy given to the commercial and domestic sector in Pakistan was at the expense of Balochistan. He has calculated that from 1964 to 2014 resources worth Rs 7.69 trillion were transferred to other parts of the country. He, therefore, recommended tripling the price of gas and creating a twenty-year, Rs 7 trillion development budget for Balochistan, lamenting that while the province was always dubbed as a 'deficit' area, yet Rs 7 trillion were extracted out of it.[32]

In a paper titled 'Oil and gas resources and rights of provinces: a case study of Sindh', Naseer Memon, the chief executive of the

Strengthening Participatory Organization (SPO), noted: 'Sindh and Balochistan together contribute more than 93 per cent of the national gas production and therefore can be considered an energy basket of Pakistan.' To prove that Punjab devours most gas, despite Article 158, he quotes the Pakistan Energy Yearbook 2008 table, which says: 'Sindh consumed only 46 per cent of its production whereas Balochistan consumed just 25 per cent [17 per cent as per other estimates] while Punjab utilized a staggering 930 per cent against its production in the national output of gas.' In 2007 Punjab produced 68,608 mmcf but utilized 638,008, or 930 per cent more than its production. This consumption is a lot higher now. Punjab has 2,162 operational CNG stations compared to only 587 in Sindh, currently, the largest producer of natural gas.[33]

The Gas Infrastructure Development Cess (GIDC) also favours Punjab by making others pay for its costs because it has the least gas production and the highest consumption. The import of liquefied natural gas (LNG) from Qatar favours Punjab as it carries additional cost for Sindh and Balochistan, which can easily meet their needs from their own production. If Article 158 of the Constitution is applied, no other province except Punjab would require imported LNG. The then minister for petroleum and later the prime minister, Shahid Khaqan Abbasi, said that commercial gas consumers, including fertilizer and other industries, will spend the upcoming winter season without natural gas everywhere except Punjab as it uses LNG. Interestingly, the other provinces pay this additional cost of the LNG.[34]

It is undeniable that cheap gas from Balochistan heralded a new chapter in the history of industry and economy of Pakistan. It was instrumental in setting up of industries all over the country except for Balochistan itself. According to the Balochistan government's Budget White Paper 2015-16, if gas from Sui was not available, the country would have to import oil as a substitute, spending at least three billion dollars per annum.[35]

Not surprisingly, the Baloch 'interpret the disparity between the value of gas produced in Balochistan and the poverty of the province as a consequence of their exploitation by outsiders'.[36] For the militants, the answer lies in forcibly preventing the Centre's exploration and extraction in regions that are resource-rich, such as the Bugti and Marri homelands.[37] Because the country so heavily depends on the supply of gas from Balochistan, its gas fields and distribution grids have become bargaining chips in the conflict. With periodic attacks on pipelines and installations disrupting gas supplies, the Baloch are determined to increase the cost of the conflict for Islamabad.[38]

The Baloch nationalists also point to the fact that the provincial government does not have any control over their resources. As an example they cite that in October 2015, without taking the provincial government into confidence, the federal government granted a one-year extension in the mining lease contract for Sui field, 'in the larger national interest as an interim arrangement to avoid disruption in gas supply'.[39] Balochistan is estimated to have 19 trillion cubic feet of natural gas reserves and 6 trillion barrels of offshore and onshore oil reserves.[40] But prospective deals with oil and gas companies have been negotiated by Islamabad without consulting Baloch stakeholders. Six new exploration concessions were signed with Pakistani and foreign companies, but with no input from the province. The government also plans to sell 51 per cent of shares in Pakistan Petroleum Limited (PPL), Sui Northern Gas Pipelines Limited (SNGPL) and Sui Southern Gas Company Limited (SSGCL), but again without consulting Baloch stakeholders.[41]

Other Resources

Pakistan is believed to have 186 billion tonnes of coal reserves as of 2013, but it is mostly of poor quality. Sindh has the largest coal reserves though Balochistan contributes more than 50 per cent to Pakistan's total coal production annually. Most of the coal is used in brick kilns and a small amount is used as an energy source. There are six developed coalfields in Balochistan.[42]

Another example of Pakistan's exploitation of the resources of Balochistan is its collaborative ventures with multinational firms in the Saindak copper and Reko Diq gold–copper projects in Chagai district. In 2002 the federal government entered into an agreement with a Chinese company to mine gold and copper from the Saindak project. Under the agreement the Chinese company would repatriate 80 per cent of total profits back home, pay 18 per cent to the federal government of

Pakistan and disburse only 2 per cent to Balochistan government as royalty charges.[43] In October 2017, the government extended the lease of the Chinese company till 2022.[44]

Reko Diq gold–copper project is the second major project in Balochistan that was given to Antofagasta of Chile and Barrick Gold of Canada. This project was meant to exploit an estimated 54 billion pounds of copper and 41 million ounces of gold.[45]

The helplessness of the provincial government can be seen from the fact that the then elected chief minister of Balochistan, Dr Abdul Malik, complained about Saindak and said: 'We have no idea how much gold and other minerals are being dug out by the Chinese company from the Saindak project.' Mir Mohammad Ali Talpur wrote that 'Saindak Metal Limited in May 2009 said that 7.746 tonnes of gold, 86,013 tonnes of copper, 11.046 tonnes of silver and 14,482 tonnes of magnetite concentrate (iron) worth $633,573 million were produced during the period 2004–08. How much more since then we should try to find out. The unmonitored over-mining by the Chinese means there will be no copper or gold in Saindak after 2017. Toxic waste will abound as for every 28 grams of gold, 79 tonnes of waste is produced.'[46]

The Baloch legitimately ask that if the elected chief minister of Balochistan did not know what the Chinese did in Saindak, what will they and the elected government know about Chinese activities in Gwadar? After all, the Chinese have now got a forty-year lease to develop a special economic zone there.

The case of fisheries is similar to that of minerals. The coast of Balochistan extends for 760 km, comprising 70 per cent of Pakistan's coastline. Fisheries are the mainstay of the population in the area, providing employment to nearly 70 per cent of the total employed persons in the coastal districts. However, it contributes less than one-sixth of the national value addition in fisheries.[47] The reason is that the thousands of tonnes of fish caught by Baloch fishermen are taken to Karachi for processing and canning, because nowhere along the Balochistan coast has any fish processing facilities been set up. In the last decade, the production of fish and domestic and export distribution has remained almost unchanged.

Similarly, tonnes of Balochistan fruit are wasted due to the absence of fruit processing industries in Balochistan.

Hub industrial estate, set up in Balochistan, has not benefitted the Baloch much as far as providing employment opportunities to the people of the province are concerned. In fact, Hub area industries are, for the most part, an extension or subsidiaries of the Karachi-based industries whose owners wanted to have tax relief by locating in Balochistan without providing employment opportunities to the people there. Moreover, the coal mines are almost all owned and operated by the non-Baloch. Balochistan's coal is sent to Punjab so the Baloch have to burn wood trucked in from Sindh. Its onyx and marble are shipped to Karachi for finishing.[48]

Banking

Another reality of Balochistan (and Khyber-Pakhtunkhwa) is that the money generated in the province is used to finance economic activities in the other two provinces. This is because the banks gave loans of Rs 16 billion against deposits of Rs 300 billion from Balochistan, or only 5.3 per cent of the deposits. In contrast, over 58 per cent of the total deposits generated from Punjab were invested there by banks. The share of Balochistan was only 0.22 per cent in the total loans disbursed by the banking sector till June 2018 out of Balochistan's 2.4 per cent share in total deposits.

Water

While the overall water situation in Pakistan is precarious,[49] it is nearing a crisis in Balochistan, which could have catastrophic consequences for the people of the province. One visible example is that of apples. More than 80 per cent of Pakistan's total apple production comes from Balochistan. However, given the water shortage, the production of varieties of apples has declined. One fruit farmer lamented: 'Since the land is not getting the required water, the apples produced are smaller in size.'[50]

The province is situated in an arid zone that receives low levels of rainfall. Despite this, the last storage dam was created thirty years ago. In 2007 Pakistan Poverty Alleviation Fund (PPAF) under the Drought Mitigation and Preparedness Program (DMPP) initiated a Rs 60 million project to construct small dams, but the project was soon marred by corruption. While the lack of rain has directly contributed to its water woes, the province has failed to preserve enough rainwater as a result of the government's faulty planning.

The United Nations Development Programme, Pakistan, had conducted a drought risk assessment study in Balochistan in 2015. It noted that 'Recurring drought is one of the major challenges faced by Balochistan province of Pakistan.' It concluded that almost 60 to 70 per cent of the population is projected to be at direct or indirect risk from droughts in the area. Droughts have led to as high as 37 per cent average livestock losses in one district only—Lasbela. It cautioned that the dry conditions in Lasbela and Gwadar had forced locals to extract groundwater excessively to sustain agriculture. As a result, groundwater levels had gone down by more than 250 feet. Due to this, seawater was making the groundwater saline, thus affecting agriculture and forcing farmers to seek other livelihood options.[51]

Quetta, the capital, is reported to be on its way to becoming a desert with its rapidly falling water table, which has dropped by up to 30 m since 1989, according to one study. Beyond Quetta, the province's water needs rank near the top of its development priorities.[52] Environmentalists warn that if concrete steps are not taken, Quetta will witness large parts of its population being displaced in the near future.[53]

As if the double whammy of lack of rain and inadequate storage wasn't enough, Balochistan also suffers from Sindh misappropriating its water. In 2016, protesting over 42 per cent water shortfall allegedly caused by Sindh irrigation authorities, the Balochistan government threatened to stay away from the meetings of the country's water regulator—the Indus River System Authority (IRSA). From 1991 to 2014, it has been alleged that Balochistan got almost 50 per cent less water than it demanded resulting in losses of around Rs 93 billion to the province.[54] In February 2018 Balochistan again accused Sindh of withholding its share of water, prompting IRSA to ask Sindh to ensure the drought-affected province got its share of water immediately. According to estimates in Balochistan, more than a quarter million acres would remain fallow due to lack of water for irrigation. The land is located in the Pat Feeder Command area in Naseerabad Division, the canal-irrigated region considered the food basket of Balochistan.[55]

According to a report submitted to the Senate by the Ministry of Water and Power, Balochistan faces a groundwater shortage of nearly catastrophic proportions. Due to excessive groundwater extraction, Balochistan's water woes could increase manifold in the coming years. 'With the introduction of deep-well pumping over the last three to four decades, groundwater resources have been rapidly depleted and levels have declined,' the report said. According to it, groundwater is being overused in ten of the nineteen sub-basins in the province. 'At this stage, groundwater use exceeds recharge by 22 per cent,' the report underlined, singling out Pishin-Loralai as the largest area of groundwater imbalance.[56]

Or, take the case of Taftan in Balochistan's Chagai district on Pakistan's border with Iran. Water apart, Taftan symbolizes government's policy of maximum extraction with little responsibility towards the people of Balochistan. Taftan tehsil has an estimated population of 25,000, of which about 7,000 live in Taftan town. Forget education and health services, the discrimination in water allocation is instructive. There is only one government tube well in Taftan town meant for supplying drinking water to its 7,000 residents. Those who can afford it use Iranian mineral water. It is not that water is not available. In fact, there is a huge water facility in Taftan whose eight tube wells supply 500 to 1,000 tonnes of water an hour, depending upon demand, for the Chinese-run Saindak copper project, a half-hour drive from Taftan town. The copper project functions 24/7 for nine months of the year.

Apart from the huge profits of the copper project, the customs post in Taftan generates substantial revenue—as much as Rs 2,211.371 million in duty in 2014 and Rs 5,249.169 million in 2015. None of this, however, is invested in Taftan or elsewhere in Balochistan to improve the quality of the people's lives by providing water, education and health facilities. Baloch reconciliation would be difficult if such irresponsible extraction continues.[57]

National Finance Commission (NFC)

The seventh National Finance Commission (NFC) award, 2009, altered the revenue distribution in favour of smaller provinces. Prior to the award, population was the sole criterion for distribution of revenue collected by the federal government from the entire country. However, in the seventh NFC the weightage of population was reduced to 82 per cent. Poverty and backwardness was given 10.3 per cent weightage, revenue generation 5 per cent and inverse population density 2.7 per cent. Balochistan was the biggest beneficiary of this new arrangement: its share in the revenues jumped from 5.11 per cent to 9.09 per cent.

Prior to the seventh NFC, the provincial budgetary outlay was Rs 71 billion and the Public Sector Development Plan (PSDP) was only Rs 16 billion for the entire province in 2009-10. The seventh NFC award considerably bolstered the financial kitty of the province. Balochistan received Rs 40 billion under the federal transfers in 2009-10; that went up to Rs 141.9 billion in 2013-14. In 2015 the development budget alone was more than Rs 86 billion. When the National Party (NP) coalition government came to power in 2013, the total budgetary outlay was less than Rs 200 billion, but by 2017 budget figures had almost doubled.[58]

This tremendous upsurge of the financial resources was an opportunity to improve services and infrastructure in the province. The moot question was whether the increase in resource availability had changed the socio-economic conditions of the people or the development deficit and infrastructure development? The simple answer is: no. While exploitation by the federal government was an irrefutable reason behind the miseries of Balochistan, apathetic plunder of the residual resources by the local bureaucracy and legislators was also a reality.

For one thing, there has been a serious problem of prioritization. Instead of completing ongoing programmes, new schemes are added every year, thus postponing the completion of the earlier projects. In 2017 alone 1,035 new projects were added, although there were already 1,258 unfinished projects.[59] Moreover, the increase in the NFC award has been mostly absorbed by the increase in development funds for legislators and payments to federal security agencies on 'internal security' duty in the province.[60]

There are also other issues with the NFC. The term of the seventh NFC award expired on 30 June 2015. The PML-N government under Nawaz Sharif and subsequently Shahid Khaqan Abbasi, whose term expired in May 2018, did not show any interest in a new NFC award.

Instead, the award was extended through presidential orders. As a result, the same old formulae are being imposed through Distribution of Revenues and Grants-in-Aid (Amendment) Order, 2015. This means that the poverty figures from 1998 are being used in 2017 even though latest poverty figures calculated by the UNDP and adopted by the planning commission are available. The continuation of the seventh NFC beyond its mandated term has adversely affected Balochistan. The reason is that the seventh NFC downplayed poverty in Balochistan. As a result, it has been calculated that Balochistan is losing up to Rs 28 billion annually from its share of the federal divisible pool due to technical wizardry.[61] Not only is this extremely unfair but the decision of the PML-N government to extend the seventh NFC formulae beyond 2015 is also considered unconstitutional.

According to Adnan Aamir, the Quetta-based editor of the online 'Baloch Voices', in the seventh NFC award, the poverty figures of all provinces were compiled from three different reports: Poverty Reduction Strategy Paper-I (PRSP-I) titled 'Accelerating Economic Growth and Reducing Poverty: the Road Ahead', published by the Finance Division in 2003 based on data of 1998-99; 'Pakistan National Human Development Report 2003' published by the UNDP; and the Province-wise HDI report published by the Statistics Division in 2008. Composite poverty figure for NFC share was calculated based on aggregate of poverty figures in these three reports. Based on this aggregate, poverty component of NFC was divided among the provinces where it was 23.17 per cent in Punjab, 23.42 per cent in Sindh, 27.83 per cent in NWFP (now KPK) and 25.62 per cent in Balochistan.[62] According to Aamir, the problem with the usage of these three poverty reports is that they were already outdated and did not represent the factual poverty situation in the country in 2009 when the seventh NFC was drafted. This resulted in unfair distribution of share from the federal divisible pool, where smaller provinces like Balochistan lost out.

He elaborates this point further by pointing out that a comparison of the poverty levels in Balochistan with other provinces shows that they were, more or less, the same as per the above reports. This was unjust for obvious reasons because there is far more poverty in Balochistan compared to the other three provinces. As a result, the 10.3 per cent share reserved for poverty and backwardness was to an extent rendered ineffective due to manipulation of data on the pretext of unavailability of latest poverty measurement reports. Resultantly, provinces with higher poverty rates did not get their due share from the NFC as they were supposed to.

In June 2016 the UNDP, Oxford Poverty and Human Development Initiative and the Federal Ministry of Planning and Development published a Report on Multidimensional Poverty 2016. This report measured poverty in the country using three indicators, health, education and standard of living, and sixteen sub-indicators. Based on these indicators, the multidimensional poverty index (MPI) was calculated for each province which, when translated into percentage, presented a much more realistic picture of poverty. According to this report, MPI is 0.394 in Balochistan, 0.25 in Khyber Pakhtunkhwa, 0.231 in Sindh and 0.152 in Punjab. These figures seem more realistic because there is a huge difference between poverty in Balochistan and other provinces.[63]

When the new poverty figures extracted from the Report on Multidimensional Poverty 2016 are used for calculating the provincial share as the seventh NFC had done, the share of Balochistan jumps from 9.09 per cent to 10.41 per cent. The estimated amount of the federal divisible pool for fiscal year 2016-17 was Rs 2.135 trillion. An increase of 1.32 per cent in share of Balochistan translates into approximately Rs 28 billion. Simply put, Balochistan has already been deprived of approximately Rs 28 billion per year from its due share in the federal divisible pool due to manipulation of poverty figures in the last three budgets. Balochistan will continue to lose an amount in similar proportion till the time a new NFC award based on accurate poverty figures is not announced.[64]

The amount of Rs 28 billion per annum that Balochistan is not getting can be used to educate approximately one million children, hire 45,000 new teachers or build 7,000 new primary schools. This is inferred from an analysis of Annual Status of Education Report and Pakistan Education Statistics Report of Idara Taleem-o-Agahi from 2011 to 2016.[65]

Another interesting aspect of the federal PSDP allocations for the Physical Planning and Housing/Housing and Works sector in

Balochistan is that, on an average, 78 per cent of allocations for schemes during the period 1990–2016 was for security agencies and federal civil administration offices and housing. In eleven of these years the average share of allocations for security agencies and federal civil administration offices and houses was 100 per cent. In fact, not one single scheme in the Balochistan component of federal PSDPs, between 1990 and 2016, was for housing for the civilian population.[66]

Whenever someone asks the federal government about how they plan to improve the economic condition in Balochistan, the standard reply these days is 'China–Pak Economic Corridor (CPEC).' The federal government proudly claims that the corridor will prove to be a game-changer and change the fate of the people of Balochistan. Unfortunately, these are nothing more than hollow claims. The proposed economic corridor will only pass through a portion of the province and can't change the lives of all the people of the province.[67] Secondly, there is no guarantee that the people of Balochistan will get jobs after the establishment of this corridor. In the past the Baloch have been ignored in mega projects such as the Saindak copper–gold project, the Reko Diq project and the Gwadar port project. As discussed in the chapter on CPEC, it is unlikely to be the solution to the employment problems, let alone the economic problems of Balochistan.[68]

10

Socio-Economic Deprivation

THE IMPACT OF THE POLITICAL and administrative marginalization and economic exploitation is clearly reflected in the socio-economic deprivation of the province. According to economist Kaiser Bengali, empirical evidence shows that Balochistan has suffered and continues to suffer systematic economic exploitation, discrimination and neglect. He laments: 'Balochistan's all-round underdevelopment is an open and festering wound. The province ranks low—and significantly so—in terms of income statistics and high—and significantly so—in terms of poverty statistics.'[1]

The deprivation of the province has been highlighted in several credible reports. To reiterate figures from the World Bank report of 2008[2] referred to earlier, Balochistan has the weakest *long-term growth, the worst quality of employment and the weakest social development* performance of all provinces. From 1972-73 to 2004-05, the economy expanded 2.7 times in Balochistan, 3.6 times in NWFP and Sindh and 4.0 times in Punjab. The growth divergence has widened historic income differences and Balochistan's per capita income level of $400 in 2004 was only two-thirds of Pakistan's level. Balochistan's rate of structural change and urbanization was also lower than elsewhere. According to the report, Balochistan scored lowest among the provinces on key indicators for education, literacy, health, water and sanitation in 2006-07. It also stood out as the province with the worst record on gender equality. Other reports and surveys confirm this grim picture of Balochistan painted by the World Bank.

Unemployment

The number of unemployed persons in Balochistan (0.06 million) in 2012 constituted about 20 per cent of the total number of unemployed persons (3.05 million) in the country, indicating a disproportionately high number given that Balochistan accounts for only 6 per cent of the total population of Pakistan.[3]

Excluding Quetta, the other districts in Balochistan provided little or no employment opportunities for the people. Agriculture was the primary source of employment in Balochistan and it has been badly affected by the water and electricity shortages. Unemployment, in fact, was increasing; a 2007 study on demographic transition, education and youth employment found that young people in Balochistan were twice as likely to be without a job as their Punjab counterparts.[4]

According to Kaiser Bengali, Balochistan is a province of only 1.5 million families and at one job per family, it needs a mere 1.5 million jobs. This, he notes, is eminently feasible, given the vast and varied agricultural, horticultural, fisheries and, in particular, mineral resources in the province. He estimates that Balochistan could become a zero-unemployment province in less than half a decade and attain single-digit incidence of poverty and illiteracy in a decade. 'That Balochistan faces mass unemployment, mass poverty, mass illiteracy and pervasive hunger is incomprehensible and inexcusable.'[5]

The impact of unemployment was obvious. For example, some police officials told a delegation of the Human Rights Commission of Pakistan that men in Panjgur and Turbat were desperate for a livelihood and such a condition forced them to accept help from any quarter; be they friendly to the state or hostile to it.[6]

Poverty

The Sustainable Development Policy Institute's (SDPI) 'Geography of Poverty' estimates poverty by using twenty-seven indicators pertaining to four dimensions of well-being, i.e., education, health, living conditions and assets ownership.[7] It looks at national, provincial and district-level trends from 2008 to 2013. The report not only highlights the districts where poverty is high but also tracks the changes in the level of poverty in individual districts over a five-year period. In 2012-13 the multidimensional poverty headcount was 62.6 per cent in Balochistan, 39.3 per cent in Khyber Paktunkhwa (KPK), 37.5 per cent in Sindh and 24.3 per cent in Punjab. Of this, 46.2 per cent of the population of Balochistan was living in extreme poverty compared to 26.6 per cent in KPK, 24.6 per cent in Sindh and 15.4 per cent in Punjab. At the national level, 18.6 per cent of the population was living in extreme poverty. While only 5.07 per cent of Pakistan's population lived in Balochistan, 10.2 per cent of the country's poor lived there in 2012-13. In the same year (2012-13) 17.8 per cent of Pakistan's poor lived in KPK and 28.0 per cent in Sindh. With 57.42 per cent population of Pakistan living in Punjab, its contribution to total poverty was 44.5 per cent in 2012-13.[8]

Based on poverty headcount ratios, districts were classified into five zones or quintiles. The geographic concentration of poverty was evident from the fact that out of fifty-six districts in the bottom two quintiles (poverty figures ranging from 72.6 per cent to 96.4 per cent in the bottom quintile and from 50 per cent to 72 per cent in the fourth quintile), twenty-three were from Balochistan, eleven from Sindh, eight from KPK and two from Punjab. Districts that were largely rural and had low population were the ones with the highest headcount ratio.[9]

The report contained another alarming detail. The entire population of the two districts of Kohlu and Kohistan—in Balochistan and KPK, respectively—lived below the poverty level. These districts were joined by almost two dozen others, which had over 72 per cent of their populations living in poverty.[10]

According to a 2016 report prepared by the United Nations Development Programme (UNDP) and Oxford Poverty and Human Development Initiative (OPHI), titled 'Multidimensional Poverty in Pakistan', Balochistan was rapidly sliding back on all human development indicators. According to it, 71.2 per cent of the population in Balochistan was victim of multidimensional poverty. Rural areas were even worse where 84.6 population lived under stifling multidimensional poverty. This explained the pathetic state of human development indicators in the province.[11]

The report held that while the China–Pakistan Economic Corridor (CPEC) could potentially boost economic activities, it also has the potential to further entrench existing inequalities by concentrating these opportunities in the already developed and least poor districts.[12]

Moreover, the Benazir Income Support Programme (BISP) that has been giving over a billion dollars a year across the country to poor families,[13] '... is systematically biased against what is by far the poorest province in the country'. Based on the 2017 census and BISP's latest data, 16 per cent of Pakistani households received unconditional transfers from BISP. The coverage level in Punjab, which has the lowest poverty level, is the lowest of the provinces at 12 per cent. The percentage of Balochistan's population covered by BISP should have been the highest given its poverty levels, but it is not. Only around 13 per cent of households in Balochistan were beneficiaries, though residents of Balochistan were more than twice as likely to be poverty-stricken as a resident of Punjab. However, 25 per cent of Khyber Pakhtunkhwa's households and 22 per cent of the far richer Sindh received BISP transfers. To achieve KPK's level of coverage, it is estimated that an additional 235,759 women in Balochistan should be getting a stipend. In other words, nearly a quarter million of Balochistan's families were being deprived of what should rightfully be theirs.

Kaiser Bengali, the first national coordinator of the BISP, notes that Balochistan's share in the total BISP disbursements in 2014-15 was substantially lower than its population share, whereas one would expect the reverse, based on relative deprivation. The reason for this, according to him, is that a larger portion of Balochistan's population wasn't surveyed in the nationwide poverty census concluded in 2011 due to their living in isolated, inaccessible settlements across the vastness of Balochistan.[14] Like in the case of the NFC award, such an obvious unjust BISP distribution has continued for more than five years without being addressed at the time of writing.

Districts and Human Development Index (HDI)

The grim picture of the persistent and continuing socio-economic deprivation in Balochistan has been recorded by a series of studies since the 1980s. These studies rank districts of Pakistan by development, deprivation or poverty levels. All of them show that districts in Balochistan have been consistently at the bottom and continue to be so. Some of these studies are:[15]

Year of Study	Authors	Findings
1982	Pasha & Hasan	9 out of 10 districts at the bottom of the ranking were from Balochistan
1990	Pasha, Malik & Jamal	14 out of 20 districts at the bottom of the ranking were from Balochistan
1996	Ghaus, Pasha & Ghaus	23 out of 30 districts at the bottom of the ranking were from Balochistan
2001	Bengali et al	24 out of 26 districts, comprising 88 per cent of the population, were in 'High Deprivation' category
2005	Jamal & Khan	8 out of 11 'Low Human Development Index' (HDI) districts were in Balochistan

The United Nations Development Programme (UNDP) created the Human Development Index (HDI) to re-emphasize that people and their capabilities should be the ultimate criterion for assessing the development of a country or a region, and not economic growth alone. The UNDP/HDI is a composite index that measures the average achievements in a country/region based on three basic dimensions: a long and healthy life, knowledge and a decent standard of living. UNDP classifies countries into low, medium, high and very high level of development according to HDI magnitudes of <0.55, >= 0.55 but less than 0.7, >= 0.7 but less than 8, and >= 0.8 respectively.

Based on 'Pakistan Social and Living Standards Measurement (PSLM)' survey for the year 2014-15, a study carried out by the Social Policy and Development Centre (SPDC), Karachi, developed regional HDIs.[16] On this basis, estimated HDI for Pakistan and the Provinces for 2014-15 was estimated as: Pakistan—0.524;

Punjab—0.550; Sindh—0.506; KPK—0.476; Balochistan—0.407. Of the bottom fifteen districts according to the estimated values of HDI, two are in KPK (Tor Ghar and Kohistan) and two in Sindh (Kashmore and Tando Mohd Khan). The remaining eleven districts belong to Balochistan. No district of Punjab is placed in this cluster of bottom fifteen districts.[17]

DISTRICTS WITH LOWEST HDI VALUE			
Province	District	HDI Value	Rank
Balochistan	Dera Bugti	0.297	113
KPK	Tor Ghar	0.323	112
KPK	Kohistan	0.330	111
Balochistan	Jhal Magsi	0.330	110
Balochistan	Qila Abdullah	0.332	109
Balochistan	Chagai	0.332	108
Balochistan	Nasirabad	0.336	107
Balochistan	Sheerani	0.338	106
Sindh	Kashmore	0.343	105
Balochistan	Harnai	0.350	104
Balochistan	Barkhan	0.356	103
Balochistan	Bolan/Kachhi	0.360	102
Balochistan	Kohlu	0.360	101
Balochistan	Jaffarabad	0.361	100
Sindh	Tando M Khan	0.361	99

Source: Estimates are based on PSLM, 2014-15 data.

The top fifteen districts of Pakistan in terms of HDI consist of twelve districts in Punjab, one in Sindh (Karachi) and two in KPK (Abbottabad and Haripur). These districts lie in the category of medium level of development. Barring Karachi, all districts of Sindh and Balochistan belong to the low level of human development.[18]

DISTRICTS WITH HIGHEST HDI VALUE			
Province	District	HDI Value	Rank
Punjab	Lahore	0.670	1
Sindh	Karachi	0.654	2
Punjab	Rawalpindi	0.646	3
Punjab	Sialkot	0.635	4
Punjab	Gujarat	0.628	5
Punjab	Jhelum	0.627	6
Punjab	Nankana Sahib	0.613	7
Punjab	Gujranwala	0.604	8
Punjab	Chakwal	0.591	9
Punjab	Sheikhupura	0.590	10
Punjab	M Bahauddin	0.590	11
Punjab	Attock	0.576	12
KPK	Abbottabad	0.573	13
KPK	Haripur	0.573	14
Punjab	T.T Singh	0.563	15

Source: Estimates are based on PSLM, 2014-15 data.

In Punjab, twenty districts are in the low level of development and sixteen in the medium; in Sindh, twenty-three districts fall in the low category and one in medium; in KPK, twenty-three districts are in low category and two in medium; and in Balochistan, all districts fall in the low HDI category. The lowest category district in Punjab is Rajanpur with an HDI of 0.425. This is higher than for twenty-four districts of Balochistan. There are only four districts in Balochistan that have a higher HDI than Rajanpur which is the lowest district in Punjab. In fact, the HDI of Dera Bugti, the lowest district in Balochistan, is 0.297 as against the 0.425 of the lowest district in Punjab.[19]

The magnitude of HDI variations shows the extent of disparities in the level of human development. In fact, approximately 75 per cent of districts in Punjab in terms of HDIs are above Quetta, the capital of Balochistan.[20] The figures also reveal intra-provincial inequalities. While the magnitude of districts' HDIs in Punjab varies from 0.43

(Rajanpur) to 0.67 (Lahore), in Balochistan it varies from 0.297 (Dera Bugti) to 0.495 (Quetta). In KPK the variation is from 0.323 (Tor Garh) to 0.534 (Peshawar) and in Sindh it is from 0.343 (Kashmore) to 0.654 (Karachi).

ESTIMATED HUMAN DEVELOPMENT INDICES FOR THE DISTRICTS OF BALOCHISTAN	
National HDI	0.524
Balochistan	0.407
Dera Bugti	0.297
Jhal Magsi	0.330
Qila Abdullah	0.332
Chagai	0.332
Nasirabad	0.336
Sheerani	0.338
Harnai	0.350
Barkhan	0.356
Kohlu	0.360
Bolan/Kachhi	0.360
Jaffarabad	0.361
Washuk	0.372
Qila Saifullah	0.378
Ziarat	0.388
Awaran	0.388
Kharan	0.392
Musakhel	0.400
Khuzdar	0.400
Nushki	0.402
Zhob	0.403
Sibbi	0.413
Lasbela	0.415
Pishin	0.416
Loralai	0.424
Kalat	0.432
Mastung	0.443
Gwadar	0.492
Quetta	0.496

Food Security and Malnutrition

According to a report, the thirteen most underfed districts in Pakistan were from Balochistan (minimum intake of food measured by calories). The entire generation of young children born in conflict in Dera Bugti in Balochistan was malnourished today. A recent report on malnutrition and food poverty disclosed that two out of three households in Balochistan could not afford a proper meal. Also, 83 per cent children in the province were facing severe malnourishment and had no access to health and education opportunities.[21]

According to Kaiser Bengali, 'I've forty years of research, I've worked all over Pakistan and the only place in Pakistan where I have found hunger is in Balochistan. There is no other place in Pakistan where I came face to face with hunger.'[22]

The situation has deteriorated so much that in May 2017 the provincial health minister Mir Rehmat Baloch felt the need to call for the imposition of a nutrition emergency in Balochistan since the mother and child nutritional situation was very serious in the province. He added that according to a survey, 52 per cent of the children in the province suffered from stunting and 40 per cent were underweight.[23] Nutrition is clearly neglected in Pakistan, especially in Balochistan. Over the decades, successive governments have paid scant attention to the issue, resulting in the current alarming statistics.

Poor spending on healthcare, weak institutions, erratic funding by donors and a culture of negligence are cited as the main reasons for the existing situation. As the *Daily Times* put it, 'Unfortunately, the ordinary citizens of Pakistan have been left at the mercy of a dysfunctional health system, negligible health facilities and often vacuous and unskilled practices of the health staff.'[24]

Electricity

Balochistan contributes 2,280 MW of power to the national grid.[25] In peak season, the electricity demand in Balochistan is around 1,800 MW but the electricity grid in Balochistan can carry only 650 MW of electricity. Ironically, the province receives less electricity than what one power plant at Uch in Balochistan generates. Thus, despite surplus electricity being available in the province, Balochistan would not get more than 650 MW unless the transmission capacity in the province is enhanced. Unfortunately, the federal government till 2018 did not allocate adequate funds to improve the capacity of the provincial grid. As a result, all districts of Balochistan, except the capital Quetta, face load shedding of more than twelve hours per day[26] despite being a surplus power producer.

In the rural areas where the bulk of the population lives, electrification is only 25 per cent compared to 75 per cent in the rest of the country.[27] As a result, the majority of the rural population still has no access to electricity and mostly use kerosene for lighting purposes. In 2008, it was estimated that Balochistan consumed about 4.1 TWh/year of electricity, which was only 5.6 per cent of the total electricity consumption in the country. Per capita yearly electricity consumption in the province was only 490 kWh.[28]

Millennium Development Goals (MDG)

Despite the tall claims, fancy promises and international commitments, Pakistan has not made much headway in fulfilling its MDG commitment. As per a UNDP report published in 2015, Balochistan was the worst performing province in most, if not all, areas of the MDGs in 2012-13. The report showed that at the current rate of progress, no MDG could be achieved in its entirety in the province. Its performance, while completely off track and below the national average for almost all indicators, was of grave concern in alleviating poverty, health- and education-related indicators. Forty per cent of children were underweight against a target of 20 per cent, reflecting a severe lag in performance. Fifty per cent of the population was below the minimum level of dietary energy consumption as against the target of 13 per cent. Similarly, in MDG 2 in all three indicators—net primary enrolment ratio, completion/survival rate and literacy rate—performance was lower than the national average and considerably behind the targets. Balochistan was also underperforming in the six indicators of child mortality with a staggeringly high infant mortality rate by national standards. In MDG 5 progress was especially lagging for all indicators—at 758 deaths per hundred thousand live births, the maternal mortality ratio deserved immediate attention.[29]

Social Indicators

Balochistan has the poorest social indicators in the country. Less educated and less urbanized than the rest of the country,[30] the province also has a far greater dependency ratio. While 43.3 per cent of Pakistan's population is below fifteen years of age, the proportion for Balochistan is 49.5 per cent. A younger population means a higher dependency ratio in terms of economic participation, and implies a larger need for educational and health facilities. A higher gender disparity in the labour force participation suggests an even greater dependency ratio for the province.

The maternal mortality rate (MMR) in Pakistan is 276 (per 100,000 live births) whereas according to 2006-07 data, as noted earlier, Balochistan had the highest MMR—758 per 100,000 live births, almost three times the national average, while MMR for Punjab stood at 227 per 100,000 live births. The current MMR and female reproductive health demographics of Balochistan can only compete with war-torn Somalia with MMR of 1,000 and Liberia with MMR 770 per 100,000 live births.

Only 43 per cent of children are fully immunized in the province against a national average of 78 per cent. According to the Extended Programme on Immunization (EPI) Coverage Survey 2001, only 35 per cent of the children in the age group of 12–23 months were fully immunized at that time, showing marked deterioration.[31] Balochistan accounted for seven out of nine districts in Pakistan with the lowest full immunization rate, including the four districts with the worst record. Balochistan's performance would look even worse without the exclusion of Dera Bugti and Kohlu in the Pakistan Social and Living Standards Measurement (PSLM) sample due to security reasons. Additionally, UNICEF reported that there was no vaccination centre in 39 per cent of the Union councils in the province. In 2011, the province recorded the highest incidence for polio cases in the world: a total of sixty-two out of a worldwide 169.[32]

The province also remains deprived of basic health facilities. High infant mortality rates (IMR) prevailed with 158 out of 1,000 children dying before five years of age. Even the Democratic Republic of Congo's average of 126 is lower, while Pakistan's national average of seventy is less than half. According to another report, the IMR in Balochistan is high with wide urban–rural and male–female variation. In rural areas, mortality rates for children under the age of five (U5MR) are at 164 per 1,000 live births, much higher than that of urban children (130 per 1,000 live births).[33]

While Pakistan as a whole lags in the social sector, Balochistan lags far behind other provinces in all indicators. The poor state of social fabric has been largely due to the failure to translate economic growth into improvement of the lot of the people. It is understandable that with such a weak social sector—with low-level literacy rate and poor and inadequate healthcare services, for instance—Balochistan cannot embark on a better economic development path.

Even the former chief justice of Pakistan, Mian Saqib Nisar, was moved to say that the situation in Balochistan was deplorable and, despite having huge mineral resources, the people of the province were demanding the provision of even basic rights. 'I personally feel a sense of embarrassment while observing this situation about Balochistan,' he said.[34]

Comparison with Punjab

A comparison of two neighbouring districts—Rajanpur, the poorest district of Punjab, and Dera Bugti, the poorest district in Balochistan—highlights the development crisis faced by Pakistan's largest province. Dera Bugti has an approximate population of 320,000 while Rajanpur has almost two million people. The food security index for the former stands at 0.23 and the incidence of caloric poverty is at 73 per cent, while the latter has a food security index of 0.58 and a 55.3 per cent incidence of caloric poverty. Only 5 per cent of girls in rural Dera Bugti were able to enrol in primary school as compared to 62 per cent in Rajanpur. The literacy rate for the 10-plus age group is 16 per cent in Dera Bugti and 39 per cent in Rajanpur, while the female literacy rate for the same age group is 1 per cent in the former and 27 per cent in the latter. Dera Bugti is rich in natural gas but the gas extracted from there is transported to other parts of Pakistan. Dera Bugti is deprived of it.[35]

TRENDS IN REGIONAL DISPARITY[36]

	Annual Growth Rate (per cent)								
	2001-02 to 2005-06			2005-06 to 2007-08			2007-08 to 2009-10		
Province	U	R	Total	U	R	Total	U	R	Total
Punjab	5.9	10.5	9.1	-1.3	-0.6	-0.9	3.4	6.7	5.6
Sindh	1.9	8.9	6.1	2.2	-9.6	-2.9	2.0	2.3	3.0
Khyber Pakhtunkhwa	9.0	8.8	9.1	-7.3	-1.5	-2.7	3.3	5.3	5.0
Balochistan	-3.0	-3.0	-2.5	8.1	-1.6	3.2	0.5	-2.5	-0.6
Pakistan	4.4	9.3	7.8	-0.3	-2.2	-1.4	2.8	5.3	4.7

U-Urban; R-Rural

Some commentators have sought to explain away the abysmal socio-economic development of Balochistan as compared with the other provinces of Pakistan as a result of its skewed land to population ratio. The greater geographical spread of the province means that the naturally scattered population needs more resources for the same effect. Just as an example, 100 km of road in the more densely populated Punjab will serve more people than in Balochistan.

Such an argument is, however, self-serving. Any enlightened government, or even a non-enlightened one, would try and bring all the provinces to one level rather than focusing only on the already developed ones, even if they have much larger populations. Thus, roads (and much longer ones) would have to be built in all the provinces. By allowing Balochistan to lag in the name of smaller population is indicative of treating the population of the province as second-class citizens. As a federation, the federal fiscal system is expected to bring about equalization among federating units, provision of public services and socio-economic development indicators.[37] This is something that Pakistan has clearly failed in doing. The consequent feeling among the Baloch of being second-class citizens is thus quite natural.

IV

CHINESE GAMBIT

11

Gwadar

THE WORD 'GWADAR' IS DERIVED from two Balochi words: Gwat (air) Darr (door or gateway). Taken together, Gwadar means 'gateway of wind'.

Gwadar is situated on a natural hammerhead-shaped peninsula forming two semicircular bays on either side on the south-western Arabian Sea coast of Pakistan. The western bay is known as the Paddi Zirr, and is generally shallow with an average depth of 12 feet, and a maximum depth of 30 feet. The eastern bay is the deep-water Demi Zirr harbour, where the Gwadar port is being built.

Historically, Gwadar was a nodal point for trade between the Indus Valley and Mesopotamian civilizations for years. In the fifteenth century the Portuguese, led by Vasco da Gama, tried to set it on fire. The then Khan of Kalat gifted Gwadar to a Muscat sultan in 1783.[1] Oman ruled the city for years and during its regime Gwadar was an active port. Remnants of structures built by the Omanis can be seen around the city even today. In 1958 Gwadar became part of Pakistan when the government formally purchased it from Oman at the cost of $3 million.[2]

Gwadar has come a long way from being just a telegraph station with a lonely, stunted tree in the nineteenth century[3] or an underdeveloped fishing village in the twentieth, to potentially becoming one of the great cities of the world in the twenty-first century. According to Robert Kaplan, 'If we can think of great place names of the past—Carthage, Thebes, Troy, Samarkand, Angkor Wat—and of the present—Dubai,

Singapore, Tehran, Beijing, Washington—then Gwadar should qualify as a great place name of the future.' However, he warns that one key to Pakistan's fate would be the future of Gwadar, 'whose development will either unlock the riches of Central Asia, or plunge Pakistan into a savage, and potentially terminal, civil war.' He adds that history is as much a series of accidents and ruined schemes as it is of great plans. Whether Gwadar becomes a new silk-route nexus or not is tied to Pakistan's own struggle against becoming a failed state.[4]

At present, however, such a 'great place name' is conspicuous by its absence. According to Abdul Wali, writing in the *Nation* in 2016, 'Presently, Gwadar has no water, decent schools, hospitals, a college for girls, or even a single university, let alone internet facilities; so, could it be a future mega city?' Gwadar's girls study in the boy's college in the evening shift; there is no university; there is a serious water crisis and the desalination plants don't work.[5] Farrukh Saleem, quoting the Pakistan Bureau of Statistics, wrote in September 2016 that Gwadar had a total of 33,680 housing units of which only 20 per cent were pucca; only 35 per cent had electricity; only 45 per cent had piped water and only 0.86 per cent had gas for cooking. A hospital operated by the Gwadar Development Authority had been lying idle for the past eight years.[6]

Gwadar and Oman

In the middle of the eighteenth century, Mir Nasir Khan, the Khan of Kalat, captured Gwadar and its surrounding areas after defeating the Gichkis and included it in the Khanate of Kalat. The local Gichki chief was, however, allowed to maintain administrative control of the area, in return for providing half the revenues. Meanwhile, Sultan bin Ahmad of the Al Said dynasty of Muscat escaped to Gwadar from Muscat in 1783 due to an internal power struggle with his brother. On arrival in Gwadar, he asked for Nasir Khan's help. Resultantly, in 1784 Nasir Khan handed over Gwadar to him for his maintenance with the understanding that the area be returned to Kalat when the Sultan acquired the throne of Muscat. Sultan bin Ahmad ascended the throne of Muscat in 1797 but did not return Gwadar to Kalat. He appointed a wali (governor) and ordered a fort to be built there. The ensuing struggle for Gwadar between the heirs of Sultan bin Ahmad and the Khan of Kalat allowed the British to intervene. After extracting concessions from the sultan for the use of the area, the British facilitated Muscat to retain Gwadar.

The British built the first ever telegraph link between Karachi and Gwadar in 1863 as part of the Indo-European Telegraph. A post office was opened in 1894 and Gwadar became a port of call for British steamers and an important base for flying boat operations.

Though the Khans of Kalat continued to reiterate their claim on Gwadar, nothing materialized since the area was under British control. In British strategic calculations, a foothold on the mainland was critical in case India became unfriendly. Surveys had also indicated the presence of oil in the area and the British realized that Gwadar could be an important port in the future. A British–American company, India Oil Concessions Ltd, was awarded a contract for oil exploration in 1939, but due to the outbreak of the Second World War, the work was suspended. The British foreign office was also unsure about independent India joining the Commonwealth and so felt that it was in their interest to keep the area under Muscat with whom they had exclusive agreements.

These agreements not only allowed Britain to use Gwadar for military and other purposes but also restrained the sultan from selling or leasing the areas under its dominion to any state other than Britain. Thus, even after its creation, Pakistan had to approach the British government for the purchase of Gwadar rather than talk directly with Muscat as two sovereign governments.

In 1954, Pakistan engaged the United States Geological Survey (USGS) to conduct a survey of its coastline. The USGS deputed the surveyor, Worth Condrick, for the survey who identified the hammerhead-shaped peninsula of Gwadar as a natural and suitable site for a new deep-sea port. This prompted Pakistan to start pressing for the return of Gwadar. Britain continued to discourage the deal till August 1958, when it finally allowed the transfer of Gwadar through a secret agreement. The agreement paved the way for purchase of Gwadar from the sultan and several concessions.

According to the agreement, if oil was found in commercial quantities in Gwadar, the government of Pakistan was bound to pay a percentage of total revenues to the sultan. Other provisions included retention of citizenship of Muscat by the residents of Gwadar without prejudice to any rights enjoyed as citizens of Pakistan; facilitation in recruitment from the area for the sultan's armed forces; training facilities for military personnel in Pakistan's technical schools, etc.[7] Gwadar formally became part of Pakistan on 7 September 1958, after 174 years of Omani rule.

Addressing the nation on Radio Pakistan on the occasion, Prime Minister Malik Feroze Khan Noon stated: 'I welcome the residents of Gwadar into the Republic of Pakistan and I would like to assure them that they will enjoy equal rights and privileges along with all other Pakistan nationals irrespective of considerations of religion, caste or creed. They will have their full share in the glory and prosperity of the Republic to which they now belong.' (Words, no doubt, that the residents of Gwadar, along with other Baloch, would wince at now.) He also thanked the British government '… for their assistance and help in bringing to a successful conclusion our negotiations with His Highness the Sultan of Muscat and Oman for the transfer of his rights in Gwadar. The negotiations were pursued with great vigour during the last six months and at every stage we received valuable advice from Her Majesty's Government in the United Kingdom.'[8]

At the time Gwadar was a small and underdeveloped fishing village with a population of a few thousand. After its incorporation, Gwadar was made a tehsil (sub-district) of Makran district in the erstwhile West Pakistan Province. Later it would become a district when Makran was upgraded into a division.

History of Gwadar's Development

Since the port's acquisition in 1958 from Oman, Pakistan has been making grand plans for its use. During the presidency of Ayub Khan in the 1960s, the thinking was to develop Gwadar as an alternative to Karachi. Gwadar, along with the port of Pasni to the east, was seen as making Pakistan a great Indian Ocean power. However, given the economic conditions of the country, such plans remained on paper.

In the 1970s, Z.A. Bhutto unsuccessfully sought to interest the US in the development of the port and offered it to the US Navy. The offer was repeated in 1974 but the US remained disinterested. In 1980 the former chairman of the US Joint Chiefs of Staff Admiral Thomas

Moorer advocated the setting up of a naval base in Gwadar.[9] However, the proposal did not get much traction.

In the 1980s the Russians evinced an interest, seeing Gwadar as the warm-water outlet to the sea that they had been looking for long. It would have allowed them to export the mineral wealth of Central Asia. However, these plans floundered as they were unable to establish control over Afghanistan. In 1988 Belgium tried its hand at developing Gwadar harbour but the port could not attract much traffic.[10]

In the 1990s with the collapse of the Soviet Union, there was a scramble to position Gwadar as a transit point for the newly independent Central Asian Republics (CARs). Nawaz Sharif in his first term and Benazir Bhutto in her second term tried to give Gwadar high visibility and billed it as the gateway to the CARs. Once again, nothing much happened. In his second term Nawaz Sharif signed an agreement with the China Harbour Engineering Corporation (CHEC) for building the first phase of the Gwadar deep-sea port. The plans were, however, derailed following Gen. Pervez Musharraf ousting him in a coup in October 1999.

The project was finally put on track in May 2001 during the visit of Chinese Premier Zhu Rongji who approved Chinese funding for developing Gwadar as a deep-sea port. As per the agreement, China would provide $250 million and Pakistan $50 million for the construction. The construction work was inaugurated in March 2002. In June 2006, the first phase was ready.

The management of the port was handed over to Port of Singapore Authority (PSA) for forty years in February 2007.[11] PSA undertook to invest $550 million over five years to develop the port further. According to former senator and current member of the Balochistan Assembly Sanaullah Baloch, the government deliberately misled the media and the public to create the impression that the Port of Singapore Authority was taking over Gwadar. However, according to him, the name 'Port of Singapore Authority' does not appear anywhere in the concession agreement signed in 2007. Instead, it was a three-week-old company PSA Gwadar Pte Ltd. The company did not even exist at the time of bidding; the bidding was done by its 'sponsors'.[12]

The port did not get off to a smooth start. The first ship—*Post Glory*—that arrived in March 2008 carrying a wheat shipment from Canada could not berth. The 14-metre draft at the time of the official opening of the port in March 2007 had reduced to 12.5 metres due to silting. Another ship had to be hired to unload some of the wheat to lighten the *Post Glory*. The then shipping minister Qamarruzzaman Kaira had to confess that the port would take three years to become operational as it lacked the required infrastructure, communication network and utilities.[13] Despite this, the port was declared 'fully functional' in December 2008.

There was a lot of criticism of the PSA operations. Ultimately, on 30 January 2013 just before the general elections, the PPP government handed over the port operations to the China Overseas Ports Holding Company Ltd (COPHCL). As per the agreement, COPHCL would execute the port's affairs through its three main companies: Gwadar International Terminal (GIT), Gwadar Marine Services Ltd (GMS) and Gwadar Free Zone Company Ltd. (GFZ). GIT would be responsible for handling business-related matters, GMS would provide port services and GFZ would develop and provide allied facilities to the investment companies in the free-zone area. After the formal handover of the free-trade zone, only the Chinese authorities would carry out all business affairs of the port.[14]

Strategic Location

Gwadar's potential is based on its location on Balochistan's Makran coast some 250 nautical miles from the Strait of Hormuz through which 40 per cent of the world's oil supply flows. Gwadar is the outlet for the China–Pakistan Economic Corridor (CPEC), providing the landlocked Xinjiang Province of China with commercial access to the Persian Gulf. It also has the potential to become a regional transit hub for trans-shipment of goods for Central Asia, apart from being an alternative to Karachi port.

Apart from trade, the port has important strategic implications for Pakistan. It is located 450 km farther from the Indian border than Karachi. At present, Karachi handles the overwhelming bulk of Pakistan's sea-borne trade. Gwadar, it is expected, will reduce the congestion at Karachi. It will also make it that much more difficult for India to blockade it, like it did in 1971 and threatened to do so again during the 1999 Kargil crisis. Consequently, the Gwadar port will provide Pakistan with crucial strategic depth along its coastline.

By making Gwadar the pivot of regional trade Pakistan claims that it would attract considerable investment into its most underdeveloped province, Balochistan. Theoretically, these funds would allow for the construction of roads and rails linking the coastal region to the rest of Pakistan, Iran and Afghanistan; would exploit the region's vast and unexplored natural resources; and would allow for the socio-economic uplift of the local Baloch through various development projects. While sounding good on paper, the reality is quite different.

Chinese Interest

Apart from a gateway to the Arabian Sea, Gwadar will provide Beijing with a listening post to monitor the strategic sea links as well as military activities of the Indian and American navies in the region. It will also provide dual-use civilian–military facilities that can be used as a base for Chinese ships and submarines. A Chinese presence at Gwadar would allow China to ensure the security of its energy-related shipments along existing routes.

A decade ago, when Musharraf offered Gwadar to the Chinese to build a port, the model was Dubai. The Chinese model for Gwadar is not Dubai but their own port of Shenzhen. Zhao Lijian, the deputy Chinese ambassador to Islamabad stated, 'Thirty-five years ago, Shenzhen was just a fishing village, like Gwadar. It has been transformed into a modern industrial city.' The challenges, however, are immense. Shenzhen's success to a great deal was due to its location next to Hong Kong whose GDP is greater than Pakistan's. Gwadar is 450 km from the nearest major city, Karachi.[15]

Many security analysts see Gwadar as an integral component of the so-called 'string of pearls' strategy of China. Interestingly, the Americans had coined the expression 'string of pearls' and not the Chinese. The US consultants Booz Allen produced a report called 'Energy Futures in Asia' for the US Defense Department in 2004 and, according to the *Washington Times*, postulated that 'China is building strategic relationships along the sea lanes from the Middle East to the South China Sea in ways that suggest defensive and offensive positioning to protect China's energy

interests, but also to serve broad security objectives.' The report listed
two of the pearls as Chittagong and Gwadar before speculating about
eavesdropping bases, a canal in Thailand, an oil pipeline in Burma and
a railway line in Cambodia. Since then the 'string of pearls' idea has
caught the imagination of strategists and is seen as a strategy to encircle
India. The Chinese projects include: Sittwe in Myanmar, Chittagong
in Bangladesh, Hambantota in Sri Lanka, Marao in the Maldives and
Woody Island near the Paracels.[16]

Yuan as Legal Tender

In a meeting of senior officials held in Islamabad on 20 November 2017
the Chinese side proposed making the Yuan legal tender in Gwadar.
This was indeed intriguing. If it was about helping the Yuan become an
international currency, why should it be legal tender only in Gwadar
and not in the rest of Pakistan?[17] For the present, Pakistan has turned
down the proposal arguing any such move would compromise its
'economic sovereignty'.[18] However, this is clearly not the last that has
been heard on the subject.

Baloch Perspective

As early as 2003, when the construction of the Gwadar port was in
its early stages, there was much public agitation. The HRCP reported
that the main grounds of criticism were: exclusion of the people and
their representatives from the planning and execution of the project;
denial of due opportunities of employment; apprehensions about
the motives of the federal government and the military leadership;
land-grabbing and fear of change in Makran's political status; and
fear of ethnic imbalance in Gwadar and of the Baloch being turned
into a minority in the region. Additional concerns were irregularities
in settlement of land titles, neglect of the traditional interests of the
fishing community, indifference to the rights of the people threatened
with displacement, inadequate representation of the local people
in the new workforce, and the local community's fears of being
swamped by settlers from other parts of the country.[19] These very
same arguments are heard even today except that they are more

strident. Clearly, nothing has been done in the past fifteen years to address any of these issues.

In a typically ham-handed manner, reflecting the insensitivity and arrogance of the federal government, the ordinary Baloch have been alienated by not being consulted about the project; and by not being given a stake in it, and are unlikely to be the beneficiaries of the project. The project is run entirely by the federal government and only a few Baloch have been employed in its construction. These are primarily unskilled labour, though even here a lot of such labour has been imported together with skilled workers like engineers.[20] Gwadar has, thus, become for the Baloch a symbol of how wrongly they have been treated.

Then there is the issue of control of the port between the provincial and the federal governments. The federal government has been running the show in Gwadar despite the Eighteenth Amendment and devolution of powers to provinces. Some crumbs have been given to the provincial government like making its nominee the chairman of the port authority. However, critical decisions remain with the federal government. Therefore, the Baloch feel threatened by the project. As the Balochistan National Party-M (BNP-M) chief Sardar Akhtar Mengal put it: 'The rights of Baloch people cannot be protected and the dream of a prosperous Balochistan cannot come true unless the control of Gwadar port is handed over to the province.'[21]

The revelation about the details of the forty-year agreement with China for the operations of Gwadar port has further increased criticism in Balochistan. The then minister for ports and shipping, Mir Hasil Khan Bizenjo, informed the Senate that under the agreement, the Chinese company, China Overseas Port Holding Company (COPHC), would carry out all the development work on the port and, as per the concession agreement, would be entitled to 91 per cent of revenue collection from the gross revenue of terminal and marine operations and 85 per cent from the gross revenue of free-zone operations. The balance would be the share of the federal government, with Balochistan getting no revenue from the port till 2048.[22]

Around the same time, Sri Lanka handed over its southern port of Hambantota to China on a ninety-nine-year lease. This had to be done after it failed to repay its debts to China. This development also rang alarm bells in Pakistan in general and Balochistan in particular. The fear is that Gwadar will eventually meet the same fate as Hambantota if Pakistan failed to repay the Chinese debts.[23]

Baloch nationalists feel that the project will adversely alter Balochistan's demography due to the influx of non-Baloch to take up prime jobs and make them a minority in their own province. However, figures vary. According to the Gwadar Development Authority, as per the plan, the existing 80,000 population, mostly fishermen, will be joined by another 2 million people over the next twenty years, including 20,000 Chinese residents. However, the Baloch apprehend that Gwadar from its current population will become a city of 10 million people, bringing major changes in the demography of the province. Baloch fears were confirmed by advertisements in the national and even international media inviting investment into Gwadar city that was initially visualized for 2.5 million people but later raised to 5 million. Given that the entire population of Balochistan (including the Pashtuns) is about 6 million, Baloch apprehensions of being converted into a minority in their own homeland and their identity being eroded are clearly justified.[24]

Such fears have been enhanced due to the announcement by the China–Pakistan Investment Corporation (CPIC) at a press conference held in London in October 2017 of a mega housing project 'China–Pak Hills' in Gwadar. The CEO of the corporation, Jian Zheng, disclosed plans to finance $500 million in the first phase of the housing project in which almost half a million white-collar Chinese would reside by 2023. The development project would encompass over 10 million square feet of built-up area. It would be a 'mixed-use gated development tailor-made for Chinese professionals in Gwadar, offering an all-encompassing lifestyle to live, work and play, with a host of facilities that will set the benchmark of future developments.' However, the federal government has called the report bogus, denying that the Gwadar Port Authority had given any such permission. Nevertheless, the CPIC has put forward documentary evidence depicting the possession of 'no objection' certificate with the company from the concerned authority.[25]

The Baloch are aware of the history of Karachi, the capital of Sindh. It had a Sindhi population of 0.5 million in 1947 but now it has more than 14 million people. Almost 90 per cent of them are non-Sindhis rendering the Sindhis a minority in their capital city.[26]

Currently, Balochistan has a fifty-one-member provincial assembly based on the population. The expected influx will lead to additional seats in the legislature, making the Baloch a minority in every respect. 'Even the chief minister will be an outsider,' fears Baloch Senator Dr Jahanzeb Jamaldini of the BNP(M)[27]. Thus, what the Baloch want are legislative guarantees like banning outsiders from getting local Computerised National Identity Cards (CNICs), domicile certificates and registration as voters, for preserving the current demographics.

According to Attaullah Mengal, 'If there are jobs in Gwadar, people would flock there, Pakistanis and foreigners alike. With time, they would get the right to vote. The problem is that one Karachi in Gwadar is sufficient to turn the whole population of Balochistan into a minority. Gwadar will end up sending more members to the Parliament than the rest of Balochistan. We would lose our identity, our language, everything. That's why we are not willing to accept these mega projects.'[28]

Recognizing the threat, the Pakistan Senate in January 2019 called on the government to take measures to preserve the demographic balance and ownership rights of the local population of Gwadar and protect the same against the expected large-scale migration into Gwadar in the wake of CPEC projects.[29] However, at the time of writing, nothing seems to have been done in this regard.

Also, Gwadar is being connected to Karachi but there are apprehensions that the federal government is dragging its feet connecting Gwadar through Turbat, Panjgur and Khuzdar to Quetta. Consequently, the rest of the province will not derive much benefit from the project. This is making the people restive as they feel that they are being converted into a landlocked province despite having the longest coastline in the country.[30]

Hence, its own people have become the port's greatest opponents. As Kaplan notes, the poor and uneducated Baloch population had been shut out of Gwadar's future prosperity. And so, Gwadar became a lightning rod for Baloch hatred of Punjabi-ruled Pakistan. Indeed, Gwadar's very promise as an Arabian Sea–Central Asian hub threatened to sunder the country.[31] Not surprisingly, when the former planning minister Ahsan Iqbal announced grandiosely that 'Gwadar will revolutionize the life of Baloch people' at a function in January 2018, there were very few takers.[32]

Water

Lack of drinking water is a key issue in Gwadar. While Gwadar is touted as the key that would unlock Pakistan's fortunes, the only key the residents of Gwadar today are looking for is adequate supply of drinking water.

According to official estimates, the average per capita water requirement is of around 18 gallons per day. On this basis Gwadar needed around 5.5 MGD of water in 2012 and 6 MGD by the end of 2017. [33] The main source of supply is the Akra dam, which could supply about 3–3.5 MGD to Gwadar and adjoining areas, including Jewani, Peshkan, Sur Bandar, Ganz and Bal Nagor. The requirement of 6 MGD was when the city had not yet expanded fully. As and when the city booms, the requirement for water will rise manifold due to the various projects and massive increase in population. The requirement for a 2.5 million population will imply a minimum 150 MGD of water and could even go as high as 250 MGD.

Gwadar, however, is an arid area known for persistent droughts. Due to periodic paucity of rain, the Akra dam dried up in 2012 and the water crisis continued for about 175 days, easing only after rains in the catchment areas of the dam. Due to the water shortage, the residents were forced to depend on private water tankers that cost Rs 15,000 per tanker. At the peak of the water crisis, one gallon of water was sold for Rs 1,000.[34] In September 2017, the price was at least Rs 17,000 per tanker or six rupees for one gallon of water.[35] The tankers fetched water from the Belar dam—a catchment area getting water from the Daramb mountain facing the Iranian border on its west. These tankers made twenty-seven trips a month, barring Fridays, to provide water to the residents of Surbandar, Peshukan, Gwadar and Jiwani.[36] The crisis turned so bad that the Pakistan Navy had to ship in around 300,000 gallons of water in two tankers.

In December 2015 the water level in Akra dam dropped drastically and a water crisis once again hit Gwadar. It continued for eighty days till March 2016. Water shortage again hit the city in December 2016 and ended in January 2017, lasting for forty days. To overcome this crisis, authorities supplied water to the people through tankers at a cost of Rs 1 billion.[37]

In 2017, due to lack of rain and the resultant drought-like situation, Gwadar was again hit by a severe water crisis. Water had to be brought from the Mirani dam located at a distance of 142 km from Gwadar. Water comes to Gwadar through tankers. It is first delivered to the waterworks town, after which it is supplied to the population through tankers.[38] Only 30–40 gallons of water are provided to each household once a week.[39] The Mirani dam was meant to be the main source of supply for Turbat. The people of Turbat have started complaining that water from the dam is supplied to Gwadar while Turbat itself has been pushed into a severe water crisis. According to the Pakistan Council of Scientific and Industrial Research (PCSIR) in Karachi, water quality tests on samples collected from Mirani dam in July 2017 revealed that the water was microbiologically not fit for human consumption.[40] Moreover, the tankers supplying water to Gwadar are the same being used to supply petrol and diesel, a fact that would make the water highly polluted.[41]

There have been intermittent problems with water tankers, largely because of non-payment of outstanding dues by the authorities. As a result, the tanker owners frequently have to face the burden of heavy loans they obtain for the payment of fuel, salaries of tanker drivers and to meet other costs to continue water supply from Mirani dam to Gwadar.[42]

The Chinese have built a small-sized desalination plant that provides one million gallons of water for the consumption of the workers at the port. Two desalination plants set up during Musharraf's tenure failed to function and got mired in corruption. Moreover, the plants require a lot of electricity to run and there is an acute shortage of it in Gwadar.[43] The Senate was told in March 2017 that up to 700 million rupees would be needed 'for repairing and re-operation'.[44]

Asks Kaiser Bengali, former economic adviser to the chief minister of Balochistan, 'How can you build a major port and a major city where there is no water?' He added, 'There are no answers to anything. Transparency is seriously lacking.' While there is talk of building more dams and a desalination plant, observers are sceptical because the country's electricity grid is about 640 km away and power is imported from neighbouring Iran, a system that leaves the area with scheduled daily blackouts.[45]

For the present, foreign investors and domestic companies have not been seriously affected since they have access to bottled water. The worst sufferers are the locals, the poor fishermen. According to an apocryphal story, when a house was burgled in Gwadar, the only items stolen were containers of fresh water—a staple that has soared in value since reservoirs dried up. According to a legislator from Gwadar city, 'Gwadar has become known to the entire world due to the multibillion CPEC project, but nobody knows how its population is suffering due to the water shortages.'[46]

If this is the situation today, the future can well be imagined. Failure to supply water may expose Gwadar to the same fate as Fatehpur Sikri[47] or Myanmar's famed capital Bagan.

Fishermen

People most affected by the development of Gwadar port are the fishermen who constitute almost 80 per cent of the local population. They have lost their prime fishing grounds located along the east bay where the port was constructed. The locals could also lose their homes if Gwadar's master plan, which was prepared with no local consultation, is implemented since they would be relocated some 15—20 km from the port area.[48]

Prior to the recent development of the port, the town's limits were basically confined to the old town. The Gwadar Development Authority (GDA) created a master plan for Gwadar's expansion in 2005 in which the whole of the old town area became part of the port. Several housing projects and markets were to be built in place of the old town. The residents of the old town were to be shifted to the north, near the coastal highway. However, now even the master plan has been junked and a Chinese company has been tasked to create a Gwadar Smart Port City. The fate of the old town at the time of writing remains unknown.[49]

The development of the Eastbay Expressway—a component of CPEC—that would connect the Makran coastal highway with the free-trade zone of the Gwadar port is also threatening to deprive local fishermen of access to the sea. The project would prevent them from fishing on Gwadar's eastern port that had been the only source of income for many members of the community for centuries. Despite an agreement with the Balochistan government and the Gwadar Port Authority that led to the fishermen calling off their protests and strikes in 2018, development of the expressway has continued as per the original plan.[50]

Tension has also been building up since the disclosure of the Federal Marine Fisheries Department's plan to issue around a hundred licences for various types of fishing vessels in its exclusive economic zone (between twenty and 200 nautical miles). The Pakistan Fisheries Exporters Association and the Pakistan Fisherfolk Forum immediately condemned the grant of licences to foreign parties in view of the likely depletion of the country's marine resources. The closure of the traditional fish harbour at Gwadar and the move to uproot the old settlement's population from their historical habitat could invite strong resistance.[51]

Recent reports indicate that trawlers from Sindh were depleting fish stocks and damaging the provincial marine ecosystem. Trawling is illegal in Balochistan but according to media reports, bribes to the fisheries departments of Balochistan and Sindh, to senior bureaucrats, politicians and other influential people—to the tune of Rs 5 billion every month—allows this practice to go unchecked. According to an official, China will also trawl the waters to send fish back to China, further depleting fish stocks.[52]

As the *Daily Times* noted, '... local communities will not derive economic benefit from the project for several years to come, which is why old sources of livelihood must be protected while CPEC projects are under construction. The Balochistan government and the Gwadar Port Authority must make good on their commitment to ensuring the fishermen's access to the Arabian sea is preserved.'[53]

Land Scam

There has been massive real estate speculation in Gwadar. Robert Kaplan quotes the cover story, 'The Great Land Robbery', from the June 2008 issue of *The Herald*, a Karachi-based investigative magazine that had alleged that the Gwadar project had '... led to one of the biggest land scams in Pakistan's history'. The locals owned the land for generations but had no documentary evidence of ownership. Taking advantage of this, influential persons could bribe revenue officials and get the land registered in their names. The land was then sold to developers from cities like Karachi and Lahore for residential and industrial schemes. Hundreds of thousands of acres were illegally allotted to civilian and military bureaucrats living elsewhere.[54]

Speculation in land sent prices skyrocketing but very few locals benefited. Officials, civil and military, and politicians cornered most of the land.[55] The Pakistan Navy was reported to have occupied a large portion of the land. In some cases, land was bought from locals for a pittance and then sold at ten to twenty times the price; government land was parcelled out to cronies who made huge profits by reselling the land to investors. However, since the port turned out to be a non-starter in the initial years, prices crashed and many people lost a lot of money.[56]

Said a Gwadar Port Authority (GPA) official, 'Gwadar's lands have been seized by state agencies, the coast guards, the navy, the paramilitaries. Every general has a plot in Gwadar. They say these plots were given because this is a federal project. But this is a land grab.'[57] Indeed, the military had sought to acquire more than 11,000 acres in Gwadar to construct what it calls a 'combined defence complex'.[58]

More recently, according to a press statement issued by the chairman of the National Accountability Bureau (NAB) Justice Javed Iqbal, investigations showed the Gwadar Industrial Estate Development Authority had completely ignored the rules in allotting commercial and industrial plots in Gwadar. Plots had been distributed among favourites and relatives with the help of revenue authorities and provincial government officials. In so doing, notes the statement, applications of eligible industrial and other investors were rejected. Even the Balochistan High Court was forced to comment: 'Nobody knows how the settled land owned by the state has been transferred to the private sector, that too for peanuts'. It also made the unsurprising observation that '… the provincial government and the Board of Revenue cannot be absolved of their responsibility in this regard'.[59]

How Safe is Gwadar?

An area of concern is the Makran Trench that is located off the coast of Pakistan, close to Gwadar. The trench is a seismically active zone in the

Arabian Sea. It is the meeting point for two tectonic plates—the Eurasian plate and the Indian plate—where one plate is inching beneath the other in a 'subduction zone'. The last major earthquake in the area was over seventy years ago in 1945. It was of a magnitude of 8.1 on the Richter scale and had triggered a tsunami that pounded Iran, the area now constituting Pakistan, Oman and India and killed around 4,000 people. In 2017 a quake of 6.3-magnitude on the Richter scale hit the area.

Despite the damage, not much is known about the zone. To find out more, a team of scientists from China and Pakistan have started to survey the area. The survey could provide critical data and enable an assessment about potential dangers. While hypothetical, given Gwadar's proximity to the trench, another major earthquake or tsunami could adversely impact, if not damage, operations of the port.[60]

Gwadar: A Military or a Commercial Project?

The Pakistan government has been at pains to stress that Gwadar is a commercial and civilian project. However, it has been pointed out that Gwadar airport has long been seen as a military base. If this were not the case, why disregard normal procedure when the 6,600 acres for the new Gwadar airport were being purchased? It was the Military Estates Officer (MEO) in Quetta instead of the Civil Aviation Authority (CAA) that bought the land for Rs 1.05 billion. Any land acquired by the Military Lands and Cantonments (MLC) makes it the property of the Pakistan Army and this fact alone thoroughly exposes the claims that Gwadar is an exclusively commercial project.[61]

Mohammad Ali Talpur makes the interesting point that Hartsfield–Jackson Airport, Atlanta, has been the world's busiest airport since 1998 and attracts more travellers than any other airport in the world with 96,178,899 passengers passing through in 2014. It also manages more aircraft movements (take-offs and landings) than any other airport in the world with 881,933 in 2014 and is built only on 4,700 acres. Gwadar airport is twice the size of London's Heathrow (2,965 acres) where a plane lands or takes off every 46 seconds at peak time, handling 73,408,442 passengers and 472,817 aircraft movements in 2014. Gwadar is clearly oversized and is being built for objectives other than what is publicized. It will clearly have a large military component.[62]

According to the *Guardian*, in theory, exporters in Xinjiang will have a much shorter journey to the Arabian Sea and international markets than via China's eastern ports. In practice, sceptics wonder whether trucking goods over one of the world's highest mountain ranges will ever be cheaper than the existing sea routes. They suspect China is more interested in Gwadar as a potential naval base near the oil supplies of the Gulf. This would fit in with acquisition of an area much larger than required for a civil airport.[63]

In fact, even when the Karakorum Highway (KKH) was being built, the then military ruler Ayub Khan had said that 'in order of priority, the first urgency was strategic and one of immediate significance' and that the 'economic and commercial importance of the highway' was only 'the second objective' for Pakistan.[64]

Chabahar

Since the early years of the new millennium Pakistan has been concerned that the development of the Iranian port of Chabahar would adversely impact Gwadar's potential as the main sea route for the Central Asian Republics (CARs) and for China, should the need ever arise. For years, India had been trying to persuade Pakistan to allow it to transport goods to Afghanistan through the land route but Pakistan did not agree. In 2002, India helped Iran develop Chabahar, located 72 km west of Gwadar. Chabahar provides India access to Afghanistan via the Arabian Sea, bypassing Pakistan. Since Islamabad views Chabahar through the prism of its relations with India, it is apprehensive about the Iranian port emerging as an alternative gateway to Central Asia apart from ending Afghanistan's dependence on Pakistan for transit.

Such concerns were heightened when, on 23 May 2016, Indian Prime Minister Narendra Modi, Iranian President Hassan Rouhani and President Ashraf Ghani of Afghanistan signed a three-way transit agreement on Chabahar. India would invest up to $500 million to develop the port and both countries planned several projects worth hundreds of millions of dollars.[65] Not only would the agreement take economic cooperation between the three countries to a new level but, as the Iranian president put it, the three-way accord '… was not merely an economic document but a political and regional one'.[66]

Three other developments have heightened Pakistan's concerns. In October 2017 India flagged off a shipment of wheat for Afghanistan through Chabahar, marking the operationalization of the port for the trans-shipment of goods from India to the landlocked country. This signalled that Afghanistan would no longer be dependent on Pakistan's Karachi port alone for trade and India could now bypass Pakistan in transporting goods to Afghanistan. Second, in February 2018 India and Iran signed a short-term lease of the first phase of Shahid Beheshti Port at Chabahar.[67] Under the agreement, Iran leased a part of the port for eighteen months to India to take over operations of existing port facilities in the first phase of the port development project. India has committed $85 million for the development of the Shahid Beheshti Port. Third, Afghanistan began exports to India through Chabahar port on 24 February 2019. As per reports, twenty-three trucks carrying fifty-seven tonnes of dry fruits, textiles, carpets and mineral products were dispatched from the western Afghan city of Zaranj to Chabahar port.[68]

In Pakistan, the 'alliance between India, Afghanistan and Iran' was seen as a 'security threat'. It was feared that such a bloc would affect Pakistan's plans for regional economic integration, restoration of internal peace and maintenance of peaceful borders as also the CPEC timelines. Some advocated that the recipe 'to break out of this encircling move' was Pakistan formalizing its defence and strategic relationship with China rather than keeping it unwritten.[69]

Pakistan's worry is threefold. First, it is concerned that as and when Chabahar port and the road/rail link to Afghanistan and beyond gets operationalized, the floodgates could be opened for Indian investment in Afghanistan. It would also improve transport connectivity and economic collaboration of India with countries in Central Asia. Second, this sea–land link allows India to bypass Pakistan and have direct access to Afghanistan, something that Pakistan has so far prevented. Likewise, it provides landlocked Afghanistan an alternative route to the outside world instead of relying solely on the whims of Pakistan. This worries Pakistan as it could be the first step in Afghanistan shaking off its dependence on its neighbour. Third, Pakistan's worry is that its 'all-weather friend' China could hedge its bets on the CPEC script. The state-run *Global Times* stated, 'There is no reason for jealousy in China about a milestone deal signed between India and Iran.' It further held that India can promote infrastructure development that will be conducive to economic development in the entire region.[70] Chinese prime minister Li Keqiang followed this up by stating that the projects (Chabahar and Gwadar) have the potential to complement each other in boosting the otherwise sluggish economies of the region and that China did not see the development of Chabahar as an attempt to undermine the Gwadar project or CPEC.[71]

Overall, the simultaneous development of Gwadar and Chabahar has caught the imagination of commentators and is projected as a contest in the Arabian Sea representing long-standing rivalries in the region that would lead to geostrategic competition.[72]

12

The China–Pakistan Economic Corridor

THE CHINA–PAKISTAN ECONOMIC CORRIDOR (CPEC) has been described as a 'game-changer' for Pakistan. Even the army chief Gen. Qamar Javed Bajwa has described CPEC in grand terms: 'This corridor is not just a collection of infrastructure and power projects—it is in fact a complete development platform that has the potential to act as a powerful springboard for shared development in the entire Central Asia–South Asia region,' he said, during his prepared remarks at a function in Karachi in October 2017.[1]

The moot question is whether it would be a game-changer for Balochistan too. Would it transform the lives of the people of Balochistan and would it be the panacea for their economic ills?

Three factors are relevant here. First—discounting for the moment doubts as to whether Balochistan is on the route of the corridor and if so, whether the route will be in phase I or II—the route will pass through only a portion of the province. It is, thus, unlikely to be a game-changer for the province. Second, as mentioned previously, there is no certainty that it will be the people of Balochistan who will be employed in the implementation of the corridor. In the past, the Baloch were passed over in mega projects like the Saindak copper–gold project, the Reko Diq project and the Gwadar port project. So, will CPEC be any different?[2]

Third, Gwadar is the critical element of the CPEC. Without an outlet from Gwadar, the CPEC will be a non-starter. And here lies the rub—as noted in the previous chapter, the Baloch have been alienated by the manner in which the development of Gwadar is taking place. The elected representative for Gwadar in the Balochistan Assembly is, for example, not convinced that the benefits of the huge investments that are planned for the people of Gwadar will actually accrue to them. He has admitted that he has not been taken on board regarding the various agreements and has gone as far as to say that it almost seems like there is a plot afoot to convert the local population into a minority in their own area. Likewise, the elected chairman of the Gwadar Municipal Committee has also complained that the opinions of local leaders and of the people of Gwadar have been disregarded in recent CPEC–related decisions. Meanwhile, the residents of Gwadar lack basic facilities like access to clean drinking water, adequate educational institutions, healthcare, and suffer prolonged power outages. The BNP-M chief Akhtar Mengal put his finger on the nub of the matter when he said that the success of CPEC was linked to the support of Baloch people.[3]

What Will CPEC Do?

According to the Economic Survey of Pakistan 2016-17, projects under the CPEC portfolio are broadly categorized into 'early harvest' projects with completion by 2018 and short- and medium-term projects, which are aimed for completion by 2020 and 2025 respectively. The intention is also to take the initiative forward under the CPEC long-term plan. The sectors of cooperation include, but are not limited to, agriculture, energy, infrastructure development in rail and road networks, development of Gwadar as a modern port city, establishment of industrial parks and improving IT connectivity through optical fibre.[4]

Out of the $21 billion worth of 'priority energy projects', there is only one project in KPK (worth $1.8 billion) and two in Balochistan (worth $1.3 billion), accounting for 8.5 per cent and 6 per cent, respectively, of the total investment categorized as 'priority'.

There have also been claims by the authorities that the debate on the installation of energy projects in any specific province is futile as electricity generated anywhere will be injected into the national grid and will be available for all the provinces without any discrimination.[5] This would be true only if all provinces had been fully connected to the national grid. At present, large swathes of rural Balochistan, FATA and KPK are not connected to the national grid. For instance, only 25 per cent of Balochistan's population has access to electricity compared to 75 per cent in the rest of the country. The existing transmission lines are weak and old and unable to sustain the additional power burden. As mentioned earlier, the peak electricity demand in Balochistan is around 1,800 MW while the transmission lines cannot carry more than 650 MW. So even if there is surplus electricity, large areas of Balochistan, owing to non-connectivity to the national grid and inadequate transmission capacity, are unlikely to benefit.

For the Sharifs (the then prime minister Nawaz Sharif and the then Punjab chief minister Shahbaz Sharif) there was an urgency to complete the 'early harvest' projects before the elections in 2018. Not surprisingly, the bulk of the projects was planned in Punjab and Sindh. Out of the $28.6-billion early-harvest projects, Punjab had the lion's share of $13 billion, Sindh $4.6 billion, KPK $1.8 billion, Islamabad $1.5 billion and Balochistan $920 million. However, by almost ramming home the projects, there was a grave danger that the mistrust the smaller provinces had with Punjab and their insecurities vis-à-vis the federation would get aggravated. Unless the smaller provinces, especially Balochistan and KPK, are given a sense of ownership, the CPEC may damage Pakistan rather than be the 'game-changer' it is billed to be. An ominous warning has been sounded by political economist Pervez Tahir: 'It would do us well to remember that investment in East Pakistan was also considered unsafe for security reasons. What are the planners of today driving the smaller provinces to?'[6]

Route Controversy

Gwadar is not the only bone of contention as far as the Baloch are concerned. The other contentious issue is the route of the CPEC from Gwadar to Kashgar in China. The original proposal envisaged a route through Balochistan and KPK. The government of Nawaz Sharif that came to power in 2013 tweaked the route to make it pass through Punjab instead. This caused a huge uproar and 'route controversy' became a contentious issue between the federal government and

Punjab on the one side and Balochistan and KPK on the other. For these provinces CPEC is increasingly turning out to be a 'China–Punjab Economic Corridor'. This is both because the bulk of the projects has been cornered by Punjab and because the route runs through the length of Punjab and, at least in the first stage of CPEC, bypasses Khyber Pakhtunkhwa completely and most of Balochistan (except the coastal areas from Gwadar to Karachi).[7]

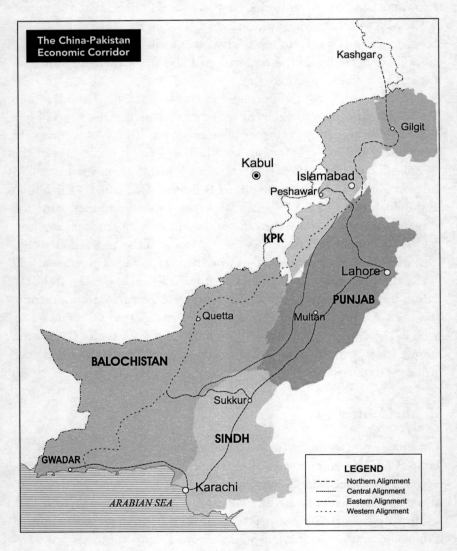

The shortest route from Gwadar to Kashgar runs through Panjgur, Quetta, Zhob (all in Balochistan), Dera Ismail Khan (KPK) and then into Punjab through Mianwali on to Islamabad and then the KKH to Xinjiang. This was also the route that was presumed to become the main CPEC artery and hence enthused the people of Balochistan and KPK who saw in it a potential to uplift areas that have until now been neglected and were underdeveloped.

In February 2014 the first reports emerged that the route had been changed. By March 2014 Baloch senators were raising objections over plans to change the route to cover Punjab and Sindh and leave the bulk of Balochistan out. The new route would also add an additional 400 km to the CPEC. By June 2014 the 'route change' had become official. Ostensibly, it was done because the original 'western route' went through very restive areas and from the point of view of security, the Punjab–Sindh route—'eastern route'—was considered much safer. That Punjab was the pocket borough of the Sharifs and their Pakistan Muslim League-Nawaz and that there were rich political and financial dividends to be gained from routing the CPEC traffic through Punjab was a very important consideration with the Nawaz Sharif government.[8]

There was also the issue of funding. The 'original route' was shortest but would also take a lot more money and time to build. According to the then CPEC point-man, Minister for Planning Ahsan Iqbal, the funds for the western route would have to come from inside Pakistan because the Chinese had refused to finance it. Later, he revealed that the Chinese wanted access to Gwadar within two years and this could only be possible if the eastern route was built first.[9]

With time the route controversy snowballed into a major one. Even as government officials claimed that the route had been changed on the request of the Chinese ambassador, the envoy himself told a leading politician that the decision on the route was taken by the Pakistan government. Senators from Balochistan and KPK not only threatened to hold protest demonstrations in front of the Chinese embassy and in front of parliament but also threatened to resign because all their concerns were falling on deaf ears in the government. Some senators even went to the extent of warning that Pakistan wouldn't remain united if the route was changed.

In the face of rising anger, the government clarified that there would be not one but three routes—western, central and eastern—connecting Gwadar to Kashgar.[10] However, to get the project up and running in the earliest possible time, the eastern route would be operationalized first by upgrading existing infrastructure. But this logic was faulted on the grounds that once the eastern route became operational, it would develop its own logic and dynamic. This would either prevent the other routes from being developed, and if developed, then they would remain underutilized and the spin-offs expected in terms of industrial and other economic activity that were to accompany the transport corridor would not happen. After both the Khyber Pakhtunkhwa and Balochistan assemblies passed resolutions against any change in the route, Chinese officials were forced to step in and issue clarifications that the so-called original route wasn't ever agreed upon by both China and Pakistan. According to the Chinese, only a single route, based on detailed feasibility studies, had been agreed upon and there was no change in that alignment.

With the routes becoming politically controversial, the government was forced to call an All Parties Conference (APC) in May 2015 to evolve a consensus on the issue. After some hectic back-room convincing by Ahsan Iqbal, during which he wooed the dissenting politicians from the smaller provinces by announcing projects that would be coming up in their provinces, the government managed to get a go-ahead. Strangely enough at the APC, Prime Minister Nawaz Sharif declared that the western route would get priority and would be constructed first![11] He had either not been briefed or, quite possibly, not understood the ramifications of the briefing.

Within days it became clear that the assurance given by the prime minister that the western route would get priority was an eyewash. The allocations for the western route were about a fifth of those made for the eastern route. There was an immediate uproar and the Senate Standing Committee on Finance demanded an explanation for what was described by one senator as 'political fudging'.[12]

Barely had the project got off the ground, reports about large-scale corruption started emerging. For example, two of the four highway projects in Balochistan inaugurated by the prime minister as part of the CPEC were awarded to the second lowest bidders instead of the lowest ones, causing a loss of over Rs 650 million. The reasoning for rejecting the lowest bidder was unsatisfactory. There were also reports about CPEC projects being billed at much higher costs than originally planned due to Chinese companies not following competitive bidding processes.[13]

Another example of the deception carried out was the inauguration with much fanfare of the 'Western route of the CPEC' by PM Nawaz Sharif at Zhob on 30 December 2015. A day later it was revealed that the two projects inaugurated were actually funded by the Asian Development Bank (ADB) as per an agreement signed in May 2015 and not through CPEC. As a journalist put it: 'In short, prime minister deceived people and political leaders of Balochistan by terming the ADB projects as CPEC funded projects ... by using ADB funds for highways in name of CPEC, PML-N government is depriving Balochistan of its due share in CPEC funds for infrastructure development, which is condemnable.'[14]

The former chief minister of Balochistan Abdul Malik Baloch's Policy Reform Unit, headed by economist Kaiser Bengali, came up with a report on 25 June 2015 titled 'China–Pakistan Economic Corridor: The Route Controversy'. The report stated that by preferring a route that passes through Punjab and Sindh rather than KPK and Balochistan, the federal government was failing to take into account the needs and desires of all federating units of the country and was trading off today's security risks against provincial discord and political instability in the future.[15] According to this report, the eastern alignment would artificially inflate the cost of the project in terms of cost of land acquisition, displacement of population, socio-economic benefits and environmental impact.

One shameful result of the wrangling and discord over CPEC was the unprecedented intervention by the Chinese embassy in Islamabad on 9 January 2016: 'We hope that relevant parties could strengthen communication and coordination, solve differences properly so as to create favourable conditions for the CPEC. We are ready to work with Pakistani side to actively promote construction of the CPEC projects, and bring tangible benefits to the peoples of the two countries.'[16]

A study that carried out a comparative cost–benefit analysis of the two routes showed that prioritizing the western route was a better option. The arguments were:

1) The western route was the shortest; 2) the costs of land acquisition and dislocation compensation were much lower along the western route compared to the eastern route; 3) many bridges would have to be built on the eastern route compared to the almost negligible number on the western route given that the former passes through rivers and canals; 4) the eastern route was vulnerable to floods in monsoon and had the 'fog' problem in winter; 5) the development of the western route would help create new growth centres and reduce the economic burden on the relatively developed big cities, thus putting a limit on existing patterns of migration; 6) the marginal return on investment in terms of improvement in living standards would be much higher on the western route compared to the eastern route; 7) security costs would be lower along the eastern route but that was offset by the interprovincial discord and weakening of federal integrity that may result from the current design of the CPEC; and 8) strategically, development of the western route would mean the addition of a safer communication line compared to the eastern route, which was closer to the Indian border and therefore vulnerable in case of an attack.

Based on the above arguments, the author of the study concluded that it was not the efficiency-based technocratic criterion alone that had created the current crisis. Instead, it was the political preferences of the ruling party and its obsession with the 2018 general elections that explained the discriminatory design of the CPEC. 'The PML-N may succeed in appeasing its political constituency and secure victory in the 2018 elections but that was likely to happen at a great cost to the already fragile federal integrity,' was the report's conclusion.[17]

Baloch View: Benefits for Balochistan?

Not only are nationalist forces opposing the project, both the treasury and opposition members of Balochistan assembly have complained that the project was being directly controlled by the federal government and that they were not even told the details of Gwadar's master plan.

Thus, the then federal minister for ports and shipping and president of the National Party (NP) Senator Mir Hasil Khan Bizenjo hedged his bets and made contradictory statements. On the one hand, he stated that he didn't know if the CPEC was in the interest of the Baloch people or not, but they were monitoring the project closely. On the other, he said that NP considered the CPEC a positive step and it was in favour of development of Balochistan.[18]

For the Baloch who have suffered at the hands of the Pakistani state since 1947-48, any assurances on CPEC are met with a lot of cynicism. Natural gas from Sui is a glaring example of how the Baloch were deprived of their resources. Even today, 80 per cent of Balochistan is deprived of gas, including Gwadar. Moreover, the development of Gwadar would adversely impact the demographic balance in the province.

Another example is that there is no working group on CPEC at the provincial level that could protect the interests of Balochistan. Such a group could have provided valuable inputs for decisions being made ostensibly in the interests of the people.[19] A prime example of how the Baloch are being ignored is the fact that the chairman of the parliamentary committee for CPEC is a Punjabi senator, Mushahid Hussain, whereas the appointment of a Baloch would have done much to assuage the feelings of the Baloch.[20]

Addressing a meeting in Quetta in September 2015, Balochistan National Party (BNP) president and former chief minister Sardar Akhtar Mengal said: 'We have researched and thoroughly read every agreement inked in recent years regarding "Gwadar–Kashgar Economic Corridor", but found nothing for Balochistan. All they are doing is build a modern Punjab and equip it with all facilities and boost its economy.'[21] In another interview in May 2017 Mengal said, 'Take my word for it, CPEC will turn out to be no different than the East India Company. The Chinese, with their huge population and all, will make Pakistan look not like a country but China Town.'[22]

In an interview to *The Friday Times* in March 2015, the veteran Baloch nationalist Mir Mohammad Ali Talpur summed up the Baloch position on the CPEC: 'They [Punjab] do not understand the Baloch people's sentiments. If the prosperity of Pakistan is essential, so are the sentiments of the people who live there. We are not against prosperity. We are against exploitation. We want our rights. Development will follow.'[23]

The worst of Baloch fears were confirmed in a report of the Federation of Pakistan Chambers of Commerce and Industry (FPCCI). It stated that given the current rate of influx of Chinese nationals into Balochistan, the local population of the area will be outnumbered by 2048. The report acknowledged that the most important apprehension of the people of Balochistan relates to change in demography. Extrapolating from the existing rate of migration from China at 0.44 persons per thousand and Baloch rate of population growth, the report predicted that the share of the Chinese in Balochistan's population would increase with the completion of the CPEC, and by 2048 Chinese population could be greater than that of Pakistanis.[24]

Likewise during a seminar on the CPEC in Lahore, the point-person for the project in the Nawaz Sharif government, Ahsan Iqbal, categorically disclosed that without China's permission no agreement on the CPEC, including Gwadar, could be made public or even shared with the government of Balochistan. This statement amply demonstrated what lay in store for Balochistan.[25]

Meanwhile, some of the CPEC projects, including two in Balochistan, have run into trouble since China has stopped their funding at the time of writing. These include the Dera Ismail Khan–Zhob Road and Khuzdar–Basima Road. Both projects were portrayed as proof by the federal government that CPEC would benefit Balochistan. However, funding for these projects has been frozen until Beijing shares its new set of financing guidelines.

In the same context a seven-member delegation of senators, including four from Balochistan, visited China in the first week of December 2017: Dr Jehanzeb Jamaldini from the Balochistan National Party (BNP), Kabir Muhammad Shahi from the National Party (NP), Daud Achakzai from the Awami National Party (ANP) and Usman Kakar from Pashtunkhwa Milli Awami Party (PkMAP). Out of these four, Kabir Muhammad Shahi and Usman Kakar belonged to the parties that were in the Government of Balochistan as well as at the Centre. On return, all these senators unequivocally stated that Balochistan was not going to get anything from the CPEC. It was significant that both the government and opposition in Balochistan were in agreement that the impoverished province would not benefit from the CPEC.[26]

Dr Jehanzeb Jamaldini said: 'It has been four years since the CPEC agreement was signed and even now the people of Gwadar don't have drinking water. It's quite clear that no tangible efforts have been made to resolve this issue.' Senator Kabir Muhammad Shahi said that all highway construction projects in Balochistan that were being given the name of CPEC were originally commenced during the Musharraf era and they were routine projects. He lamented that he did not have any clue about the CPEC agreements despite being a member of the parliamentary committee on CPEC. 'Why should I praise CPEC when I am not sure what the agreements entail for Balochistan?'[27]

In fact, in December 2018 even the Balochistan Chief Minister Jam Kamal Khan said, while chairing a meeting to review the progress of development projects under CPEC, that the provincial government was still 'blind' as to what exactly existed in the CPEC.[28] As the *Dawn* put it, there was outrage in the Balochistan cabinet after it was revealed in a briefing of CPEC projects that no progress has been made in any projects outside Gwadar and that the overall portfolio of CPEC projects in the province was meagre. What was of special concern was that no progress has been made on projects that would connect the western route, a goal that was supposed to bring most benefits to the economy and was supposed to be the government's top priority.[29]

Security Issues

The surge in economic activity has attracted new threats in a province that already has myriad security challenges. Apart from the Baloch insurgency, Balochistan has seen the rise of sectarian and Islamist militancy. With the expansion of the Chinese footprint in Pakistan where there are over 30,000 Chinese working,[30] pre-existing threats could fuse with new strands of militancy to create an even greater threat. As the *Dawn* put it: 'There is no realistic scenario in which Pakistan can wage a full-scale war against all those threats at the same time in the same province.'[31]

Security issues came to be highlighted from about 2004 when Chinese engineers and workers started being directly attacked. Three

Chinese engineers were killed and nine injured in a car bomb blast in Gwadar in May 2004. The next month there were four serial blasts in the town but no casualties. A month later, three 'home-made' bombs exploded in the city, once again without causing any damage or casualty except for creating a sense of insecurity. A little later, three Chinese engineers were killed and eleven people, including two Pakistanis, were injured in Gwadar.[32] In 2005 there were two sets of multiple bomb explosions within days of one another. Once again, there were no casualties or damage. In 2006 three Chinese engineers were shot dead in an ambush in Hub, Balochistan. In 2010 Chinese engineers had a narrow escape when there was a rocket attack from a boat off the coast on the Pearl Continental Hotel in Gwadar, where they were staying.[33] In 2013 several tankers carrying oil for Saindak project were attacked and partially damaged at Jorkain area of Noshki Balochistan. The tankers were on their way to supply oil for electricity generators and other machinery at Saindak gold and copper project in Chagai.[34] In 2016 the Chinese government said it was 'highly concerned' after Allah Nazar Baloch, leader of the Balochistan Liberation Front (BLF), threatened to target CPEC projects and the several thousand Chinese nationals working on them.

On 11 August 2018 a bus carrying eighteen Chinese engineers escorted by Frontier Corps troops to the Dalbandin airport from the Saindak copper and gold mines was attacked on the Quetta–Taftan Highway by a suicide bomber. This was perhaps the first suicide attack by a Baloch nationalist. He tried to drive his explosives-laden vehicle into the bus. As a result, six persons including three Chinese engineers, two FC soldiers and the bus driver were injured. The Baloch Liberation Army (BLA) claimed responsibility saying it was carried out '… to warn China to vacate Balochistan and stop plundering its resources'. Jiand Baloch, a 'spokesperson' for BLA, stated, 'We targeted this bus which was carrying Chinese engineers. We attacked them because they are extracting gold from our region, we won't allow it.' In a statement issued on Twitter the militant group identified the suicide bomber as Rehan Baloch, the elder son of BLA's 'senior commander' Aslam Baloch. In his pre-recorded message, Rehan Baloch stated, 'Through this act, I want to make China and its people realize [that] whosoever will try to meddle in Baloch issues without Baloch nation's consent will face the wrath of Baloch nation.'[35] In a significant development, different nationalist Baloch leaders and groups endorsed the suicide attack on the convoy of Chinese engineers.

On 23 November 2018 militants of the Baloch Liberation Army (BLA) attacked the Chinese consulate in Karachi. In the ensuing shoot-out, four people were killed—two policemen and two civilians. No Chinese nationals were hurt in the attack. The three attackers were also killed. The BLA later claimed responsibility for the attack in a tweet that included a photo of three attackers identified as Azal Khan Baloch, Razik Baloch and Rais Baloch.

The attack was the first time the Baloch insurgents directly attacked the Chinese diplomatic mission. It showed that the BLA had expanded its operations from Balochistan to Karachi and, most significantly, it used suicide-bombing methods for the operation. As important as this indicator was the potential that the unresolved conflict in Balochistan could have in causing tensions between China and Pakistan in case of additional attacks on Chinese interests.[36]

On 14 December 2018, less than a month after the attack on the Chinese consulate in Karachi, there was a joint attack by the three Baloch armed groups, the BLA, the Baloch Liberation Front and the Baloch Republican Guards, in Turbat district bordering Iran. At least six personnel of the Frontier Corps were killed. This attack in a mountainous region bordering Iran created tensions between the two countries.[37]

The Chinese are clearly aware of the dangers to their interests posed by the restiveness among the Baloch who have made no bones about targeting the Chinese. According to a report titled 'China woos Pakistan militants to secure Belt and Road projects', published on 19 February 2018, the *Financial Times* claimed that China had been in contact with 'Pakistani tribal separatists' for more than five years. The objective of the talks was to protect its investments in the China–Pakistan Economic Corridor (CPEC). The report cited three unnamed persons who had knowledge of these talks.[38] Some support for the report was available from a statement of the Chinese ambassador to Pakistan Yao Jing who claimed in an interview to BBC Urdu on 2 February 2018 that the Baloch militant organizations were no longer a threat to the CPEC.[39]

On 22 February 2018, however, China rejected reports that it has been engaged in a dialogue with Baloch separatists to secure the CPEC project. China's foreign ministry spokesperson when asked about such reports asserted, 'I have never heard of such things as you mentioned.'[40] On 23 February 2018 Pakistan also denied the reports that China was holding talks with Baloch insurgents to ensure the security of CPEC projects. According to the official spokesman, China was in 'direct contact' with Pakistan and 'did not need to discuss security with Baloch leaders'.[41] Likewise, Sher Muhammad Bugti, a representative of a separatist group the Baloch Republican Party, also denied having any negotiations with China.[42]

Nevertheless, what the *Financial Times* report did underline is the growing scepticism of the Chinese in Pakistan's ability to handle the Balochistan insurgency, prompting them to undertake a direct outreach to the separatists. 'This clearly reflects a weakness of the Pakistani government in bringing the Baloch to the negotiation table,' writes Malik Siraj Akbar. He also makes the important point that the Chinese interest is primarily in the region around the Gwadar port. Here, the only group that has substantial influence is the Baloch Liberation Front led by Dr Allah Nazar Baloch.[43]

However, it wasn't only in Balochistan that Chinese engineers and civilians were being targeted. They were attacked in different parts of Pakistan, which made the security of Chinese citizens one of the primary concerns of the Chinese government in their negotiations with Pakistani authorities. On 9 October 2004 two Chinese engineers were kidnapped while working at the Gomal Zam dam project in the South Waziristan Agency where a large-scale Pakistani military operation was underway against al-Qaeda fighters. The kidnapping led to a rescue operation that left one of the engineers dead, while the mastermind, former Guantanamo Bay inmate Abdullah Mehsud, remained at large. While Beijing vowed that such incidents will not deter it from engaging in development projects, work on the dam project was suspended.

In May 2016 a low-intensity bomb injured a Chinese engineer in Karachi. The Sindhudesh Revolutionary Party claimed responsibility and, in a pamphlet recovered from the blast site denounced CPEC as an 'anti-Sindh project'. It also accused China of 'looting Sindh's resources'. In February 2018 a forty-six-year-old Chinese executive was killed in

Karachi after an unknown gunman fired on his car. He worked for Cosco Shipping Lines Pakistan, a company unconnected with CPEC.[44]

Groups like Tehreek-e-Taliban Pakistan (TTP), al-Qaeda and IS have all threatened to target Chinese nationals as a warning to China over its treatment of Muslims. A TTP faction claimed responsibility in March 2012 for the killing of a Chinese woman in Peshawar in retaliation for China's killing of Uighur Muslims in Xinjiang.[45] In a video released in March 2017 IS vowed to '… shed blood like rivers' in attacks on Chinese nationals in order to avenge Beijing's treatment of Uighurs. It followed up on that threat by kidnapping two Chinese language teachers from the supposedly secure zone in Quetta on 24 May 2017. They were subsequently killed.

The incident raised disturbing questions since it came a week after the security forces had conducted an operation against the IS–Lashkar-e-Jhangvi nexus in Splinji, Mastung, as part of Operation Raddul Fasaad. According to reports, several top commanders of the IS from different parts of the country, who had assembled in the Mastung area, were killed. This revealed the unpleasant truth that the IS was not a peripheral threat, and that the militancy in Balochistan was not limited to the nationalists alone.[46] As China steps up its repressive policies in Xinjiang, more attacks on its nationals and projects in Pakistan are possible.

In October 2017 the Chinese embassy in Pakistan requested additional security for its ambassador in the wake of information that he was likely to be attacked. The embassy named one Abdul Wali belonging to the banned East Turkestan Independence Movement (ETIM), an extremist group operating in Xinjiang.[47] For the ETIM, it may be easier to target Chinese interests in Pakistan than in Xinjiang where security is very tight. In December 2017 the Chinese embassy in Islamabad warned its citizens in Pakistan to be on alert after receiving intelligence reports about a 'series of terror attacks' targeting the Chinese. It urged its citizens to stay inside and avoid crowded places.[48]

In the light of the growing threat, Pakistan announced the setting up of a 12,000-strong force called 'Special Security Division (SSD)', comprising both civilian and military personnel which would be led by an officer of the rank of a Lt. General. The mandate of the force was to provide protection to the entire CPEC. The security plan was later expanded by making it a four-layered plan in which some 32,000 security personnel (including the SSD) would guard the Chinese working in different capacities on projects in Pakistan. The force would include over 500 Chinese security personnel as well. On a visit to the SSD on 19 February 2016, former army chief Gen. Raheel Sharif stated, 'The military is ready to pay any price to turn this ambitious project into reality.'[49]

An ominous aspect of this four-layered plan was the repercussion it would have on residents of Gwadar, whose worst fears regarding Chinese involvement in the port project could well be coming true. The plan involves issuing of residence cards to local inhabitants, and all outsiders coming into the city would be registered at entry points with records of outsiders maintained and updated regularly. The Chinese are apparently pushing for a sixty-five-mile fence around the whole town, with a special permit required for anyone—including locals—to enter, according to Pakistani and Chinese officials. Gwadar, in effect, would become a separate enclave limited for the Chinese with special rules and regulations. The Pakistanis, however, believe they can provide sufficient security without a fence.[50]

Apart from the Special Security Division, the Pakistan Navy has allocated a special marine battalion at the Gwadar port for surveillance. These marines will safeguard sea links used for communication and provide protection to ships entering and exiting the port in the near future.[51]

The *Guardian* quoted Kaiser Bengali, former economic adviser to the Balochistan chief minister, saying that the notion that the two special brigades formed by the army will be enough to protect road traffic was 'laughable'. 'If every convoy of trucks has to be accompanied by half a dozen tanks, armoured carriers and helicopters, the cost is going to be exorbitant.' In an interview, the noted economist made the following points. (i) Instead of a game-changer, CPEC may signify a game over. 'I see the Corridor creating threats for local businesses and fear that it won't be a win-win situation for both countries.' (ii) 'Gwadar cannot become Dubai. It is a seaport built for the purpose of re-exporting Chinese products brought into Pakistan via a land route. I think it is not possible to establish industrial zones and a mega city in Gwadar because there is no water available to support this development.'[52]

Commenting on CPEC, former chief minister Dr Malik said that it would not be a game-changer for the people of Balochistan: 'There is no hope for changing their destiny.' He said that it was now known that 91 per cent of CPEC profit would be siphoned off to China and the remaining 9 per cent would be taken away by the federal government, with Balochistan remaining empty-handed.[53]

It is obvious that the way CPEC has been planned and implemented, it has not even tried to address the sense of deprivation faced by the people of Balochistan. Since they are neither participants of the CPEC process nor its beneficiaries, a feeling of resentment and frustration among the Baloch is natural. Worse, while articulating their grievances regarding CPEC, the Baloch find that the project has been raised to the level of an ideological issue and anybody who asks for a reconsideration of any of its parts or even asks for a clarification of one point or another is branded as a subversive element.[54]

Taking note of the Baloch scepticism over the CPEC, the army chief Gen. Qamar Bajwa proposed in January 2017 that a 'people-centric approach based on local ownership' should be adopted as far as securing the 'ongoing developmental activity and future trade' in Balochistan under CPEC is concerned. He also acknowledged that the province has been 'unfortunately' neglected in the past for a host of reasons but said that was not the case anymore. Given that the army has had a free run of state policies in Balochistan, Bajwa's statement was clearly a frank acknowledgement of the army's failures.[55]

The *Daily Times* sounded an ominous warning that 'CPEC will be a failure if it fails to accommodate all concerned parties, especially Gwadar's local population. The project cannot be executed successfully if the local populace views it with mistrust.'[56]

V

RELENTLESS
PERSECUTION

13

Human Rights Violations

THE MOST DISTRESSING ASPECT OF the situation in Balochistan is the sharp increase in the number of human rights (HR) violations. While both sides have been guilty of it, it is the army that has been guilty of violating human rights systematically as an instrument of policy to crush the insurgency. This is borne out by reports of human rights organizations, think tanks as well as journalists who have had access to the region.

There are four impediments in discussing the HR violations. First, as the Human Rights Commission of Pakistan noted, 'The human rights abuses in the province receive only limited attention as certain areas remain virtually inaccessible to the national media and civil society, while many parts of the rest of the province are poorly connected to major cities elsewhere in Pakistan. Human rights violations are, therefore, poorly documented and patchily reported.'[1] The media has been denied access even to the internally displaced people in the Bugti area where hundreds are believed to have died due to inadequate medical facilities and poor sanitation.

Second is the lack of serious international attention. As noted by Declan Walsh, the Baloch insurgency that has gone on intermittently for decades is often called Pakistan's Dirty War, because of the rising numbers of people who have disappeared or have been killed on both sides. But it has received little attention internationally, in part because most eyes are turned toward the fight against the Taliban and al-Qaeda in Pakistan's north-western tribal areas.[2] The government was able to take '... advantage of the more permissive attitude towards human rights violations by the international coalition fighting the "war on terror" to subject its political opponents, including Sindhi and Baloch nationalists, to enforced disappearance'.[3]

Third, as Walsh notes, the forces of law and order are curiously indifferent to the plight of the dead men. Not a single perpetrator has been arrested or prosecuted; in fact, police investigators openly admit they are not even looking for anyone. As he puts it: 'The stunning lack of interest in Pakistan's greatest murder mystery in decades becomes more understandable, however, when it emerges that the prime suspect is not some shady gang of sadistic serial killers, but the country's powerful military and its unaccountable intelligence men.'[4]

Fourth, the statistics relating to human rights violations vary given the enormous difficulties in documenting them. Despite this, the common link in these violations is the crude attempt at suppressing the growing independence movement in Balochistan.

In spite of these constraints and Pakistan's efforts to keep its brutality in Balochistan under wraps, it has failed to do so due to the determination of the human rights organizations and of the Baloch to bring to light what the army is doing to the people.

Casualty Figures

According to the South Asia Terrorism Portal (SATP) database, the province has recorded at least 6,726 fatalities since 2004 (data till 29 April 2018) which included 4,055 civilians. Of these, at least 1,167 have been attributable to one or the other terrorist/insurgent outfits. Of these, 396 civilian killings (226 in the south and 170 in the north) have been claimed by Baloch separatist formations, while Islamist and sectarian extremist formations—primarily LeJ, TTP and Ahrar-ul-Hind (Liberators of India)—claimed responsibility for another 771 civilian killings, 688 in the north (mostly in and around Quetta) and eighty-three in the south. The remaining 2,888 civilian fatalities—1,696 in the south and 1,192 in the north—remain 'unattributed'. A large proportion of the 'unattributed' fatalities, particularly in the southern region, are believed to be the result of enforced disappearances carried out by state agencies, or by their proxies, prominently including the

Tehreek-e-Nafaz-e-Aman, Balochistan (TNAB, Movement for the Restoration of Peace, Balochistan). The large number of unattributed civilian fatalities is a clear indication that strengthens the widespread belief of the security agencies indulging in kill-and-dump operations against local Baloch dissidents.[5]

According to the Federal Ministry of Human Rights, at least 936 dead bodies of 'disappeared' persons, often mutilated and bearing the signs of torture, were found in Balochistan since 2011. Figures obtained from the Federal Ministry of Human Rights by the BBC Urdu on 30 December 2016 pointed to large-scale extra-judicial killings by state agencies and their proxies. Most of the bodies were dumped in Quetta, Kalat, Khuzdar and Makran—areas where the separatist insurgency has its roots.[6]

In 2015 the provincial government revealed that the bodies of 800 people linked to the insurgency were recovered between 2011 and 2014.[7] It also estimated 950 people were still missing, although some claims go as high as 14,000 according to a 2013 report by a UN fact-finding team.[8]

Human Rights Commission of Pakistan (HRCP)

The HRCP report titled 'Conflict in Balochistan: HRCP fact-finding missions, December 2005–January 2006' made the following points:

(i)   There were widespread instances of disappearances, of torture inflicted on people held in custody and on those fleeing from their house and hearth in fear:

(ii)   The security forces and decision-makers were completely unaccountable for the gross human rights violations in the province;

(iii)   The present situation in parts of Balochistan, including Dera Bugti and Kahan, 'can be described as armed conflict' where non-combatants have been killed and where the use of force was disproportionate, excessive and employed indiscriminately;

(iv)   There was a sharp rise in disappearances of those suspected of nationalist sympathies or links with the militants. Baloch dissidents have been the main victims of what the HRCP secretary-general described as a 'barbaric and inhuman practice';[9]

(v) There were alarming accounts of summary executions, some allegedly carried out by paramilitary forces. HRCP received credible evidence that showed such killings had indeed taken place; and

(vi) Despite constraints in documentation, there was a consistent pattern of abuse of human rights in the province.[10]

Amnesty International

In its 2008 report 'Denying the Undeniable' the Amnesty International (AI) put its finger on the problem of documentation of human rights violations.[11] According to it, '... enforced disappearances were characterized by an official shroud of secrecy' making it difficult to establish just how many people the government had abducted. Relatives, too, remained silent about the disappearance for fear of reprisals on the 'disappeared', or themselves.[12] Another difficulty was that some who were declared released were, in fact, not released while others were subjected to renewed enforced disappearance. The report underlined that hundreds of people alleged to be linked to terrorist activities were arbitrarily detained, '... denied access to lawyers, families and courts, and held in undeclared places of detention run by Pakistan's intelligence agencies, with the government concealing their fate or whereabouts'.

The AI report also highlighted, with examples, some of the tactics used by the army to conceal enforced disappearances. These included the failure to obey judicial directions, concealing the identity of detaining authorities, hiding the detained, silencing victims of enforced disappearance by threatening the relatives of the disappeared.

Reports by Journalists

In an article in the *Guardian*, Declan Walsh wrote: 'The bodies surface quietly, like corks bobbing up in the dark. They come in twos and threes, a few times a week, dumped on desolate mountains or empty city roads, bearing the scars of great cruelty. Arms and legs are snapped; faces are bruised and swollen. Flesh is sliced with knives or punctured with drills; genitals are singed with electric prods. In some cases the bodies are unrecognizable, sprinkled with lime or chewed by wild animals. All have a gunshot wound in the head.' According to him, this was 'Pakistan's dirty little war'. The victims, men between twenty and forty years, were nationalist politicians, students, shopkeepers and labourers. In several cases they were kidnapped in broad daylight by a combination of uniformed soldiers and plain-clothes intelligence men.[13]

Writes human rights activist Zohra Yusuf, 'The victims are primarily political activists and students, as well as the intelligentsia and religious minorities. Almost all the dead bodies found are of victims of enforced disappearance, mostly idealistic young political activists fighting for Baloch rights, not necessarily for separatism.[14]

Voice of Baloch Missing Persons (VBMP)

Jalil Reki Baloch was abducted in February 2009 from Quetta and his dead body turned up two years later. This incident compelled Jalil's seventy-year-old father Abdul Qadeer Reki to rally other families whose sons had gone 'missing' to form an organization—the Voice of the Baloch Missing Persons (VBMP). The VBMP comprises the family members of abducted Baloch activists, and its objective is to collect the data of all abducted and extra-judicially killed Baloch persons. They stormed into the limelight when led by Qadeer—also called Mama—fifteen of them started on a long march from Quetta to Karachi and from Karachi to Islamabad in October 2013 to protest against and draw attention to the issue of enforced disappearances and extra-judicial killings in Balochistan that had reached alarming proportions.[15] The long march certainly caught the imagination of the population in Sindh and south Punjab. The reaction in central and northern Punjab, the Punjabi heartland as it were, was far more restrained if not hostile.[16]

Even prior to the long march, the activities of the VBMP had succeeded in attracting international attention. A team of UN Working Group on Enforced and Involuntary Disappearances (WGEID) visited Pakistan and Balochistan in September 2012. This was the first ever visit of a high-level UN mission to Balochistan in connections with the issue of missing persons. They did detailed interviews with leaders of VBMP and families of the victims.[17]

Interestingly, the VBMP does not ask for the release of the missing persons. Instead, they want the authorities to try them in court and punish them if guilty. Their grouse is that it is precisely this that the authorities do not do, and they have not been able to get justice from any quarter in Pakistan, including the judiciary.

According to the group, there have been more than 2,825 documented cases of enforced disappearances of Baloch activists since 2005. In January 2016 Nasrullah Baloch, chairman of the VMBP, said that approximately 463 people had forcefully disappeared while 157 mutilated bodies were found from Balochistan in 2015. He, however, added that the number of enforced disappearances in 2015 could be higher as the government had recently admitted to having arrested 9,000 people under National Action Plan from Balochistan last year. In 2014, while the government claimed that 164 mutilated bodies were found, the VBMP held that 435 people were abducted and 455 mutilated bodies were found from Balochistan in 2014.[18]

According to VMBP, Pakistani security forces had abducted 480, killed twenty-six persons including women and children, and torched at least 500 properties in more than 100 offensives just in March 2017. Only thirty persons among those abducted had been released. On 8 July 2017, three civilians were killed and 265 were abducted by the army from Dera Bugti and Mastung. The army also reportedly 'stole' civilian property and valuables, including 300 camels.[19] None of the abducted persons were presented before any court or given the right to defend themselves. Balochistan's Dasht, Tump, Mand, Dera Bugti, Kohlu, Quetta and Makran regions have been the most affected areas, where Pakistani military carried out attacks and offensives against Baloch civilians. Leaders of the VBMP say more than 18,000 Baloch men have been abducted by security agencies since the killing of prominent Baloch leader Nawab Akbar Bugti in August 2006. After cities in Balochistan, Karachi is fast becoming a dumping ground for bodies of missing Baloch persons.[20]

Qadeer was stopped at Karachi airport in March 2015 from leaving Pakistan for a talk in New York organized by expatriate Pakistanis on the situation in Balochistan, saying he was on the Exit Control List (ECL). The ECL is a roster of people barred by the government from leaving the country. Pakistani government officials confirmed that Qadeer Baloch was prevented from boarding the flight saying that he was on the ECL.[21]

Enforced Disappearances

The most harrowing of all the human rights violations in Balochistan are enforced disappearances. It has become an explosive issue given that more people have gone missing in the province than in any other part of Pakistan.

The HRCP has ample evidence to support the allegations of the families of victims that the perpetrators of enforced disappearances are intelligence agencies and security forces. Senior officials and politicians in authority have also conceded this. A HRCP mission learnt that in several incidents even public figures in power were unable to secure relief or assurances that such incidents will stop. These public figures cited a number of incidents of disappearances in which, on the basis of credible evidence, they approached the intelligence agencies and the security forces only to be met with a bland denial.[22] The mission also received information about arbitrary arrests and reports of endemic torture at unauthorized cells whose existence was confirmed by public figures.

The consequences of such atrocities were well articulated by the veteran Baloch leader, Attaullah Mengal, when he told Nawaz Sharif in December 2011: 'Baloch youth don't want such a Pakistan in which they receive mutilated bodies of their compatriots. It is for them to decide [about their future], because they are being systematically eliminated and forced to seek refuge in the mountains.' An ominous note followed: 'But if atrocities continue, the Baloch will never accept a united Pakistan.' Sharif termed Attaullah Mengal's concerns legitimate, conceding that atrocities were being committed in Balochistan. He said his party would also talk to Baloch youth. About the assassination of Akbar Bugti, Nawaz Sharif said the 'killers must be called to account'.[23]

The HRCP started noticing this issue in 2004 when the number of missing persons from Balochistan rose sharply. By 2006, Balochistan accounted for an overwhelming majority of persons reported missing in a year in Pakistan. In the cases of enforced disappearance brought before it, the mission found that there were credible allegations and material on record to substantiate the involvement of state security forces, particularly the Frontier Corps.[24]

While first information reports (FIRs) had been registered with the local police in many cases of enforced disappearance, there had been no efforts by the police to investigate them. Quite likely since the involvement of the state security agencies, particularly the FC, was well known, the police did not take any action. According to the HRCP, 'This indicated that there was either an unstated policy not to interfere with actions of the FC or the civil law enforcement authorities themselves feared the military and paramilitary forces.'[25]

In one particular case a young man named Abid Saleem was picked up from Chitkar Bazaar in Panjgur on 23 January 2011, together with five other men who had no connection with him. Everyone present in that part of the bazaar saw uniformed FC personnel together with plain-clothes men take the boys into custody. An FIR was registered on 26 January 2011 with Panjgur Police Station and FC personnel were listed for the disappearance. Instead of making any efforts to recover the disappeared persons, the police did not even ask any questions of the FC personnel. At least one of the persons picked up along with Abid Saleem was found alive. He had been severely tortured, shot and thrown by the roadside along with the dead body of another person who had disappeared with him on 23 January. His tormentors had apparently thought that he too had died after being shot in the throat. There had been no investigation in this case by the police. No medical records were collected even though the survivor did receive medical treatment.[26]

The HRCP Report 2009 made the important point that while in the rest of the country most of the missing persons were picked up due to involvement in terrorism, in Balochistan many belonged to areas where no terrorist activity was reported. The inescapable conclusion, according to it, was that a large number of Balochistan's missing persons were targeted for their legitimate political activities/opinions.[27] The perception had also gained ground that only ethnic Baloch were being targeted in incidents of enforced disappearance and none of the disappeared was a 'settler'.[28]

The situation had become so bad and attracted such international opprobrium that Pakistan was compelled to allow a UN mission in September 2012. The mission spent ten days in Balochistan meeting with government officials and private citizens to investigate the fate of disappeared persons in Balochistan. Some of the witnesses who met with the delegation told its members that they had been 'threatened or intimidated'.[29] However, neither the Inter-Services Intelligence (ISI) nor the Frontier Corps that are blamed for most of the disappearances met the delegation.[30] The UN mission did succeed in drawing international attention to the issue of enforced disappearances. The United States and the United Kingdom also expressed concerns over the human rights situation in Balochistan during the nineteenth session of the United Nations Human Rights Council.[31]

The Legal Situation

Enforced disappearance is defined in Article 2 of the International Convention for the Protection of All Persons from Enforced Disappearance, which the UN General Assembly adopted in December 2006, as: '... the arrest, detention, abduction, or any other form of deprivation of liberty by agents of the state or by persons or groups of persons acting with the authorization, support, or acquiescence of the state, followed by a refusal to acknowledge the deprivation of liberty or by concealment of the fate or whereabouts of the disappeared person, which place such a person outside the protection of the law.'[32]

Part II of the Constitution of Pakistan dealing with Fundamental Rights and Principles of Policy states: '(1) No person shall be detained in custody without being informed, as soon as may be, of the grounds for such arrest, nor shall he be denied the right to consult and be defended by a legal practitioner of his choice. (2) Every person who is arrested and detained in custody shall be produced before a magistrate within a period of twenty-four hours of such arrest to the court of the nearest magistrate, and no such person shall be detained in custody beyond the said period without the authority of a magistrate.' There are provisions for preventive detention but here too: 'No such law shall authorize the detention of a person for a period exceeding three months,' unless approved by the appropriate Review Board.[33] All these constitutional guarantees have been systematically and repeatedly abused by the state.

For example, Munir Mengal, director of a proposed Baloch television channel, was illegally detained in April 2006. He was released in September 2007 on orders of the Balochistan High Court after he was exonerated of all charges. However, according to his family, he was again detained by the intelligence agencies at an unknown location.[34]

Despite undeniable evidence of 'disappearances', successive governments have consistently denied subjecting anyone to enforced disappearance or knowing anything of their fate or whereabouts. In September and December 2006, after Amnesty International released reports documenting dozens of cases of enforced disappearances, President Musharraf responded by stating: 'I don't even want to reply to that; it is nonsense, I don't believe it, I don't trust it.' He added that; 700 people had been detained but that all were accounted for.[35] In March 2007 President Musharraf asserted that the allegation that hundreds of persons had disappeared in the custody of intelligence agencies had 'absolutely no basis' but that these individuals had been recruited or lured by 'jihadi groups' to fight for their 'misplaced causes': 'I am deadly sure that the missing persons are in the control of militant organizations,' he said.[36]

The security forces when confronted by the Supreme Court and the provincial high courts about enforced disappearances have resorted to a variety of falsehoods to avoid being exposed. Not surprisingly, the refusal of the state to meaningfully and truthfully respond to Supreme Court directions has stalled the tracing of persons subjected to enforced disappearance in Pakistan. More wide-ranging damage is being done by giving the intelligence agencies immunity to commit such grave human rights violations and collaborating in their cover-up. The state has also sent a dangerous signal that it condones the impunity of committing, condoning or concealing such human rights violations.[37]

In July 2011 the Human Rights Watch published a report named 'We Can Torture, Kill, or Keep You for Years—Enforced Disappearances by Pakistan Security Forces in Balochistan'. It starts with a summary that gives the account of the person who witnessed the disappearance of Abdul Nasir in June 2010: 'Even if the president or chief justice tells us to release you, we won't. We can torture you, or kill you, or keep you for years at our will. It is only the army chief and the [intelligence] chief that we obey.'[38]

During consultations with the families of the disappeared people in Quetta, the HRCP found that families of missing persons living in remote areas, and in not so remote areas such as Kalat, did not have the means to register their complaints; most did not know how to access redressal channels and families were unaware of the cases in courts.[39] As a result, Balochistan today has the dubious distinction of being the world capital of enforced disappearances where more than 2,000 journalists, singers, teachers and lawyers have been forcibly abducted, tortured, killed and dumped since 2009—in just five years as many as in Chile during the reign of Augusto Pinochet. In 2014 alone, as many as 455 people, who were forcibly abducted, were tortured and killed by the Pakistani security forces and intelligence services, and their bodies dumped, according to Nasrullah Baloch, chairman of the VBMP.[40]

Sabeen Mehmud

During a discussion titled 'Un-Silencing Balochistan (Take 2)' in Karachi on 24 April 2015 organized by Sabeen Mahmud, a prominent Pakistani women's rights activist, Mama Qadeer noted, 'Today when I am addressing this conference, the number of missing persons from Balochistan is over 21,000. This is the figure for 2014. We are writing up the figures for 2015 and [will] release them every six months together. So until 2014, over 21,000 missing persons and over 6,000 tortured bodies have also been found. We knocked on every door for the missing person's issue.'[41]

Sabeen Mahmud had organized the discussion after a planned talk by Mama Qadeer at the Lahore University of Management Sciences (LUMS) was abruptly cancelled. The university said this was 'on orders from the government'. Some faculty members said the order came from the military's Inter-Services Intelligence (ISI). The government and the military declined to comment.

Sabeen Mahmud was to pay with her life that very night for organizing such a discussion at her café 'The Second Floor'. She was shot dead by two 'unknown' assailants. The provocation clearly was her temerity of going ahead with the discussion after LUMS had cancelled the same talk. The attack on Sabeen Mahmud for bringing the Baloch plight into the limelight was no aberration. Exactly a year ago, top Pakistani journalist Hamid Mir barely returned from the brink of death after he was attacked on 19 April 2014, soon after he left Karachi's Jinnah International Airport on the way to his Jang group-owned Geo

TV's office to interview Mama Qadeer. Mir alleged that elements of
the ISI were behind the attack. The link with his interview of Mama
Qadeer Baloch was obvious. The treatment of journalists and civil
society activists who dared speak out on the situation in Balochistan
was clear evidence of the government being rattled.

Helplessness of Civilian Governments

The PPP government that came to power in the province in 2008 as
well as the coalition PML-N government in 2013 had promised an
end to the conflict in Balochistan. But both found that the army was
unwilling to relinquish its heavy-handed strategy for Balochistan. With
both the federal and the provincial governments being helpless in the
face of the army conducting day-to-day counter-insurgency operations,
brooking no civilian control, the space for easing the human rights
situation has receded enormously.

Consequently, there has been no change. In November 2010 the
chief minister of Balochistan, Aslam Raisani, publicly accused the
security forces of abductions and extra-judicial killings. He told the
BBC that the security forces were 'definitely' guilty of some killings;
the province's top lawyer Salahuddin Mengal told the Supreme Court
that the FC was 'lifting people at will'. He resigned a week later.[42]

Dr Abdul Malik Baloch, who was Balochistan's chief minister from
2013 to December 2015, conceded that his government had failed to
overcome the issue of missing persons in the province. 'Although its
intensity has come down, the matter is still alive and this is possibly
the only area where we have failed to achieve our target,' the outgoing
chief minister said at a press conference.[43] The fact of the matter is that
the civilian politicians are powerless to restrain the military's counter-
insurgency operations.[44] In December 2013 Dr Malik acknowledged
that state agencies were responsible for 'illegal confinement' of Baloch
activists including, he believed, the secretary-general of his own
National Party that was part of Balochistan's coalition government.[45]

Selig Harrison has called these violations 'slow motion genocide',
which, unlike the humanitarian crises in Darfur and Chechnya, have not
troubled the conscience of the world yet. But as he notes, 'as casualty
figures mount, it will be harder to ignore the human costs of the Baloch

independence struggle and its political repercussions in other restive minority regions of multi-ethnic Pakistan'.[46] His conclusion was that the current revival of Baloch nationalism may pose a far greater threat to Pakistan than any of the previous insurgencies.

The dehumanizing nature of the violence is evidenced not just in the ways people are tortured—with holes drilled in the head and bodies mutilated beyond recognition—but also in the way their bodies are discarded. One note accompanying a decomposed corpse said, 'Eid gift for the Baloch'.[47]

Violations by the Nationalists

Human rights abuses are not limited to the army. The nationalists too have been responsible for violations including targeting 'settlers'—unarmed civilians, mostly from neighbouring Punjab, many of whom have lived in Balochistan for decades. Declan Walsh, quoting government figures, wrote that 113 settlers—civil servants, shopkeepers and miners—were killed in 2010. On 21 March 2011 militants killed eleven workers in a camp of construction workers; the Baloch Liberation Front claimed responsibility.[48] According to one estimate, until 2011, around 1,200 settlers were killed in Balochistan mostly in 'hit-and-run incidents' and grenade attacks on their businesses and homes. Such killings created an atmosphere of fear and terror among the settlers and led to an exodus. Estimates vary, but between 2008 and 2011 it is believed that about 100,000 to 200,000 settlers left Balochistan for other provinces. Along with settlers, the militants also started targeting teachers, doctors and lawyers from other provinces. While Quetta still hosts a substantially large population of Punjabi and other settlers, few remain in the Baloch areas of the province. Even in Quetta, the settlers are afraid of going to the Baloch-dominated neighbourhoods.[49]

The killings have continued intermittently. Thus, on 4 May 2018, six ethnic Punjabi labourers were killed and one injured in an incident of firing in the Laijay area of Kharan District. On 31 October 2018 five construction workers of non-Baloch ethnicity were shot dead, while another three suffered injuries in an attack near Ganz, some 15 km west of Jiwani in Gwadar District, on 31 October 2018. According to official sources, the labourers were working at a China–Pakistan Economic

Corridor (CPEC)-related private housing scheme on Peshkan–Ganz road, which links Gwadar with Jiwani, when a group of unidentified assailants riding motorcycles appeared on the scene and opened fire.[50]

The *Dawn* quoted Muhammad Khalid of the Balochistan Punjabi Ittehad saying '… the militants began to target the Punjabi settlers after Nawab Bugti was taken out by the military (in August 2006). Before that there were occasional incidents in which Punjabis were targeted'. According to a Balochistan Students Organisation (BSO) activist: 'How can you expect us to let your people live in peace when our own land has been turned into a hell for us?'[51] One apparent reason for this appears to be the government's insistence on constructing new cantonments because the army, seen as an instrument of suppression, is predominantly Punjabi. Denouncing the Punjab as a 'colonial' power and the army as the 'Punjab army',[52] 'Baloch militants are now targeting Punjabi settlers,' says the International Crisis Group (ICG). In the wake of Akbar Bugti's killing '… resentment against Punjabis has reached extreme levels', said a Quetta-based journalist. 'Since Bugti's death, there is also a visible social segregation between the Baloch and the Punjabis; even in schools and universities.'[53]

Then there have been attacks on education: twenty-two schoolteachers, university lecturers and education officials have been assassinated since January 2008, causing another 200 to flee their jobs.[54]

Cases

Some representative cases are listed below.

Three local political leaders, Gul Muhammad, chairman of Baluchistan National Movement (BNM), his associate Lala Munir, and Sher Muhammad Bugti, a leader of the Balochistan Republican Party (BRP)—all prominent in the nationalist movement—were seized from a small legal office in Turbat in April 2009. They were handcuffed, blindfolded and hustled into a waiting pickup truck in front of their lawyer and neighbouring shopkeepers. Their bodies riddled with bullets—badly decomposed in the scorching heat—were found in a date palm grove five days later. Government officials said the men were being prosecuted for activities against the state but denied any involvement in their deaths.

People were not convinced and said that while the men supported independence, they were not involved in the armed struggle. Mir Kachkol Ali, their lawyer from whose office the three were abducted, said the killings represented a deepening of the campaign by the Pakistani military to crush the Baloch nationalist movement. 'Their tactics are not only to torture and detain, but to eliminate,' he said. After telling his story to the press, Ali was harassed by military intelligence, who warned him his life was in danger. He fled the country. 'In Pakistan, there is only rule of the jungle,' he said by phone from Lørenskog, a small Norwegian town where he got asylum. 'Our security agencies pick people up and treat them like war criminals,' he said. 'They don't even respect the dead.'[55]

There appears to be a link in these abductions with the kidnapping in February of an American citizen, John Solecki, the head of the United Nations refugee organization in the provincial capital Quetta. The abduction was carried out by a breakaway group of young radicals who wanted to draw international attention to their cause and to exchange their captive for the Baloch being held by the security services. Though Solecki was released, Baloch leaders speculate that the intelligence agencies may have killed Gul Muhammad and his colleagues to provoke the kidnappers into murdering the American, which would have branded the Baloch nationalists as terrorists.

Instead, '… the killing of these three has centralized the national movement of Balochistan', said Kachkol Ali. He and others said they had no doubt that the intelligence services were responsible. 'They were persons of the agencies,' Mr Ali said. 'They were in plain clothes, but from their hairstyles, their language, we know them.'[56]

Another case is of the credible allegations of the extra-judicial execution of a ten-year-old boy Chakar Baloch in Turbat. Four plain-clothes men accompanied by four uniformed personnel from the Frontier Corps picked him up as he was walking to Turbat market, according to eyewitnesses. Chakar Baloch's family registered a complaint about the abduction with the police in Turbat. However, apart from registering the complaint, the police did not appear to take any further steps as in practice, they have virtually no power to investigate allegations against the Frontier Corps. Three days later on 10 January, Chakar Baloch's body was recovered from Kech Kaor River, a kilometre from where he was last seen alive. According to a medical examination carried out at the District Headquarters Hospital in Turbat, Chakar Baloch's body bore torture marks and four bullet wounds to the head, chest and left arm, fired at close range.[57]

A Baluch doctor, Bari Langove, thirty-six, said he had examined a student leader, Dr Allah Nazar Baloch, in a prison ward in Quetta and found him so debilitated that he could neither walk nor talk at first. 'He was mentally exhausted and wholly unable to speak,' Dr Langove said in an interview in Quetta. 'We examined him and found he had post-traumatic stress disorder, symptoms of loss of short-term memory, insomnia, loss of appetite and energy.'[58] The victim, Allah Nazar Baloch, would go on to set up one of the most effective militant groups fighting the Pakistan Army. Speaking at a book launch, noted human rights activist I.A. Rehman said that Allah Nazar did not choose the path of rebellion: 'We forced him to it. So, if we keep treating them like we treated Bengalis, the consequences won't be any different either.'[59]

In its 2007 report the ICG mentioned that since December 2005 when military operations began, at least 84,000 people were displaced by the conflict in Dera Bugti and Kohlu districts alone. According to a UNICEF internal assessment in July-August 2006 that was leaked to the media, the displaced persons, mostly women (26,000) and children (33,000), were living in makeshift camps without adequate shelter in Jafarabad, Naseerabad, Quetta, Sibi and Bolan districts. Of the five-year-old children, 28 per cent were acutely malnourished and more than 6 per cent were in a state of 'severe acute malnourishment', with their survival dependent on receiving immediate medical attention. Over 80 per cent of deaths among those surveyed were among children under five.[60]

Mass Graves

There was a staggering rise in recoveries of tortured bodies in 2014, primarily accounted for by the discovery of three mass graves in the Totak area of Khuzdar District. Between 25 January 2014 and 2 April 2014 a total of at least 103 bodies were recovered from these graves (local sources claimed that 169 bodies were found). The bodies were too decomposed for identification.[61]

The Frontier Corps reportedly cordoned off the area surrounding the graves soon after their discovery, preventing civil society and the local community from monitoring activity at the gravesites. The Frontier Corps also prevented some relatives of enforced disappearance victims from visiting a local hospital to inspect the recovered bodies to see if they could identify their missing relatives.

14

The Judiciary

THE SUPREME COURT OF PAKISTAN started seeking explanations from the Musharraf government at the end of 2005 and made rigorous efforts to find the whereabouts of the 'missing persons'. The court summoned representatives of the government, military and intelligence agencies but they simply denied any knowledge of either the whereabouts of missing persons or the name of the detaining authority. Gen. Musharraf, on the other hand, tried to pressurize the judiciary into dropping these investigations. He even attempted to blackmail the judges. In March 2007 Musharraf ousted the chief justice of the Supreme Court Iftikhar Muhammad Chaudhry for making efforts to look into the 'missing persons' cases. Though Justice Chaudhry was reinstated and the court hearings on the 'missing persons' or 'enforced disappearances' continued, it was clear that the government was doing all it could to stop the judiciary from meddling into its affairs.

In a constitutional petition filed before the Supreme Court of Pakistan in March 2007 the HRCP submitted a verified list of 148 missing persons, the overwhelming majority from Balochistan, and asserted that the law enforcement and intelligence agencies were responsible. The petition stated that some who had disappeared but were subsequently released had told the HRCP that they were held incommunicado and physically and mentally tortured by intelligence personnel to extract confessions and other evidence against themselves, their family or friends. Some were allegedly coerced into spying for the intelligence agencies. The mistreatment was said to have included sleep deprivation, severe beatings, electric shocks and humiliations such as being stripped naked.[1]

The Supreme Court set up a commission to investigate these cases. By November 2007 about half of the persons listed as missing by HRCP had been traced. The hearings stopped in November 2007 and were revived after the chief justice was restored to his office.[2]

Initially, the commission recorded only ninety cases from Balochistan even though the number was far higher. However, gradually it started receiving new complaints. The number of cases of missing persons it was dealing with went up in 2013 to 122—many of these people had gone missing in earlier years. The figure had jumped to 265 by July 2016.[3] Even so, the VBMP held that the official figures did not reflect the actual number of missing persons—the total standing at 3,700 in their reckoning at that time. The HRCP too has questioned the Commission of Inquiry on Enforced Disappearances reports that claimed there were 2,116 unresolved cases of forcible disappearances as of 30 November 2018, saying the number was far higher.[4] This discrepancy was possibly due to relatives not reporting the disappearance of their family members.

As the Amnesty International had noted earlier, it was difficult to determine how many people the government had subjected to enforced disappearance. Many remained silent about their relatives' disappearance for fear of repercussions for the 'disappeared' or themselves. Despite a civilian government taking office after the general elections of 2008, there was very little impact on the continuing enforced disappearance and kill-and-dump policy in Balochistan.

While the Supreme Court has heard cases about the 'enforced disappearances' and formed several commissions, it has been unsuccessful in pushing the authorities to either release the victims or hold a transparent investigation into the issue.[5] The Supreme Court has also been unable to enforce its decisions. For example, it had ordered the return of more than 178,000 persons who had been displaced from the Dera Bugti area as a result of military action in 2005, but they were not allowed to return home by the Frontier Corps.[6]

The Supreme Court has repeatedly warned that it would initiate legal action against persons responsible for enforced disappearances. Fearful of being held to account, intelligence agencies sought to prevent the truth emerging by threatening relatives of the 'disappeared' to withdraw petitions and to silence people being released. Such threats may also account for the fact that only a few of the released persons have submitted affidavits to the Supreme Court. 'It is believed that families of "disappeared" persons were contacted by intelligence agencies with assurances that their relatives would be returned, if they kept quiet. Consequently, many people might have preferred silence to coming out in the open about a "disappearance" and risk upsetting a government agency holding a missing relative.'

The active connivance of the state intelligence and security agencies, including the local police, in enforced disappearances is undeniable. Whenever a court was petitioned in a missing person's case, it issued notices through the Quetta capital city police officer (CCPO), the top police officer in the provincial capital, to the security and intelligence agencies. Subsequently on the court's query, the CCPO would inform the court that no reply had been received from the agencies. In a stereotype reply the investigating officer would submit that military officials had verbally refused to join the investigation and the police lacked the capacity to force them to comply.[7]

The clout of the intelligence agencies can be gauged from an interesting case in July 2006, during a habeas corpus petition at the Sindh High Court. The defence secretary stated that the ministry had only administrative, not operational, control over its own intelligence agencies, including the Inter-Services Intelligence and Military Intelligence (MI), so could not enforce their compliance with court directions.[8]

Not surprisingly, there is growing frustration with the judiciary. In the words of Mohammad Sadiq Reesani, the then president of Balochistan Bar Association: 'In the past four years, the Balochistan Bar Association has filed more than 500 petitions in the Balochistan High Court for disappeared persons, but the judges have not taken them seriously. Baloch people have lost confidence in the legislature and judiciary and are indifferent to these institutions.'[9]

The lawyers in Balochistan told the HRCP that the courts had abdicated their responsibility and jurisdiction by failing to ensure compliance with their orders. They stated that the military and paramilitary forces ignored the orders of the court and that was responsible for the spread of 'blatant anarchy'. They said that throwing dead bodies of the disappeared persons in deserted areas was a vile method of making the habeas corpus petitions seeking their recovery infructuous. They said that the disappeared youth now 'reappeared' as dead bodies within days of their abduction.[10]

Moreover, a recurring problem is that perpetrators have been rarely caught. Even when they are, no prosecution has resulted from it. The HRCP mission noted that in fifty-two cases decided by the anti-terrorism court (ATC), all the accused had been set free due to lack of witnesses.[11]

While judicial action on the ground has been wanting, verbally the courts have repeatedly admonished the state agencies. For example, on 1 March 2012 the Supreme Court reprimanded the intelligence agencies by telling them that they were not above the law.[12] The then chief justice Iftikhar Muhammad Chaudhry also termed them as the biggest violators of the law of the country. While commenting on the role of the intelligence agencies in Balochistan he said, 'You are an arsonist. You have set Balochistan on fire.'[13]

Irked by the apathy of the government towards preventing Balochistan from sliding into chaos, the chief justice, while heading a three-judge bench of the apex court hearing a case on the volatility of the security situation in Balochistan, issued an ominous warning: if the prime minister doesn't take steps to improve the law and order, the Constitution will declare a state of emergency. He added, 'The judiciary is an organ of the state. It'll not allow violation of the Constitution. We want to save Pakistan.' He cautioned, 'Why don't we implement the Constitution before the Army imposes martial law?'[14]

According to the HRCP, while the law provides sufficient guarantees from arbitrary arrest, these have become meaningless in the absence of an effective judicial mechanism. In addition, it noted the absence of specific legal machinery—including laws and oversight bodies—for the effective accountability of law and security agencies, including penal sanctions and stopping the culture of impunity. Its lament was that superior courts in the country had not been able to uphold the principles of the rule of law.[15]

While the Supreme Court has not really been successful in making the security forces respect the law, it cannot be denied, as Frederic Grare notes, it '... has been instrumental in shedding light on the

Balochistan issue'.[16] It has held a large number of hearings on the situation and also issued orders for the implementation of the law and the Constitution.'[17] Though it has exposed its own impotency due to lack of implementation of its orders, but in the process it has underlined the total absence of accountability of the security establishment and the impunity with which they operate in Balochistan. The hearings, therefore, '... have contributed more than any other official body to informing the Pakistani press, public opinion, and the international community about the situation in Balochistan'.[18]

15

The Media

Not being dead is a victory in today's Balochistan if you are a journalist. Worse, there is little or no hope of prosecuting the killers, let along sentencing them. Most deaths of journalists go unpunished as a norm. This is the price our media has to pay for keeping the torch alive.[1]

THESE CHILLING WORDS PENNED BY analyst Raza Rumi encapsulates what the media is going through in Balochistan. Despite being Pakistan's largest province, Balochistan receives the least amount of editorial space in the mainstream national media. Editors routinely censor stories filed by Balochistan-based correspondents under the pretext of 'national security'. 'For a reporter covering Balochistan, it is often frustrating that your editors and publishers censor so much of your reporting that the government no longer needs officials to perform this job [of censorship],' says Malik Siraj Akbar.[2]

There are two major reasons for such strong censorship and the targeting of journalists and newspapers in Balochistan. For one, the army wants to put a lid on what it is doing and ensure that its brutal suppression of Baloch activists and massive violations of human rights are not reported, especially in the international media. The second is that the army wants to continue to manipulate the national narrative on Balochistan. The narrative that they have developed over the decades depicts that a small minority of 'miscreant' Baloch, by trying to seek 'provincial autonomy' and ownership of their natural resources, are playing into the hands of the 'enemies of Pakistan' and are 'foreign agents'. The linked argument is that Pakistan is in Balochistan to 'modernize' and 'develop' the Baloch. This is contrary to the Baloch narrative that sees Pakistan's policy as one of trying to plunder Balochistan's mineral wealth and treat the province as a Punjabi colony. A relatively free media would expose the fact that the army's narrative is unacceptable to the Baloch, and hence the crackdown on the media.[3]

Not surprisingly, critical media reports have been frowned upon. Scores of local journalists who exposed enforced disappearance, torture, extra-judicial executions and other human rights violations by Pakistan security forces have been threatened, assassinated or have just disappeared themselves.

As the examples of Sabeen Mahmud and Hamid Mir mentioned in a previous chapter showed, even discussing Balochistan is not tolerated. Journalists and columnists outside Balochistan writing about Balochistan face pressures, so the conditions in Balochistan can well be imagined.[4] As a result, the Pakistan media fears to openly and fully report what is really happening in Balochistan. The net effect has been blanketing of the seven-decade old Baloch tragedy.

The figures speak for themselves. Twenty-two journalists were killed in Balochistan in four years (2008–12).[5] In February 2014 the annual report of Reporters Without Borders stated that of the seven reporters killed in Pakistan in 2013, four were from Balochistan. According to an article in November 2017 quoting Khalil Ahmed, president of the Balochistan Union of Journalists, forty-three journalists have been killed in Balochistan, including by bomb blasts and targeted killings.[6]

Some examples of what the media and journalists have to endure is enumerated in the following paragraphs.

- In 2009, the FC laid siege to three newspaper offices in Quetta— *Daily Asaap, Azadi* and *Balochistan Express*. The FC personnel posted outside *Asaap*'s offices eventually forced it to stop publication.
- In November 2011 the body of Javed Naseer Rind, a *Daily Tawar* editor and columnist, was found two months after he disappeared in his home town of Hub in Baluchistan.
- In September 2012 ARY TV reporter Abdul Haq Baloch was killed as he was leaving the Khuzdar Press Club in Khuzdar, Balochistan.

Baloch was the secretary-general of the Khuzdar Press Club. In protest his fellow journalists stopped performing their professional duties and locked the Khuzdar Press Club. According to journalist Hamid Mir, the Baloch Musalah Diffa Army (BMDA or the Armed Baloch Defence) had threatened Baloch in 2011. Later, the BDMA released a hit list carrying the names of journalists, which also included that of Abdul Haq Baloch. The BDMA was reportedly being run under the patronage of a government-backed senator from Balochistan. Baloch had been killed because security forces were upset that he was working with the families of the missing Baloch on presenting cases before the Quetta bench of the Supreme Court of Pakistan.[7]

- In March 2013 Haji Abdul Razzaq Baloch, a copy editor for the *Daily Tawar*, a pro-Baloch nationalist paper acting as the voice of Baloch nationalists, was abducted in Karachi. His body was found in the Surjani Town area of Karachi on 21 August 2013. His face was mutilated and his body showed signs of strangulation and torture. The case was highlighted by the Committee to Protect Journalists (CPJ) whose Asia programme coordinator Bob Dietz said, 'The pattern of violence directed against the *Daily Tawar* and its staff is undeniable. The government must act to protect the paper and its journalists even if they voice opinions that the government resists.'

- In April 2013 a large group of unidentified men entered the Karachi bureau of the Urdu-language *Daily Tawar* (headquartered in Quetta) in Lyari, Karachi and stole computers and other equipment, burned records and archives before leaving the premises.[8]

- Razzaq Sarbazi, blogger, senior TV news producer and documentary filmmaker, escaped to the West after his life came under constant threat in Pakistan. Later he said, 'Journalism in Pakistan was like an unending nightmare for me. The price my colleagues and I paid for the written word is embedded in my memory like a deep wound.' At least four of Sarbazi's colleagues in *Daily Tawar*—Haji Razzaq Baloch, Razzaq Gul, Abdul Khaliq and Javed Naseer Rind—were killed by the Pakistani intelligence services since 2011. In his work as a journalist, he exclusively covered the war in Balochistan, including enforced disappearances. 'The issue of enforced disappearances in Balochistan is such that before daring to highlight it, a journalist has to count his days on earth,' Sarbazi said. 'I remained faithful to my pen and paid a price for it.'[9]

- Other journalists who have been killed include senior journalist Irshad Mastoi, his trainee reporter Abdul Rasool Khajak, and accountant Mohammad Younus in their office in Quetta's Jinnah Road area; Mumtaz Alam in April 2014; Abdul Qadir Hajizai, and Mohammad Afzal Khawaja, a reporter for *The Balochistan Times* and its sister publication *Zamana* in February 2014 along with his driver

- The Balochistan Union of Journalists (BUJ) has stated that 'Balochistan has become a cemetery for journalists, who perform their journalistic duties honestly and bravely.' Added a journalist, 'Our voices are unheard in mainstream national media, and we (journalists) when faced (with) threats don't get them published.' Highlighting the tragedy, Saleem Shahid, the bureau chief of a leading daily English newspaper commented, 'Those journalists in Balochistan, who have written and reported about injustices, have themselves become news.'[10]

The foreign media has also been targeted. The Al Jazeera quoted an Irish journalist saying, 'The Balochistan story is one of the most difficult to cover in Pakistan. The authorities don't like foreign journalists entering the province unaccompanied and are rarely given permission to do so. They say this is for security reasons. But they also don't want reporters snooping around in an area where so much militant activity is taking place—Taliban, sectarian and nationalist—and where the security agencies either lack control, or have historical ties with some of these groups.'[11]

Carlotta Gall, who worked for the *New York Times*, was beaten up in Quetta in 2006 by men who identified themselves as members of a special branch of the Pakistan police and who accused her of 'being in Quetta without permission'.[12] Ahmed Rashid, writer and commentator told Al Jazeera that some journalists exercise 'self-censorship' and 'tend not to report on the issue for sheer survival. And if it's not in the Pakistani media, it will hardly reach the outside world, as Western media basically relies on Pakistani sources.'[13]

As a result of the insecurity among journalists, the BBC in 2012 asked its Quetta correspondent Ayub Tarin to shift to Islamabad. A Quetta-based Voice of America (VOA) journalist Naseer Kakar left Balochistan after being threatened by security forces.[14]

Malik Siraj Akbar, a Baloch writer and the editor of an online newspaper in English on Balochistan's issues, and living in exile in the US, was quoted as saying, 'The Western media covers the whole Afghanistan–Pakistan region with a special focus on the 'war on terror,' Islamic fundamentalism and issues of religious terrorism. There is scant realization that the Baloch nationalist movement is absolutely different from the Taliban movement. In fact, the Baloch movement is the antithesis of the Taliban and Islamic movements,' said Akbar. He added that the Western media often sees the Baloch movement as a 'by-product' of the war in Afghanistan, or treats it as a domestic Pakistani issue.[15]

The HRCP has also documented the condition of the journalists. Almost every journalist that met the HRCP team complained of threats that they had received from intelligence agencies. A few of them narrated incidents in which they were picked up and then released a day later, after having been warned. Journalists complained that persons claiming to be representatives of the secret services threatened to kidnap their family members unless they succumbed to their demands.[16]

The HRCP lamented that the national media ignored Balochistan issues in its coverage. Moreover, newspapers had lost their national character and had become regional in news coverage. The news that appeared in *Jang*, Quetta, did not appear in other editions of the newspaper. There was no representation of Balochistan in the media at the national level. The incidents of enforced disappearance, targeted killings and tortured bodies found on the streets were not reported in mainstream newspapers and electronic media. In Balochistan the media was seen as biased along ethnic and sectarian lines. The Hazara-Shia community in Balochistan also complained that the media did not report the rampant target killings of their members.[17]

This was not only because of the number of journalists who had been killed in the province in connection with their work but also because media persons were forced to navigate threats emanating from multiple quarters in order to stay alive. As the *Dawn* noted, 'There are feuding tribes with shifting allegiances, extremist organizations and ruthless insurgent groups, as well as instruments of the state, including the

Frontier Corps, intelligence agencies and the military; all of which want to use the media to further their agendas.' What this means for the media is an impossible balancing act of trying to please one group without displeasing a mutually hostile group. Thus, 'journalism in Balochistan, especially where local papers are concerned—and about Balochistan in the case of national dailies—has thus been virtually reduced to a farce'. Not surprisingly, self-censorship is widespread; human rights violations go unreported; and editorializing is extinct in the local papers, since no editor can hope to express a point of view and survive.[18]

In an interview with the *Diplomat*, Hamid Mir, a famous anchor in Pakistan, shared his ordeals during a reporting trip to Khuzdar in Balochistan in March 2013 in the wake of the killing of Abdul Haq Baloch. He called this as one of the scariest days of his life. According to Mir, a deputy inspector general of police asked him why he had endangered his life by visiting Khuzdar. He then asked Mir to sit in his vehicle. No sooner had he done so, the vehicle was surrounded by a group of armed men. What was shocking was that the high-ranking police officer appeared confused and helpless and requested the militia, known as the 'death squad' in Balochistan, not to harm Mir. He was allowed to go after he agreed to give coverage to a few females, supposedly widows of soldiers. The entire episode happened close to a security check post.[19]

Fateh Jan, who now lives in a refugee camp in Germany and previously worked as a journalist in Balochistan, told the *Diplomat*, 'I have witnessed my colleagues being killed by the religious extremist group and a banned terrorist organization Baloch Musalla Difa Tanzeem (BMDT). They have killed Munir Shakir, Javed Naseer and Khan Mohammed. They all worked with me.' In a worried tone Jan added, 'I had a good career back in Pakistan with a promising bright future. But no career is worth dying for, so I left Pakistan to have a safe and sound life. Though I am living in a refugee camp in Germany, I am safe here.'[20]

The separatists too have been guilty of pressurizing the media. In 2011 a pamphlet by the Balochistan Liberation Front was delivered to several Quetta-based journalists. It warned them against becoming a part of the 'dirty game' being played by Pakistan's security forces against the Baloch freedom movement. 'Do not try to cover up the Pakistani security forces' black deeds against the Baloch. Do not also try to play down the forces' losses at the hands of the BLF,' it said.[21] In October 2017, according to media reports, the Balochistan Liberation Front and the United Balochistan Army (UBA) threatened action against local newspapers if they refused to publish their points of view. This led to the forcible shutting down of twenty-four press clubs and warning to hawkers and distributors against selling newspapers. The affected dailies were *Azadi*, *Tawar*, *Intekhab*, *Bolan*, *Jasarat*, *Jang* and *Dawn*. Hawkers and distributors stopped newspaper circulation in Baloch-majority districts, including Pasni, Turbat and Gwadar. This situation continued for several months.[22]

VI

ENDURING
INSURRECTION

16

The Separatist Challenge

We have a distinct civilization, we have a separate culture like that of Iran and Afghanistan. We are Muslims but it is not necessary that by virtue of our being Muslims we should lose our freedom and merge with others. If the mere fact that we are Muslims requires us to join Pakistan, then Afghanistan and Iran, both Muslim countries, should also amalgamate with Pakistan ... Pakistan's unpleasant and loathsome desire that our national homeland, Balochistan, should merge with it is impossible to concede. It is unimaginable to agree to such a demand ... We are ready to have friendship with that country on the basis of sovereign equality but by no means ready to merge with Pakistan ... We can survive without Pakistan. We can prosper outside Pakistan. But the question is what Pakistan would be without us? ... We want an honourable relationship, not a humiliating one. If Pakistan wants to treat us as a sovereign people, we are ready to extend the hand of friendship and cooperation. If Pakistan does not agree to do so, flying in the face of democratic principles, such an attitude will be totally unacceptable to us, and if we are forced to accept this fate, then every Baloch son will sacrifice his life in defence of his national freedom.[1]

Mir Ghaus Bakhsh Bizenjo

BIZENJO'S REMARKS WERE TO PROVE prophetic. Festering alienation has been transformed into violent insurgency periodically in 1948, 1958, 1962, 1973–77 and since the early 2000. The response of the state to each insurgency has fuelled the next.

Moderates and Separatists

The Baloch nationalist movement is not a single, unified one. The nationalists can be grouped into two categories: (a) the moderates who seek maximum provincial autonomy within Pakistan. They believe in the political process—dialogue and participation in elections—to achieve their demands; (b) The separatists who seek independence from Pakistan. For them, the time for a political process—a dialogue with the government—or taking the parliamentary route is long over. They have put their faith in militant means to achieve their objectives. Given the centralizing policies of the government, both moderates and separatists have a common meeting ground in asserting a distinct Baloch identity and expressing frustration with Pakistan over its failure to acknowledge the historical identity of the Baloch people.

In fact, given the popularity of the insurgency, even the moderate elements have had to adopt a harder line—at least rhetorically—or else lose the support of their constituencies. As early as 2006, former chief minister of Balochistan—Balochistan National Party elder statesman Attaullah Mengal—had to declare that 'the days to fight political battles are over.'[2] Later, he told Abida Hussain, a politician from south Punjab, that his heart still beats for Pakistan. He hoped that the heart of his sons and grandsons would beat in the same way, but he suspected that their hearts were souring and the assassination of Nawab Akbar Bugti was a wound inflicted on the hearts of all Baloch, including himself.[3] In January 2006, Nawab Bugti, a former governor and head of the Jamhoori Watan Party (JWP), had said: 'The denial of democratic rights and economic deprivation have compelled people to take up arms. It is war now.'[4]

The difference between the ideologies of the two groups is that the Baloch political parties continue to pin their hopes on a political solution and on a constitutional path. The militants, on the other hand, faced with continued suppression and betrayals by the Pakistan state, have taken to violence to prevent further extraction of resources and to raise the economic cost for Islamabad in trying to do so. Consequently, pipelines and installations have become prime targets, disrupting gas supplies all over the country. The variance between the militants and the nationalist parties, said Sardar Akhtar Mengal, was that the former 'do not think they can achieve anything through democratic and constitutional means', while the 'Baloch nationalists are still optimistic about engaging in the democratic process, they are increasingly frustrated'.[5]

The students, perhaps, best represent the dilemma. The HRCP reported in 2011 that student groups in particular were insistent that the Baloch had no option but to demand independence from Pakistan. Many of the political groups did not support violence as part of the struggle for independence, but were very clear that the struggle was legitimate and that their right to self-determination should be a part of the political discourse on Balochistan. There were, however, those who felt that violence was justified as part of the struggle for an independent Balochistan in the face of aggression and repression by the security forces in the province. The representatives of one such group that met with the mission were extremely bitter because of what they saw as 'the injustices by the Punjab'.[6]

The Moderate Case

Major grievances of the moderate Baloch nationalists include the following:[7]

(i)   Pakistan's political system is not democratic and representative of the people, but is dominated by a single ethnic community—the Punjabi;

(ii)   The Baloch are not represented in the power structure at Islamabad;

(iii) Institutions of the state are perpetrating excesses against the Baloch people, political activists in particular, leading to their killings, arbitrary arrests, enforced disappearances and humiliation;

(iv) The Islamabad establishment is not trustworthy as it has backed out of its promises time and again and killed Baloch leaders, including Akbar Bugti;

(v)   The Baloch do not have control over their resources and Punjab has been exploiting them for decades;

(vi) Balochistan needs political autonomy and control over natural and economic resources, and not a mere financial relief package; and

(vii) The Pakistani establishment is patronizing the Taliban movement and has helped them establish their sanctuaries in Baloch areas with a view to pitting them against the Baloch.

Based on these grievances, the key demands of the moderates are provincial control over the resources of the province, ending economic exploitation, insisting that development projects like Gwadar port are linked with local ownership and benefit, devolving genuine provincial autonomy to the province, empowering the provincial government so that crucial decisions on issues like law and order and mega projects are not monopolized by the military. For example, as a Baloch leader said, 'We want to live as an equal partner in the federation, with our democratic rights respected, including the ownership of our resources; these resources belong to the people of Pakistan'.[8]

The growing disenchantment among the moderates is, however, visible. For example, according to the late Baloch leader Habib Jalib Baloch: 'Our main demand is the right of self-determination and self-rule. We appeal to the United Nations and other international organizations to help us. We want peaceful resolution of our dispute with Pakistan and to avoid bloodshed. We urge the UN to send peacekeeping forces here to expel Pakistani forces from this region and then start talks for peaceful settlement of the issue.'[9] Likewise, a HRCP mission that visited Balochistan in 2011 noted the absence of a political discourse amongst the political elements in the province. Some of them even told the mission that the time for politics was over, and '... now even within the province there was a polarization of views on whether politics in the context of Pakistan was of any relevance.'[10]

One reason for this, of course, is that due to political engineering under Gen. Musharraf, the alliance of religious parties known as the

Mutahida Majlis-i-Amal (MMA) dominated politics in Balochistan between 2002 and 2008. Then, the major nationalist parties of the province boycotted the 2008 elections, which resulted in their non-representation in the national and provincial assemblies between 2008 and 2013. Due to this moderate political vacuum, the separatists who were opposed to parliamentary politics got greater legitimacy.[11]

Moderate Political Parties

The key moderate political parties are:

The Balochistan National Party (BNP). It was formed by Sardar Attaullah Mengal, the head of the Mengal tribe, as a result of the merger of Mengal's own Balochistan National Movement (BNM) and Ghaus Bakhsh Bizenjo's Pakistan National Party (PNP). While Attaullah Megal's son Sardar Akhtar Mengal now heads the party, the BNP's Central Executive Committee has very few sardars. Its demands include maximum provincial autonomy, an increase in Balochistan's share of revenue from provincial resources and limiting the federal government's authority to four subjects: defence, foreign affairs, currency and communications. Akhtar Mengal had stated: 'It is not the government's writ that has been challenged. It is the writ of the people which is challenged'.[12] Musharraf had targeted Akhtar Mengal who was imprisoned in November 2006 on terrorism charges. During the trial, he was subjected to humiliating confinement in the courtroom in a cage-like structure that prevented any contact with his lawyer.[13]

In 2012 Akhtar Mengal presented a 'six-point agenda' for the peaceful resolution of the Baloch conflict. These included: immediate suspension of all overt and covert military operations in Balochistan; production of all missing persons before a court of law; disbanding of all proxy death squads operating under the supervision of the Inter-Services Intelligence and Military Intelligence; allowing the Baloch political parties to function freely; and rehabilitation of displaced persons as a confidence-building measure.[14] Following the July 2018 elections, the BNP-M decided to support the ruling party in Islamabad—Imran Khan's Pakistan Tehreek-e-Insaf (PTI)—on the basis of a six-point agreement.

The key element of this was addressing the issue of missing persons on a priority basis.[15]

The National Party (NP). It was formed with the merger of the Balochistan National Movement and the Balochistan National Democratic Party. It is led by Abdul Malik Baloch who was the chief minister of the province from 2013 to 2015 in coalition with the PML-N. It is a moderate, centre-left Baloch nationalist party that claims to represent the middle class. It has usually participated in the electoral process but boycotted the 2008 elections. It strongly opposes the Central government's projects in the Makran belt such as Gwadar port without Baloch participation, demands that the Baloch should have the right to control their own resources and to determine their own priorities, political and economic. With its educated, non-tribal cadre, the National Party is opposed to the sardari system. Yet, it rejects the Musharraf government's claims that the sardars are solely responsible for all of Balochistan's ills. Instead, the National Party places the blame for the crisis squarely on the military's shoulders.[16]

The Jamhoori Watan Party (JWP). It was formed by Nawab Akbar Khan Bugti in 1990. The JWP's support base is largely limited to the Bugti tribe. However, his defiant stand against the government in his later years had won him the support of many other Baloch. Defending Nawab Bugti, Sardar Akhtar Mengal insisted: 'If Bugti was a turncoat, he would not be in the mountains; he could have made a deal (with Musharraf), which he did not'.[17] After Bugti's killing, he is seen as a martyr for the Baloch cause.

Baloch Haq Talwar. Like Nawab Bugti's JWP, Nawab Khair Bakhsh Marri's Baloch Haq Talwar is also largely tribal in its membership and structures. However, the Marris have been at the forefront of the fight against military rule. As such, politics for them have taken a back-seat.

These four political parties—BNP, NP, JWP and Haq Tanwar—had joined together in 2003 to form the Baloch Ittehad or Alliance that demanded an end to military action and advocated Baloch rights within a democratic, federal, pluralistic framework. One of the Ittehad leaders, Dr Baloch of the NP, stated that the Ittehad would 'stand the test of time', stressing that when 'we see trouble from outside our nation, we stand as one'. Admitting that the four parties 'still had political differences', BNP leader Akhtar Mengal said, 'on the Balochistan issue, we are one'.[18]

Balochistan Students Organisation (BSO). It was formed in 1967. It represents the educated Baloch middle class and students and has emerged as an independent political force, with its demands for the Baloch youth and recognition of Balochi as a medium of instruction in the province. It is divided into four factions: BSO (Awami), BSO (Azad), BSO (Mengal) and BSO (Pajjar). These factions have, however, united in the face of the challenges facing the Baloch. Although the BSO is not politically aligned with any nationalist party, like them it strongly opposes military rule.[19]. It has been responsible for training and producing many nationalist leaders and is an important vehicle for entry into the nationalist movement.

The Separatist Case

The separatist case hinges on the following:

- The Baloch territory and the people were forcibly integrated into Pakistan without the approval of the Baloch representatives;
- Both the Pakistani state and civil society are not trustworthy and are inimical to the cause of the Baloch people. The parliament and the judiciary cannot be helpful in the Baloch cause;
- The Baloch do not want to live in Punjabi-dominated Pakistan and want separation to form their nation state;
- Military and paramilitary forces must be removed from the province as a demonstration of a genuine commitment to end 'occupation' of the province;
- All 'settlers' must be evicted from the province, especially the Punjabis and Afghan refugees who had settled in the province, since this would change the demography of the province;
- The traditional Baloch territories, like Jacobabad and DG Khan, should be restored to Balochistan;
- Organizations that want to help the Baloch people should raise the issue of human rights violations at the international level, especially in the United Nations; and

- International support for independence of Balochistan is welcome irrespective of who offers that, be it the United States or India.[20]

A separatist, in an interview, unambiguously expressed the gravity of the current situation: 'We're an oppressed nation. There is no other choice but to fight … No matter how hard they try to turn Gwadar into Dubai, it won't work. There will be resistance. The pipelines going to China will not be safe. They will have to cross through Baloch territory, and if our rights are violated, nothing will be secure.'[21]

As Brahamdagh Bugti, Akbar Bugti's grandson, told journalist Carlotta Gall: 'The people are angry and they will go to the side of those using violence, because if you close all the peaceful ways of struggle, and you kidnap the peaceful, political activists, and torture them to death and throw their bodies on roadsides, then definitely they will go and join the armed resistance groups.' He saw little hope of change from within Pakistan and sought intervention by the United Nations and Western nations. 'We have to struggle hard, maybe for one year, two years, twenty years,' he said, 'We have to hope.' 'Ninety-nine per cent of the Baloch now want liberation,' he said.[22]

Separatist Groups

Like the moderate Baloch groups and parties, the separatists, too, are divided into several factions. However, given the shadowy nature of these organizations, it is very difficult to determine their leadership and structure. Due to necessity, their structure is fluid and it is their mobility that helps them evade detection and gives them the element of surprise.[23] As Human Rights Watch notes, the extent to which Baloch political leaders maintain control of militant groups remains unclear.[24]

According to media reports, more than fourteen major and minor militant Baloch separatist groups operate in the province. The main groups are the Balochistan Liberation Army, Baloch Republican Army, Baloch Liberation Front, and Lashkar-e-Balochistan.[25]

Balochistan Liberation Army (BLA): The precursors of the BLA were two militant groups that were active in the 1960s and 1970s— the Balochistan People's Liberation Front (BPLF) and the Balochistan Liberation Front (BLF). At that time, the Marri, Mengal and Bugti tribes carried out armed resistance activities under the umbrella of these groups. However, as the BPLF dissipated during the exile years in Afghanistan, the armed supporters of the Marri tribe were organized under a new organization—the BLA. According to Naseer Dashti, during the initial years of the current insurgency it provided logistic support and training to the other armed resistance groups.[26] Reportedly, Marri as well as Bugti tribesmen form the bulk of the BLA's cadre, some of whom participated in the 1970s' insurgency, and others have taken up arms for the first time. The BLA also reportedly draws its strength from underemployed, alienated and politicized Baloch youth in Quetta and other towns.[27] It started its militant activities in 2002.

On 9 April 2006 the Musharraf government banned the BLA as a terror organization, threatening to arrest anyone with links to it, a move that was seen by many as the first step in a systematic campaign to clamp down on Baloch dissent.[28] Since then, scores of Baloch nationalist leaders and activists have been charged with links to the BLA.[29]

In the initial years of the insurgency the BLA claimed credit for most attacks on government installations and personnel and on communication links and energy grids province-wide.[30] Despite this, very little is known about its leadership, command structures or manpower. No Baloch nationalist political party or tribal group publicly admits knowledge of or links to the militant group, and with good reason. Nawab Bugti described the BLA, the BLF and the BPLF as 'different groups or organizations'. Denying any links to them, he said: 'Whatever name you give to these groups, they are not under our control. They are not beholden to anyone. Whatever they do, they do on their own. They don't ask anyone.'[31] The leader of the opposition in the Balochistan Assembly, Kachkool Ali Baloch, concurred that there were multiple militant groups with different tactics but an identical goal—to protect the Baloch people from an oppressive and exploitative Centre.[32]

According to Baloch journalist Malik Siraj Akbar, the BLA 'is not owned by any one sardar. No nationalist leader, including Bugti, Marri, and Mengal, accepts responsibility for leading the Baloch Liberation Army even though all of them admit to backing the outfit's activities.[33] And neither the assassination of Balach Marri nor of Akbar Bugti, the two main leaders of the initial phase of the current insurgency, ended the conflict between Balochistan and the Centre.[34]

Among its high-profile attacks were the 15 June 2013 attack on the Ziarat Residency where Mohammad Ali Jinnah had spent his last days. The BLA mainly operates in the Marri area although like the other insurgent groups, its area of operations is not rigidly defined. [35]

Balochistan Liberation Front (BLF). The BLF, reputed to be the most organized of the resistance groups, represents a new phenomenon in Balochistan in that it is the only militant organization led by educated middle-class segments of the Baloch society. Till the present fifth phase of Baloch insurgency, the national struggle was led by tribal sardars. This is no longer true. The volunteers of the BLF are mostly educated and come from the BSO (Azad). According to Naseer Dashti, young nationalist activists under the leadership of Ghulam Mohammad Baloch, Dr Allah Nazar and Wahid Kamber formed the BLF in 2003. Initially, it allied itself with the BLA and its volunteers reportedly received militant training from BLA instructors. The BLF is the only resistance group in Balochistan that is overt. Dr Allah Nazar, who belongs to a middle-class family from Mashkay in district Awaran, is the declared leader of the organization. The security forces, including the Pakistan Air Force, have targeted him on several occasions.[36] He is the only prominent leader among the various insurgent groups who is engaged in actual fighting on the ground in Balochistan. This accounts for his popularity among the younger Baloch.[37] The BLF's area of operations includes Awaran, Panjgur, Washuk, Turbat and Gwadar districts in southern Balochistan. Here, the sardari system does not exist. BLF's cadres include a large number of Zikris who are concentrated in the Makran belt.[38]

The Baloch Republican Army (BRA): After the killing of Akbar Bugti in 2006, his Jamhoori Watan Party splintered and his grandson Brahamdagh Bugti set up the Baloch Republican Party (BRP). The security agencies claim that BRA is the militant wing of BRP and Brahamdagh is running it. This has been vehemently and repeatedly denied by him and he has accused the agencies of finding an excuse for the crackdown on the activities of BRP inside Balochistan. The BRP has also denied any link with militancy and claimed to believe in a peaceful struggle for the liberation of Balochistan.[39] The BRA advocates the independence of a 'greater Balochistan' and opposes any sort of political dialogue, calling upon the international community to intervene to halt a 'genocide'.

The BRA is composed mainly of Bugti tribesmen who were followers of Akbar Bugti. In recent years its membership has expanded with volunteers from other parts of Balochistan joining it. The group has been successful in disrupting gas supplies from Sui to other parts of the country on many occasions and is believed to be one of the most potent resistance groups in the contemporary conflict.[40] Among its high-profile attacks was the one on 24 January 2015, when it bombed two electricity transmission lines in Naseerabad district, plunging much of the country into darkness.[41]

United Baloch Army (UBA): After the death of Balach Marri in 2007, differences were reported to have arisen between his successors. These differences caused divisions in the rank and file of the BLA. Resultantly, in 2012, the BLA split and according to Naseer Dashti, with the blessings of Khair Bakhsh Marri a new organization called the UBA was announced. Like the BLA, the UBA too is mostly composed of fighters from the Marri tribe but there are also people in its ranks from other tribes in Sarawan and Bolan regions. The security agencies have frequently accused Mehran Marri as leading the group but this has been strongly denied by him. Mehran Marri, who spends his time between London and UAE has, in fact, been articulating the Baloch case effectively in the UN Human Rights Commission in Geneva. Among UBA's deadly attacks was the bombing of a Rawalpindi-bound train at Sibi station in April 2014, which killed at least seventeen people.[42]

Lashkar-e-Balochistan (LeB): Formed in 2008 the LeB recruits volunteers from the Mengal tribe though today its volunteers come from more than just the Mengal area. Its main area of operations is in the Jhalawan and Makran regions. The security agencies have frequently accused Javed Mengal, the elder brother of Akhtar Mengal, the head of the BNP, as leading this militant group. The BNP has, however, denied any link with the LeB and has asserted that it is has no role in the armed struggle. It has made clear that its declared objective is to achieve the rights of the Baloch through political means. Javed Mengal who lives in exile in London and UAE has also denied any links with the LeB. Like Mehran Marri, Javed Mengal and his son Noordin Mengal have been active in pleading the Baloch case and highlighting the human rights situation in Balochistan in different international forums. Noordin has been active in the Unrepresented People's Organisation (UNPO) and been instrumental in organizing some events in the US on the Balochistan issue.[43]

Curiously, the Balochistan home department had announced bounties for ninety-nine members of banned militant organizations ranging between Rs 500,000 and Rs 15 million. These included militants belonging to the Baloch Liberation Army, Baloch Republican Army, Baloch Liberation Front, United Baloch Army and Lashkar-e-Balochistan. However, names of their alleged leaders like Brahamdagh Bugti, Hairbyar Marri, Mehran Marri and Javed Mengal, who are accused of instigating terrorist activities in Balochistan, were not included in the list.[44] This says something about all the allegations against such leaders.

Nature of the Conflict

Since its forced accession to Pakistan and till the 1970s the Baloch conflict with the state was limited largely to tribal pockets. It lacked mass national participation. Things started changed during 1970s when due to the brutal suppression of the insurgency, a Baloch national consciousness started taking firmer roots. As a result, today the nature of the Baloch resistance is qualitatively different from the earlier periods. According to Naseer Dashti, 'Now it has acquired many dimensions that are necessary for a national resistance movement to flourish and survive.' According to him, 'The perception of running out of time among the Baloch intellectuals and opinion makers is fuelling the sentiments of "national salvation in our life time"' among the politically conscious elements. The Baloch universally share the belief that as a nation they are at the verge of becoming extinct.[45]

Frederic Grare makes an important point: 'It was the state's repressive response that radicalized most elements of the "nationalist movement"' and 'as soon as it became clear that the military regime was seeking the elimination of the nationalist leadership', the possibility of political compromise greatly diminished.[46] The impact of this has been that the position of the nationalist political parties who hoped for a constitutional and political solution has been undermined. It is not only the militants who don't believe that a political solution is possible any longer but the ordinary Baloch are also becoming convinced that there is no political solution and the gun is the only way.

Unlike the past resistance movements, the ongoing Baloch insurgency has created serious challenges for Pakistan for several reasons. First, as of 2019 the insurgency is now in its fourteenth year. It has lasted longer than any of the past resistance movements and is continuing at the time of writing. It shows no signs of dissipating despite everything that the army has thrown against it. Even though low-key and not yet a threat to the state, it has a momentum of its own.

Second, geographically the insurgency extends far beyond the tribal areas and has reached the length and breadth of Balochistan. Today, it is no longer confined to the domain of one or two tribes. Instead, it has spread into non-tribal regions such as the southern Makran belt, cutting across society and age groups, from the rural, mountainous regions to the city centres. As Grare puts it, the insurgency has shifted '... from rural to urban areas and from the north-east of the province to the south-west. Sometimes it spills over to cities like Karachi.' As evidence he cites the fact that '... many leaders now come from the urbanized districts of Kech, Panjgur and Gwadar (and to a lesser extent from Quetta, Khuzdar, Turbat, Kharan and Lasbela). They are well-connected to Karachi and Gulf cities, where tribal structures are nonexistent.'[47] In fact, the insurgency seems to concentrate mainly in the hilly terrain of Turbat, Panjgur, Gwadar and Awaran districts.

Third, Baloch women and children have become involved in the insurgency. They have supported the armed groups through regular protest rallies. This indicates that the insurgency has permeated the ordinary people who are fighting not for the sake of a sardar but for the cause of Balochistan. As Declan Walsh noted: '... this insurgency seems to have spread deeper into Baloch society than ever before. Anti-Pakistani fervour has gripped the province. Baloch schoolchildren refuse to sing the national anthem or fly its flag; women, traditionally secluded, have joined the struggle. Universities have become hotbeds of nationalist sentiment.'[48]

The impact was felt even in Islamabad. In April 2009 a Baloch senator dropped a bombshell in the Senate stating that the Pakistan national anthem was no longer sung in schools of Balochistan.[49] By

2010 in most of Balochistan, books on 'Pakistan Studies' had been banned, the national flag could no longer be flown in any school or any other building, and singing the national anthem had been prohibited by the militants.[50]

Fourth, for a considerable time, especially under Musharraf, the international community did not understand the threat posed by the army's Islamist allies, domestically and externally. Though belatedly, the insurgency seems to have caught the attention of the international community. For example, in February 2012 US Congressman Dana Rohrabacher convened a hearing on Balochistan and supported the demand for a free Baloch land. He moved a resolution that was co-sponsored by House Representatives Louie Gohmert and Steve King. It asserted that the people of Balochistan that were '… currently divided between Pakistan, Iran and Afghanistan, have the right to self-determination and to their own sovereign country', adding that they 'should be afforded the opportunity to choose their own status among the community of nations'.[51] The European Parliament has held several debates on the issue of Balochistan, while the matter is frequently raised in the sessions of the Human Rights Council in Geneva. In 2018 there were poster campaigns in Geneva, London and New York creating greater awareness about the situation in Balochistan.

Fifth, Marri, Bugti and Mengal tribes had dominated the insurgency in the initial phases, but today the ranks of the insurgency include a large numbers of educated, middle-class Baloch. The bulk of them is said to be under the age of thirty. An observer has noted: 'Previous insurgencies were led by sardars but today's insurgency is spearheaded by ordinary, middle-class Baloch.'[52] Nationalist fervour, he said, is driving it; factors such as poverty, unemployment and underdevelopment are of secondary importance. 'The insurgents,' he said, 'include doctors, lawyers, traders and teachers. They can all make a living but they have chosen to fight because they see their rights violated and [Balochistan's] resources plundered.'[53] According to Baloch politician Abdul Rauf Mengal, 'It is not just the three tribes but all Baloch people are fighting [for their rights], and most of them are ordinary Baloch.'[54]

The educated middle class that is leading the movement is underrepresented in the higher echelons of the Pakistan state structure—both military and civil, as noted in an earlier chapter, and it provides a substantial cadre to the Baloch nationalist movement.[55] The middle class is also a unifying factor due to its opposition to separate agreements, individual or collective, between Islamabad and the tribal chiefs. Not surprisingly, the Pakistan Army has targeted the middle class to dent the growing consolidation of Baloch nationalism.[56]

Dr Allah Nazar, leader of the BLF, best represents the change in the epicentre of the insurgency. According to author Mahvish Ahmad, Nazar's rise represented a fundamental shift within the hierarchy of the movement. 'From one led by sardars, or tribal leaders, it is becoming one spearheaded and populated by a non-tribal cohort of middle-class Baloch. Nazar's leadership exemplifies the shift of the movement's epicentre from Balochistan's north-east—home to the Marris and Bugtis, and known for its longstanding separatist sentiments—to the remittance-rich, urbanizing south, which is home to a burgeoning educated and professional class, which has historically remained on the sidelines of the province's politics.'[57]

Sixth, while it is true that tribal unity in Balochistan has been a chimera and one of the banes for the nationalists, several events provide a glimmer of hope. The first was the 2003 four-party alliance called the Baloch Ittehad of Abdul Hayee Baloch's NP, Sardar Akhtar Mengal's BNP, Nawab Akbar Bugti's JWP and Nawab Khair Bakhsh Marri's Baloch Haq Talwar. The alliance stayed together for a while but later disintegrated. The second was provided in the wake of the killing of Akbar Bugti when the former Khan of Kalat called a grand Baloch Jirga on 21 September 2006 and again on 2 October 2006 in which about 380 leaders, including eighty-five sardars, participated. This put paid to Musharraf's boast that all except three sardars supported him.[58] For a while at least, there was a semblance of unity. The Baloch sardars even called upon the Pakistan government to vacate Baloch areas. In 2013 the Khan of Kalat and Hyrbyair Marri joined forces and announced that a united the Balochistan 'charter' would be launched. This, however, did not materialize. Key exiled figures such as the Baloch representative at the United Nations Human Rights Council (UNHRC) Mehran Marri, Brahamdagh Bugti and Javed Mengal refused to endorse the document.

More recently, almost all Baloch groups supported the suicide attack on the bus carrying Chinese workers at Dalbandin, mentioned in an earlier chapter. Likewise, a joint action by three Baloch groups was carried out on a Frontier Corps camp. Finally, Baloch probably realize that they cannot take on the Pakistan Army in a regular war. Hence, the strategy is jointly to increase the cost of holding on to Balochistan and preventing the exploitation of its resources.

Causes of the Insurgency

The myriad causes of Baloch alienation have been noted in earlier chapters. These can be summarized briefly as follows.

Historical: A basic cause for the Baloch to frequently break out in rebellion is the fact that, as Bizenjo put it so articulately in 1947, they did not want accession to Pakistan in the first place. The alienation engendered by the forced accession that many believe was illegal, since the Khan had no authority to do so, has been greatly enhanced by subsequent behaviour of the Pakistan state.

Legacy of betrayal: The solemn promises made on the Koran that were broken by the Pakistan Army in 1950 and 1959; the indiscriminate use of air-power by the Pakistani and Iranian forces on Baloch villages, women and children in 1973–77; and the killing of Nawab Akbar Bugti in 2006 have all left a bitter legacy of hatred.

Economic exploitation: Mounting anger over the exploitation of Balochistan's resources to benefit Punjab, and the denial of the benefits of the natural gas and mineral resources to the Baloch in the form of increased royalty payments and their use for the benefit of the Baloch.

Gwadar and CPEC: The denial of any meaningful role to the Baloch in decisions relating to the construction and administration of the Chinese-aided Gwadar port and CPEC.

Fear of becoming a minority: The influx of a large number of Punjabis and other non-Baloch into the province to work in the construction of the Gwadar port raises fears of being converted into a minority.

Administrative marginalization: The continuing discrimination against the Baloch in matters of recruitment to the armed forces and various civilian departments of the government, both at the federal and provincial levels.

Army presence: The overbearing presence of the security forces and the establishment of more cantonments in the province that are perceived to facilitate the extraction of Balochistan's resources.

Perceptional differences: For the Baloch the current violence is a product of decades of exploitation that has reduced them to 'slaves and third grade citizens' in their own land. The Central government, on the other hand, labels the violence in Balochistan as the work of a small band of 'miscreants', led by a few militant tribal leaders. They, according to the government, do not represent the majority of the Baloch population and their efforts to undermine the development of Balochistan are purely aimed at maintaining the 'backward' feudal tribal system from which they garner their great power and wealth.[59]

Control over own resources: The Baloch desire a greater say and less interference with their political and economic destiny, especially over resources like gas and mega projects like Gwadar.

Timing: The above factors have combined with the province's increased strategic significance due to the construction of Gwadar port and the CPEC to exponentially increase the efforts by the Central government to exert its authority inside Balochistan. This renewed interest in Balochistan, which has included an influx of foreign workers and an increased military presence, has ignited the smouldering belief among Baloch nationalists that the Central government seeks only to subjugate the Baloch people and exploit their resources for the benefit of the Central government. The result has been an increased sense of 'colonialization' on the part of the Baloch population that has spawned a violent backlash by Baloch militants.

The Killing of Nawab Akbar Bugti

For Musharraf, it was the seventy-nine-year-old Nawab Akbar Bugti who was behind the Baloch unrest. In an interview with *Herald* Akbar Bugti had said: 'Now our options are clear: resist and die or die without resisting. The people have chosen the former ... They are fighting for Baloch honour and for their motherland and its resources.'[60] On 15 January 2006 Nawab Akbar Bugti told an audience at the Karachi Press Club's Meet the Press programme over telephone that the Pakistani government is committing 'genocide' in Balochistan, adding, 'As a war has been imposed on Baloch people, they have every right to defend themselves against the onslaught by the government forces.'[61]

The army finally trapped Bugti in his mountain hideout in Kohlu district and killed him on 26 August 2006. It was his killing and the manner in which it was done that intensified the insurgency and brought the simmering alienation among the Baloch to the fore. Instead of crushing the insurgency, his killing made him a martyr and gave the insurgents an icon. *The Newsline* commented editorially that it was a cover-up of ludicrous proportions. It warned that the army needed to sort itself out in order to grasp the consequences of what was possibly about to hit them.[62]

Bugti clearly had a premonition about what was coming. From the cave where he was hiding, he told Abida Hussain via satellite phone, 'I have clocked nearly eighty years and it is time for me to go. And your Punjabi army is going to kill me, which will convert me into the spirit of liberated Balochistan. That would be a befitting end for me with no regrets.'[63] Pakistani journalist Hamid Mir wrote in one of his articles that the last time he talked to Nawab Akbar Bugti on his satellite phone, Bugti had told him, 'Your commando general will rest only after he martyrs me, but after my martyrdom he will be held responsible. So, now it's up to you people to either choose Musharraf or Pakistan. The choice is yours.'[64]

Bugti's killing led to widespread violence in Balochistan, especially in Quetta. Vehicles and petrol pumps were burnt and roads were blocked. In Kalat a telephone exchange was set on fire. There was a total 'wheel-jam' strike in Balochistan on 28 August 2006.

Bugti's killing proved to be a seminal moment in Baloch history and a major mistake by Musharraf. The HRCP mission in 2011 noted that almost everyone that they met said that the killing of Nawab Akbar Bugti had been the turning point in Balochistan and that it had led many Baloch to support the call for independence.[65]

Calling Bugti's killing a huge disaster as much for Balochistan as for Pakistan, National Party (NP) leader Abdul Hayee Baloch said that the Baloch '... have all been devastated by the magnitude of the crime the government had committed. If this is what they could do to him, just imagine what they are doing to ordinary Baloch men, women and children every day'. According to him, hundreds had been killed, thousands arrested and scores disappeared. 'If this sort of barbarity does not constitute state terrorism, what does?' His lament was that helicopter gunships were used to kill 'a frail 80-year man' whose 'only fault was that he was struggling for his people's rights'.[66] According to Bugti's son Jamil: 'The dictator thought that by killing my father he would extinguish the whole movement. He has been proved wrong; the intensity of the insurgency has increased.'[67]

In the wake of Bugti's killing, the Khan of Kalat, Mir Suleman Daud, called a Grand Jirga of all tribal chiefs on 21 September 2006 in Kalat. Eighty-five tribal chiefs and around 300 'elders' attended it. A declaration adopted called for an end to the army's brutal military operation and spoke about the 'colonial occupation of Baloch lands by Punjab in violation of the accord signed by the state of Kalat and the Government of Pakistan in 1948'. The jirga also rejected the mega development projects being promoted by the federal government in the province. Condemning Bugti's killing, the jirga appealed to the International Court of Justice (ICJ) in The Hague against the 'violation of ... territorial integrity, exploitation of Balochistan's natural resources, denial of the Baloch right to the ownership of their resources and the military operation in the province'.[68] While the ICJ has no jurisdiction to take up the petition, Baloch nationalists maintain that the jirga succeeded in its twin objectives: to raise the Baloch cause internationally and to unite Baloch tribes and factions.[69] A sardar who participated said that armed BLA fighters had dominated the proceedings with calls for Balochistan's independence. 'It is these youth, and not the sardars, who are now leading the resistance.' The hatred for Pakistan voiced at the jirga, he said, 'would have left the intelligence agencies aghast'.[70]

To operationalize the jirga's declaration, the Khan of Kalat convened another jirga on 2 October 2006. This formed a 'sovereign supreme council' comprising the Khan himself and five other members. The council was mandated to approach the ICJ. In addition, the jirga also established a national council comprising the Baloch chiefs, political leaders, intellectuals, lawyers and students. This national council was to meet every six months to take stock of the problems facing the Baloch people.

By killing Bugti, Gen. Musharraf earned the enmity of not just the Baloch rebels but the wider Baloch population, who may not have believed in taking up arms but were still frustrated with Islamabad for its failure to develop the province. He clearly underestimated the power of Baloch nationalism that had led to four wars with the Pakistan Army in the past.[71] The increased violence pushed the Baloch far beyond their original demands for greater autonomy and recognition of their rights and towards an armed independence movement. Those who were calling for separation were mostly young, educated Baloch who no longer saw a future for themselves in Pakistan.

While the insurgency got a major fillip, politically Bugti's party, the Jamhoori Watan Party, went into decline and suffered several splits. Bugti's relatives like Mir Ghulam Haider Khan Bugti and Haji Juma Khan Bugti went their own way, enticed undoubtedly by offers from the government. These problems reduced the JWP to a shadow of the political force it was under Akbar Bugti.

Current Insurgency

Sporadic incidents of violence had taken place in Balochistan from the late 1990s. For example, insurgents had triggered a series of bomb blasts at Chagai, the testing site of Pakistan's nuclear device, on 28 May 1998. As a result, the main railway lines between Quetta and the rest of Pakistan were disrupted at two points. In addition, there were seven blasts in Quetta as well as blasts in Mastung, Khuzdar, Sui and Kohlu on May 28-29. The Balochistan Liberation Army (BLA) that seemed to have re-emerged after the 1970s claimed responsibility for the attacks and said in a statement: 'These attacks were to remind Punjabi Pakistanis that we the sons of the soil will not forget the great injustices and especially the nuclear test in the heart of our Fatherland Balochistan... We will avenge and free our country from Pakistani slavery.'[72]

In July 2000 there were three bomb explosions on the same day in Quetta, including one in the cantonment area that killed over half-a-dozen soldiers.[73] The Quetta cantonment came under rocket attacks from the surrounding hills and on one particular occasion, the roof of an empty classroom of the Command and Staff College collapsed after taking a direct rocket hit.[74]

What gave these sporadic and intermittent incidents of violence a certain direction was what the Baloch perceived as a grave provocation. This was the 2001 arrest of Khair Bakhsh Marri on the murder charges of a high court judge. The Baloch nationalists perceived this as a deliberate state policy of humiliating respected Baloch leaders and attacking their honour and dignity. This incident is perceived by many Baloch to be the turning point of Baloch resistance after a pause of two decades.[75] Not surprisingly, between 2001 and 2002 there were nearly two dozen rocket attacks directed at the gas infrastructure. Consequently, there were major disruptions in the supply of gas to Punjab causing hardship to domestic consumers as also inflicting a heavy cost on industry and the gas companies. One report estimated that suspension of gas from Sui (which at that time was supplying 45 per cent of the total gas used in Pakistan) cost the Sui Northern Gas Pipelines Ltd a daily loss of Rs 60 million.[76]

Between 2002 and 2004 intermittent attacks continued. During 2004 there were 626 rocket attacks, of which 379 attacks targeted the Sui gas fields while others targeted power pylons and railway tracks. In addition, there were 122 bomb explosions on the gas pipeline.[77] The BLA launched a massive attack in 2004 that damaged the Pakistan Petroleum Limited (PPL) property and Sui area in Pakistan. A peace deal was then brokered with the help of Shujaat Hussain, leader of the Pakistan Muslim League (Quaid) (PML-Q). In August 2004 the BLA ambushed an army van in Khuzdar killing six soldiers. A day later, militants attacked the convoy of the chief minister in Khuzdar killing two soldiers. On Pakistan's Independence Day in 2004, the BLA carried out ten coordinated bomb blasts in Quetta. Though these were low-intensity bombs and did not cause casualties, the message of the militants was obvious.[78]

In December 2004 the Pakistan government-owned company Oil and Gas Development Corporation Limited (OGDCL) was granted a licence for gas exploration in Balochistan. The area they wished to explore was the Kohlu district that belonged to the Bugti tribe who were not offered any part of the substantial revenue that would arise from the discovery. It was estimated that there was as much as 22 trillion cubic feet of gas in that area, which would fetch the company billions of dollars over the years. Nawab Akbar Bugti opposed the exploration without any promise of adequate compensation. Several Baloch leaders including Sardar Attaullah Mengal, Nawab Khair Bakhsh Marri and Nawab Khan Bugti initiated talks with the military regime in an effort to diffuse mounting tensions. But Musharraf had other plans.

Nothing would deter him and the army to militarily achieve their ends in Balochistan.

To counter opposition from the Baloch tribes, Gen. Musharraf announced the setting up of more cantonments and military posts in Balochistan. By the beginning of 2005 the Pakistan Army was itching for action against the Baloch, particular the Bugti tribesmen. As Baloch opposition mounted, Gen. Musharraf issued his famous warning: 'Don't push us. It isn't the 1970s when you can hit and run and hide in the mountains. This time you won't even know what hit you.'[79] This was much like what Ayub Khan had threatened in the 1960s.

Against such a backdrop and the accompanying incidents of violence in 2003-04, the situation erupted on 2 January 2005 due to the rape of Dr Shazia Khalid, a lady doctor working at Pakistan Petroleum Limited (PPL) at Sui. Nawab Akbar Bugti accused an army officer, Captain Emad, of the offence. The PPL and the government tried to cover up the incident. The captain was allowed to give a lengthy statement on Pakistan Television, presenting his side of the story, and President Musharraf publicly vouched for the captain's innocence.

Failure of the government to bring the guilty to book sparked attacks on the Sui gas fields by Baloch tribesmen for whom a crime like rape was only punishable with death. Hundreds of rockets and mortar shells were fired and there was a heavy gun battle. According to Pakistan government sources, the rebels fired 14,000 rounds of small arms, 436 mortars and sixty rockets in four days of fighting. Large-scale damage was inflicted on the property of the PPL; on 18 January 2005 a major attack disrupted Sui's output.

In the aftermath of the attack, the government rushed hundreds of troops to the area. At least eight people died in the violence, which caused a production loss of more than 43,000 tonnes of urea and a daily electricity shortfall of about 470 megawatts.[80] Sui Northern Gas Pipelines Ltd subsequently halted natural gas supplies to 118 power plants in Lahore–Sheikhupura, Bhai Phero and Gujranwala regions, forcing textile mills to halt their operations for an indefinite period. A Sui Northern Gas Pipelines official, however, claimed that the shut-off was because of adverse weather conditions.

Violence continued throughout 2005. According to the federal government's tally, in 2005 there were more than 275 rocket attacks on government installations, seventeen bombings and eight attacks on gas pipelines.[81] According to the *Dawn* newspaper, there were at least 261 bomb blasts and 167 rocket attacks in 2005, while Baloch militants—prominently the Balochistan Liberation Army—have made claims that there were five times those numbers.[82]

A major development took place in December 2005 when Baloch militants rocketed a meeting attended by President Musharraf in Kohlu. A few days later, rockets were fired at a helicopter carrying the commander of the Frontier Corps, Balochistan. By mid-December press reports indicated that Pakistani military and paramilitary forces were engaged in 'a full-scale military campaign' against militant Baloch tribesmen. The government played down the fighting and denied that the Pakistani Army was even deployed in Baluchistan, saying that it was merely using the Frontier Corps to run a police operation to stem violence. However, according to Carlotta Gall, 'One visit makes it clear that, despite official denials, the government is waging a full-scale military campaign here…. During a 24-hour trek on camel, horse and foot across the rugged, stony terrain in early March, the fighting was plain to see. Military jets and surveillance planes flew over the area, and long-range artillery lighted up the distant night sky.'[83]

If, as the government claimed, the conflict prior to 2005 was confined to only 7 per cent of the area of Balochistan (parts of Kohlu and Dera Bugti districts), from 2006 onwards it now engulfed more than half the area of the province.[84] In January 2006, the BLA targeted railway links in Dera Ghazi Khan, Punjab. On 5 January the army had to be deployed at Dera Ghazi Khan airport after an abortive attempt on an electricity pylon. In Jacobabad in Sindh, which also houses a significant Baloch population, there were a series of attacks on gas pipelines.[85]

In 2009, 792 attacks resulting in 386 deaths were recorded; approximately 92 per cent of the attacks were linked to Baloch nationalist militants. Violence increased in 2010, with 730 attacks carried out resulting in 600 deaths. The insurgents were even able to attack the main gas pipeline in the heart of Punjab near Pattoki, thereby indicating that the fire ignited in Balochistan was spreading. During 2006–10 there were more than 1,600 casualties in a total of 1,850 incidents—nearly 50 per cent civilians, 23 per cent militants and 22 per cent security forces.

Some of the incidents included the killing of three Chinese engineers working on the Gwadar port project; the attack on the chief minister's convoy; the attack on Sui airport building; regular disruption of power transmission lines and railway lines; and attacks on military and government installations. On 9 April 2014 a bomb blast ripped through an Islamabad market killing twenty-five and injuring dozens. The little-known United Baloch Army (UBA) claimed responsibility for the attack. The blast came following a military operation in Khuzdar and Kalat districts of Balochistan that killed roughly forty people including separatists. Baloch groups allege that children as young as six years old were also killed as helicopter gunships attacked homes. The UBA specifically linked the violence of the army to the attack.[86] 'We carried out the attack in Islamabad in response to the military operation against us,' said UBA spokesman Mureed Baloch, and warned that there would be more.[87]

The Islamabad blast was significant because it is the first time that a Baloch group had attacked non-military targets outside of Balochistan. The government dismissed the UBA's claim. In a text message to reporters, the interior ministry spokesman implied that foreign intervention, rather than an indigenous insurgency, was behind the attack—a long running claim by the government, which primarily blamed India, but also Afghanistan and the US, for fomenting a fabricated Baloch insurgency.[88]

An important aspect of the militant tactics is the attack on gas infrastructure. Since the bulk of the gas is sent out of Balochistan, the militants have targeted gas extraction and infrastructure to prevent the depletion of this resource. With periodic attacks on pipelines and installations disrupting gas supplies, the Baloch seem determined to increase the cost of the conflict for Islamabad. 'We might not defeat the Pakistani army but we will drain out the Pakistani economy,' Sardar Attaullah Mengal told the ICG.[89]

Repeated government claims over the past decade that the insurgency has been crushed have proved false. Attacks continue, as before, on government targets—installations and personnel and on economic symbols like pipelines.

Levels of Violence in Balochistan

According to partial data collated by the South Asia Terrorism Portal (SATP), 62,485 people have died in terrorist violence across Pakistan from 2005 to March 2019. Out of these, 43,697 casualties have occurred in FATA and KPK alone, followed by Sindh (mainly Karachi) with 8,284 casualties, Balochistan with 7,102 casualties and Punjab with 2,396 casualties. In proportional terms, Balochistan, FATA and KPK together account for 81.29 per cent of the total fatalities that occurred in Pakistan between 2005 and March 2019. Besides the loss of human lives, the sociocultural, economic and political fabric of these regions has been severely damaged.[90]

According to SATP, at least twenty-eight security force personnel were killed till 24 March 2019. During the corresponding period of 2018 the number of such fatalities was twenty-seven. The overall fatalities among security force personnel had increased in 2018 as compared to 2017—from seventy-seven to seventy-nine. While the first half of 2018 (January to June) recorded forty-seven such fatalities, the second half (July to December) accounted for another thirty-two.

Balochistan: North-South security force personnel fatalities

Year	Balochistan	North	South
2011	122	79	43
2012	178	116	62
2013	137	79	58
2014	83	60	23
2015	90	61	29
2016	153	130	23
2017	77	60	17
2018	80	56	23
2019	28	24	4
Total	947	665	282

Out of the twenty-eight security force personnel killed in the province in 2019, at least twenty-four were killed in north Balochistan, while the remaining four were killed in the south. Since 2011, out of 947 security personnel killed in Balochistan, the north accounted for

665 fatalities (70.22 per cent), while the south recorded 282 fatalities (29.77 per cent). Security force fatalities in each of these nine years have been consistently higher in the north.

North Balochistan is afflicted by Islamist terrorist groups like the TTP, LeJ and the ISIS. Baloch nationalist insurgent groups operate largely in the south. Despite the bulk of the casualties being in the north, the army has been targeting ethnic Baloch insurgent groups in the south with much greater ferocity and viciousness.

Weapons

It is undeniable that Balochistan is awash with weapons of all kinds. All tribal chiefs carry private armed guards and some maintain private militias.[91] A HRCP mission in 2012 was shocked at the glut of sophisticated firearms in Balochistan and the people's easy access to them. A rocket, for example, could be bought in Balochistan for less than Rs 1,000.[92] The mission questioned how huge quantities of weapons could pass through a series of check posts when common citizens were stopped from even carrying a knife. Its conclusion was that had there been sincere efforts to curtail the free flow of weapons, they would certainly have made a difference.[93]

In an interview before he was killed, Akbar Bugti admitted that there was no dearth of arms and ammunition in Balochistan. According to him, the Americans had offloaded huge caches of weapons and sums of money to fund the jihad in Afghanistan. Much of this inevitably ended up in the arms markets. He quoted the example of the Ojhri camp that was destroyed specifically to cover up shady arms transfers.[94]

Weaknesses

Despite the recent spread of the insurgency and growth of anti-Pakistan feeling across the province, the Baloch insurgency is characterized by several weaknesses. First, the small population size of the Baloch relative to the land is a major impediment. Even if the Baloch remain united, their small numbers will be a major handicap vis-à-vis the Pakistani state. They just do not have the critical mass to be able to assert their rights. Militarily too, they do not have the manpower or the hardware to take on the professional Pakistan Army in a conventional war.

Second, the leadership of the Baloch national movement remains highly fractured. The lack of unity among the tribes is a major disadvantage especially because the tribal system continues to be prevalent in some parts of the province. The intertribal rivalries have proved to be a major impediment in the development of a united resistance among the Baloch. This explains their failure to come on one single platform to put forward their demands. The multiplicity of armed groups has also made it difficult for them to properly coordinate with each other. Consequently, there is little unity in tactics. According to the Jinnah Institute—an Islamabad-based think tank—the multiplicity of Baloch leaders with competing motivations has exacerbated the violence, making deciphering the conflict landscape increasingly difficult. According to it, 'Making sense of this conflict requires parsing the growing categories of violence inflicted by a multiplicity of actors with competing motivations.'[95]

Third, because of the disunity, the Baloch have not been able to come up with a blue-print for governance. The closest was the effort of the Khan of Kalat and Hyrbyair Marri to work out a united Balochistan charter. This effort came to naught as other Baloch leaders did not evince much enthusiasm. Resultantly, the Baloch case is marked by a lot of criticism of the Pakistan state without presenting a viable alternative. Quite possibly the major hurdle in such an endeavour would be the contradiction between the old bugbear of the tribal system and the fresh impetus of the non-tribal, middle-class Baloch who seek a modern and democratic system. Whatever the reason, without clarity on the positives of what they seek to achieve and establish, the nationalist struggle will remain handicapped.

Fourth, the various groups are engaged in internecine fighting. While the killing of Nawab Akbar Bugti in August 2006 gave a big boost to the insurgency, there have been major disagreements over who would be his successor. Though his grandson Brahamdagh was his chosen political successor, several other relatives have thrown their hat in the ring. These include his cousin Shahzain Bugti,[96] another cousin Mir Aali Bugti and the former provincial home minister Sarfaraz Bugti, one of Brahamdagh's worst tribal and political enemies.[97] Likewise, following the demise of Nawab Khair Bakhsh Marri in June 2014 differences broke out between the Marri brothers on the question of who would succeed the senior Marri.

Fifth, the Baloch insurgents have started targeting Baloch politicians both inside and outside Balochistan. They have alienated the moderate Baloch political parties opposed to violence by questioning their patriotism and commitment to the 'national cause'.

Sixth, Baloch nationalists have lost a lot of sympathy due to their targeting of non-Baloch 'settlers', primarily Punjabi teachers. Even though the killing of Nawab Akbar Bugti and the atrocities of the army possibly provoked such attacks, yet, human rights groups have been critical of such killings. In fact, an intrinsic element of the Baloch culture is the centuries-old concept of protection that enjoins the safety of the life of a 'settler' or an 'outsider' in a Baloch area. These attacks clearly contradict the Baloch code of conduct, known as Balochmayar, and they also alienate supporters of Balochistan who live outside the province and the country.[98]

Finally, any separatist movement in Balochistan is impaired by the fact that the two countries bordering it—Iran and Afghanistan—have sizeable Baloch populations of their own. Both are apprehensive of a spillover of Baloch nationalism from Pakistan that could create unrest amongst their own Baloch. They also view any movement towards the consolidation of a 'Greater Balochistan'—Baloch areas in Pakistan, Iran and Afghanistan—as a direct threat to their territorial sovereignty. Thus, neither Iran nor Afghanistan would desire, let alone support, an independent Balochistan. For its part, Afghanistan has its own historical claim to parts of Balochistan, territories it lost to the British during the colonial period. The Durand Line as an international border is disputed by the Afghans, who regard the frontier with Pakistan as drawn by the British being agreed to by the Afghans only under duress.[99]

Surrenders

An interesting development in the ongoing insurgency are the intermittent reports about surrenders of Baloch militants. Such surrenders were initiated soon after the 2006 military operation that

led to the killing of Akbar Bugti. For example, a typical such report
is that '... the Inter-Services Public Relations (ISPR), the media wing
of Pakistan's armed forces, recently confirmed that at least twenty
Baloch insurgents, including a Parrari commander, have surrendered to
Pakistan Rangers Punjab'. According to another report, '... under the
political reconciliation scheme launched in Balochistan, 1,025 militants,
belonging to various proscribed outfits, have surrendered before the
provincial government during the past year. Among the surrendered
militants are a dozen key militant commanders, who have laid down
their arms before provincial officials,' said secretary, home and tribal
affairs Akbar Hussain Durrani. More recently, 265 militants belonging to
different proscribed organizations were supposed to have surrendered
on 18 September 2018,[100] seventy on 20 November 2018[101] and 560
militants on 2 January 2019.[102]

According to figures released by the National Action Plan Review
2017, some 2,000 Baloch separatists had surrendered to the security
forces over the last two years. As part of the amnesty scheme, the
surrendered separatists were to be given money and government jobs.
The 200–300 who did surrender in January 2018 were reportedly given
Rs 0.1 million for doing so. However, in none of the cases of surrender,
details were provided about either the commanders or the militant and
neither were any of them identified.[103]

In an interview, Baloch rights leader Mir Mohammad Ali Talpur
rubbished the government claims about the surrenders. According
to him, the government had claimed that there were only a handful
of misguided Baloch who resisted progress at the behest of foreign
hands. However, despite the large number of surrenders, why were the
attacks still going on? For him, these were 'rent a crowd surrenders,'
and quite pointless'.[104]

For the army, the 'surrenders' were quite useful in that they could
arrange alleged 'confessions' that pointed to foreign funding. This,
in turn, provided the army an alibi for its own failures to prevent
the continuing violence from essentially home-grown militants.[105]
However, as the *Nation* puts it, 'Every now and then, some militants
lay down their weapons voluntarily or are arrested, yet the situation
on the ground has never changed because of such surrenders or arrests.

The problem of separatism must be tackled from its roots; the causes for its existence must be addressed, instead of fighting tooth and nail for territory against our own people.'[106]

The *Daily Times* pertinently remarked: '... how do we know who exactly is surrendering?' '... This incentive driven "inclusion" of certain sections of Baloch society will do nothing to quell the resentment of a people who have been routinely exploited by the country's larger provinces,' adding, '... piecemeal experimentation rarely works. What the province needs is an all-out effort by the Pakistani state to ensure that its political and economic marginalization ends. The priority for now should be to gain the trust of ordinary Baloch by ushering in a set of reforms that will ensure provincial autonomy in letter and spirit.'[107]

17

The Response of the Government

THREE TRACKS CAN BE NOTED in the overall response of the state to the insurgency in Balochistan. One is the response of the provincial government in Quetta, the second is the response of the federal government in Islamabad and the third is the response of the army. As far as the nationalist leaders are concerned, the civil governments, both at the Centre and the province, are not in charge, having abdicated their constitutional responsibilities to the security agencies led by the army.[1]

The Provincial Government

One of Balochistan's misfortunes has been that its political leadership has been handicapped either by not being able to fully govern the province or because it has found it simpler to follow the diktats of Islamabad rather than implement policies for the benefit of the people. This was especially so under Musharraf when Balochistan's provincial government was a subsidiary arm of the Centre, working at its behest and following its directives. 'The provincial government,' said Abdul Hayee Baloch, a Baloch nationalist politician, 'is the tool of the federal establishment.' There is no '... provincial purview [over] political and economic decisions. All our decisions are made for us' by Islamabad.[2] The provincial legislature's sessions, for instance, were repeatedly cancelled under Central pressure to prevent the opposition from discussing the direction and impact of the conflict. Even administrative appointments and transfers were made in Islamabad.[3] The Balochistan chief minister is reported to have publicly stated that the military officials did not listen to him. Despite the restoration of democracy after the exit of Pervez Musharraf, the military continued to remain the dominant political force paying little heed to the provincial government.

Following the May 2013 elections, a tribal chief for the first time did not lead the provincial government. The HRCP Mission in 2013 was told that the government formation was considered to be a positive step that could lead to an opportunity for ending grave human rights violations in the province. The National Party (NP) that formed a coalition in Balochistan with the Pakistan Muslim League-Nawaz (PML-N) after the 2013 elections was expected to focus on three issues: that of missing persons; reversing the policy of kill-and-dump[4]; and reaching out to the leadership of the Baloch militants apart from tackling at least some of the issues of socio-economic development in Balochistan. The two-and-a-half years of Abdul Malik Baloch's chief ministership that ended in December 2015 unfortunately did not make much of a dent on any of the three issues. Nor did the succeeding government of the PML-N make much of a difference.

To be fair, the provincial government did not have much authority to tackle these issues, which were in the domain of the army. The 2013 HRCP mission had cautioned that they did not see many signs of a change in policy within the security and intelligence agencies as the kill-and-dump policy continued.[5] Despite this, Abdul Malik Baloch did actively try to engage with the exiled Baloch leadership to find a political solution to all issues. However, he carried little credibility with them since they were sceptical of his authority in taking decisions. Neither could the provincial government make much of a dent on the issue of missing persons. The army's kill-and-dump policy continued apace and persons kept going 'missing' with sickening frequency.

In fact, it is well recognized that all chief ministers of Balochistan have been powerless on such issues. As Jamil Bugti, the son of late Akbar Bugti, put it, the status of the chief minister of Balochistan was nothing more than that of a munshi or clerk as everything was remotely controlled from Islamabad. 'He has to run to Islamabad every month to get the salaries for his employees in the secretariat. So, he is given a cheque for the month's salaries and sent home to return again next month with palms outstretched.'[6] As a journalist put it:

'Balochistan is the only province whose total budget is [based] on loans. Provincial budgets are prepared purely on the basis of imagination and presumption; there is not even a modicum of reality in them'.[7]

The ground realities in Balochistan are such that economic resources and political power are concentrated in the hands of the federal government despite devolution of powers to the provincial government under the Eighteenth Constitutional Amendment. The situation in Balochistan is, however, worse than in the other provinces since even the maintenance of law and order has been taken over by the federally controlled paramilitary troops and not the local police. According to Zahid Hussain, a *Newsline* columnist, 'The master–servant relationship is starker here than in any other province. The return of military rule further aggravated the situation. Even the present pro-military provincial government does not have any real power.'[8]

Take the case of Abdul Quddus Bizenjo, who became the chief minister of Balochistan in 2018 after a 'coup' was engineered against the PML-N chief minister Sanaullah Zehri. Bizenjo had won his provincial seat from Awaran district by securing just 544 votes out of a total of 57,656 registered votes in the constituency, or just about one per cent. What credibility would his mandate have and could he really be said to represent the aspirations of the people of the constituency, let alone of the province?[9]

This situation has generated the general belief among the Baloch nationalists that the governments in Islamabad, especially those dominated by the army, have either confronted the political forces in the province or tried to marginalize them.[10] A HRCP mission in 2011 confirmed this state of affairs. It noted the absence of the political government and the civil authorities from critical areas of decision-making. It made the following points: (i) The political government had abdicated its responsibility towards the people and hid behind its own helplessness in the face of domination of the military and intelligence agencies in the decision-making process in the province. (ii) The political government had failed to protect the rights and fundamental freedoms of the people since extra-judicial killings and other lawless actions of the security forces continued unabated. (iii) All authority in the province was vested in the security forces who enjoyed complete immunity and had complete disregard towards the political government and the civil authorities. (iv) The government officials at the higher level did not even attempt to negotiate on behalf of the people. (v) The military authorities did not take the civil government on board; neither did they share information which made administration of law and order by the civil authorities impossible. (vi) The security forces were totally inaccessible to the people and even to the civil authorities. For example, the local Frontier Corps commander in Makran became unavailable for any meeting called by the Divisional Commissioner and attended only when it suited him, regardless of the importance of the matters on the agenda. (vi) Despite this, people continued to approach the civil authorities and the political elements for redressal. (vii) Finally, the use of force rather than political engagement or dialogue remained the preferred approach. Promises made in the Balochistan package about concrete reform, like inquiry into the murder of Baloch leaders and release of missing persons, remained little more than promises.[11]

One of the key points in the National Action Plan, formulated in the wake of the killing of schoolchildren in Peshawar on 16 December 2014, was 'empowering Balochistan government for political reconciliation with complete ownership by all stakeholders'. As a former IG of Balochistan Police noted, this disregarded the fact that there was only one player that had the final say in Balochistan—the military-led security establishment, including the intelligence agencies. They would never let the civilian provincial government formulate a policy of bringing the Baloch sub-nationalists into the mainstream of the strategically important province.[12] Thus, the high-sounding action point was a non-starter since the provincial government was not empowered to resolve the issue of the missing persons, could not prevail on the security forces to abandon the kill-and-dump strategy, and neither did it have cards to get the Baloch nationalists on the negotiating table.

The helplessness of the provincial government can be evaluated from the fact that even on key development issues, like the Gwadar deep-sea port, CPEC, awarding and renewal of mineral licences, it is not even consulted by the federal government. The simple fact is that Balochistan is seen as a resource-rich colony and every civilian, politician or provincial government is helpless against the Pakistan state's strategy of putting down by force any opposition to the exploitation of the province.

Lack of Governance

Even in areas that the provincial government has the authority to act independently, it has failed miserably. Take for example the capital city Quetta. This is how a journalist described its condition: 'Living in the provincial capital has become a nightmare. Streets routinely remain inundated by sewage water; roads reduced to dusty pathways with gaping manholes. Streetlights do not work and when they do, many people get killed from electrocution because of water around lamp posts. Major road arteries are actually mosaics of potholes. And this is Quetta, a city whose nine MPAs have been given Rs 2.25 billion in the name of development funds (Rs 250 million each), not to mention Rs 1 billion given by the federal government for Quetta's "beautification". Ministers are reported to take ten to twenty per cent upfront from contractors as their cut from development funds and issue them completion certificates without even an iota of actual work on ground.'[13]

Education

Education is another area the pitiable condition of which has been noted in an earlier chapter. Over the last six years the Balochistan government had consistently increased the percentage share of education in the provincial budget. From 13 per cent in 2010-11 to 20 per cent in 2015-16, it showed the commitment of successive governments to improve the state of education in the province. However, in 2016-17, after the PML-N headed the provincial government, the percentage share of education was reduced substantially to 17 per cent of the provincial budget. Advisor to Balochistan chief minister on information Sardar Raza Muhammad Bureech said that 17 per cent of the provincial budget outlay for education was insufficient to get rid of the education crisis even in the next fifty years.[14] Likewise, in 2015-16, out of the education budget, a sum of Rs 7.5 billion was apportioned for education development purposes. In 2016-17 the development budget was slashed by 42 per cent to Rs 4.4 billion.[15]

The major cut in the education budget pertained to primary and secondary schools with the focus being on higher secondary, college and university education. Projects for primary and middle education made up only 22 per cent of the budget. The misplaced priorities can be gauged from the fact that Balochistan had the highest percentage of out-of-school children at 70 per cent; among the under-ten children only 28 per cent were literate; the ratio for girls was even worse at only 16 per cent. In rural areas only 10 per cent girls were educated. Without prioritizing primary education, especially girls' education, Balochistan would continue to remain far behind in literacy than the other provinces. Moreover, instead of completing ongoing projects, 66 per cent of the funds were allocated to new projects. As a result, education development projects initiated during the last two years would not only take longer to complete but there would be cost overruns too.[16]

Police

The provincial police were in as pitiable a condition as the provincial government. A provincial police chief told the Human Rights Commission of Pakistan that cases had surfaced in which police officers who tried to check cars with tinted windows landed up in jail. The owners/occupants of these cars clearly had protection of the intelligence agencies.[17] Another officer said that the greatest threat to the police was from within and that the sectarian Lashkar-e-Jhangvi had indoctrinated sections of the force. He cited the case where black paint was thrown on the pictures of Shia policemen killed in action. Such pictures were displayed in the offices of senior police officers where only police personnel had access. Not surprisingly, he lamented, 'In Quetta we have to keep coffins and flags ready at all times. That is how frequently police officers are killed.'[18]

The death toll of Balochistan police in Quetta had risen above twenty in 2017 and there were seventy terrorist attacks in Quetta alone in 2017. This does raise doubts about the improving law and order situation in the area.[19]

The Federal Government

The federal government's performance in responding to the challenge posed by Balochistan has been as bad as that of the provincial government. The basic argument of the federal government, taking a cue from the army, was that the Baloch leaders were opposed to development projects and wanted to keep the province 'backward' for the sake of their vested interests to maintain the traditional sardari system. The violence in Balochistan was dubbed the work of a small band of 'miscreants' unrepresentative of the larger Baloch population and a 'law and order' issue. Musharraf, for example, in a speech in January 2006, stated: 'The tribal chiefs have held this country hostage for the past thirty to forty years for their interests. These tribal chiefs have no interest whatsoever in the well-being and progress of the common man and subject their own sub-tribesmen to torture because of their pro-development thinking.'[20]

Such arguments, as pointed out earlier, have lacked credibility because it does not factor in the reality that a large number of Baloch have taken up arms. The government is at a loss to explain the reason for its message not finding acceptance with the population, while the message of the tribal chiefs is doing so. With the entry of middle-class Baloch the argument about tribal chiefs has become even weaker.

Issue of Development

The issue of 'development' has become a major bone of contention between the nationalists and the government. According to a Baloch leader, 'It is totally a wrong concept that we oppose development. The basic question is about the nature and modalities of development. That is why the basic demand of Balochistan's political parties is that provinces must be given maximum autonomy. Trust them and give them the authority to undertake development projects.'[21]

Musharraf and his successors have insisted that the Gwadar project demonstrated the government's commitment to developing Balochistan.[22] However, as noted in an earlier chapter, since the Baloch are not stakeholders or beneficiaries, they strongly oppose it, perceiving the project as yet another Central government scheme to exploit Balochistan's resources, while also altering the province's demographic composition to their disadvantage.[23] Moreover, in far-flung areas of Balochistan there was hardly any 'development'. In the words of Jamaat-e-Islami leader Abdul Mateen, '... the coastal highway does not pass through even a single union council of Makran district; it has been built for the benefit of civil and military bureaucracy.'[24] Not surprisingly, for many Baloch the continued emphasis on mega projects contrasts adversely with the failure of previous development announcements to materialize. Hence, the Baloch do not feel confident that their circumstances will improve.

Rejecting the argument that the government's development schemes had sparked the insurgency and that the conflict was confined to the tribal territories of a few sardars, an opposition parliamentarian said: 'If the federal government claims that the troubled areas in Balochistan are only 7 per cent of the province, then why is there no development in the rest of the 93 per cent?'[25] The secretary-general of Nawab Bugti's party stressed: 'If the (dissenting) sardars are guarding their self-interest, then they would side with the government, not confront it,' adding, 'only when you have the support of the masses and are fighting for the people can you can confront the government'.[26]

'Packages'

To offer some political sops to the Baloch, Musharraf's government, under the chairmanship of Chaudhury Shujaat Hussain, president of the Pakistan Muslim League-Q (PML-Q), formed a parliamentary committee consisting of sixteen senators and twelve members of the National Assembly in September 2004. Its task was to 'examine the current situation in Balochistan and make recommendations thereon'. The committee was split into two subcommittees. Wasim Sajjad (leader of the house in the Senate) chaired one that was to make recommendations to promote provincial harmony and to protect the rights of the provinces with a view to strengthening the federation. Senator Mushahid Hussain chaired the other that was mandated to examine the current situation in Balochistan and make recommendations. While nothing was heard about the recommendations of the Wasim Sajjad subcommittee, the Hussain subcommittee did make several recommendations, the key among which were:

- review the check posts manned by the Frontier Corps and the Coast Guards in interior Balochistan;

- halt construction of military cantonments until all major issues are resolved;
- increase royalties to the gas-producing districts of Balochistan, with the federal government paying arrears;
- address underdevelopment in Gwadar, Quetta and Sui;
- strictly implement the 5.4 per cent employment quota for Baloch workers in all federal ministries, divisions, corporations and departments; and
- create parity between the Baloch and Pashtuns in Balochistan in all spheres of life.

However, most of the recommendations were only suggestions, with no specific mechanisms for their execution. Its recommendation about convening a special task force to ensure the implementation was never implemented.[27]

In fact, Baloch nationalist leaders were disappointed that the committee did not mention the withdrawal of military forces or the release of political prisoners languishing in Pakistani jails. Instead, the recommendations were seen as providing a cover to the military and paramilitary forces to mobilize and eliminate the political representatives of Balochistan. They were also concerned about its recommendations of 'parity' between the Baloch and the Pashtuns in the province, perceiving it as part of Islamabad's long-standing policy of divide-and-rule.[28]

Shaukat Aziz, the then prime minister, doomed the recommendations when he echoed the military's line that 'stern measures' would be taken against Baloch 'miscreants' and 'the writ of the government would be ensured at every cost'. A disappointed Mushahid Hussain said: 'The sense of engagement, involvement and inclusion is missing. We see it as a far-off territory meant to be controlled. I think there was criminal negligence when it came to its implementation by both civil and military bureaucracy. We have never learnt any lessons from the mistakes we made in the 1973 insurgency.... But nothing changed.'[29]

In November 2009 yet another reform package called the Aghaz-e-Haqooq-e-Balochistan (Start of Rights of Balochistan Package) meant to address Baloch grievances was announced with much fanfare by the PPP government. The intention was to correct the wrongs done to Balochistan by successive governments over the years. The army chipped in by giving up the idea of building a military cantonment, deciding instead to establish a military college with reserved seats for the Baloch. On paper, at least, the package seemed to meet several of the Baloch demands including the return of political exiles, the release of jailed Baloch political activists, creation of jobs, etc. However, the major grievances of retrieving missing persons, stopping the kill-and-dump policy, exploitation of resources and denial of control over the resources were not addressed.

Hence, the package failed to meet the expectations of the nationalists. According to the HRCP mission in 2011, almost everyone they met said that the package was meaningless in the context of the situation in the province and that even the things promised under the package had not been delivered. For example, the 5,000 jobs given under the package were not of much value as these were one-year contracts and offered no permanent solution to the acute unemployment amongst the Baloch youth.[30] Likewise, more than 3,000 posts reserved in the federal government for Baloch domicile holders under the package remained vacant since the announcement. This again reflected the lack of political will that ensured paltry implementation of decisions.[31]

Even otherwise, by its own admission, the government could implement only fifteen of the sixty-one proposals contained in the package. In February 2013 a ten-member special cabinet committee said that desired results were not achieved despite unprecedented allocation of funds.[32]

The Eighteenth Amendment to the Constitution and the seventh National Finance Commission (NFC) Award did open a window of opportunity to rectify two of the main grievances of the Baloch. The amendment, on paper, devolved greater power on the provinces, especially making them partners in oil and gas resources. However, if the complaints of the chief ministers of Sindh and KPK are to be believed, clearly the Eighteenth Amendment has not made much of a difference in practice. The reason for the scepticism is that the implementation of the devolution of power to the provinces has not taken full effect. According to Peter Jacob, a human rights activist: 'Operating in an environment of lack of trust and lack of civil society input, the constitutional review process has been marred by bottlenecks and the failure of the government to appoint a body to supervise the devolution of ministries from the federal to the provincial level.'[33]

The NFC Award, as noted earlier, took into account multiple criteria including backwardness, poverty, etc., and not merely population as before. This has certainly benefited Balochistan. As a result, the province's share of revenue was increased from 5.11 per cent to 9.09 per cent, making more funds available for development. However, given Balochistan's accumulated deprivation since 1947, it would take decades before a dent is made, provided the funds are used judiciously. Furthermore, the continuation of the seventh NFC award after its expiration on 30 June 2015, as noted in a previous chapter, has not only been unconstitutional but has put Balochistan in an unfavourable position. This is because the seventh NFC award used obsolete and manipulated figures of poverty that downplayed poverty in Balochistan. As a result, Balochistan is losing up to Rs 28 billion annually.[34]

On 6 August 2015 Prime Minister Nawaz Sharif approved another package called the Pur-aman (Peaceful) Balochistan programme. Given the past record, however, there was a question mark against the potential success of this programme as well. According to Mohammad Ali Talpur, the Pur-aman Balochistan programme of the two Sharifs isn't a development programme but is a 'pacification' one, based solely on brute force to ensure security for the Chinese working on CPEC. It is in pursuance of this pacification plan that the formation of a special security division became necessary despite the presence of 50,000 plus Frontier Corps personnel there.[35] Even if these programmes brought some development to the region, this would be too little too late. Indeed, as Brahamdagh Bugti observed on 26 August 2015, 'Development in Balochistan is irrelevant, as a democratic government is not present in the Province and the Baloch people were not included in the decision.'[36]

In late 2017 Shahid Khaqan Abbasi, who took over as prime minister after the Supreme Court disqualified Nawaz Sharif in July 2017, announced an 'equalization package' for Balochistan, the estimated value of which was reported to be Rs 20 billion over a span of ten years. It was meant for the provision of gas, electricity, education and clean drinking water.[37] However, it was unlikely that a cash package of this sort would placate the Baloch who were looking not for handouts but for their rights.[38] Moreover, what was notable was that the Centre would only contribute half the money, with the balance to be made up by the provincial government. It was also a bit late in the day for the PML-N government, which at that time had only a few months left of its mandated time, to realize that basic services were needed in Balochistan.

The basic problem with all the 'packages' has been that they ignore why the Baloch were so alienated. There has been little understanding of the strong perception among the Baloch that they have been and are being treated as a colony, unable to use their own resources for their own benefit. As the *News* puts it, 'Tackling that requires not just a package of economic development but political reforms. That would require the state to listen to Balochistan's leaders rather than just announcing a package and believing that will solve problems that have existed for decades.'[39]

The task for the government is quite clear. According to the World Bank–sponsored Balochistan Economic Report, mentioned in an earlier chapter, the province needs 158,000 jobs and a growth rate of 6.5 per cent annually to lift a significant percentage of the poverty-stricken population above the poverty line. Unfortunately, the growth rate in Balochistan is only 2.9 per cent. To bring Balochistan up to the level of other provinces would require massive investments in a wide variety of sectors. However, given Balochistan's geography and demography, no political government in Islamabad has been willing to make such investments. For a politician, greater investment in Balochistan does not translate into electoral gains given that Balochistan sends only twenty MNAs (sixteen general seats and four reserved seats for women) to parliament. The return on the investment is much higher in high-density provinces like Punjab and Sindh. Not surprising, therefore, Balochistan has remained neglected, underdeveloped and marginalized. It risks continuing to face the same fate under any government.[40]

This is also borne out by the fact that the mainstream political parties of Pakistan do not really consider the province to be a stakeholder in the power structure of Pakistan. In fact, these mainstream parties like the Pakistan Peoples Party (PPP), various shades of the Muslim Leagues and the Pakistan Tehreek-e-Insaf (PTI) have little roots in the province. The parliamentarians of these parties also do not take the authority of the parties' central leaderships seriously. Balochistan governments are perceived as pawns of the establishment.[41] As a result, all the major political parties have restricted themselves to only maintaining a token presence in the province. The absence of the federal parties' involvement in the politics of Balochistan is one of the elements preventing normalcy to return to the province.

Since assuming office in 2013 and till his removal in July 2017, former prime minister Nawaz Sharif hardly held any political gathering in the province. His visits to Balochistan were fly-in-fly-out ones to inaugurate a few projects. Other central leaders of the PML-N also did not bother to visit the province and involve themselves in its politics. A few PML-N leaders did visit Quetta prior to the Senate election in March 2015 to ensure that candidates who were nominated got votes. This marked the apathy of the PML-N towards the politics and problems of Balochistan. Prime Minister Abassi visited in January 2018 to try and unsuccessfully prevent the collapse of the PML-N government in the province.

The PPP has not behaved any differently with Balochistan. The PPP's tenure as the government in the province from 2008 to 2013 was marked with corruption, bad governance and nepotism. Once it was booted out of power, the interest of the central leadership in the province dwindled. In February 2017 Asif Zardari visited Balochistan for the first time since his tenure as president ended, primarily to meet the potential 'winning horses' from Balochistan.

The attitude of the PTI has not been any different. It conducted a political gathering in Quetta in April 2012 but since then Balochistan has fallen off its radar. Even during the dharna politics of the PTI, the party's leadership from Balochistan was not involved. The central leadership showed little commitment to strengthen the political structure of the party in Balochistan. After becoming prime minister, Imran Khan visited the province a few times to inaugurate some projects but had done little else.

The nationalist and religious parties based in Balochistan have maintained a similar stance. The Pashtunkhwa Milli Awami Party (PkMAP) and National Party are two parties that play the Pashtun and

Baloch ethnic card respectively. These parties remained busy enjoying the bounties of the government and their political activities were restricted to attaining maximum benefits till the end of their tenure.

The Jamiat Ulema-i-Islam-Fazlur (JUI-F) was the leading opposition party in the province. It has a vast network in the province—mainly through religious seminaries. However, the party was in the government at the federal level so they were not involved in any serious political activities that aimed to challenge the provincial government. This only left the Balochistan National Party–Mengal (BNP–M), which is also a nationalist party, but with limited representation even in Balochistan it proved to be ineffective.

The nationalist parties of Balochistan have their influence only at the provincial level. They do not exert any influence at the federal level given the small share of Balochistan in parliament. On the other hand, the major problems of Balochistan are federal-centric in nature and cannot be solved at the provincial level. If the mainstream political parties of Pakistan keep on ignoring Balochistan, the problems in the province are unlikely to be resolved.[42]

The cynicism of the Baloch is not surprising given the fact that they have seen Islamabad-based leaders mouthing homilies without taking action on the ground. For example, soon after he assumed power, Gen. Musharraf promised to alleviate the growing sense of deprivation among the smaller provinces and he even offered an apology to the people of Balochistan for 'past mistakes'. Similarly, President Asif Ali Zardari started off with a public apology to Balochistan and promised to reverse the wrongs of the past, adding that his Baloch roots would reinforce his commitment to that goal. However, on the ground nothing much changed. If anything, 'the situation in Balochistan is worse than before and the Baloch insurgency is a throwback to their armed struggle in the 1970s, during Zulfikar Ali Bhutto's tenure'.[43] The situation under Imran Khan, at the time of writing, is no different.

According to Mushahid Hussain, 'These recurring problems, during different governments, point to a deep-seated mindset which is a major impediment to granting the Baloch their legitimate rights under the 1973 Constitution as equal partners of the federation.' According to him, it was this mindset that impelled rulers like Bhutto and Musharraf to commit monumental mistakes in Balochistan, including the tragic

killing of the sons of Sardar Attaullah Mengal in 1975 and Nawab
Akbar Bugti in 2006. He calls this mindset 'not only colonial, callous
and bureaucratic, but it is also outmoded, refusing to reason with those
who dare to challenge the status quo'. He admits that the track record of
the federal government in dealing with Balochistan was truly abysmal,
irrespective of whether the ruler was in khaki or in mufti.[44]

18

The Response of the Army

THE RESPONSE OF THE ARMY is fundamental to the situation in Balochistan. Despite the restoration of democracy in Pakistan, the Baloch issue continues to be handled militarily rather than politically.

The army's approach to the situation in Balochistan is dictated by three factors: one, the insecurity bred by the knowledge that the people of Balochistan have not embraced Pakistan wholeheartedly since its forced accession in 1948. Two, the continuing hangover of the creation of Bangladesh. The trauma of the secession of East Pakistan has been such that the army fears that it could be repeated in Balochistan. Thus, the ruling elite, especially the army, has become increasingly wary of accommodating even legitimate ethno-national demands, seeing dissent as a threat to the integrity of the country. Three, the army refuses to comprehend that the persisting Baloch insurgency is due to the legitimate grievances of the Baloch. Instead, the security establishment has sought to mask the demands by projecting disaffection as externally sponsored to destabilize Pakistan or to disrupt the China–Pakistan Economic Corridor (CPEC).

The army has thus sought to crush any national movement believing that the only way to deal with dissent is 'a military solution', i.e., a physical suppression coupled with a media blackout on developments there. As has been well put, the Pakistan army, '… has earned the dubious distinction of being an army that keeps trying to conquer its own people when they refuse to follow its diktats.'[1] It is this simplistic militarized approach to security in Balochistan that has become ingrained in the mindset and is in reality a fundamental part of the problem and not a solution.² The army's continuing domination of the polity even when it is not in power has ensured that a change in policy over handling Balochistan is unlikely.

Musharraf exemplified the mentality of the army. Ruling out any compromise with 'miscreants' trying to sabotage peace and development in Balochistan, he reiterated, in an address to the nation, that '... the time has come to end the sway of these sardars and establish the writ of the government to protect national assets and installations ... there will be no political settlement with these cruel Baloch sardars who remained involved in anti-government, anti-democracy and even anti-state activities in the past'.³

Currently, the construction of the Gwadar deep-sea port, the CPEC and the need for the protection of the Chinese has given the army a further excuse to accelerate the military operation against the Baloch.

Army Tactics

The Army has adopted several tactics to tackle the insurgency.

Use of Excessive Force

Force, much more than required, has been indiscriminately used by the army. Several commentators and organizations have testified to this. As Selig Harrison noted, 'The wanton use of superior firepower by the Pakistani and Iranian forces, [during the 1973–77 insurgency] especially the indiscriminate air attacks on Baluch villages, left a legacy of bitter and enduring hatred. Since nearly all Baluch felt the impact of Pakistani repression, the Baluch population is now politicized to an unprecedented degree. In mid-1980, I found a pervasive mood of expectancy among the Baluch, a widespread desire to vindicate Baluch martial honour, and a readiness to renew the struggle when and if circumstances appear to be favourable.'⁴ The Human Rights Commission of Pakistan reported that 'indiscriminate bombing and strafing' by F-16s and Cobra gunships are again being used to draw the guerrillas into the open. Six Pakistani army brigades, plus paramilitary forces totalling some 25,000 men, are deployed in the Kohlu mountains and surrounding areas where the fighting is most intense.'[5]

Kill-and-Dump and Enforced Disappearances[6]

In addition to brute force, the army has also resorted to abductions or enforced disappearances, killing hapless individuals and then dumping their bodies—acts that are widely referred to as kill-and-dump operations. The corpses invariably bear marks of severe torture. Such victims have included students, doctors, lawyers and journalists—the emerging middle class—who have been detained by intelligence agencies without being produced before any court of law. The exact number of such enforced disappearances is disputed but would run into thousands. The army has, of course, denied any involvement in these kill-and-dump operations.

Downplaying the Insurgency

Many a time the army has sought to downplay the insurgency asserting that actually there was no insurgency. It has even denied that the army was deployed in Balochistan, saying that it was merely using the Frontier Corps to run a police operation to stem violence. For example, Maj. Gen. Shaukat Sultan, the former director general, Inter-Services Public Relations (ISPR), in an interview to *Daily Times* on 15 September 2004 said that no military operation was taking place in Balochistan and that life there was normal. Whenever a terrorist attack occurred, the provincial government called out troops to aid civil authority.[7] More recently, the then commander, Southern Command, Lt Gen. Aamer Riaz told a gathering, 'There is no insurgency in Balochistan, but a bit of misguided militancy.'[8]

From the perspective of the Pakistan Army a 'military operation' takes place when tanks and helicopters as well as weaponry are employed to accomplish a goal. On the other hand, the Baloch equate extra-judicial killings, disappearances, and even the checking at check posts with 'operation'.[9]

Islamization

Another element of the army's strategy has been to try and supplant the Baloch ethnic identity by a common Muslim identity through Islamization. Like the rest of the country, Balochistan too could not escape Zia-ul-Haq's Islamization zeal. However, as discussed in an earlier chapter, in the past decade there has been an obvious effort to radicalize the province using Deobandi groups as well as the Ahle Hadis Jamaat-ud-Dawa (JuD)/Lashkar-e-Taiba (LeT). For example, during the earthquake of October 2015 only the JUD was allowed to be on the frontline of relief efforts.[10] The state has encouraged the Deobandi and Salafi militant organizations to operate in the nineteen Baloch districts of Balochistan, especially in the districts of Mastung and Lasbela. As mentioned in an earlier chapter, some Brahvi youth have reportedly joined the sectarian groups and are being used to target the Shia Hazaras and the Baloch nationalists.

The state has 'inserted' JuD assets in Balochistan as a means of countering nationalist/separatist sentiment. It even deployed its favourite 'strategic asset', viz., Jamaat-ud-Dawa chief Hafiz Saeed to control the situation in Balochistan. He visited Quetta in December 2016 and was accorded full protocol. However, his presence did not create many waves in Balochistan.[11]

Counter-Nationalists

Another strategy adopted by the army is to employ counter-nationalists. An organization, Tehreek-e-Nefaz-e-Aman Balochistan (TNAB; movement for the restoration of peace in Balochistan), has been formed by intelligence agencies to crush the national movement. TNAB is said to be the armed wing of Mutahida Mahaz Balochistan (United Front of Balochistan), a political party headed by Siraj Raisani, the brother of the former provincial chief minister Aslam Raisani. The armed wing claims to have support of the establishment to restore peace in Balochistan.[12] Interestingly, Aslam Raisani, who was a Balochistan Awami Party (BAP) candidate for the July 2018 elections, was killed in a suicide blast at a political rally in Mastung on 13 July

2018. More than 130 people were also killed in the terrorist incident believed to have been carried out by the Daesh.[13]

The HRCP noted another armed vigilante outfit calling itself the Baloch Musallah Difa'a Tanzeem that was openly threatening the people with dire consequences if they tried to register cases with the police about disappearances or recovery of dead bodies of missing persons. The threats were made on the phone by callers who claimed to be Baloch. However, when addressed in the local Balochi or Brahvi languages, they failed to answer. This led the people to believe that they were not Baloch. The police have not made even half-hearted efforts to investigate the cases or even question the accused in cases where the families of the missing persons had revealed that personnel of security agencies were responsible for the abduction of their relatives.[14]

The army has naturally denied such allegations. Despite this, reports in the Pakistani media continue to highlight the use of 'death squads', resembling the notorious Al Shams and Al Badr militias that the Pakistan Army had used during the Bangladesh liberation war in 1971.[15]

A representative of one of the political parties told the HRCP that such extremist elements had scores of cars with tinted windows, which passed unchecked through different check posts in the province. It was claimed that some of them carried cards stamped by the intelligence agencies that served as permits for illegal weapons and unregistered cars.[16] In one case in Mastung, residents nabbed an attacker who was carrying an ISI identity card. Some senior public figures confirmed this incident in their interviews with the fact-finding mission.[17] A lawmaker said that even if such extremists were caught by the police and produced in court, they were released due to lack of evidence and were back roaming the streets within days. Not even one of these state-sponsored elements had been tried in court despite hundreds of violent incidents, and attacks continued despite the presence of thousands of Frontier Corps and police personnel in the province.[18]

Some, if not all, of these outfits have links with sectarian terrorist elements. Many of them have joined the ISIS and the Lashkar-i-Jhangvi (LeJ) and have become an even bigger threat to the state than the Baloch insurgents. In five recent attacks claimed by the Islamic State (ISIS) in 2017 over 220 people were killed and many more injured.

One of these proxies—Shafique Mengal—who was used to target Baloch militants went rogue after he was discarded. He went on to assume a prominent position in the Lashkar-i-Jhangvi al-Alami that has been responsible for several terrorist incidents in Balochistan.

The 'Foreign Hand'

When the insurgency began, Musharraf and the army described it as the work of a few 'miscreants', the reference being to a few tribal sardars. However, when the insurgency spread to non-tribal areas the narrative started changing to the 'foreign hand'. The public was informed that foreign powers, especially India, had set out to impede the development of the Gwadar port and the CPEC. The state's information machinery kept releasing stories that emphasized Indian 'interference' in Balochistan's affairs.[19] However, as the Daily Times commented aptly, 'It is not enough to simply outsource responsibility to CPEC—as if this is a one-size-fits-all panacea for every occasion. No, the Pakistani state must get its own house in order. And that means not only focusing on the front lawn seen mostly by visitors. But that back garden, too. For both fall within the picket fencing of national borders.[20]

In reality, '… denouncing international conspiracies has become a barometer to judge when the army feels they are unable to control the situation'.[21] By harping on this bogey of 'foreign hand' the government hopes to wean away those sympathetic towards the Baloch struggle. It also provides them with a handle to justify to the international audiences the brutal crackdown in the form of missing persons and the terrible kill-and-dump policy.[22]

In the 1960s and '70s the favourite whipping boys were Afghanistan and Soviet Union. Today it is India. Allegations about Indian support have been frequent. The then Balochistan chief minister, Jam Mohammed Yousaf, accused India on 13 August 2004 of supporting terrorists and maintaining forty training camps in Balochistan.[23] These allegations were repeated by the then director general of ISPR, Maj. Gen. Shaukat Sultan, in an interview to the Daily Times on 15 September 2004.[24] Two years later, Balochistan governor Owais Ghani accused India of financing the insurgency, and Afghan warlords and drug barons of arming the militants.[25] In February 2006 Musharraf presented the visiting Afghan president Hamid Karzai with 'proof' that India was using bases within Afghanistan to 'foment trouble in Balochistan and FATA'.[26] Pakistan Senator Mushahid Hussain took those accusations one step further in an April 2006 interview with the *News* when he accused Indian agencies of establishing training camps near the Pakistan–Afghanistan border in order to train Baloch dissidents in the use of explosives and sophisticated weapons. Hussain further claimed that India was using its five diplomatic missions within Afghanistan as 'launching pads for undertaking covert operations' in both the NWFP (now KPK) and Balochistan.[27]

In April 2009 the then advisor to the prime minister on interior affairs, Rehman A. Malik, alleged in the Pakistan Senate that India was backing the Balochistan Liberation Army (BLA) for fuelling insurgency in the province and creating unrest.[28] On 3 June 2012 the then inspector general of the Frontier Corps, Maj. Gen. Ubaidullah Khan Khattak, told the press that some 121 training camps run by Baloch dissidents were active in Balochistan and supported by 'foreign agencies', twenty of which were directly operating in the province. While suspicions invariably fall on India, they are also directed at Afghanistan and the United States.[29] Coming to the present, speaking at a seminar in Quetta, former army chief Gen. Raheel Sharif said foreign adversaries were more than eager to exploit any opportunity to destabilize Pakistan by '… harbouring, training and funding dissidents and militants' and that 'Terrorists were externally supported and internally facilitated'.[30]

Little hard evidence of substantive foreign funding or cross-border sanctuaries and bases has, however, been presented. The Baloch themselves have emphasized that the militancy was an 'indigenous, nationalist movement'.[31] As Selig Harrison puts it, 'Instead of recognizing the political dimensions of the issue and acting to resolve them, Pakistan has taken the easier route by accusing India of using its consulates in Afghanistan to assist Baloch insurgents. However, evidence of this, in the public domain, is woefully missing.'[32] Or as Grare puts it, despite the widespread allegations of the Pakistani authorities, the hardliners do not seem to enjoy any significant foreign support, which is likely to change the provincial balance of forces in their favour.[33]

According to media reports, the current favourite story is about a former Indian naval officer Kulbhushan Jadhav. According to the narrative, Jadhav was a serving Indian naval officer working for an Indian intelligence agency and was caught by Pakistani security forces in 2016 in Pakistan. 'In his recorded confessional statement, Jadhav accepted that he had been assigned by the Indian intelligence agency to promote unrest in Balochistan and Karachi and had been working with the Baloch student organizations and insurgents and terrorist groups for the purpose.'[34] This is touted as 'proof' of Indian interference and state-sponsored terrorism in Balochistan. The fact of the matter is that Jadhav was not given consular access despite repeated requests of the Indian high commission in Islamabad, and the so-called 'confession' was clearly made under duress as was obvious to everyone who watched the TV programme. Though Jadhav has been sentenced to death by a military court, at the time of writing the matter is pending in the International Court of Justice (ICJ).

Significantly, Baloch human rights activist Mama Qadeer Baloch in an interview confirmed that Kulbhushan Jadhav was kidnapped in Iran, he was not a spy, he never entered Balochistan and that he was convicted without evidence. Giving details, he said that an Iranian cleric Mulla Umer Balochi Irani of the Jaish-ul-Adl group (an outfit known to be on the Pakistan Army's payroll) had kidnapped Jadhav at Sarbaaz in Iran and sold him for Rs 40–50 million.[35] These revelations clearly put paid to the army's elaborate charade about an Indian spy.

It is, of course, possible that the Baloch operations are financed through illegal trade across the borders with Afghanistan and Iran. However, more plausible is that the prosperous Baloch Diaspora, especially in the Gulf States, is the major source of financing.[36]

Targeting Families

The army has not hesitated in targeting the families of prominent Baloch leaders to pressurize them. In this, they are repeating what had been done during the 1970s insurgency. In 1973 the Baloch poet laureate Gul Khan Naseer's house was attacked and his brother killed.[37] Asad Mengal, son of the former chief minister of Balochistan Attaullah

Mengal, was abducted by the security agencies in the mid-1970s and his body was never found.

Coming to the present, Akbar Bugti's son, Jamil Bugti, was arrested on charges of treason for 'speaking against the army and the government' at a press conference in October 2006 at which he had said that the 'fighters on the mountains' were waging a war for the Baloch people, and '... it is the responsibility of every Baloch to support them according to his capability'.[38] In July 2006 bank accounts of forty-two alleged 'BLA members', twenty-five from Akbar Bugti's family, were frozen. Also included were Khair Bakhsh Marri's sons, granddaughters and daughters-in-law.[39] In November 2006 two granddaughters of Akbar Bugti were accused of links with the BLA and their bank accounts frozen.[40] While Brahamdagh Bugti managed to escape to Switzerland via Afghanistan in 2011, his sister had to pay the price. She was married to Nawabzada Bakhtiar Khan Domki, a provincial legislator, and had a daughter. On 30 January 2012 unidentified assailants gunned her down together with her daughter and her driver in the heart of Karachi.[41] In 2015 the brother and nephew of Dr Allah Nazar were killed by the Frontier Corps.[42]

Frontier Corps

The paramilitary Frontier Corps (FC), technically under the federal interior ministry, is as per the Frontier Corps Ordinance 1959, deemed to be in 'active service' against external aggressor or enemy, against hostile tribes, raiders or other hostile persons, or persons co-operating with or assisting them. In theory, the provincial home department requests the federal interior ministry to come to the aid of the provincial government. However, given the highly centralized system of governance in Pakistan, the Centre takes the decision and the provinces simply back it.[43]

A bone of contention and bitterness about the FC are the nearly 500 check posts established by it all over the province. The HRCP noted that many people complained about the abuses by those running these posts. The complaints ranged from extortion, humiliation, threats and outright use of lethal force without any provocation.[44] Incidents were reported where the FC personnel manning these checkpoints insulted the people by shaving their moustaches, tearing the traditional Baloch shalwar and making other gestures derogatory to their culture and bearing.[45] The HRCP quoted a political activist saying 'The FC is here to kill us, not to protect us.'[46] Another complaint was that the security presence in the sparsely populated province was undeniably overwhelming, and most security personnel were not locals.

Even the Balochistan chief minister Aslam Raisani blamed the FC for running a 'parallel government' within the province. Ministers in his cabinet accused the FC of sabotaging every attempt to politically reconcile with the enraged Baloch leaders.[47]

———•———

As the Baloch nationalists point out with some justification, the cantonments, which are largely in Balochistan's interior, have little to do with protecting Pakistan 'against external aggression or threat of war', the military's primary constitutional role, but are aimed primarily at subduing Baloch dissent and enabling the Centre to exploit the province's natural resources.[48] As Attaullah Mengal told PML-N chief Nawaz Sharif on 19 December 2011, 'This is not Pakistan Army. It is Punjabi army that is indulging in such inhuman acts against the Baloch people.'[49]

Pakistan's past efforts in assuaging the Baloch does not inspire confidence. The army generals seem only intent in suppressing the insurgency. In the process they have succeeded in intensifying it. Since the army does not believe in using 'soft power' and instead relies on coercion, its policies can only beget more violence. Baloch history shows that the attempt to bury the idea of Baloch nationalism is unlikely to succeed.

Conclusion

ESSENTIALLY, PAKISTAN'S BALOCHISTAN CONUNDRUM IS that the state is trying to resolve a serious political issue militarily; instead of a surgeon's delicate and deft touch, Pakistan is using a butcher's cleaver. The roots of Baloch alienation and resentment run deep. The state, led by the army, just cannot or does not want to understand the import and depth of Baloch nationalism. Having learnt very little from the past, the Pakistan state, led by the army, sees the insurgency as a law and order problem that needs to be tackled militarily.

The army does not see that the insurgency is not the real problem but is the result of a problem, and the problem is political. It goes to the heart of what kind of a state Pakistan is and whether minority nationalities like the Baloch can be accommodated equitably or will have to live subserviently under the dominant Punjabis. The army being overwhelmingly Punjabi is also part of the problem. In Punjab the army is seen as a friend but in Balochistan, or Sindh for that matter, the army is not a friend but a force of oppression.

The results of tackling a political problem militarily are there for all to see. The International Crisis Group (ICG) perhaps summed it up best when it noted, 'The military can retain control over Balochistan's territory through sheer force, but it cannot defeat an insurgency that has local support ... its policy directions will likely undermine the remaining vestiges of state legitimacy in the troubled province ... The insurgency is not likely to recede, nor will Islamabad manage to dampen the Baloch'.[1]

There is no doubt that Balochistan poses a complex problem and it is this complexity that poses a challenge to the military mind that is used to seeing things in black and white. Even so, the fact that the problem in the province resurrects after a hiatus of few years must make the leadership, including that of the army, think why this happens. The simple answer is because political remedies have always been ignored.

If there is one thread running through the problem, it is the memory of the forced accession of Balochistan in 1948 and the economic exploitation of the province for the benefit of Punjab leading to severe deprivation, which, in turn, has fuelled political alienation. The Baloch believe that their land is rich but they have been kept poor by the state. As Kaiser Bengali puts it: 'The province has, for seventy years, suffered a situation where the country has taken much from and given little to it. That the province can be rich in natural resources and yet abjectly poor is a testimony to long years of neglect and exploitation. It is a saga of resource transfer on a massive scale, a saga of colonial style political and economic management.'[2] Haunting deprivation, discrimination and disenchantment are starkly evident and cannot be callously refuted by merely alleging that it's the handiwork of a few sardars, or of foreign hands.

Politically and socially, the Baloch believe that their secular democratic mindset is not compatible with religious fundamentalism and dictatorial behaviour of the state's ruling elite.[3] According to Naseer Dashti, '... the essence of the Baloch national struggle is the assertion that the Baloch have their separate cultural, social and historical identity which is markedly different from the fundamentalist ideology of the religious-based state of Pakistan.' Baloch nationalist politics has always been based on secular principles and they have not politicized religion that has remained in the personal sphere and tradition.[4]

In the initial decades, alienation provoked by the above factors was limited to a few tribes who intermittently broke into rebellion. Now, since the basic issues have been aggravated instead of being resolved, the insurgency has spread to all parts of the province. The fact is, in large parts of Balochistan, the Pakistani state is considered an illegitimate actor.[5]

The army seems to be unwilling to concede that unlike in the 1970s, the insurgency in Balochistan today is not limited to a handful of sardars. The insurgency is truly a nationalist one with the participation of a wider spectrum of the Baloch. They are not fighting to preserve individual sardari rights but to become masters of their own destiny, of their own resources and be responsible for their own political, economic and social empowerment. According to a Baloch nationalist, the military cannot crush the insurgency, since 'there is no single messianic leader whose removal will end it. This movement is based on an ideology that cannot be wiped out, and that ideology is Baloch nationhood'.[6] Even those Baloch who are participating in the political process are just as concerned about the narrowing space for the Baloch in Pakistan as those who have taken up arms against the state. It is just that their methods are different.

In the collective Baloch memory, injustices of the Pakistani (read Punjabi) state began with the creation of Pakistan itself, when they lost their independence, when their distinct national identity was snuffed out. Over the decades, the injustices have been fuelled by broken promises, and betrayals like the arrest, imprisonment and execution of Baloch leaders after the revolts of 1948 and 1958 despite solemn guarantees of amnesty and safe passage, sworn on the Koran. This was followed by the arbitrary dismissal of three democratically elected provincial governments, especially the one in 1973 that led to the four-year insurgency. Compounding matters was the killing of Nawab Akbar Khan Bugti in August 2006 that has become a defining moment in the current insurgency. Other injustices include: the lack of, or inadequate representation of the Baloch in the state and administrative structures of Pakistan; the continued exploitation of the province's natural gas and other resources for the benefit of other provinces, especially Punjab; the appalling socio-economic indices of the province; the construction of mega projects like Gwadar deep-sea port and the CPEC that do not factor in Baloch aspirations and ownership and could turn them into a minority in their own province. Topping it all are the brutal tactics of enforced disappearance and especially the wanton kill-and-dump operations adopted by the army. The weight of such past and present injustices cannot be lightly brushed under the carpet by touting distant development goals.

Perhaps the former chief justice Iftikhar Muhammad Chaudhry summed up the conundrum best during a hearing on the law and order situation when he remarked: 'We are all responsible for the destruction of Balochistan ourselves.'[7]

Facing absorption and subjugation, a growing section of the Baloch seem to have had no other choice than to resort to arms. They have chosen the option to fight to be alive rather than being submissive and becoming extinct. As Declan Walsh put it, 'Balochistan's dirty little war … highlights a very fundamental danger—the ability of Pakistanis to live together in a country that, under its Islamic cloak, is a patchwork of ethnicities and cultures.' He quotes Haris Gazdar, a Karachi-based researcher, saying, 'Balochistan is a warning of the real battle for Pakistan, which is about power and resources and if we don't get it right, we're headed for a major conflict.'[8]

The roots of these problems lie in Pakistan's failure to acknowledge and accommodate its ethnic diversity, economic disparities and provincial autonomy. In the process of constructing a national ideology based on a purely mechanical unity and simplistic idea of religious homogeneity, the ruling classes of Pakistan neglected the diversity of its people and ignored the interests of ethnic and regional minorities. This gave a deathblow to Pakistan as it was created in 1947. A majority of its people broke away to form a separate country in 1971—Bangladesh. The remainder of Pakistan is marred by ethnic and sectarian conflicts, religious terrorism and economic inequality.[9]

For Pakistan the dilemma is that given the economic and strategic importance of Balochistan, it cannot afford to fail. Loosening of the links with Balochistan would be a signal for other nationalities, like the Sindhis especially, to put forward claims for independence of their own. However, continuation of the conflict, let alone its escalation, could seriously impact the image of stability and could potentially raise doubts about its territorial integrity. Thus for Pakistan, Balochistan is a test case of its resolve not only to hold Pakistan together but also to weld the various nationalities into a larger whole. However, the way it is doing so is ensuring just the opposite.

As the equations stand today, the needs and interests of the state establishment and the Baloch are diametrically opposed to one another. The Baloch are fighting for their identity and their cultural, historical, geographical and economic rights. The state, including the army, is concerned with making an artificial Islamic nation, politically marginalizing the Baloch and ruthlessly exploiting Baloch resources. For the army, to reverse the course in Balochistan will not be easy given its mindset.

The moot question is whether the situation in Balochistan is irretrievable for Pakistan? Will the insurgency dissipate with economic development and improvement in social indicators? Will the state put an end to the policy of kill-and-dump and release those in illegal captivity? Will Balochistan see a lessening of the presence of security forces? Will the state ensure provincial rights and autonomy, allowing the Baloch to genuinely use their resources for their benefit first?

While the jury is out on this, what is clear is that such measures are unlikely to be taken and will certainly not be taken simultaneously. For one thing, the military is averse to provincial rights and autonomy. For another, Pakistan has gone too far down the road in terms of commitments to the Chinese on Gwadar and the CPEC to tweak the projects to give the Baloch a stake. For most of the Baloch themselves, the struggle seems to have gone beyond economics.

In any case, the Baloch have come to view development projects as more examples of the exploitation of the resources of Balochistan for the sake of the Punjabi state. For most of them, it is now about their honour, their survival with dignity on their own lands, about preserving their national identity, culture and language—in a word, about independence. Pushed to the wall, facing marginalization and subjugation, an increasing number of Baloch are now willing to pick up the gun for the sake of preserving their rights.

There is also a huge trust deficit. The people in general and the militant groups in particular no longer trust the government because of the frequent betrayals, military operations and the continuing policy of systematic enforced disappearances. Blood has been spilled; among others, the killing of Nawab Akbar Bugti, the mysterious killing of Balach Marri, the brutal murder of three Baloch leaders in 2009 and so on. For the Baloch, revenge is a key element in their honour code, Balochmayar. Clearly, one of the biggest obstacles in stabilizing the situation is the repugnant policy of enforced disappearance and kill-and-dump.[10] The trust deficit is too huge; moreover, the establishment is totally intransigent because it believes, as it did in East Pakistan, that they are powerful enough to crush people's aspirations in Balochistan.[11]

Not surprisingly, the HRCP warned that the decades-long history of neglect and betrayal combined with systematic human rights abuses carried out with impunity had made a vast number of Baloch people desperate. In such a situation '... a large section the Baloch youth has been driven into repudiating their allegiance to the state. When the people's will is being broken, their voice ruthlessly stifled and their bodies charred in torture cells; where mothers are dying to hear any news of their disappeared children, the state cannot expect any other reaction but one of rebellion.'[12]

There were windows of opportunities for peace in the past but were squandered through arrogance and ignorance; the best among them was the 1972-73 Attaullah Mengal government. In September 2008 the Baloch militant groups unilaterally observed ceasefire but there was no response and in January 2009 they ended the ceasefire.

The current spate of insurgency is the fifth in Balochistan. In other words, in the seventy years since the creation of Pakistan, almost every successive generation of the Baloch have risen in revolt, having lost faith that their grievances could be addressed within the political system. Every time the Baloch have risen, they have been put down militarily without any attempt to address their basic problems and issues and without giving them an equal opportunity to become stakeholders in Pakistan. As a result, these issues have festered and erupted whenever the Baloch have thought they were strong and able to assert their rights.

What is the likelihood of the establishment of an independent Balochistan? Despite Baloch determination and resolve to preserve their specific and unique identity and not be subsumed into a larger Pakistani identity, the political realities are indeed very challenging and pose major obstacles to the realization of their hopes. Many analysts have argued that Balochistan is an unlikely candidate for a successful separatist movement. Stephen Cohen, for example, has written that it lacks a middle class, a modern leadership, and that the Baloch are a tiny fraction of Pakistan's population—and even in their own province are faced with a growing Pashtun population. Further, neither Iran nor Afghanistan shows any sign of encouraging Baloch separatism because such a movement might encompass their own Baloch population.[13]

Selig Harrison remarked that the insurgency itself is scattered and weak but enough to keep a portion of the Pakistan Army tied down. Earlier, the insurgency was tribal-based but now, in the last decade, there has been a greater political awareness among the common people about their exploitation and hence there has been greater political mobilization. Even the moderate Baluch politicians have to articulate issues of provincial rights, missing persons, etc.[14]

At present levels, therefore, the conflict is unlikely to threaten the integrity of the state. Pakistan's military is large with well-trained troops and sophisticated weapons, making it capable of holding the country. The Pakistan Army will manage to outfight the Baloch fighters. Whether it will manage to outlast a people who are fighting to protect their identity and their homeland is a different matter altogether. What is likely is that protracted violence will continue to afflict Balochistan. The Baloch insurgents cannot defeat the army but as they have demonstrated, they can certainly defy the writ of the state, increase the cost for the army to maintain its grip on the province and prevent further exploitation of their resources.[15] The resistance groups have come to view the conflict with Pakistan as a prolonged struggle and are devising appropriate methodologies, involving both political mobilization and armed resistance.[16]

For Pakistan the question is what cost would it have to pay for holding on to Balochistan for the present and in the future. So far, previous military 'victories' have not resolved the Baloch question and there is nothing to suggest that another military 'victory' will either. If anything, the way the government and the army are handling mega projects, making the Baloch a minority in their own province, will increasingly ensure that in the future more and more ordinary Baloch will be alienated and take to armed insurrection.

Thus, neither the army nor the Pakistan state can get much comfort from the situation. Even at its present level, the insurgency is enough to target various pipelines and other infrastructure that gives the impression of instability to the outside world. The Chinese would be especially worried since they are investing huge sums of money.

A comparison with the situation in the then East Pakistan is instructive. The Bengali discontent that led to their independence in 1971 was driven by economic as well as political grievances. Baloch alienation, too, is driven by much the same grievances with the addition of historical wrongs. Speaking at a function in February 2018 in Karachi, former diplomat Jehangir Ashraf Qazi said that it was criminal governance not bad governance and sustained transfer of income from East Pakistan to West Pakistan, without benefits in proportion, that led to a kind of alienation, which was widespread and legitimate. He warned: 'The same process is taking place in Balochistan today,' adding that 'unlike East Pakistan, the population in Balochistan was lesser and there was a tendency to say that they can be crushed because there are just pockets of rebellion and resistance'.[17]

The difference between the two is that the Bengalis were relatively homogenous, had a significant middle class, a well-established cultural and literary life, a standardized language, a broad base of nationalist activists and a history of mass politicization that dated back to the struggle against the British Raj.[18] The Baloch nationalist movement, on the other hand, was built on 'uncertain social and cultural foundations of a fragmented tribal society' that had only a minuscule middle class, widespread illiteracy, underdeveloped literature, only a narrow base of nationalist activists and no real history of mass participation in the political process.[19] Moreover, the Bengalis obtained the support of India while the Baloch do not have a foreign backer. Resultantly, they have not been able to pose a grave threat to the Central government's hold on power.

The Baloch have, however, come a long way from the 1970s. The nature of the Baloch society is evolving. With the gradual dismantling of the age-old 'sardari nizam' (tribal structures), a new generation of leaders is taking root and these young and dynamic leaders are at the forefront of the Baloch struggle now. As the Foreign Policy Centre notes: 'The Baloch have also started defining their nationhood consciously and have assumed greater international visibility now than ever before. While there are many weaknesses within the movement, the spirit of independence and the will to fight, partly induced by the undemocratic and excessive measures by the Pakistani state, may turn the tide in favour of the Baloch, but only if there is exemplary leadership, unity among the ranks, a long-term strategy and resources to keep the movement alive.'[20]

Where would Balochistan be, say, ten years from now? How will its political dynamics play out when the Baloch become a marginalized and impoverished minority in their own province and the demography shifts decisively in favour of other groups? What about the Baloch youth? These questions need answers. However, answering them today can only be hypothetical given that there could be many variables in the developing situation.

One thing that is clear is that unless resolved the insurgency in Balochistan, even at current levels, will eat the innards of Pakistan. Unfortunately, Pakistani leaders have selective memories and learn selective lessons from history. For them, there is hardly any incentive to resolve such issues, given the fact that they are invariably bailed out by the US/West (and now by China) on the one hand, and on the other, the insurgency is not of such intensity yet as to threaten Pakistan's existence. However, what they seem to overlook is that it took nineteen years for the language riots in the then East Pakistan that broke out in 1952 to mature into the creation of Bangladesh in 1971. During this period, resentment among the Bengalis continued to grow unabated, just as it has been growing in Balochistan.

The overall prognosis has to be that given the current military capability of the Baloch and without a catalyst like massive international support, Balochistan is unlikely to break away. However, having sustained the insurgency for over a decade, it has developed a momentum of its own. Hence, military force alone will not break Baloch resistance. Pakistan would have to be prepared for a long haul unless there is a radical change in the way the army decides to deal with the Baloch. This, at present, seems unlikely.

For the long term, the Pakistani state will have to compromise with the Baloch. Continuing to seek a military solution to a political problem may make sense tactically in softening the opposition. But it can never be the long-term solution. One of the key factors for the future development of Pakistan would be a just solution to the Balochistan conundrum, a solution that puts the Baloch in the centre rather than the resources of the province. Failure to do so will slowly but inexorably exacerbate the crisis in Balochistan till it explodes with dire consequences for Pakistan.

Notes

Balochistan at a Glance

1. Government of Balochistan: Budget White Paper 2015-16, p. 6, https://balochistan.gov.pk/index.php?option=com_docman&task=cat_view&gid=1414&Itemid=677, (accessed on 27 February 2018).
2. Report of the Parliamentary Committee on Balochistan (November 2005) cited in Human Rights Commission of Pakistan (HRCP), 'Conflict in Balochistan', Report of the HRCP Fact-Finding Mission, August 2006, p. 39, http://hrcp-web.org/hrcpweb/wp-content/pdf/ff/20.pdf, (accessed on 3 March 2018).

Preface

1. Human Rights Commission of Pakistan (HRCP), 'Hopes, Fears and Alienation in Balochistan', Report of the HRCP Fact-Finding Mission, May 2012, http://hrcp-web.org/hrcpweb/wp-content/pdf/ff/12.pdf, p. 8, (accessed on 3 March 2018).
2. Banari Mengal, 'What have we received from the people of Pakistan except neglect and torment?' *The Express Tribune*, 5 May 2015, https://blogs.tribune.com.pk/story/27534/what-have-we-received-from-the-people-of-pakistan-except-neglect-and-torment/, (accessed on 27 February 2018). The author is the daughter of the president of the Balochistan National Party and a former chief minister of Balochistan, Sardar Akhtar Mengal.

Introduction

1. Government of Balochistan Budget White Paper 2015-16, https://balochistan.gov.pk/index.php?option=com_docman&task=cat_view&gid=1414&Itemid=677, p. 5, (accessed on 27 February 2018).

2.   Around one-third of the drugs from Afghanistan are smuggled via the coastal region of Balochistan. According to the United Nations Office on Drugs and Crime (UNODC)'s World Drug Report 2012, approximately $30 billion worth of drugs are smuggled from Afghanistan via Pakistan to other countries. Similarly, there is a substantial market for smuggling arms and weapons from Afghanistan into Balochistan and on to other parts of Pakistan. Balochistan is also the principal route for smuggling migrants from Central Asia, Afghanistan and Iran to destinations in Europe and beyond. See Ali Dayan Hasan, 'Balochistan: Caught in the Fragility Trap', USIP, June 2016, https://www.usip.org/publications/2016/06/balochistan-caught-fragility-trap, (accessed on 27 February 2018).
3.   Declan Walsh, 'Pakistan's Secret Dirty War', *The Guardian*, 29 March 2011, https://www.theguardian.com/world/2011/mar/29/balochistan-pakistans-secret-dirty-war, (accessed on 27 February 2018).
4.   Naveed Hussain, 'Fiddling While Balochistan Burns', *The Express Tribune*, 14 August 2012, https://tribune.com.pk/story/422060/fiddling-while-balochistan-burns/, (accessed on 27 February 2018).
5.   Human Rights Commission of Pakistan (HRCP), 'Pushed to the Wall', Report of the HRCP Fact-Finding Mission to Balochistan, October 2009, p. 5, http://hrcp-web.org/hrcpweb/wp-content/pdf/ff/14.pdf, (accessed on 3 March 2018).
6.   Syed Sharifuddin Pirzada, *Foundations of Pakistan, AIML Documents, Vol. II 1924–47*, Indian Edition, New Delhi: Metropolitan Book Co., 1982, p. 329.
7.   Maulana Abul Kalam Azad's interview to Shorish Kashmiri for *Chattan*, in April 1946. Reproduced in http://www.newageislam.com/books-and-documents/maulana-abul-kalam-azad-the-man-who-knew-the-future-of-pakistan-before-its-creation/d/2139, (accessed on 27 February 2018).
8.   Adeel Khan, 'Baloch Ethnic Nationalism in Pakistan: From Guerrilla War to Nowhere?', *Asian Ethnicity*, Vol. 4, No. 2 (June 2003), p. 286.
9.   Selig S. Harrison, *In Afghanistan's Shadow: Baloch Nationalism and Soviet Temptations*, Washington: Carnegie Endowment for International Peace, 1981, p. 151.
10.   Lawrence Ziring, 'Pakistan's Nationalities Dilemma: Domestic and International Implications', in L. Ziring (ed.), *The Subcontinent in World Politics*, New York, 1978, p. 96, cited in Urmila Phadnis, 'Ethnic Movements in Pakistan', in Pandav Nayak (ed.), *Pakistan Society & Politics*, Jaipur: South Asia Studies Centre, University of Jaipur, 1984, p. 192.
11.   Selig S. Harrison, *In Afghanistan's Shadow*, p. 64.
12.   Selig S. Harrison, 'Baluch Nationalism and Superpower Rivalry', *International Security*, Vol. 5, No. 3, (Winter 1980/81), https://thebaluch.com/documents/Baluch%20Nationalism%20and%20Superpower%20Rivalry.pdf, (accessed on 3 March 2018).
13.   A Pashtun from Quetta, Mohd Isa, attended the session though.
14.   HRCP Report 2009, p. 11.
15.   Detailed in chapter 5: History till Partition.
16.   Inayatullah Baloch, *The Problem of Greater Baluchistan: A Study of Baluch Nationalism*, Stuttgart: Steiner Verlag Wiesbaden Gmbh, 1987, pp. 191–92.

17. 'Interview Nawab Khair Baksh Marri', *Newsline*, September 2009 https://newslinemagazine.com/magazine/interview-nawab-khair-bakhsh-marri/, (accessed on 3 March 2019).

18. Human Rights Commission of Pakistan (HRCP), 'Human Rights in Balochistan and Balochistan's Rights', Report of a HRCP Fact-Finding Mission, October 2003, p. 59, http://hrcp-web.org/hrcpweb/wp-content/pdf/ff/20.pdf, (accessed on 3 March 2018).

19. HRCP Report, 2009, p. 5.

20. Muhammad Ijaz Laif and Muhammad Amir Hamza, 'Ethnic Nationalism in Pakistan: A Case Study of Baloch Nationalism during Musharraf Regime', *Pakistan Vision*, Vol. 10, No. 1, http://pu.edu.pk/images/journal/studies/PDF-FILES/Artical%20-%204.pdf, (accessed on 3 March 2018).

21. Mushahid Hussain, 'Has the Rubicon Been Crossed', *Newsline*, June 2009, http://newslinemagazine.com/magazine/the-final-showdown/, (accessed on 3 March 2018).

22. Manzoor Ahmed and Akhtar Baloch, 'Political Economy of Balochistan, Pakistan: A Critical Review', *European Scientific Journal*, May 2015, Vol. 11, No. 14, https://eujournal.org/index.php/esj/article/viewFile/5688/5508, (accessed on 3 March 2018).

23. 'Imperialism, Oil and the Balochistan Revolution', *Jabal*, July 1977, p. 6, cited in Selig S. Harrison, *In Afghanistan's Shadow*, p. 171.

24. Selig S. Harrison, *In Afghanistan's Shadow*, p. 47.

25. Malik Siraj Akbar, 'Why Pakistan Is Embarrassed to Talk About Balochistan', Huffington Post, 13 March, 2014, http://www.huffingtonpost.com/malik-siraj-akbar/why-pakistan-is-embarrass_b_4937159.html, (accessed on 2 March 2018).

26. HRCP Report 2003, p. 59.

27. Selig S. Harrison, *In Afghanistan's Shadow*, p. 4.

28. Carlotta Gall, 'In Remote Pakistan Province, a Civil War Festers', *The New York Times*, 2 April 2006, http://www.nytimes.com/2006/04/02/world/asia/02pakistan.html?_r=0&pagewanted=all, (accessed on 2 March 2018).

29. Marvin and Bernard Kalb, *Kissinger*, Boston: Little, Brown, 1974, pp. 63–64, cited in Selig S. Harrison, *In Afghanistan's Shadow*, p. 1.

PART I   AN ANCIENT CIVILIZATION

1: The Land

1. Taj Mohammad Breseeg, *Baloch Nationalism: Its Origin and Development*, Karachi: Royal Book Company, 2004, pp. 74–77.

2. *Imperial Gazetteer of India*, Provincial Series, Baluchistan, London: Clarendon Press, 1960. This edition, Lahore: Sang-e-Meel Publications, 1991, p. 13.

3. Cited in International Forum for Rights and Security (IFFRAS), *Balochistan: Denial of Destiny*, London: European Media Ltd, 2012, p. 13.

4. Talha Zaheer, 'Learning from Alexander', *Dawn*, 23 November 2009, https://www.dawn.com/news/813064/learning-from-alexander, (accessed on 2 March 2018).

5.　　*Imperial Gazetteer of India*, pp. 21–22.
6.　　Syed Iqbal Ahmed, *Balochistan: Its Strategic Importance*, Karachi: Royal Book Co, 1992, p. 2.
7.　　Mary Anne Weaver, *Pakistan: In the Shadow of Jihad and Afghanistan*, Straus and Girous, USA, 2002, Indian Viking edition, New Delhi: Penguin Books India, 2003, p. 90; David O. Smith, *The Quetta Experience: A Study of Attitudes and Values in the Pakistan Army*, Washington D C: Wilson Centre, 2018, p. 25.
8.　　Inayatullah Baloch, *The Problem of Greater Baluchistan: A Study of Baluch Nationalism*, Stuttgart: Steiner Verlag Wiesbaden Gmbh, 1987, pp. 19–23.
9.　　Edward Wakefield, *Past Imperative: My Life in India, 1927-1947*, London: Chatto and Windus, 1966, p. 98 cited in Inayatullah Baloch, *The Problem of Greater Baluchistan*, p. 21.
10.　Mir Ahmed Yar Khan Baluch, *Inside Baluchistan: A Political Autobiography of His Highness Baiglar Baigi: Khan-E-Azam-XIII*, Karachi: Royal Book Company, 1975, pp. 263–64.
11.　Ainslie T. Embree (ed.), *Pakistan's Western Borderlands: The Transformation of a Political Order*, New Delhi: Vikas Publishing House Pvt Ltd, 1977, p. xii.
12.　Government of Balochistan, http://www.balochistan.gov.pk/index.php?option=com_content&view=article&id=37&Itemid=783, (accessed on 3 March 2018).
13.　*Imperial Gazetteer of India*, p. 3.
14.　T. Holdich, *The Gates of India*, Quetta: Gosha-e-Adab, 1977, pp. 285 and 289, cited in Syed Iqbal Ahmed, *Balochistan: Its Strategic Importance*, p. 3.
15.　Robert D. Kaplan, 'Pakistan's Fatal Shore', *The Atlantic*, May 2009, http://www.theatlantic.com/magazine/archive/2009/05/pakistans-fatal-shore/307385/, (accessed on 2 March 2018).
16.　Selig S. Harrison, *In Afghanistan's Shadow: Baluch Nationalism and Soviet Temptations*, Washington DC: Carnegie Endowment for International Peace, 1981, p. 8.
17.　*Imperial Gazetteer of India*, p. 89.
18.　Mary Anne Weaver, *Pakistan: In the Shadow of Jihad and Afghanistan*, p. 116.
19.　Ibid., p. 90.
20.　Captain Harry Willes Darell de Windt, *A Ride to India across Persia and Baluchistan*, 1891, cited in IFFRAS, *Balochistan: Denial of Destiny*, p. 26.
21.　Taj Mohammad Breseeg, *Baloch Nationalism: Its Origin and Development*, Karachi: Royal Book Company, 2004, pp. 78–79.
22.　Cited in Sylvia A. Matheson, *The Tigers of Balochistan*, Karachi: Oxford University Press (OUP henceforth), 1997, p. 11.
23.　*Imperial Gazetteer of India*, p. 10.
24.　Ainslie T. Embree (ed.), *Pakistan's Western Borderlands: The Transformation of a Political Order*, p. xi.
25.　Syed Muhammad Abubakar, 'Embattled Balochistan is now up against a different foe', *The Express Tribune*, 22 July 2017, https://tribune.com.pk/story/1463981/embattled-balochistan-now-different-foe/, (accessed on 27 February 2018).

26. Muhammad Sardar Khan Baluch, *History of Baluch Race and Baluchistan*, Quetta: Khair-un-Nisa, Nisa Traders, third edition 1984, p. 26, cited in Taj Mohammad Breseeg, 'Heterogeneity and the Baloch Identity', 20 September 2011, http://intellibriefs.blogspot.in/2010/10/heterogeneity-and-baloch-identity.html, (accessed on 3 March 2018).
27. Sylvia A. Matheson, *The Tigers of Balochistan*, pp. 11–12.
28. Taj Mohammad Breseeg, *Baloch Nationalism*, p. 79.
29. Inayatullah Baloch, *The Problem of Greater Baluchistan*, pp. 22–23.
30. *Imperial Gazetteer of India*, pp. 53–57.
31. Inayatullah Baloch, *The Problem of Greater Baluchistan*, p. 23.
32. Government of Balochistan, 'Education Sector Plan, 2013–17', p. 9, http://aserpakistan.org/document/learning_resources/2014/Sector_Plans/Balochistan%20Sector%20Plan%202013-2017.pdf, (accessed on 3 March 2018).
33. R.N. Frye, 'Baluchistan', *The Encyclopaedia of Islam*, Vol. 1, p. 1005, cited in Inayatullah Baloch, *The Problem of Greater Baluchistan*, p. 19.
34. *Encyclopaedia Britannica*, Vol. 2, p. 8, cited in Inayatullah Baloch, ibid.
35. G.N. Curzon, *Persia and the Persian Question*, Vol. 2, p. 255, cited in Inayatullah Baloch, ibid.
36. Mir Ahmed Yar Khan Baluch, *Inside Baluchistan*, p. 107.
37. Sir Olaf Caroe, *The Pathans 550 BC—AD 1957*, Karachi: OUP, 1958, p. 372.
38. Inayatullah Baloch, *The Problem of Greater Baluchistan*, p. 31.
39. *Encyclopaedia Britannica*, 'Balochistan', 1911, cited in IFFRAS, *Balochistan: Denial of Destiny*, pp. 22–23.
40. Mary Anne Weaver, *Pakistan: In the Shadow of Jihad and Afghanistan*, p. 95.
41. *Imperial Gazetteer of India*, pp. 77–78.
42. Human Rights Commission of Pakistan (HRCP), 'Conflict in Balochistan', Report of the HRCP Fact-Finding Mission, August 2006, p. 41, http://hrcp-web.org/hrcpweb/wp-content/pdf/ff/20.pdf, (accessed on 3 March 2018).
43. The levy system was started by Sir Robert Sandeman who, as deputy commissioner of the Dera Ghazi Khan district in 1867, employed a small number of tribal horsemen from the Marri and Bugti tribes. He extended the system to Balochistan by giving tribal leaders allowances for maintaining a certain number of armed horse and foot soldiers to keep order in their tribes and to produce offenders when crimes occurred.
44. Saleem Shahid, 'Plan to re-organise Levies Force approved', *Dawn*, 12 September 2018, https://www.dawn.com/news/1432412/plan-to-re-organise-levies-force-approved, (accessed 3 January 2019).
45. HRCP Report, 2006, p. 41.
46. Human Rights Commission of Pakistan (HRCP), 'Balochistan: Giving the People a Chance', Report of the HRCP Fact-Finding Mission, June 2013, p. 31, http://www.hrcp-web.org/hrcpweb/wp-content/pdf/Balochistan%20Report%20New%20Final.pdf, (accessed on 3 March 2018).
47. Ibid.
48. Government of Balochistan, 'Budget White Paper 2015–16', p. 10. https://balochistan.gov.pk/index.php?option=com_docman&task=cat_view&gid=1414&Itemid=677, (accessed on 27 February 2018).

49.   'Odd foreign policy priority', *Dawn*, 19 October 2015, https://www.dawn.
       com/news/1213936, (accessed on 27 February 2018).

50.   Hasnaat Malik, 'Sindh says India wants ban on houbara hunts', *The Express
       Tribune*, 8 January 2016, https://tribune.com.pk/story/1023863/desperate-
       measures-sindh-says-india-wants-ban-on-houbara-hunts/, (accessed on 2
       March 2018).

51.   A Baloch proverb, cited in Farhan Hanif Siddiqi, *The Political Economy of
       The Ethnonationalist Uprising in Pakistani Balochistan, 1999–2013*, Quaid-
       i-Azam University, Islamabad, January 2015, https://www.researchgate.
       net/publication/272183981_Political_Economy_of_the_Ethno-
       nationalist_Uprising_in_Pakistani_Balochistan_1999-2013, (accessed on
       3 March 2018).

52.   Gas from Sui is in a league by itself, as discussed in detail in a later
       chapter.

53.   Maqbool Ahmed, 'Magic Mountain: The Reko Diq Gold and Copper Mining
       project', *Herald*, September 2017, https://herald.dawn.com/news/1153283,
       (accessed 3 March 2018).

54.   Yousaf Ajab Baloch, 'Plunder of Saindak's Gold and Copper', *Daily Times*,
       14 October 2013, https://dailytimes.com.pk/107284/plunder-of-saindaks-
       copper-and-gold/, (accessed on 2 March 2018).

55.   Rehan Khattak, 'Rs 6 billion Generated from Chamalang Coal Mines Project',
       Associated Press of Pakistan, 21 June 2015, https://defence.pk/pdf/threads/
       balochistans-socioeconomic-development-updates-discussions.302433/
       page-4, (accessed on 27 February 2018).

56.   Seymour M. Hersh, 'The Iran Plans: Would President Bush go to war to stop
       Tehran from getting the bomb?' *The New Yorker*, 17 April 2006, https://
       www.newyorker.com/magazine/2006/04/17/the-iran-plans, (accessed on 27
       February 2018).

57.   Selig S. Harrison, *In Afghanistan's Shadow*, p. 7.

58.   Robert G. Wirsing, 'Baloch Nationalism and the Geopolitics of Energy
       Resources: The Changing Context of Separatism in Pakistan', April 2008,
       https://permanent.access.gpo.gov/websites/ssi.armywarcollege.edu/pdffiles/
       PUB853.pdf', (accessed on 3 March 2018).

59.   Ibid., p. 30.

60.   Ibid., pp. 6–7.

61.   Ibid., p. 6.

62.   Ibid., p. 10.

63.   Ibid.

64.   Khalid Mustafa, 'Shelving of IP gas project: Iran threatens to take Pakistan
       to The Hague', *The News*, 28 February 2018, https://www.thenews.com.pk/
       print/286409-shelving-of-ip-gas-project-iran-threatens-to-take-pakistan-to-
       the-hague, (accessed on 2 March 2018).

65.   'Bonhomie marks opening of TAPI gas pipeline', *Dawn*, 24 February 2018,
       www.dawn.com/news/1391340/bonhomie-marks-opening-of-tapi-gas-
       pipeline, (accessed on 2 March 2018).

2. The People

1. Cited in International Forum for Rights And Security (IFFRAS), *Balochistan: Denial of Destiny*, London: European Media Ltd, 2012, fn. 5, p. 62.

2. Government of Balochistan, 'Balochistan Education Sector Plan 2013-2017', http://aserpakistan.org/document/learning_resources/2014/Sector_Plans/Balochistan%20Sector%20Plan%202013-2017.pdf, (accessed on 3 March 2018).

3. Abdul Wahab, 'A Province in Peril', *Newsline*, June 2009, http://newslinemagazine.com/magazine/the-final-showdown/, (accessed on 2 March 2018).

4. *Imperial Gazetteer of India*, Provincial Series, 'Baluchistan', London: Clarendon Press, this edition, Lahore: Sang-e-Meel Publications, 1991, p. 29.

5. G.P. Tate, *Seistan: A Memoir on the History, Topography, Ruins and People of the Country*, (in four parts, Part IV, *The People of Seistan*), Calcutta, 1912, p. 365, cited in Taj Mohammad Breseeg, *Baloch Nationalism: Its Origin and Development*, Karachi: Royal Book Company, 2004, p. 5.

6. Taj Mohammad Breseeg, *Baloch Nationalism*, 2004, p. 75.

7. J. Hansman, 'A Periplus of Magan and Melukha', in *Bulletin of the School of Oriental and African Studies*, (BSOAS), London, 1973, p. 555; H.W. Bailey, 'Mleccha, Baloc, and Gadrosia', in *BSOAS*, No. 36, London, 1973, pp. 584–87, cited in Taj Mohammad Breseeg, *Baloch Nationalism*, p. 75.

8. Interview with Munir Ahmad Gichki, in Taj Mohammad Breseeg, *Baloch Nationalism*, p. 75.

9. Muhammad Sardar Khan Baluch, *History of Baluch Race and Baluchistan*, pp. 14–16, cited in Taj Mohammad Breseeg, *Baloch Nationalism*, p. 75.

10. Mir Khuda Bakhsh Bijarani, *Searchlight on Baloches and Balochistan*. pp. 9–10, cited in Taj Mohammad Breseeg, *Baloch Nationalism*, p. 75.

11. Taj Mohammad Breseeg, 'Hetrogenity and the Baloch Identity', *Hanken, Annual Research Journal*, The Department of Balochi, Faculty of Languages and Literature, University of Balochistan, Quetta, Volume No.1, 2009, pp. 51–65, published online, 4 October 2010.

12. Taj Mohammad Breseeg, *Baloch Nationalism*, p. 131.

13. Mir Ahmed Yar Khan Baluch, *Inside Baluchistan: A Political Autobiography of His Highness Baiglar Baigi: Khan-E-Azam-XIII*, Karachi: Royal Book Company, 1987, pp. 255–96.

14. Ibid., p. 51.

15. Hittu Ram, *Tarikh-e-Baluchistan*, pp. 10–11, cited in Inayatullah Baloch, *The Problem of Greater Baluchistan: A Study of Baluch Nationalism*, Stuttgart: Steiner Verlag Wiesbaden Gmbh, 1987, p. 35.

16. H.H. Risley, *Census of India 1901*, Vol. 1, 'Ethnographic Appendices', p. 68, cited in Inayatullah Baloch, *The Problem of Greater Baluchistan*, p. 35.

17. Inayatullah Baloch, *The Problem of Greater Baluchistan: A Study of Baluch Nationalism*, Stuttgart: Steiner Verlag Wiesbaden Gmbh, 1987, p. 41.

18. Cited in Mary Anne Weaver, *Pakistan: In the Shadow of Jihad and Afghanistan*, Straus and Girous, USA 2002, Indian Edition, Viking, Penguin Books India, 2003, p. 88.
19. Sylvia A. Matheson, *The Tigers of Balochistan*, Karachi: OUP, 1997, first published 1967, p. 2.
20. Selig S. Harrison, *In Afghanistan's Shadow: Baluch Nationalism and Soviet Temptations*, Washington DC: Carnegie Endowment for International Peace, 1981, p. 9.
21. Mary Anne Weaver, *Pakistan: In the Shadow of Jihad*, p. 113.
22. Justin S. Dunne, 'Crisis in Baluchistan: A Historical Analysis of the Baluch Nationalist Movement in Pakistan', Monterey, California: Naval Postgraduate School, June 2006, p. 16, https://calhoun.nps.edu/bitstream/handle/10945/2755/06Jun_Dunne.pdf?sequence=1&isAllowed=y, (accessed on 3 March 2018).
23. Denis Bray, *The Life History of a Brahvi*, Karachi: Royal Book Company, 1913; M.B. Emeneau, *Brahvi and Dravidian Comparative Grammar*, Berkeley: University of California Press, 1962, cited in Tariq Rehman, 'The Balochi/Brahvi language Movements in Pakistan', *Journal of South Asian and Middle Eastern Studies*, Vol. XIX, No. 3, Spring 1996, cited in Taj Mohammad Breseeg, *Baloch Nationalism*, p. 144.
24. Sherbaz Khan Mazari, *A Journey to Disillusionment*, Karachi: OUP, 1999, p. xii.
25. Taj Mohammad Breseeg, *Baloch Nationalism*, p. 124.
26. Foreign Policy Centre, *Balochis of Pakistan: On the Margins of History*, London: Foreign Policy Centre, November 2006, p. 32, https://fpc.org.uk/publications/balochis-of-pakistan-on-the-margins-of-history/, (accessed on 3 March 2018).
27. Taj Mohammad Breseeg, *Baloch Nationalism*, pp. 109–10.
28. Human Rights Commission of Pakistan (HRCP), 'Conflict in Balochistan', Report of the HRCP Fact-Finding Mission, August 2006, p. 42, http://hrcp-web.org/hrcpweb/wp-content/pdf/ff/20.pdf, (accessed on 3 March 2018).
29. Taj Mohammad Breseeg, *Baloch Nationalism*, pp.106–07.
30. Mansoor Akbar Kundi, 'Tribalism in Balochistan: A Comparative Study' in Pervaiz Iqbal Cheema and Maqsudul Hasan Nuri (eds), *Tribal Areas of Pakistan: Challenges and Responses*, Islamabad: Islamabad Policy Research Institute, 2005, p. 20.
31. Martin Axmann, *Back to the Future: The Khanate of Kalat and the Genesis of Baloch Nationalism 1915-1955*, Karachi: OUP, 2008, p. 79.
32. Syed Iqbal Ahmed, *Balochistan: Its Strategic Importance*, Karachi: Royal Book Company, 1992, p. 41.
33. Foreign Policy Centre, *Balochis of Pakistan*, p. 31.
34. Mary Anne Weaver, *Pakistan: In the Shadow of Jihad*, p. 93.
35. Janmahmad, 'Essays on Baloch National Struggle in Pakistan', p.164, cited in Taj Mohammad Breseeg, *Baloch Nationalism*, p. 106.
36. Akhlaq Ullah Tarar, 'Policing in Balochistan—an account', *The Nation*, 6 October 2018, https://nation.com.pk/06-Oct-2018/policing-in-balochistan-an-account, (accessed 27 February 2019).

37. Ibid.
38. *Provincial Assembly of Baluchistan Debates*, Vol. II (7th June to 4th July 1972), https://sites.google.com/site/gulkhannasir/speeches-interviews/speech-against-the-tribal-system-on-the-floor-of-the-provincial-assembly-of-balochistan-on-june-8th-1972, (accessed on 3 March 2018).
39. Human Rights Commission of Pakistan (HRCP) 'Human Rights in Balochistan and Balochistan's Rights', Report of the HRCP Fact-Finding Mission, October 2003, p. 56, http://hrcp-web.org/hrcpweb/wp-content/pdf/ff/20.pd, (accessed on 3 March 2018).
40. Taj Mohammad Breseeg, *Baloch Nationalism*, p. 45.
41. Henry Pottinger, *Travels in Beloochistan and Sinde*, Oxford: OUP, 2003 reprint, p. 57, cited in Justin S. Dunne: 'Crisis in Baluchistan', p. 15.
42. Sherbaz Mazari, *A Journey to Disillusionment*, p. 16.
43. A.B. Awan, *Baluchistan: Historical and Political Processes*, London: New Century Publishers, 1985, p. 2.
44. Nina Swidler, 'Beyond Parody: Ethnography Engages Nationalist Discourse', in Paul Titus (ed.), *Marginality and Modernity: Ethnicity and Change in Post-Colonial Balochistan*, Karachi: OUP, 1996, p. 177.
45. Inayatullah Baloch, *The Problem of Greater Baluchistan*, p. 80.
46. Sherbaz Khan Mazari, *A Journey to Disillusionment*, pp. xii–xiv.
47. Sylvia A. Matheson, *The Tigers of Balochistan*, p. 12.
48. Mian Abrar, 'Balochistan: Tentative peace prevails but new challenges may be ahead', *Pakistan Today*, 19 February 2016, http://www.pakistantoday.com.pk/2016/02/19/news/balochistan-tentative-peace-prevails-but-new-challenges-may-be-ahead/, (accessed on 2 March 2018).
49. Rafiullah Kakar, 'Understanding the Pashtun Question in Balochistan', *The Express Tribune*, 5 June 2015, https://tribune.com.pk/story/897858/understanding-the-Pashtun-question-in-balochistan/, (accessed on 2 March 2018).

3. Religion

1. Inayatullah Baloch, *The Problem of Greater Baluchistan: A Study of Baluch Nationalism*, Stuttgart: Steiner Verlag Wiesbaden Gmbh, 1987, p. 70.
2. Shah Meer, 'The Noorani attack proves Pakistan will continue being religiously intolerant', The Express Tribune Blogs, 14 November 2016, http://blogs.tribune.com.pk/story/42909/the-noorani-attack-proves-pakistan-will-continue-being-religiously-intolerant/, (accessed on 2 March 2018).
3. Inayatullah Baloch, *The Problem of Greater Baluchistan*, p. 75.
4. E. Oliver, *Across the Border*, p. 24, cited in Inayatullah Baloch, *The Problem of Greater Baluchistan*, p. 71.
5. Inayatullah Baloch, *The Problem of Greater Baluchistan*, p. 75.
6. E. Oliver, *Across the Border*, p. 24, cited in Inayatullah Baloch, *The Problem of Greater Baluchistan*, p. 71.
7. Riccardo Redaelli, *The Father's Bow: The Khanate of Kalat and British India 19th, 20th century*, Florence: Maestrale, 1997, p. 21, cited in Naseer Dashti,

The Baloch Conflict with Iran And Pakistan, Bloomington: Trafford Publishing, 2007, p. 28.

8.   Inayatullah Baloch, *The Problem of Greater Baluchistan*, p. 75.
9.   Nina Swidler, 'Beyond Parody: Ethnology Engages Nationalist Discourse', in Paul Titus (ed.), *Marginality and Modernity: Ethnicity and Change in Post-Colonial Balochistan*, Karachi: OUP, 1996, p. 169.
10.   Sharif Khan, '85,000 enrolled in 1,095 seminaries in Balochistan', *The Nation*, 18 August 2017, http://nation.com.pk/national/18-Aug-2017/85-000-enrolled-in-1-095-seminaries-in-balochistan, (accessed on 2 March 2018).
11.   Frederic Grare, 'Balochistan: The State Versus the Nation', Carnegie Endowment for International Peace, April 2013, http://carnegieendowment.org/2013/04/11/balochistan-state-versus-nation-pub-51488, (accessed on 3 March 2018).
12.   International Crisis Group (ICG), Pakistan: The Worsening Conflict in Balochistan, *Asia Report*, No. 119, 14 September 2006, pp. i-ii, https://d2071andvip0wj.cloudfront.net/119-pakistan-the-worsening-conflict-in-balochistan.pdf, (accessed on 2 March 2018).
13.   Human Rights Watch, 'We Are the Walking Dead: Killings of Shia Hazaras in Balochistan, Pakistan', Annex II, 2014, www.hrw.org/sites/default/files/reports/pakistan0614_ForUplaod.pdf; (accessed on 2 March 2018).
14.   Ali Dayan Hasan, 'Balochistan: Caught in the Fragility Trap', *United States Institute of Peace (USIP)*, June 2016, https://www.usip.org/publications/2016/06/balochistan-caught-fragility-trap, (accessed on 27 February 2018).
15.   Syed Shaoaib Hasan, 'Sectarian Militancy Thriving in Balochistan', *Dawn*, 11 April 2012, https://www.dawn.com/news/709603, (accessed on 2 March 2018).
16.   The provincial chief of the Lashkar-e-Jhangvi, Osman Shaifullah Kurd, on death row in a cantonment, was simply allowed to go.
17.   Katja Riikonen, 'Sect in Stone', *Herald*, 16 October 2012, http://www.cssforum.com.pk/general/news-articles/71893-herald-magazine.html, (accessed on 2 March 2018).
18.   Ibid.
19.   Farid Kasi, 'Feeding the forces of Extremism', *Newsline*, February 2014, http://newslinemagazine.com/magazine/feeding-the-forces-of-extremism/, (accessed on 2 March 2018).
20.   Naseer Dashti, 'Resolving the Baloch National Question: Aspects of a Negotiated Settlement', https://www.thebaluch.com/050708_article.php, (accessed on 2 March 2018).
21.   Human Rights Commission of Pakistan (HRCP), 'Hopes, Fears and Alienation in Balochistan', Report of the HRCP Fact-Finding Mission, May 2012, p. 45, http://hrcp-web.org/hrcpweb/wp-content/pdf/ff/12.pdf, (accessed on 3 March 2018).
22.   Muhammad Akbar Notezai, 'Spiral into Chaos', *Dawn*, 16 August 2017, https://www.dawn.com/news/1351870/spiral-into-chaos, (accessed on 2 March 2018).
23.   B.L.A. Malik, 'LeJ responsible for Balochistan unrest', *Dawn*, 2 August 2012, https://www.dawn.com/news/739179, (accessed on 2 March 2018).

24. Waqar Ahmed, 'Tackling Daesh threat assuming urgency', *The News*, 17 July 2018, https://www.thenews.com.pk/print/342578-tackling-daesh-threat-assuming-urgency, (accessed on 28 July 2018).

25. Umar Cheema, 'Law enforcers in control of Balochistan situation', *The News*, 26 September 2018, https://www.thenews.com.pk/print/373129-law-enforcers-in-control-of-balochistan-situation, (accessed on 30 September 2018).

26. Inayatullah Baloch, 'Islam, the State, and Identity: The Zikris of Balochistan', in Paul Titus (ed.) *Marginality and Modernity*, p. 224.

27. Ibn Khaldun, *The Muqaddimah*, 1958, p.156, cited in Inayatullah Baloch, 'Islam, the State, and Identity', p. 224.

28. Ibid.

29. Ibid., p. 225.

30. Ibid., p. 226.

31. Ibid., p. 224.

32. Taj Mohammad Breseeg, *Baloch Nationalism: Its Origin and Development*, Karachi: Royal Book Company, 2004, p. 95.

33. Inayatullah Baloch, 'Islam, the State, and Identity', p. 229.

34. 'Zikri leader's murder', editorial in *Dawn*, 9 October 2016, http://www.dawn.com/news/1288960/zikri-leaders-murder, (accessed on 2 March 2018).

35. Inayatullah Baloch, 'Islam, the State, and Identity', pp. 223–24.

36. For details see chapter on The Separatist Challenge.

37. Inayatullah Baloch, 'Islam, the State, and Identity', p. 246.

38. Though not all Hazaras are Shias, the majority are.

39. Human Rights Commission of Pakistan (HRCP), 'Balochistan: Giving the People a Chance', Report of the HRCP Fact-Finding Mission, June 2013, p. 5, http://www.hrcp-web.org/hrcpweb/wp-content/pdf/Balochistan%20Report%20New%20Final.pdf, (accessed on 3 March 2018).

40. Mushtaq Rajpar, 'No end in sight', *The News*, 19 October 2017, https://www.thenews.com.pk/print/238136-No-end-in-sight, (accessed on 2 March 2018).

41. Farid Kasi, 'Feeding the forces of Extremism'.

42. Mushtaq Rajpar, 'No end in sight', *The News*, 19 October 2017.

43. 'Hazara killings', editorial in *Dawn*, 12 September 2017, https://www.dawn.com/news/1357041/hazara-killings, (accessed on 2 March 2018).

44. HRCP Report 2013, p. 28.

45. Human Rights Commission of Pakistan (HRCP), 'Pushed to the Wall', Report of the HRCP Fact-Finding Mission to Balochistan October 2009, pp. 18–19, http://hrcp-web.org/hrcpweb/wp-content/pdf/ff/14.pdf, (accessed on 3 March 2018).

46. Ibid., p. 19.

47. Human Rights Commission of Pakistan (HRCP), 'Blinkered Slide into Chaos', Report of the HRCP Fact-Finding Mission, Lahore, June 2011, p. 16, http://hrcp-web.org/hrcpweb/wp-content/pdf/ff/6.pdf, (accessed on 3 March 2018).

48. Human Rights Commission of Pakistan (HRCP), 'Hopes, Fears and Alienation in Balochistan', Report of the HRCP Fact-Finding Mission, May 2012, p.

10, http://hrcp-web.org/hrcpweb/wp-content/pdf/ff/12.pdf, (accessed on 3 March 2018).

49.   HRCP Report, 2013, pp. 28–29.
50.   Inayatullah Baloch, *The Problem of Greater Balochistan*, p. 73.
51.   Human Rights Commission of Pakistan (HRCP), 'Human Rights in Balochistan and Balochistan's Rights', Report of the HRCP Fact-Finding Mission, October 2003, p. 63, http://hrcp-web.org/hrcpweb/wp-content/pdf/ff/20.pd, (accessed on 3 March 2018).
52.   HRCP Report 2009, p. 22.
53.   Ibid., p. 23.
54.   HRCP Report 2011, p. 15.
55.   HRCP Report 2013, pp. 29–30.

4. Language

1.   Government of Pakistan, The 1981 Census Report of the Balochistan Province, Islamabad: Population Census Organization, Statistics Division, 1984.
2.   J.H. Elfenbein, 'Baluchi', in *Encyclopaedia of Islam*, Vol. I, A–B, Leiden: E.J. Brill, *1960*, p. 1006, cited in Inayatullah Baloch, *The Problem of Greater Baluchistan: A Study of Baluch Nationalism*, Stuttgart: Steiner Verlag Wiesbaden Gmbh, 1987, p. 50.
3.   Selig S. Harrison, 'Baloch Nationalism and Superpower Rivalry', *International Security*, Vol. 5, No. 3, (Winter 1980–81) pp. 152–63, https://thebaluch.com/documents/Baluch%20Nationalism%20and%20Superpower%20Rivalry.pdf, (accessed on 27 February 2018).
4.   Inayatullah Baloch, *The Problem of Greater Baluchistan: A Study of Baluch Nationalism*, Stuttgart: Steiner Verlag Wiesbaden Gmbh, 1987, p. 51.
5.   Taj Mohammad Breseeg, *Baloch Nationalism: Its Origin and Development*, Karachi: Royal Book Company, 2004, pp. 86–87.
6.   Ibid., pp. 143–44.
7.   Mohan Guruswamy, 'Yes, let's talk Balochistan!' Hardnews, 31 July 2009, http://www.hardnewsmedia.com/2009/07/3124, (accessed on 2 March 2018).
8.   Tariq Rahman, 'The Balochi/Brahvi Language Movements in Pakistan, in *Journal of South Asian and Middle East Studies*, Vol. XIX, No. 3, Spring 1996, p. 88.
9.   Selig S. Harrison, 'Baloch Nationalism and Super Power Rivalry'.
10.   Interview with Agha Naseer Khan Ahmadzai, cited in Taj Mohammad Breseeg, *Baloch Nationalism*, p. 142.
11.   Nina Swidler, 'Beyond Parody: Ethnology Engages Nationalist Discourse', in Paul Titus (ed.), *Marginality and Modernity: Ethnicity and Change in Post-Colonial Balochistan*, Karachi: OUP, 1996, p. 169.
12.   Cited in Taj Mohammad Breseeg, *Baloch Nationalism*, p. 143.
13.   Nina Swidler, 'Beyond Parody', p. 169.
14.   Janmahmad, *Essays on Baloch National Struggle in Pakistan*, p. 17, cited in Taj Mohammad Breseeg, *Baloch Nationalism*, p. 143.

15. Taj Mohmmad Breseeg, *Baloch Nationalism*, pp. 145–46.
16. Interview with Dawood Khan Ahmadzai, cited in Taj Mohammad Breseeg, *Baloch Nationalism*, p. 150.
17. Express Telegram from AGG Balochistan to the Foreign Office, New Delhi, dated 27 April 1932, IOR R/1/34/57, cited in Inayatullah Baloch, *The Problem of Greater Baluchistan*, p. 35.
18. India Office Records, L/P+S/12/3174, cited in Inayatullah Baloch, ibid.
19. Taj Mohammad Breseeg, *Baloch Nationalism*, p. 85.
20. Taj Mohammad Breseeg, *Baloch Nationalism*, pp. 215–16.
21. Nadir Qambrani, 'Brahvi Adabi Akabereen', *Pakistan Studies*, Vol. I: No. 1, 1990, pp. 13–21, cited in Taj Mohammad Breseeg, *Baloch Nationalism*, pp. 212–13.
22. Syed Abdul Quddus, *The Tribal Balochistan*, p. 72, cited in Taj Mohammad Breseeg, *Baloch Nationalism*, pp. 212–13.
23. Interview with Anwar Sajidi, cited in Taj Mohammad Breseeg, *Baloch Nationalism*, p. 214.
24. Tariq Rehman, *Language and Politics in Pakistan*, Karachi: OUP, first published 1997, third impression 2003, pp. 168–69.
25. Brian Spooner, *Baluchistan: Geography, History, and Ethnography*, p. 599, cited in Taj Mohammad Breseeg, *Baloch Nationalism*, p. 86.
26. Taj Mohammad Breseeg, *Baloch Nationalism*, p. 214.
27. Carina Jahani, 'Poetry and Politics: Nationalism and Language Standardization in the Balochis Literary Movement' in Paul Titus (ed.), *Marginality and Modernity*, p. 106.
28. Taj Mohammad Breseeg, 'Heterogeneity and the Baloch Identity', *Hanken*, Annual Research Journal From the Department of Balochi, Faculty of Languages and Literature, University of Balochistan, Quetta, Vol. 1, 2009, pp. 51–65, published online, 4 October 2010.
29. Sajid Hussain, 'Faith and politics of Balochi script', *Balochistan Times*, 18 March 2016, http://balochistantimes.com/faith-and-politics-of-balochi-script/, (accessed on 2 March 2018).
30. Ibid.
31. Ibid.
32. Ibid.

II: TIMES GONE BY

5. History till Partition

1. Inayatullah Baloch, *The Problem of Greater Baluchistan: A Study of Baluch Nationalism*, Stuttgart: Steiner Verlag Wiesbaden Gmbh, 1987, p. 95.
2. Janmahmad, *Essays on Baloch National Struggle in Pakistan*, pp. 157–63, cited in Taj Mohammad Breseeg, *Baloch Nationalism: Its Origin and Development*, Karachi: Royal Book Company, 2004, pp. 154–55.
3. Muhammad Sardar Khan Baluch, *The Great Baluch*, p. 113, cited in Taj Mohammad Breseeg, *Baloch Nationalism*, p. 160.

4.   Muhammad Sardar Khan Baluch, *A Literary History of Baluchis*, p. 73, cited in Taj Mohammad Breseeg, *Baloch Nationalism*, p. 160.

5.   Selig S. Harrison, *In Afghanistan's Shadow: Baluch Nationalism and Soviet Temptations*, Washington DC: Carnegie Endowment for International Peace, 1981, p. 16.

6.   Foreign Policy Centre, 'Balochis of Pakistan: On the Margins of History', London: *Foreign Policy Centre*, 2006, p. 12, https://fpc.org.uk/publications/balochis-of-pakistan-on-the-margins-of-history/, (accessed on 3 March 2018).

7.   Selig S. Harrison, 'Baloch Nationalism and Superpower Rivalry', *International Security*, Vol. 5, No 3, pp. 152–63, https://theBaloch.com/documents/Baloch%20Nationalism%20and%20Superpower%20Rivalry.pdf, (accessed on 27 February 2018).

8.   Ibid.

9.   Mir Ahmed Yar Khan Baluch, *Inside Baluchistan: A Political Autobiography of His Highness Baiglar Baigi: Khan-E-Azam-XIII*, Karachi: Royal Book Company 1975, p. 264.

10.   Paul Titus, Preface in Paul Titus (ed.), *Marginality and Modernity: Ethnicity and Change in Post-Colonial Balochistan*, Karachi: OUP, 1996, p. ix.

11.   Adeel Khan, 'Baloch Ethnic Nationalism in Pakistan: From Guerrilla War to Nowhere?' *Asian Ethnicity*, Vol. 4, No. 2, June 2003, p. 283.

12.   Selig S. Harrison, *In Afghanistan's Shadow*, p. 19.

13.   Sir Henry Rawlinson (1810–95) came to India in 1827, was later an MP. He served in the India Council and was President of the Royal Asiatic Society and Royal Geographical Society.

14.   Sir Alfred Lyall (1835–1911) was the foreign secretary of the Government of India and Lieutenant-Governor in the North-West Frontier Province.

15.   Sir Henry Rawlinson, *England and Russia in the East*, London: John Murray, 1875, p. 14, cited in Ainslie T. Embree, 'Pakistan's Imperial Legacy', in Ainslie T. Embree (ed.), *Pakistan's Western Borderlands: The Transformation of a Political Order*, New Delhi: Vikas Publishing House Pvt Ltd, 1977, pp. 25–26.

16.   Sir Alfred Lyall, 'Frontiers and Protectorates', *The Nineteenth Century*, Vol. 30, 1891, p. 315, cited in Ainslie T. Embree, 'Pakistan's Imperial Legacy', p. 26.

17.   Ibid., p. 27.

18.   Justin S. Dunne, 'Crisis in Baluchistan: A Historical Analysis of the Baluch Nationalist Movement in Pakistan', Monterey, California: *Naval Postgraduate School*, 2006, p. 19, https://calhoun.nps.edu/bitstream/handle/10945/2755/06Jun_Dunne.pdf?sequence=1&isAllowed=y, (accessed 3 March 2018).

19.   Ainslie T. Embree, 'Pakistan's Imperial Legacy' in Ainslie T. Embree (ed.), *Pakistan's Western Borderlands*, p. 36.

20.   James W. Spain, 'Political Problems of a Borderland' in Ainslie T. Embree (ed), *Pakistan's Western Borderlands*, p. 2.

21.   Nina Swidler, 'Beyond Parody: Ethnography Engages Nationalist Discourse', in Paul Titus (ed.), *Marginality and Modernity*, p. 179.

22.   Fred Scholz, *Nomadism and Colonialism: A Hundred Years of Balochistan 1872–1972*, Oxford: OUP, 1974, p. 91, cited in Justin S. Dunne: 'Crisis in

Baluchistan: A Historical Analysis of the Baluch Nationalist Movement in Pakistan', Monterey, California: Naval Postgraduate School.

23. Mir Ahmed Yar Khan Baluch, *Inside Baluchistan*, p. 281.

24. Martin Axmann, *Back to the Future: The Khanate of Kalat and the Genesis of Baloch Nationalism 1915–1955*, Karachi; OUP, 2008, p. 30.

25. Ainslie T. Embree, 'Pakistan's Imperial Legacy' in Ainslie T. Embree (ed) *Pakistan's Western Borderlands:* pp. 33–34.

26. James W. Spain, 'Political Problems of a Borderland' in Ainslie T. Embree (ed.), *Pakistan's Western Borderlands*, p. 11.

27. Nina Swidler, 'Beyond Parody', in Paul Titus (ed.), *Marginality and Modernity*, p. 182.

28. Olaf Caroe, *The Pathans 550 BC—AD 1957*, Karachi: OUP, 1958, p. 375.

29. Ibid., p. 376.

30. 'Baluchistan Under the British', http://www.globalsecurity.org/military/world/pakistan/baloch-brits.htm, (accessed on 3 March 2018).

31. Rafiullah Kakar, 'Making sense of the CPEC controversy—III', *The Express Tribune*, 11 February 2016, http://tribune.com.pk/story/1045140/making-sense-of-the-cpec-controversy-iii/, (accessed on 2 March 2018).

32. Inayatullah Baloch, *The Problem of Greater Baluchistan*, p. 29.

33. Ibid., pp. 30–31.

34. Selig S. Harrison, 'Nationalism and Superpower Rivalry', pp. 152–63.

35. Taj Mohammad Breseeg, *Baloch Nationalism*, 2004, p. 181.

36. Ibid., p. 216.

37. Ibid., p. 219.

38. Ibid., pp. 221–23.

39. Ibid., pp. 233, 235.

40. Adeel Khan, 'Baloch Ethnic Nationalism in Pakistan: From Guerrilla War to Nowhere?' *Asian Ethnicity*, Vol. 4, No. 2, June 2003, p. 285.

41. Stephen Cohen, *The Idea of Pakistan*, Washington DC: Brookings, 2006, p. 219.

6. Accession to Pakistan

1. Martin Axmann, *Back to the Future: The Khanate of Kalat and the Genesis of Baloch Nationalism 1915-1955*, Karachi; OUP, 2008, p. 176.

2. Naseer Dashti, *The Baloch and Balochistan*, Bloomington, Indiana, USA: Trafford Publishing, 2012, p. 326.

3. India Office Records IOR R/1/34/63, cited in International Forum for Rights and Security (IFFRAS), *Balochistan: Denial of Destiny*, London: European Media, 2012. pp. 56-57.

4. IOR.LVP+S/13/1847 cited in Taj Mohammad Breseeg, *Baloch Nationalism: Its Origin and Development*, Karachi: Royal Book Company, 2004, p. 246.

5. Mir Ahmed Yar Khan Baluch, *Inside Baluchistan: A Political Autobiography of His Highness Baiglar Baigi: Khan-E-Azam-XIII*, Karachi: Royal Book Company 1975, pp. 255–56.

6. Ibid., pp. 275–79.

7.   Ibid., p. 306.
8.   Ibid., p. 146.
9.   Ibid, p. 147.
10.   Inayatullah Baloch, *The Problem of Greater Baluchistan: A Study of Baluch Nationalism*, Stuttgart: Steiner Verlag Wiesbaden Gmbh, 1987, p. 256.
11.   Foreign Policy Centre, 'Balochis of Pakistan: On the Margins of History', London: *Foreign Policy Centre*, November 2006, pp. 17–18, https://fpc.org.uk/publications/balochis-of-pakistan-on-the-margins-of-history/, (accessed on 3 March 2018).
12.   Yaqoob Khan Bangash, *A Princely Affair: The Accession and Integration of the Princely States of Pakistan, 1947-1955*, Karachi: OUP, 2015, p. 168.
13.   Abdul Majeed Abid, 'The question of Kalat', *The Nation*, 21 December 2015, http://nation.com.pk/columns/21-Dec-2015/the-question-of-kalat, (accessed on 2 March 2018).
14.   Ziauddin to Jinnah, 8 July 1947, PS-77, *Jinnah Papers*, Vol III, cited in Yaqoob Khan Bangash, *A Princely Affair*, p. 165.
15.   Yaqoob Khan Bangash, ibid.
16.   Mountbatten to Listowel, Personal Report No 14, 25 July 1947, L/PO/6/123, IOR, cited in Yaqoob Khan Bangash, *A Princely Affair*, pp. 165–66.
17.   Yaqoob Khan Bangash, *A Princely Affair*, p. 167.
18.   Ibid.
19.   Memo on Kalat', R/1/1/4922, IOP, cited in ibid.
20.   Yaqoob Khan Bangash, *A Princely Affair*, pp. 171 and 179.
21.   Mir Ahmed Yar Khan, '*Baluch kaum ke naam Khan-e-Baluch ka paigam*', cited in Inayatullah Baloch, *The Problem of Greater Baluchistan*, p. 61.
22.   Yaqoob Khan Bangash, 'Recalling Baloch History', *The Express Tribune*, 14 June 2011, http://tribune.com.pk/story/188798/recalling-baloch-history/, (accessed on 2 March 2018).
23.   Inayatullah Baloch, *The Problem of Greater Baluchistan*, pp. 181–82.
24.   Ibid., p. 184.
25.   Ibid.
26.   Ibid., p. 182.
27.   Martin Axmann, *Back to the Future*, p. 180.
28.   *Dawn*, 18 July 1946, cited in Yakoob Khan Bangash, *A Princely Affair*, p. 190.
29.   Foreign Policy Centre, *Balochis of Pakistan*, p. 23.
30.   Ibid, pp. 23–24.
31.   Martin Axmann, *Back to the Future*, p. 197.
32.   Selig S. Harrison, *In Afghanistan's Shadow: Baluch Nationalism and Soviet Temptations*, Washington D.C.: Carnegie Endowment for International Peace, 1981, p. 24.
33.   R.C. Money also recorded a detailed note on Balochistan's economy as would be seen in a later chapter.
34.   Inayatullah Baloch, *The Problem of Greater Baluchistan*, p. 174. Incidentally, according to Baloch, the file of Gen. R.C. Money was regarded a confidential, secret file in the War Office Library.
35.   Foreign Policy Centre, *Balochis of Pakistan*, p. 22.
36.   Naseer Dashti, *The Baloch and Balochistan*, p. 336.

37. International Forum for Rights and Security (IFFRAS), *Balochistan: Denial of Destiny*, London: European Media Ltd, 2012, p. 59.

38. Narendra Singh Sarila, *The Shadow of The Great Game: The Untold Story of India's Partition*, NOIDA, HarperCollins India, 2005, p. 28.

39. Naseer Dashti, *The Baloch and Balochistan*, pp. 334–35.

40. IOR L/P+S/13/1846 cited in Inayatullah Baloch, *The Problem of Greater Baluchistan*, p. 257.

41. Yogeena Veena, 'How Balochistan became a part of Pakistan—a historical perspective', *The Nation*, 5 December 2015, http://nation.com.pk/blogs/05-Dec-2015/how-balochistan-became-a-part-of-pakistan-a-historical-perspective, (accessed on 2 March 2018).

42. Aslam to Ikramullah, 29 October 1947, 2(20) S/47, SAFRON, (States and Frontier Regions Ministry), cited in Yaqoob Khan Bangash, *A Princely Affair*, p. 178.

43. Yogeena Veena, 'How Balochistan became a part of Pakistan—a historical perspective'.

44. Abdul Majeed Abid, 'The question of Kalat'.

45. Mir Ahmed Yar Khan Baluch, *Inside Baluchistan*, p. 162.

46. Ibid.

47. Martin Axmann, *Back to the Future*, p. 299.

7. Post-Accesssion Insurgencies

1. Paul Titus and Nina Swidler, 'Knights, Not Pawns: Ethno-Nationalism and Regional Dynamics in Post-Colonial Balochistan', *International Journal of Middle East Studies*, Vol. 32, No. 1, February 2000, pp. 47–69, http://www.jstor.org/stable/259535, (accessed on 3 March 2018).

2. Inayatullah Baloch, *The Problem of Greater Baluchistan: A Study of Baluch Nationalism*, Stuttgart: Steiner Verlag Wiesbaden Gmbh, 1987, pp. 195–96.

3. Selig S. Harrison, *In Afghanistan's Shadow: Baluch Nationalism and Soviet Temptations*, Washington DC: Carnegie Endowment for International Peace, 1981, p. 26.

4. Ibid., p. 27.

5. Ibid., p. 47.

6. Ibid., p. 28.

7. Taj Mohammad Breseeg, *Baloch Nationalism: Its Origin and Development*, Karachi: Royal Book Company, 2004, p. 301.

8. Selig S. Harrison, *In Afghanistan's Shadow*, p. 28.

9. Mir Ahmed Yar Khan Baluch, *Inside Baluchistan: A Political Autobiography of His Highness Baiglar Baigi: Khan-E-Azam-XIII*, Karachi: Royal Book Company, 1975, p. 189.

10. Mir Mohammad Ali Talpur, 'Seeds and soil' *The News on Sunday* (TNS), 12 November 2017, http://tns.thenews.com.pk/seeds-soil/#.WgfgaYhx3IU, (accessed on 2 March 2018).

11. Parrari is the Baloch word used to describe a person(s) whose grievances cannot be solved through talks.

12.   Selig S. Harrison, *In Afghanistan's Shadow*, p. 30.
13.   Ibid., p. 33.
14.   Sabir Shah, 'NAP was banned twice by Yahya and Bhutto', *The News*, 3 May 2015, https://www.thenews.com.pk/print/38435-nap-was-banned-twice-by-yahya-and-bhutto, (accessed on 2 March 2018).
15.   Selig S. Harrison, *In Afghanistan's Shadow*, p. 35.
16.   Taj Mohammad Breseeg, *Baloch Nationalism*, pp. 324–25
17.   Paul Titus and Nina Swidler, 'Knights, Not Pawns', pp. 47–69.
18.   Selig S. Harrison, *In Afghanistan's Shadow*, p. 72.
19.   Paul Titus and Nina Swidler, 'Knights, Not Pawns', p. 62.
20.   Selig S. Harrison, *In Afghanistan's Shadow*, p. 37.
21.   Ibid., p. 33.
22.   Ibid.
23.   The Hyderabad Conspiracy Case was the name given to the trial of opposition politicians of the National Awami Party in Hyderabad Jail on the charges of treason that was instituted by Z.A. Bhutto after he dismissed the government in Balochistan.
24.   Roedad Khan, *Pakistan: A Dream Gone Sour*, Karachi: OUP, 1997, p. 86.
25.   Selig S. Harrison, *In Afghanistan's Shadow*, p. 4.
26.   Ibid.
27.   *People's Front*, Vol. 2, No. 67, London, 1975, p. 4, cited in Taj Mohammad Breseeg, *Baloch Nationalism*, pp. 340–41.
28.   Selig S. Harrison, *In Afghanistan's Shadow*, p. 71.
29.   Naseer Dashti, *The Baloch Conflict with Iran and Pakistan*, Bloomington: Trafford Publishing, 2007, pp. 161–62.
30.   Ibid., pp. 165–66.
31.   Urmila Phadnis and Rajat Ganguley, *Ethnicity and Nation Building in South Asia*, New Delhi: Sage, 1989, p. 189, cited in Rahul Mukand, 'Ethnicity and Nationalism in Balochistan', Pakistan Security Research Unit (PSRU), Brief Number 34, Department of Peace Studies at the University of Bradford, UK, 24 May 2008.
32.   For a succinct account of political developments during the 1980s–1990s, see Nasir Dashti, *The Baloch Conflict with Iran and Pakistan*, pp.169–98.

III: THE ROOTS OF ALIENATION

8. Political and Administrative Marginalization

1.   Manzoor Ahmed and Akhtar Baloch, 'Political Economy of Balochistan, Pakistan: A Critical Review', *European Scientific Journal*, May 2015, Vol. 11, No. 14.
2.   Malik Siraj Akbar, 'Why Pakistan Is Embarrassed to Talk About Balochistan', Huffington Post, 13 March, 2014, http://www.huffingtonpost.com/malik-

siraj-akbar/why-pakistan-is-embarrass_b_4937159.html, (accessed on 2 March 2018).

3. Mozaffar Shaheen, 'The Politics of Cabinet Formation in Pakistan: A Study of Recruitment to the Central Cabinets. 1947–1977', Ph.D. dissertation, Miami University, Ohio, 1980, cited in Urmila Phadnis, 'Ethnic Movements in Pakistan', in Pandav Nayak (ed.), *Pakistan Society & Politics*, South Asia Studies Centre, University of Jaipur, 1984, p. 193.

4. Kaiser Bengali, *A Cry for Justice: Empirical Insights from Balochistan*, Karachi: OUP, 2018, p. 127.

5. Tahir Mehdi, 'Obfuscating Balochistan', op-ed in *Dawn*, 30 March 2018, https://www.dawn.com/news/1398427/obfuscating-balochistan, (accessed on 4 April 2018).

6. Ibid.

7. Selig S. Harrison, *In Afghanistan's Shadow: Baloch Nationalism and Soviet Temptations*, Washington: Carnegie Endowment for International Peace, 1981, p. 160.

8. Urmila Phadnis 'Ethnic Movements in Pakistan', pp. 194–95.

9. Mumtaz Alvi, 'Balochistan schools abandon national anthem, Senate told', *The News*, 30 April 2009, https://defence.pk/pdf/threads/pakistans-national-anthem-not-allowed-abandoned-in-balochistan.27576/, (accessed on 27 February 2018).

10. Urmila Phadnis, 'Ethnic Movements in Pakistan', p. 193.

11. Saleem Shahid, 'How ghost employees plague Balochistan's government departments', *Herald*, 3 October 2017, https://herald.dawn.com/news/1153869, (accessed on 2 March 2018).

12. Mir Mohammad Ali Talpur, 'Not the Brinjals' Servant', *Daily Times*, 13 September 2015, http://www.dailytimes.com.pk/opinion/13-Sep-2015/not-the-brinjals-servant], (accessed on 27 February 2018).

13. Irfan Ghauri, 'Changing demographics fuel ethnic tensions-II', *The Express Tribune*, 30 November 2015. http://tribune.com.pk/story/1000901/changing-demographics-fuel-ethnic-tensions-ii/, (accessed on 27 February 2018).

14. 'Nadra officials issued 90,000 cards to foreigners in Balochistan, reveals detained employees', report in *Daily Times*, 7 May 2016, http://dailytimes.com.pk/balochistan/07-May-16/nadra-officials-issued-90000-cards-to-foreigners-in-balochistan-reveals-detained-employees, (accessed on 27 February 2018).

15. Sharif Khan, 'CNICs of 45,000 Balochistan employees found fake', *The Nation*, 21 May 2017 http://nation.com.pk/national/21-May-2017/cnics-of-45-000-balochistan-employees-found-fake, (accessed on 27 February 2018); Saleem Shahid, 'How ghost employees plague Balochistan's government departments'.

16. Saleem Shahid, 'How ghost employees plague Balochistan's government departments'.

17. 'Most posts in Balochistan bureaucracy vacant', *Dawn*, 27 October 2016, http://www.dawn.com/news/1292509/most-posts-in-balochistan-bureaucracy-vacant, (accessed on 27 February 2018).

18. Saleem Shahid, 'Balochistan to fill 20,000 vacant posts in 90 days', *Dawn*, 30 December 2016, http://www.dawn.com/news/1305306/balochistan-to-fill-20000-vacant-posts-in-90-days, (accessed on 27 February 2018).

19. Kaiser Bengali, *A Cry for Justice*, pp. 97, 99 and 103.

20. Saleem Shahid, 'Balochistan PA slams "bias" over jobs', *Dawn*, 21 September 2017, https://www.dawn.com/news/1359070/balochistan-pa-slams-bias-over-jobs, (accessed on 27 February 2018).

21. Riazul Haq, '3,431 posts for Balochistan vacant in different ministries', *The Express Tribune*, 15 October 2017, https://tribune.com.pk/story/1531749/3431-posts-balochistan-vacant-different-ministries/, (accessed on 27 February 2018).

22. 'SC drivers earning more than Balochistan doctors: CJP', *The Nation*, 11 April 2018, https://nation.com.pk/11-Apr-2018/sc-drivers-earning-more-than-balochistan-doctors-cjp, (accessed on 15 April 2018).

23. Selig S. Harrison, *In Afghanistan's Shadow*, p. 22.

24. Stephen Cohen, 'Security Decision-Making in Pakistan', Report prepared for the office of External research, Department of State, September 1980, p 40, cited in Urmila Phadnis, 'Ethnic Movements in Pakistan', p. 193.

25. Asaf Hussain, 'Elite Politics in an Ideological State: The Case of Pakistan', Kent 1979, p. 129, Table 14, cited in Urmila Phadnis, ibid., p. 193.

26. K.B. Sayeed, 'Pathan Regionalism', *The South Asia quarterly*, Vol. 63, No. 4, Autumn 1964, Table 14. Even later, there were hardly any Baloch in the armed forces ranks. See Urmila Phadnis, ibid.

27. Tariq Ali, *Can Pakistan Survive?* Bungay, Suffolk: Penguin Books, 1983, p. 117.

28. 'Growing regional disparity in incomes', *Dawn*, 14 February 2005, https://www.dawn.com/news/382393, (accessed on 27 February 2018).

29. Hasan Askari Rizvi, *The Military and Politics in Pakistan 1947–86*, Lahore: Progressive Publishers, 1986, p. 242.

30. Mohammad Zafar, 'COAS calls for harnessing Balochistan's human resource', *The Express Tribune*, 8 December 2017, https://tribune.com.pk/story/1578643/1-army-chief-says-believes-democracy-selfless-service/, (accessed on 27 February 2018).

31. Monthly Balochi Labzan, *Hub* (Balochistan), September 1997, p. 6, cited in Taj Mohammad Breseeg, *Baloch Nationalism: Its Origin and Development*, Karachi: Royal Book Company, 2004, p. 118.

32. *Dawn*, 14 January 2006, cited in Human Rights Commission of Pakistan (HRCP), 'Conflict in Balochistan, Report of the HRCP Fact-Finding Mission', August 2006, p. 42, http://hrcp-web.org/hrcpweb/wp-content/pdf/ff/20.pdf, (accessed on 3 March 2018).

33. Shahzada Zulfiqar, 'Land-Mine', *Newsline*, August 2004, p. 58.

34. HRCP Report 2006, p. 41.

35. Human Rights Commission of Pakistan (HRCP), 'Human Rights in Balochistan and Balochistan's Rights', Report of the HRCP Fact-Finding Mission, October 2003, p. 57, http://hrcp-web.org/hrcpweb/wp-content/pdf/ff/20.pd, (accessed on 3 March 2018).

36. Manzoor Ahmed and Akhtar Baloch, 'Political Economy of Balochistan.

37. '35pc children out of schools in Balochistan: Minister', *The Nation*, 2 March 2017, http://nation.com.pk/newspaper-picks/02-Mar-2017/35pc-children-out-of-schools-in-balochistan-minister, (accessed on 27 February 2018).

38. Monis Ali, 'The education crisis in Balochistan', *Daily Times*, 27 October 2016, http://dailytimes.com.pk/opinion/27-Oct-16/the-education-crisis-in-balochistan, (accessed on 27 February 2018).

39. Syed Fazl-e-Haider, 'Education in Balochistan fails to keep pace', *Pakistan and Gulf Economist*, 31 July 2017, http://www.pakistaneconomist.com/2017/07/31/education-in-balochistan-fails-to-keep-pace/, (accessed on 27 February 2018).

40. Mohammad Zafar, '75 per cent Girls Out Of School In Balochistan', *The Express Tribune*, 4 July 2016, https://tribune.com.pk/story/1135714/provincial-govt-challenge-75-per-cent-girls-school-balochistan/, (accessed on 27 February 2018).

41. Ibid.

42. Alif Ailaan, 'The State of Education in Balochistan', https://d3n8a8pro7vhmx.cloudfront.net/alifailaan/pages/496/attachments/original/1473163108/, (accessed on 3 March 2018).

43. Mohammad Zafar, 'No record of 15,000 teachers, 900 ghost schools in Balochistan: Minister', *The Express Tribune*, 21 May 2016, http://tribune.com.pk/story/1107409/no-record-15000-teachers-900-ghost-schools-balochistan-minister/, (accessed on 27 February 2018).

44. Government of Balochistan, Balochistan Education Sector Plan 2013–2017, http://aserpakistan.org/document/learning_resources/2014/Sector_Plans/Balochistan%20Sector%20Plan%202013-2017.pdf, (accessed on 3 March 2018).

45. Adnan Aamir, 'Balochistan is being cheated out of its share by HEC', *The Nation*, 8 January 2016, http://nation.com.pk/blogs/08-Jan-2016/balochistan-is-being-cheated-out-of-its-share-by-hec/, (accessed on 27 February 2018).

46. Shaukat Ali Mazari, 'Wisdom at Higher Education Commission of Pakistan', *Daily Times*, 20 March 2019, https://dailytimes.com.pk/367261/wisdom-at-higher-education-commission-of-pakistan/, (accessed 21 March 2019).

47. Adnan Aamir, 'Balochistan is being cheated out of its share by HEC'.

48. Hussain Nadim, 'Balochistan Matters', *The Express Tribune*, 13 March 2016, https://tribune.com.pk/story/1065052/balochistan-matters/, (accessed on 27 February 2018).

49. Mary Anne Weaver, *Pakistan in the Shadow of Jihad and Afghanistan*, New York: Farrar, Straus and Giroux, 2002, p. 105.

50. 'A word of caution', editorial in *Daily Times*, 25 November 2015, http://www.dailytimes.com.pk/editorial/25-Nov-2015/a-word-of-caution, (accessed on 27 February 2018).

51. Zohra Yusuf, 'Trigger-happy in Balochistan', *The Express Tribune*, 9 June 2011, http://tribune.com.pk/story/184794/trigger-happy-in-balochistan/, (accessed on 27 February 2018).

52. Kill-and-dump refers to the gruesome practice of the security forces abducting Baloch youth, killing the individuals with extreme violence and then dumping their bodies.

53. Mama Qadeer, whose real name is Abdul Qadeer Reki, set up an organization of family members of abducted Baloch activists called the Voice of the Baloch Missing Persons (VBMP). Their objective is to collect data of all abducted, missing and extra-judicially killed Baloch persons.

54. Hashim bin Rashid, 'Why Punjab doesn't talk about Balochistan', *The Friday Times*, 17 April 2015, http://www.thefridaytimes.com/tft/why-punjab-doesnt-talk-about-balochistan/#sthash.scfDSWvS.dpuf, (accessed on 27 February 2018).

55. Hussain Nadim, 'Balochistan Matters'.

56. Human Rights Commission of Pakistan (HRCP), 'Conflict in Balochistan', Report of the HRCP Fact-Finding Mission, August 2006, p. 59, http://hrcp-web.org/hrcpweb/wp-content/pdf/ff/20.pdf, (accessed on 3 March 2018).

57. HRCP Report, 2009, pp. 5 and 10.

58. 'Publisher apologises for "offensive" content in sociology textbook', *Dawn*, 14 March 2016, http://www.dawn.com/news/1245561/publisher-apologises-for-offensive-content-in-sociology-textbook], (accessed on 27 February 2018).

59. Zaigham Khan, 'Insult the Baloch', *The News*, 21 March 2016, http://www.thenews.com.pk/print/106819-Insult-the-Baloch, (accessed on 27 February 2018).

60. International Crisis Group (ICG), telephone interview, Islamabad, August 2007, 'Pakistan: The Forgotten Conflict in Balochistan', Brussels, 22 October 2007, p. 9, https://www.crisisgroup.org/asia/south-asia/pakistan/pakistan-forgotten-conflict-balochistan, (accessed on 3 March 2018).

61. ICG Report 2007, p. 9.

62. Zoya Anwer, 'Balochistan has no say in national policy making', *The News*, 12 February 2018, https://www.thenews.com.pk/print/279759-balochistan-has-no-say-in-national-policy-making, (accessed on 27 February 2018).

63. Saleem Shahid, 'Census results hurting Baloch interests won't be accepted, warns NP', *Dawn*, 24 April 2017, https://www.dawn.com/news/1328842/census-results-hurting-baloch-interests-wont-be-accepted-warns-np, (accessed on 27 February 2018).

64. Shezad Baloch, 'Problems with census in Balochistan', *The Express Tribune*, 31 March 2017 https://tribune.com.pk/story/1370062/problems-census-balochistan/, (accessed on 27 February 2018).

65. Mubarak Zeb Khan, 'Number of Balochi-speaking people in Balochistan falls', *Dawn*, 11 September 2017, https://www.dawn.com/news/1356899/number-of-balochi-speaking-people-in-balochistan-falls, (accessed 27 February 2018).

9. Economic Exploitation

1. General Money's memorandum (unpublished), cited in Inayatullah Baloch, *The Problem of Greater Baluchistan: A Study of Baluch Nationalism*, Stuttgart: Steiner Verlag Wiesbaden Gmbh, 1987, p. 25.

2. Inayatullah Baloch, *The Problem of Greater Baluchistan: A Study of Baluch Nationalism*, Stuttgart: Steiner Verlag Wiesbaden Gmbh, 1987, pp. 25–27.

3. Maneck B. Pathawalla, *The Problem of Baluchistan*, pp. 3–4, cited in Inayatullah Baloch, ibid., p. 27.

4.   World Bank, 'Pakistan–Balochistan Economic Report: From Periphery to Core', Report No. 40345, May 2008, https://openknowledge.worldbank.org/handle/10986/8082, (accessed on 3 March 2018).
5.   Government of Balochistan, Budget White Paper 2015-16, p. 8, www.kcci.com.pk/Rnd/wp-content/uploads/2017/07/White-Paper-2015-16-2.pdf, (accessed on 27 February 2018).
6.   Ibid.; Government of Balochistan, Budget White Paper 2016-17, http://www.balochistan.gov.pk/index.php?option=com_docman&gid=1474&Itemid=677; Government of Balochistan, Budget White Paper 2017-18, http://www.balochistan.gov.pk/index.php?option=com_docman&gid=1680&Itemid=677, (accessed on 27 February 2018).
7.   Kaiser Bengali, *A Cry For Justice: Empirical Insights From Balochistan*, Karachi: OUP, 2018, p. 21.
8.   Ibid., p. 23.
9.   Ibid., p. 49.
10. Government of Balochistan, Budget White Paper 2017-18, pp. 8–9.
11. Ibid., p. 11.
12. Selig S. Harrison, *In Afghanistan's Shadow: Baluch Nationalism and Soviet Temptations*, Washington DC: Carnegie Endowment for International Peace, 1981, p. 8.
13. Abdul Wahab, 'A Province in Peril', *Newsline*, June 2009, http://newslinemagazine.com/magazine/the-final-showdown/, (accessed on 2 March 2018).
14. Government of Balochistan, Budget White Paper 2017–18, p. 12.
15. Abdul Wahab, 'A Province in Peril'.
16. Kaiser Bengali, *A Cry for Justice*, p. 43.
17. Abdul Wahab, 'A Province in Peril'.
18. 'Rs.100 Billion for Balochistan road network, says Musharraf', *Daily Times*, 4 April 2005, cited in International Crisis Group, Pakistan (ICG), 'The Worsening Conflict in Balochistan', *Asia Report* No. 119, 14 September 2006, p. 18, https://d2071andvip0wj.cloudfront.net/119-pakistan-the-worsening-conflict-in-balochistan.pdf, (accessed on 2 March 2018).
19. Ibid., p.18.
20. World Bank Group, Country Partnership Strategy (CPS) 2015-19, 'Balochistan Consultations', Quetta, 23–24 September 2013, http://documents.worldbank.org/curated/en/520931468086941207/Balochistan-consultations-report-World-Bank-Group-WBG-Country-Partnership-Strategy-CPS-2015-19, (accessed on 3 March 2018).
21. Kaiser Bengali, *A Cry for Justice*, p. 1.
22. Ibid.
23. Frederic Grare, 'Pakistan: The Resurgence of Baluch Nationalism', South Asia Project Number 65, January 2006, p. 5, Washington DC: Carnegie Endowment for International Peace, http://carnegieendowment.org/files/CP65.Grare.FINAL.pdf, (accessed on 27 February 2018).
24. Iftikhar Firdous, 'Deprived province: 59 per cent of Balochistan without natural gas', *The Express Tribune*, 26 May 2014, https://tribune.com.pk/

story/713135/deprived-province-59-of-balochistan-without-natural-gas/, (accessed on 2 March 2018).

25. Government of Balochistan, White Paper 2015–16, p. 8.
26. Frederic Grare, 'Pakistan: The Resurgence of Baluch Nationalism', p. 5.
27. Ibid.
28. Government of Balochistan, Budget White Paper 2016–17, p. 19.
29. Ibid.
30. Pakistan Institute of Legislative Development and Transparency (PILDAT), 'Balochistan: Civil–Military Relations', Islamabad, March 2012, http://www.pildat.org/publications/ublication/cmr/issuepaperbalochistanconflictcmr.pdf, p. 15, (accessed on 3 March 2018).
31. Syed Fazle Haider, 'Higher poverty in Balochistan', Dawn, 6 February 2006, cited in International Crisis Group, 'Pakistan: The Worsening Conflict in Balochistan', 2006, p. 17.
32. Kaiser Bengali, A Cry for Justice, pp. 9 and 17.
33. Mir Mohammad Ali Talpur, 'Confronting Injustices', Daily Times, 20 September 2015, https://dailytimes.com.pk/98359/confronting-injustices/, (accessed on 3 March 2018).
34. Ibid.
35. Government of Balochistan, Budget White Paper 2015–16, p. 19.
36. Paul Titus, 'Introduction' in Sylvia Matheson, The Tigers of Baluchistan, Karachi: OUP, second editions, 1997, p. xx.
37. Explaining why the Marris opposed oil exploration in their lands, Nawab Khair Bakhsh Marri said: 'We saw what happened in the Bugti area, where they have "developed" the Sui gas, 80 per cent of which goes out of Balochistan to make others rich.', Selig S. Harrison, In Afghanistan's Shadow, p. 47.
38. ICG Report, 2006, p. 16.
39. Zafar Bhutta, 'Balochistan presses for share in PPL dividends', The Express Tribune, 27 December 2015. http://tribune.com.pk/story/1016701/looking-to-reap-benefits-balochistan-presses-for-share-in-ppl-dividends/, (accessed on 3 March 2018).
40. Frederic Grare, 'Pakistan: The Resurgence of Baluch Nationalism', p. 4.
41. Khaleeq Kiani, 'Emerging gas market, privatisation and the CCI', Dawn, 17 July 2006, https://www.dawn.com/news/201698, (accessed on 27 February 2018).
42. Government of Balochistan, Budget White Paper 2015–16, p. 9.
43. Muhammad Ijaz Laif and Muhammad Amir Hamza, 'Ethnic Nationalism in Pakistan: A Case Study of Baloch Nationalism during Musharraf Regime', Pakistan Vision, Vol. 10, No. 1, p. 64, http://pu.edu.pk/images/journal/studies/PDF-FILES/Artical%20-%204.pdf, (accessed on 3 March 2018).
44. Shah Meer Baloch, 'I was the first chief minister to address the existence of death squads in Balochistan: Abdul Malik Baloch', Herald, 24 December 2017, https://herald.dawn.com/news/1153954/i-was-the-first-chief-minister-to-address-the-existence-of-death-squads-in-balochistan-abdul-malik-baloch, (accessed on 27 February 2018).

45. Maqbool Ahmed, 'Magic Mountain: The Reko Diq Gold and Copper Mining project', *Herald*, September 2017, https://herald.dawn.com/news/1153283, (accessed 3 March 2018).

46. Mir Mohammad Ali Talpur, 'Not the Brinjals' Servant', *Daily Times*, 13 September 2015, http://www.dailytimes.com.pk/opinion/13-Sep-2015/not-the-brinjals-servant, (accessed on 27 February 2018).

47. Government of Balochistan, Balochistan Education Sector Plan 2013–2017, http://aserpakistan.org/document/learning_resources/2014/Sector_Plans/Balochistan per cent20Sector per cent20Plan per cent202013-2017.pdf, (accessed on 3 March 2018).

48. Mary Anne Weaver, *Pakistan: In the Shadow of Jihad and Afghanistan*, Straus and Girous, USA 2002, Indian edition, New Delhi: Viking, Penguin Books India, 2003, pp. 105–06.

49. See the author's *Pakistan: Courting the Abyss*, NOIDA: Harper Collins India, 2016, pp, 207–27.

50. Kashif Shaikh & Ashfaq Ahmed, 'Water shortage: How long will Balochistan have to suffer?' *The Express Tribune* Blogs, 3 December 2016, http://blogs.tribune.com.pk/story/43563/water-shortage-how-long-will-balochistan-have-to-suffer/, (accessed on 27 February 2018).

51. UNDP, Pakistan, 'Drought Risk Assessment in the Province of Balochistan, Pakistan', 15 January 2016, http://www.pk.undp.org/content/pakistan/en/home/library/crisis_prevention_and_recovery/drought-risk-assessment-in-balochistan-province--pakistan.html, (accessed 3 March 2018).

52. 'Water for Balochistan', editorial in *Dawn*, 5 January 2019, https://www.dawn.com/news/1455550/water-for-balochistan, (accessed on 20 February 2019).

53. 'Quetta's water crisis', editorial in *Dawn*, 2 September 2018 https://www.dawn.com/news/1430495, (accessed 20 February 2018).

54. Zafar Bhutta, 'Balochistan accuses Sindh of stealing its water', *The Express Tribune*, 22 September 2016. http://tribune.com.pk/story/1186158/water-indent-balochistan-accuses-sindh-stealing-water/, (accessed on 27 Februaery 2018).

55. 'Parched realities', editorial in *The Nation*, 4 February 2018, https://nation.com.pk/04-Feb-2018/parched-realities, (accessed on 27 February 2018).

56. Khawar Ghumman, 'Balochistan losing groundwater, warns report', *Dawn*, 26 October 2015, http://www.dawn.com/news/1215455/balochistan-losing-groundwater-warns-report, (accessed on 27 February 2018).

57. Farman Kakar, 'Extraction without responsibility', *The News*, 20 March 2016, http://tns.thenews.com.pk/extraction-without-responsibility/#.Vu709Pl97IU, (accessed on 27 February 2018).

58. Mushtaq Rajpar, 'The political economy of Balochistan', *The News*, 24 June 2017, https://www.thenews.com.pk/print/212514-The-political-economy-of-Balochistan, (accessed on 2 March 2018).

59. Ibid.

60. Government of Balochistan, Balochistan Education Sector Plan 2013–2017, p. 10.

61. Adnan Aamir, 'What Nawaz Sharif did for Balochistan', *Daily Times*, 5 August 2017, http://dailytimes.com.pk/opinion/05-Aug-17/what-nawaz-sharif-did-for-balochistan, (accessed on 2 March 2018).

62. Adnan Aamir, 'Balochistan's under-reported poverty', *The News on Sunday*, (TNS), 28 May 2017, http://tns.thenews.com.pk/balochistans-reported-poverty/#.WSpc7WiGPIU, (accessed on 2 March 2018).
63. Ibid.
64. Ibid.
65. Ibid.
66. Kaiser Bengali, *A Cry for Justice*, p. 60.
67. Adnan Aamir, 'Unemployment in Balochistan', *The News*, 27 April 2015, http://www.adnan-aamir.com/2015/04/unemployment-in-balochistan.html, (accessed on 2 March 2018).
68. Ibid.

10. Socio-economic Deprivation

1. Kaiser Bengali, *A Cry for Justice: Empirical Insights from Balochistan*, Karachi: OUP, 2018, pp. 49, 134.
2. World Bank, 'Pakistan–Balochistan Economic Report: From Periphery to Core', No. 40345-PK May 2008, p. 148, https://openknowledge.worldbank.org/handle/10986/8082, (accessed on 3 March 2018).
3. Pakistan Institute of Legislative Development and Transparency (PILDAT), 'Balochistan: Civil–Military Relations', Islamabad, March 2012, http://www.pildat.org/publications/publication/cmr/issuepaperbalochistanconflictcmr.pdf, p. 15, (accessed on 3 March 2018).
4. Sher Baz Khan, 'Unemployment on rise, says ADB', *Dawn*, 22 May 2007, https://www.dawn.com/news/248191, (accessed on 27 February 2018).
5. Kaiser Bengali, *A Cry for Justice*, p. xix.
6. Human Rights Commission of Pakistan (HRCP), 'Balochistan: Giving the People a Chance', Report of a HRCP Fact-Finding Mission, June 2013, p. 35, http://www.hrcp-web.org/hrcpweb/wp-content/pdf/Balochistan per cent20Report per cent20New per cent20Final.pdf, (accessed on 3 March 2018).
7. Arif Naveed, Geof Wood and Muhammad Usman Ghaus, 'Geography of Poverty in Pakistan—2008-09 to 2012-13: Distribution, Trends and Explanations', Pakistan Poverty Alleviation Fund & Sustainable Development Policy Institute (SDPI), Islamabad, 2016, p. iii, http://www.ppaf.org.pk/doc/regional/6-PPAF_SDPI_Report_%20Geography_of_Poverty_in_Pakistan.pdf, (accessed on 3 March 2018).
8. Ibid.
9. Ibid., p. iv.
10. Ibid., p. iii.
11. Naseer Memon, 'The Balochistan conundrum', *The News*, 16 April 2017 http://tns.thenews.com.pk/balochistan-conundrum/#.Wr-gY62B06g, (accessed on 2 March 2018).
12. Arif Naveed, Geof Wood and Muhammad Usman Ghaus, 'Geography of Poverty in Pakistan', p. vii.

13. Deserving families are selected via a nationwide poverty census (last completed in 2011) and receive Rs 4,700 a quarter, paid to the woman of the house.

14. Assad Ahmad, 'Balochistan's missing poor', *Dawn*, 24 March 2018, https://www.dawn.com/news/1397227/balochistans-missing-poor, (accessed on 31 March 2018).

15. Kaiser Bengali, *A Cry for Justice*, p. 27.

16. Haroon Jamal, 'Quantifying sub-national human development indices from household survey data', Social Policy and Development Centre (SPDC), Karachi, May 2016, http://www.spdc.org.pk/Data/Publication/PDF/RR-96.pdf, p. 1, (accessed on 3 March 2018).

17. Ibid., pp. 5–6.

18. Ibid., p. 7.

19. Ibid., p. 8.

20. Ibid., p. 9.

21. Dr Sadia Ali, 'The poor daughter of Balochistan', *The News*, 17 August 2016, https://www.thenews.com.pk/print/142987-The-poor-daughter-of-Balochistan, (accessed on 3 March 2018).

22. Syeda Shehrbano Kazim, 'Balochistan can become the only part of the world with full employment', *Dawn*, 26 October 2018, https://www.dawn.com/news/1441342, (accessed 20 February 2019).

23. Saleem Shahid, 'Call for Nutrition Emergency In Balochistan', *Dawn*, 1 May 2017, https://www.Dawn.Com/News/1330316/Call-For-Nutrition-Emergency-In-Balochistan, (accessed on 2 March 2018).

24. 'Malnutrition in Balochistan', editorial in *Daily Times*, 2 May 2017, www.dailytimes.com.pk, , (accessed on 2 March 2018).

25. Kaiser Bengali, *A Cry for Justice*, p.7.

26. Adnan Aamir, 'What Nawaz Sharif did for Balochistan', *Daily Times*, 5 August 2017, http://dailytimes.com.pk/opinion/05-Aug-17/what-nawaz-sharif-did-for-balochistan, (accessed on 2 March 2018).

27. Syed Fazl-e-Haider, 'Higher poverty in Balochistan', *Dawn*, 6 February 2006, https://www.dawn.com/news/177446, (accessed on 3 March 2018).

28. Khanji Harijana, Mohammad A. Uqailib, Mujeebuddin Memona and Umar K. Mirza, 'Potential of On-shore Wind Power in the Coastal Areas of Balochistan, Pakistan', *Wind Engineering*, Vol. 34, No. 2, 2010, pp. 167–79.

29. UNDP Pakistan, 'Pakistan: Millennium Development Goals—Provincial Status, 2012–13', http://www.pk.undp.org/content/pakistan/en/home/library/mdg/mdgs-status-for-districts-in-balochistan.html, (accessed on 3 March 2018).

30. The 2017 census indicated that only 27.62 per cent of Balochistan's population is urban, while the national urban population is 32.5 per cent.

31. Abdul Wahab, 'A Province in Peril', *Newsline*, June 2009, http://newslinemagazine.com/magazine/the-final-showdown/, (accessed on 2 March 2018).

32. Government of Balochistan, Balochistan Education Sector Plan 2013–2017, http://aserpakistan.org/document/learning_resources/2014/Sector_Plans/

Balochistan per cent20Sector per cent20Plan per cent202013-2017.pdf, p. 8, (accessed on 3 March 2018).

33. Abdul Wahab, 'A Province in Peril'.
34. Saleem Shahid, 'Situation in Balochistan deplorable: CJP', *Dawn*, 11 December 2018, https://www.dawn.com/news/1450699, (accessed on 4 January 2019).
35. Qazi Azmat Isa, 'Building a cohesive state', *Dawn*, 22 August 2015, http://www.dawn.com/news/1201962/building-a-cohesive-state], (accessed on 2 March 2018).
36. Various reports.
37. PILDAT, 'Balochistan: Civil–Military Relations', p. 15.

IV: CHINESE GAMBIT

11. Gwadar

1. 'The Mega Follies', *Dawn*, 31 January 2008, https://www.dawn.com/news/409575, (accessed on 27 February 2018).
2. Naseer Memon, 'Killing fields of Balochistan', *The News*, http://tns.thenews.com.pk/killing-fields-balochistan/#.WSpcvmiGPIU, (accessed on 27 February 2018).
3. Captain Harry Willes Darell de Windt, *A Ride to India across Persia and Baluchistan*, 1891, cited in International Forum for Rights and Security (IFFRAS), *Balochistan: Denial of Destiny*, London: European Media Ltd., 2012, p. xxiv.
4. Robert D. Kaplan, 'Pakistan's Fatal Shore', *The Atlantic*, May 2009, http://www.theatlantic.com/magazine/archive/2009/05/pakistans-fatal-shore/307385/, (accessed on 27 February 2018).
5. Abdul Wali, 'Gwadar isn't a "mega city", it isn't even a city yet!', *The Express Tribune*, 20 March 2016. http://blogs.tribune.com.pk/story/32247/gwadar-isnt-a-mega-city-it-isnt-even-a-city-yet/, (accessed on 27 February 2018).
6. Farrukh Saleem, 'Gwadar', *The News*, 11 September 2016, https://www.thenews.com.pk/print/149434-Gwadar, (accessed 27 February 2018).
7. Azhar Ahmad, 'Unravelling Gwadar town', *The Frontier Post*, 4 May 2013, https://web.archive.org/web/20130929104602/http://www.thefrontierpost.com/article/10194.htm, (accessed on 27 February 2018).
8. Rai Muhammad Saleh Azam, 'Gwadar's Accession to Pakistan', *Pakistan Defence*, 21 April 2015, https://defence.pk/pdf/threads/gwadars-accession-to-pakistan.371824/, (accessed on 27 February 2018).
9. Christophe Jaffrelot, 'A Tale of Two Ports', Yale Global Online, 7 January 2011, ,http://yaleglobal.yale.edu/content/tale-two-ports, (accessed on 27 February 2018).
10. 'Rs 894 million Pak-Belgian contract to build Gwadar port', *Dawn*, 18 July 1988; Abdul Majeed, 'Comments: truth about Gwadar port project', *The*

News, 30–31 July 2006, cited in Sushant Sareen, 'Balochistan: Forgotten War, Forsaken People', Vivekananda International Foundation, New Delhi, September 2017, http://www.vifindia.org/sites/default/files/Balochistan-Forgotten-War-Forsaken-People.pdf,, (accessed on 27 February 2018).

11. 'Singapore to run Gwadar port', *The Post*, 23 December 2006, cited in Sushant Sareen, 'Balochistan: Forgotten War, Forsaken People'.

12. Sanaullah Baloch, 'The Gwadar deal' *The News*, 13 February 2016, http://www.thenews.com.pk/print/97926-The-Gwadar-deal, (accessed on 27 February 2018).

13. Syed Fazl-e-Haider, 'Non-functional Gwadar Port', *Dawn*, 30 June 2008, https://www.dawn.com/news/309512, (accessed on 27 February 2018).

14. Peer Muhammad, 'Gwadar's free-trade zone: Pakistan to hand over 2,281 acres to Chinese on Nov 11', *The Express Tribune*, 10 November 2015, http://tribune.com.pk/story/988331/gwadars-free-trade-zone-pakistan-to-hand-over-2281-acres-to-chinese-on-nov-11/, (accessed on 27 February 2018); 'Chinese firm gets land for free-trade zone in Gwadar', *The Express Tribune*, 12 November 2015, http://tribune.com.pk/story/989763/chinese-firm-gets-land-for-free-trade-zone-in-gwadar/, (accessed on 27 February 2018).

15. Saheed Shah, 'Big Chinese-Pakistani Project Tries to Overcome Jihadists, Droughts and Doubts', *The Wall Street Journal*, 10 April 2016, http://www.wsj.com/articles/big-chinese-pakistani-project-tries-to-overcome-jihadists-droughts-and-doubts-1460274228, (accessed on 27 February 2018).

16. Tim Willasey-Wilsey, 'Gwadar and the "String of Pearls"', *Gateway House*, 8 January 2016 https://www.gatewayhouse.in/gwadar-and-the-string-of-pearls-2/, accessed on 27 February 2018.

17. Khurram Husain, 'China's road through Pakistan', *Dawn*, 23 November 2017, https://www.dawn.com/news/1372349/chinas-road-through-pakistan, (accessed on 27 February 2018).

18. Shahbaz Rana, 'Pakistan rejects use of Chinese currency', *The Express Tribune*, 21 November 2017, https://tribune.com.pk/story/1564050/2-pakistan-rejects-use-chinese-currency/, (accessed on 27 February 2018).

19. Human Rights Commission of Pakistan (HRCP), 'Human Rights in Balochistan and Balochistan's Rights', Report of a HRCP Fact-Finding Mission, October 2003, p. 65, http://hrcp-web.org/hrcpweb/wp-content/pdf/ff/20.pd, (accessed on 3 March 2018).

20. M.A. Niazi, 'Running out of options', *The Nation*, 19 August 2016, http://nation.com.pk/columns/19-Aug-2016/running-out-of-options, (accessed on 27 February 2018).

21. 'Mengal asks govt to hand over Gwadar port to Balochistan', *Dawn*, 23 November 2015, http://www.dawn.com/news/1221621/mengal-asks-govt-to-hand-over-gwadar-port-to-balochistan, (accessed on 27 February 2018).

22. Adnan Aamir, 'The Baloch's concerns', *The News*, 31 December 2017, http://tns.thenews.com.pk/balochs-concerns/#.Wkhv7d-WbIU, (accessed on 27 February 2018).

23. Ibid.

24. Muhammad Ijaz Laif and Muhammad Amir Hamza, 'Ethnic Nationalism in Pakistan: A Case Study of Baloch Nationalism during Musharraf Regime',

Pakistan Vision, Vol. 10, No. 1, p. 65, http://pu.edu.pk/images/journal/studies/PDF-FILES/Artical%20-%204.pdf, (accessed on 03 March 2018).

25. Mohsin Saleem Ullah, 'Gwadar: China's next abode by 2023', *The Nation*, 29 November 2017, http://nation.com.pk/29-Nov-2017/gwadar-china-s-next-abode-by-2023, (accessed on 27 February 2018); Murtaza Ali Shah, '500,000 Chinese professionals expected in Gwadar by 2023', *The News*, 21 October 2017, https://www.thenews.com.pk/print/238644-500000-Chinese-professionals-expected-in-Gwadar-by-2023, (accessed on 27 February 2018).

26. International Crisis Group, Pakistan (ICG), 'The Worsening Conflict in Balochistan', *Asia Report* No. 119, 14 September 2006, p. 15, https://d2071andvip0wj.cloudfront.net/119-pakistan-the-worsening-conflict-in-balochistan.pdf, (accessed on 3 March 2018).

27. Irfan Ghauri, 'Changing Demographics Fuel Ethnic Tensions—II', *The Express Tribune*, 30 November 2015, https://tribune.com.pk/story/1000901/changing-demographics-fuel-ethnic-tensions-ii/, (accessed on 27 February 2018).

28. Idrees Bakhtiar, 'Mega projects are a conspiracy to turn the Balochis into a minority in their own homeland', *The Herald*, August 2004, cited in Foreign Policy Centre, 'Balochis of Pakistan: On the Margins of History', London: *Foreign Policy Centre*, 2006, p. 55, https://fpc.org.uk/publications/balochis-of-pakistan-on-the-margins-of-history/, (accessed on 3 March 2018).

29. Mumtaz Alvi, 'Senate calls for steps to preserve Gwadar's demographic balance', *The News*, 22 January 2019 https://www.thenews.com.pk/print/421930-senate-calls-for-steps-to-preserve-gwadar-s-demographic-balance, (accessed on 27 February 2019).

30. Foreign Policy Centre, 'Balochis of Pakistan', p. 54.

31. Robert Kaplan, 'Pakistan's Fatal Shore'.

32. 'Balochistan: Present & Future', editorial in *The Nation*, 31 January 2018, https://nation.com.pk/31-Jan-2018/balochistan-present-future, (accessed on 27 February 2018).

33. Kalbe Ali, 'Govt lethargy stalls Gwadar's projects, Senate body told', *Dawn*, 30 December 2017, https://www.dawn.com/news/1379722/govt-lethargy-stalls-gwadars-projects-senate-body-told, (accessed on 27 February 2018).

34. Behram Baloch, 'Gwadar in grip of severe water crisis', *Dawn*, 21 December 2015, http://www.dawn.com/news/1227817/gwadar-in-grip-of-severe-water-crisis, (accessed on 27 February 2018).

35. Muhammad Akbar Notezai, 'Thirsty in Gwadar' *Dawn*, 10 September 2017, https://www.dawn.com/news/1356787/thirsty-in-gwadar, (accessed on 27 February 2018).

36. Behram Baloch, 'Gwadar in grip of severe water crisis'.

37. 'Water crisis again hits Gwadar', *Dawn*, 22 May 2017, https://www.dawn.com/news/1334634/water-crisis-again-hits-gwadar, (accessed on 27 February 2018).

38. Ibid.

39. Syed Muhammad Abubakar, 'Welcome to thirsty Gwadar', *The News*, 1 July 2018, http://tns.thenews.com.pk/welcome-thirsty-gwadar/#.WzjJJe5AvIU, (accessed on 24 December 2018).

40. Muhammad Akbar Notezai, 'Thirsty in Gwadar'.
41. Syed Muhammad Abubakar, 'Welcome to thirsty Gwadar'.
42. Behram Baloch, 'Gwadar water woes worsen as supply from Mirani dam halted', *Dawn*, 5 February 2018, www.dawn.com/news/1387425/gwadar-water-woes-worsen-as-supply-from-mirani-dam-halted, (accessed on 27 February 2018).
43. Muhammad Akbar Notezai, 'Thirsty in Gwadar'.
44. Maqbool Ahmed, 'CPEC: Hopes and fears as China comes to Gwadar', *Herald*, 14 March 2017, https://herald.dawn.com/news/1153685, (accessed on 27 February 2018).
45. Saeed Shah, 'Big Chinese-Pakistani Project Tries to Overcome Jihadists, Droughts and Doubts'.
46. P.M. Baigel, 'Gwadar port reels under water shortages', *Dawn*, 16 February 2016, http://www.dawn.com/news/1239912] , (accessed on 27 February 2018).
47. Saher Baloch, 'Gwadar's long wait for water', *Dawn*, 6 March 2016, http://www.dawn.com/news/1243899/footprints-gwadars-long-wait-for-water, (accessed on 27 February 2018).
48. 'Impact of development on fisheries sector in Gwadar', cited in ICG Report 2006, p. 15.
49. Maqbool Ahmed, 'CPEC: Hopes and fears as China comes to Gwadar'.
50. 'CPEC and Gwadar fishermen', editorial in *Daily Times*, 18 March 2019, https://dailytimes.com.pk/366412/cpec-and-gwadar-fishermen/ (accessed 21 March 2019).
51. I.A. Rehman, 'Baloch concerns revisited', *Dawn*, 28 July 2016, http://www.dawn.com/news/1273557/baloch-concerns-revisited, (accessed on 27 February 2018).
52. Shah Meer Baloch, 'What matters most', *Dawn*, 6 May 2018 https://www.dawn.com/news/1405970/what-matters-most, (accessed on 27 February 2018).
53. CPEC and Gwadar fishermen', editorial in *Daily Times*.
54. Robert Kaplan, 'Pakistan's Fatal Shore'.
55. Aqil Shah, 'The brewing storm of discontent', *Dawn*, 21 June 2006, http://www.dawn.com/news/1064691, (accessed on 27 February 2018).
56. Malik Siraj Akbar, 'Gwadar's real estate boom busts', *Daily Times*, 29 November 2008, http://archives.dailytimes.com.pk/national/29-Nov-2008/gwadar-s-real-estate-boom-busts, (accessed on 27 February 2018).
57. ICG Report, 2006, p. 15.
58. Arif Rana, 'Army seeks 11,000 acres of land for "Defence Complex" at Gwadar', *Business Recorder*, 6 September 2007, cited in International Crisis Group (ICG), 'Pakistan: The Forgotten Conflict in Balochistan', *Asia Report*, 22 October 2007, p. 10, https://www.crisisgroup.org/asia/south-asia/pakistan/pakistan-forgotten-conflict-balochistan, (accessed on 2 March 2018).
59. 'The Gwadar land scam', editorial in *Business Recorder*, 3 January 2018, https://epaper.brecorder.com/2018/01/03/20-page/691717-news.html, (accessed on 27 February 2018).

60. Sarah Zheng, 'Danger in the deep that could derail Belt and Road plan', *South China Morning Post*, 11 February 2018, http://www.scmp.com/news/china/diplomacy-defence/article/2132833/danger-deep-near-chinas-multibillion-dollar-port, (accessed on 27 February 2018).

61. 'The Mega Follies', *Dawn*, 31 January 2008.

62. Mir Mohammad Ali Talpur, 'Gwadar conundrum', *Daily Times*, 22 November 2015, http://www.dailytimes.com.pk/opinion/22-Nov-2015/gwadar-conundrum, (accessed on 27 February 2018).

63. Jon Boone and Kiyya Baloch, 'A new Shenzhen? Poor Pakistan fishing town's horror at Chinese plans', *The Guardian*, 4 February 2016, http://www.theguardian.com/world/2016/feb/04/pakistan-new-shenzhen-poor-gwadar-fishing-town-china-plans, (accessed on 27 February 2018).

64. Mahnaz Isphani, *Roads and Rivals*, New York: Cornell University Press, 1989, p. 201, cited in Andrew Small, *The China Pakistan Axis: Asia's New Geopolitics*, New Delhi: Random House India, 2015, paperback edition, pp. 105–06.

65. 'Iran, India, Afghanistan sign transit accord on Chabahar port', *Dawn*, 23 May 2016, http://www.dawn.com/news/1260176, (accessed on 27 February 2018).

66. 'Three-way transit accord, an isolated Pakistan', editorial in *Pakistan Today*, 25 May 2016, http://www.pakistantoday.com.pk/2016/05/25/comment/three-way-transit-accord/, (accessed on 27 February 2018).

67. Chabahar contains two separate ports called Shahid Kalantari and Shahid Beheshti.

68. Saud bin Ahsen, 'Operationalization of Chabahar Port', *Daily Times*, 27 February 2019, https://dailytimes.com.pk/359138/operationalisation-of-chabahar-port/, (accessed on 31 March 2019).

69. 'How to Lose Friends, and add to enemies', editorial in *Pakistan Today*, 1 June 2016, http://www.pakistantoday.com.pk/2016/06/01/comment/how-to-lose-friends/, (accessed on 27 February 2018); Harris Khalique, 'Affairs Not So Foreign', *The News*, 1 June 2016, http://www.thenews.com.pk/print/124238-Affairs-not-so-foreign, (accessed on 27 February 2018).

70. 'China not "jealous" of Chabahar port deal', *DNA* 29 May 2016, http://www.dnaindia.com/money/report-china-not-jealous-of-chabahar-port-deal-beneficial-for-china-2217689, (accessed on 27 February 2018).

71. 'Projects in Iran, Pakistan can complement each other: China', *Dawn*, 2 June 2016, http://www.dawn.com/news/1262242/projects-in-iran-pakistan, (accessed on 27 February 2018).

72. Christophe Jaffrelot, 'A Tale of Two Ports'.

12. The China–Pakistan Economic Corridor

1. Khurram Husain, 'Army chief says economy showing mixed indicators', *Dawn*, 12 October 2017, https://www.dawn.com/news/1363192/army-chief-says-economy-showing-mixed-indicators, (accessed on 27 February 2018).

2. Adnan Aamir, 'Unemployment in Balochistan, *The News*, 27 April 2015, http://www.thenews.com.pk/Todays-News-9-315006-Unemployment-in-Balochistan, (accessed on 27 February 2018).

3. 'Powerless people trying to hold talks with nationalists: Mengal', *Dawn*, 18 January 2016, http://www.dawn.com/news/1233750/powerless-people-trying-to-hold-talks-with-nationalists-mengal, (accessed on 27 February 2018).

4. Government of Pakistan, Pakistan Economic Survey 2016–17, http://www.finance.gov.pk/survey/chapters_17/Pakistan_ES_2016_17_pdf.pdf, (accessed on 3 March 2018).

5. Ahmed Noorani, 'Three confusions on CPEC confronted with reality check', *Geo News*, 11 January 2016, http://www.geo.tv/latest/9271-Three-confusions-on-CPEC-confronted-with-reality-check#sthash.B8gGktK7.dpuf, (accessed on 27 February 2018).

6. Pervez Tahir, 'Whither CPEC?', *The Express Tribune*, 14 January 2016, http://tribune.com.pk/story/1027518/whither-cpec/, (accessed on 27 February 2018).

7. "PTI MNA terms CPEC as China–Punjab Economic Corridor', *The News*, 23 November 2015, http://www.thenews.com.pk/print/74906-pti-mna-terms-cpec-as-china-punjab-economic-corridor, (accessed on 27 February 2018).

8. Ejaz Hussain and Ghulam Ali, 'Pak-China Economic Relations', *Daily Times*, 25 February 2010, https://dailytimes.com.pk/101508/pakistan-china-economic-relations/, (accessed on 27 February 2018).

9. Shahbaz Rana, 'Altered trade route strikes provincialism chord', *The Express Tribune*, 12 June 2014, http://tribune.com.pk/story/720692/altered-trade-route-strikes-provincialism-chord/, (accessed on 27 February 2018).

10. 'Ahsan reveal three routes of corridor', *Dawn*, 15 May 2015, http://www.dawn.com/news/1182074/ahsan-revealsthree-routes-of-corridor, (accessed on 27 February 2018).

11. 'Ahsan Iqbal succeeds in hammering out consensus on CPEC route', *The News*, 30 May 2015, http://www.thenews.com.pk/print/12743-ahsan-iqbal-succeeds-in-hammering-out-consensus-on-cpec-route, (accessed on 27 February 2018).

12. Shahbaz Rana, 'Budget 2015-16: 12% of approved funds goes to CPEC's western alignment', *The Express Tribune*, 2 June 2015, http://tribune.com.pk/story/895940/budget-2015-16-12-of-approved-funds-goes-to-cpecs-western-alignment/, (accessed on 27 February 2018); Khaleeq Kiani, 'Govt violating APC decision on China corridor', *Dawn*, 12 June 2015, http://www.dawn.com/news/1187722/govt-violating-apc-decision-on-china-corridor, (accessed on 27 February 2018).

13. Andleeb Abbas, 'Curious Case of the CPEC', *The Daily Times*, 17 January 2016, https://dailytimes.com.pk/95883/curious-case-of-the-cpec/, (accessed on 27 February 2018).

14. Adnan Aamir, 'CPEC: The deception continues', *The Nation*, 1 January 2016, http://nation.com.pk/blogs/01-Jan-2016/cpec-the-deception-continues, (accessed on 27 February 2018).

15. Mir Mohammad Ali Talpur, 'Not the Brinjals Servant', *Daily Times*, 13 September 2015, http://www.dailytimes.com.pk/opinion/13-Sep-2015/not-the-brinjals-servant], (accessed on 27 February 2018).

16. Obaid Abrar Khan, 'Pak political parties must hammer out rifts: China', *The Daily Times*, 10 January 2016, http://www.thenews.com.pk/print/89216-

Pak-political-parties-must-hammer-out-rifts-China, (accessed on 27 February 2018).

17. Rafiullah Kakar, 'Making sense of the CPEC controversy—III', *The Express Tribune*, 11 February 2016, http://tribune.com.pk/story/1045140/making-sense-of-the-cpec-controversy-iii/, (accessed on 27 February 2018).

18. Saleem Shahid, 'Census results hurting Baloch interests won't be accepted, warns NP', *Dawn*, 24 April 2017, https://www.dawn.com/news/1328842/census-results-hurting-baloch-interests-wont-be-accepted-warns-np, (accessed on 27 February 2018).

19. Shezad Baloch, 'Is Balochistan being ignored again?', *The Express Tribune*, 18 December 2015, http://tribune.com.pk/story/1011795/is-balochistan-being-ignored-again/, (accessed on 27 February 2018).

20. Ibid.

21. 'Govt must give Baloch people a say in mega projects: Mengal', *Daily Times*, 15 September 2015, http://www.dailytimes.com.pk/national/21-Sep-2015/govt-must-give-baloch-people-a-say-in-mega-projects-mengal], (accessed on 27 February 2018).

22. Shazia Hasanin, 'Killing of labourers in Gwadar seen as attempt to split Sindhi-Baloch unity', *Dawn*, 28 May 2017, http://epaper.dawn.com/DetailImage.php?StoryImage=28_05_2017_121_005, (accessed on 27 February 2018).

23. Raza Wazir, 'The road to Gwadar passes through Balochistan', *The Friday Times* 13 March 2015, http://www.thefridaytimes.com/tft/the-road-to-gwadar-passes-through-balochistan/#sthash.eOWmMSkd.dpuf, (accessed on 27 February 2018).

24. Fawad Yousafzai, 'Chinese to outnumber Baloch natives by 2048, says FPCCI', *The Nation*, 29 December 2016, http://nation.com.pk/national/29-Dec-2016/chinese-to-outnumber-baloch-natives-by-2048, (accessed on 27 February 2018).

25. Sanaullah Baloch, 'The Gwadar deal', *The News*, 13 February 2016, http://www.thenews.com.pk/print/97926-The-Gwadar-deal, (accessed 27 February 2018).

26. Adnan Aamir, 'The Baloch's concerns', *The News*, 31 December 2017, http://tns.thenews.com.pk/balochs-concerns/#.Wkhv7d-WbIU, (accessed on 27 February 2018).

27. Ibid.

28. Mohammad Zafar, 'Balochistan reviews progress on CPEC': *The Express Tribune*, 01 December 2018 https://tribune.com.pk/story/1857619/1-balochistan-reviews-progress-cpec/, (accessed 20 February 2019).

29. 'Shockers In CPEC', editorial in *The Nation*, 12 December 2018, https://nation.com.pk/12-Dec-2018/shockers-in-cpec, (accessed on 20 February 2019).

30. '30,000 Chinese Working on CPEC, Other Projects in Pakistan: Ambassador Khalid', Associated Press of Pakistan, 24 August 2017, http://www.app.com.pk/30000-chinese-working-on-cpec-other-projects-in-pakistan-ambassador-khalid/, (accessed on 27 February 2018).

31. 'Chinese victims', *Dawn*, 11 June 2017, https://www.dawn.com/news/1338772, (accessed on 27 February 2018).

32. Sarfaraz Ahmed, 'The latest hotspot: Gwadar', *Daily Times*, 5 May 2004, http://archives.dailytimes.com.pk/national/05-May-2004/comment-the-latest-hotspot-gwadar, (accessed on 27 February 2018).

33. *Daily Times*, cited in 'Chinese Engineers in Gwadar Escape Rocket Attacks', Chennai Centre for Chinese Studies, 10 July 2010, https://www.c3sindia.org/geopolitics-strategy/chinese-engineers-in-gwadar-escape-rocket-attacks/, (accessed on 27 February 2018).

34. Archen Baloch, 'Balochistan: Saindak project oil Tankers attacked in Noshki', *Balochwarna News*, 30 September 2015, http://balochwarna.com/2015/09/30/balochistan-saindak-project-oil-tankers-attacked-in-noshki/, (accessed on 2 March 2018).

35. Raffaello Pantucci, 'The lesson of the Pakistan suicide attack: China will have to pay a high price for its infrastructure plan', *South China Morning Post*, 27 August 2018, ww.scmp.com/news/china/diplomacy-defence/article/2160918/lesson-pakistan-suicide-attack-china-will-have-pay-high, (accessed on 31 August 2018).

36. Malik Siraj Akbar, 'Blind spots in Balochistan', *The News*, 23 December 2018, http://tns.thenews.com.pk/blind-spots-balochistan/#.XB9EpVwzbIU, (accessed on 6 January 2019).

37. Ibid.

38. 'China in direct contact with Baloch separatists', *Financial Times*, 19 February 2018, cited in *The Balochistan Post*, 19 February 2018, http://thebalochistanpost.net/2018/02/china-direct-contact-baloch-separatists-financial-times/, (accessed on 27 February 2018).

39. Tusar Ranjan Mohanty, 'Chinese Checkmate', *South Asia Intelligence Review*, Vol. 17, No. 10, 3 September 2018, https://www.satp.org/south-asia-intelligence-review-Volume-17-No-10, (accessed 27 February 2019).

40. 'China says not in talks with Baloch separatists', *Daily Times*, 23 February 2018, https://dailytimes.com.pk/206278/china-says-not-talks-baloch-separatists/, (accessed on 27 February 2018).

41. Shafqat Ali, 'Contacts with Baloch Nationals: China not bypassing Pakistan govt', *The Nation*, 20 February 2018, https://nation.com.pk/20-Feb-2018/contacts-with-baloch-nationals-china-not-bypassing-pakistan-govt, (accessed on 27 February 2018).

42. Ayesha Tanzeem, 'China Denies Contacts with Separatist Militants in Pakistan', Voice of America, 22 February 2018, https://www.voanews.com/a/china-separatist-militants-in-pakistan/4265611.html, (accessed 27 February 2018).

43. Malik Siraj Akbar, 'Beijing to Balochistan', *The News*, 4 March 2018, http://tns.thenews.com.pk/beijing-balochistan/#.WpubwOhubIU, (accessed on 12 December 2018).

44. 'Chinese National Shot in Karachi's "Targetted" Attack Dies', *Dawn*, 5 February 2018, https://www.dawn.com/news/1387470, (accessed on 27 February 2018).

45. 'Tehreek-e-Taliban Pakistan claims responsibility for killing Chinese tourist', *The Express Tribune*, 2 March 2012, https://tribune.com.pk/story/344297/tehreek-e-taliban-pakistan-claims-responsibility-for-killing-chinese-tourist/, (accessed on 27 February 2018).

46. Talat Farooq, 'Security for CPEC', *The News*, 18 June 2017, https://www.thenews.com.pk/print/211243-Security-for-CPEC, (accessed on 27 February 2018).

47. 'Chinese embassy says its envoy may be attacked', *The News*, 22 October 2017, https://www.thenews.com.pk/print/238869-Chinese-embassy-says-its-envoy-may-be-attacked, (accessed on 27 February 2018).

48. 'Chinese citizens in Pakistan warned of possible terror attacks', *Dawn*, 8 December https://www.dawn.com/news/1375350/chinese-citizens-in-pakistan-warned-of-possible-terror-attacks, (accessed on 27 February 2018).

49. Muhammad Ali Ehsan, 'Protectors of the CPEC', *The Express Tribune*, 25 February 2016, http://tribune.com.pk/story/1054692/protectors-of-the-cpec, (accessed on 27 February 2018).

50. Saheed Shah, 'Big Chinese-Pakistani Project Tries to Overcome Jihadists, Droughts and Doubts', *The Wall Street Journal*, 10 April 2016, http://www.wsj.com/articles/big-chinese-pakistani-project-tries-to-overcome-jihadists-droughts-and-doubts-1460274228, (accessed on 27 February 2018).

51. Irfan Ghauri, 'Pakistan Navy increases surveillance at Gwadar port', *The Express Tribune*, 14 February 2016, https://tribune.com.pk/story/1046498/coast-guard-navy-increases-surveillance-at-gwadar-port/, (accessed on 27 February 2018).

52. Shahzada Irfan Ahmed, 'CPEC is not a game-changer, it's game over', *The News on Sunday*, 2 September 2017, http://tns.thenews.com.pk/cpec-game-changer-game/#.Wa1SaK2B2u5, (accessed on 27 February 2018).

53. Owais Qarni, 'Iran, Saudi rivalry affects Balochistan: Dr Malik', *The Express Tribune*, 18 December 2017, https://tribune.com.pk/story/1586477/1-iran-saudi-rivalry-affects-balochistan-dr-malik/, (accessed on 27 February 2018).

54. I.A. Rehman, 'Baloch concerns revisited', *Dawn*, 28 July 2016, https://www.dawn.com/news/1273557, (accessed on 27 February 2018).

55. Abbas Nasir, 'Will Gen. Bajwa walk the talk?' *Dawn*, 7 January 2017, http://www.dawn.com/news/1306805/will-gen-bajwa-walk-the-talk, (accessed on 27 February 2018).

56. 'CPEC and Gwadar fishermen', editorial in *Daily Times*, 18 March 2019,https://dailytimes.com.pk/366412/cpec-and-gwadar-fishermen/, (accessed on 21 March 2019).

V: RELENTLESS PERSECUTION

13. Human Rights Violations

1. Human Rights Commission of Pakistan (HRCP), 'Conflict in Balochistan', Report of the HRCP Fact-Finding Mission, August 2006, p.7, http://hrcp-web.org/hrcpweb/wp-content/pdf/ff/20.pdf, (accessed on 3 March 2018).

2. Declan Walsh, 'Pakistan's Secret Dirty War', *The Guardian*, 29 March 2011, https://www.theguardian.com/world/2011/mar/29/balochistan-pakistans-secret-dirty-war, (accessed on 27 February 2018).

3. Amnesty International, 'Denying the Undeniable: Enforced Disappearances in Pakistan, 2008', https://www.amnesty.org/download/Documents/.../asa330182008eng.pdf, (accessed on 2 March 2018).

4. Declan Walsh, 'Pakistan's Secret Dirty War'.

5. Tushar Ranjan Mohanty, 'Balochistan: Insecure Security', *South Asia Intelligence Review*, Vol. 16, No. 44, 30 April 2018, https://www.satp.org/south-asia-intelligence-review-Volume-16-No-44, (accessed on 15 May 2018).

6. 'About 1,000 bodies found in Balochistan in six years', *The News*, 30 December 2016, https://www.thenews.com.pk/print/175521-About-1000-bodies-found-in-Balochistan-in-six-years, (accessed on 27 February 2018).

7. Naseer Memon, 'The Balochistan conundrum', *The News on Sunday*, 16 April 2017, http://tns.thenews.com.pk/balochistan-conundrum/#.WPN5pdKGPIU, (accessed on 27 February 2018).

8. Jon Boone and Kiyya Baloch, 'A new Shenzhen? Poor Pakistan fishing town's horror at Chinese plans', *The Guardian*, 4 February 2016, https://www.theguardian.com/world/2016/feb/04/pakistan-new-shenzhen-poor-gwadar-fishing-town-china-plans, (accessed on 27 February 2018).

9. HRCP Report, 2006, pp. 2, 13 .

10. Ibid., p. 2.

11. Amnesty International, 'Denying the Undeniable: Enforced Disappearances in Pakistan, 2008.

12. The HRCP also noted an acute sense of fear in the province, in particular among those whose relatives had gone missing or had been released after their enforced disappearance. People were hesitant to pursue the cases for fear that other members of their family might be targeted. See Human Rights Commission of Pakistan (HRCP), 'Blinkered Slide into Chaos, Report of the HRCP, Fact-Finding Mission', Lahore, June 2011, http://hrcp-web.org/hrcpweb/wp-content/pdf/ff/6.pdf, (accessed on 3 March 2018).

13. Declan Walsh, 'Pakistan's Secret Dirty War.

14. Zohra Yusuf, 'Trigger-happy in Balochistan., *The Express Tribune*, 9 June 2011, http://tribune.com.pk/story/184794/trigger-happy-in-balochistan/, (accessed on 27 February 2018).

15. Faiz M. Baluch, 'Background Notes on the Voice for Baloch Missing Persons March', *The Naked Punch*, 21 November 2013, http://www.nakedpunch.com/articles/189#sthash.qLiG7Tnq.dpuf, (accessed on 27 February 2018).

16. Hamid Mir, '72-year-old Mama Qadeer Baloch breaks record of Gandhi after 84 years', *The News*, 25 February 2014, https://www.thenews.com.pk/archive/print/636350-72-year-old-mama-qadeer-baloch-breaks-record-of-gandhi-after-84-years, (accessed on 27 February 2018).

17. Faiz M. Baluch, 'Background Notes on the Voice for Baloch Missing Persons March'.

18. 'Balochistan: Enforced Disappearances Reach Alarming Records in 2015', UNPO, 5 January 2016, http://www.unpo.org/article/18818, (accessed on 2 March 2018).

19.   Tushar Ranjan Mohanty, 'Pakistan: Ethnic Carnage in Balochistan', *South Asia Intelligence Review* (SAIR), 28 November 2017, https://www.satp.org/satporgtp/sair/Archives/sair16/16_22.htm, (accessed on 27 February 2018).

20.   'Two missing Baloch men found dead in Karachi', *Dawn*, 21 August 2013, https://www.dawn.com/news/1037320, (accessed on 27 February 2018).

21.   'Mama Qadeer barred from foreign travels', *The News*, 6 March 2015, https://www.thenews.com.pk/print/27595-mama-qadeer-barred-from-foreign-travels, (accessed on 27 February 2018).

22.   Human Rights Commission of Pakistan (HRCP), 'Pushed to the Wall', Report of the HRCP Fact-Finding Mission to Balochistan, October 2009, p. 5, http://hrcp-web.org/hrcpweb/wp-content/pdf/ff/14.pdf, (accessed on 3 March 2018).

23.   'Balochistan at point of no return, Mengal tells Nawaz', *Dawn*, 20 December 2011, https://www.dawn.com/news/681889, (accessed on 27 February 2018).

24.   HRCP Report, 2011, p. 3.

25.   Ibid., p. 4.

26.   Ibid.

27.   HRCP Report, 2009, p. 13.

28.   HRCP Report, 2011, p. 12.

29.   Declan Walsh, 'UN Presses Pakistan Over the Fate of Hundreds of Missing People', *The New York Times*, 20 September 2012, https://www.nytimes.com/2012/09/21/world/asia/united-nations-presses-pakistan-on-disappearances.html, (accessed on 27 February 2018).

30.   According to the *Baluch Sarmachar* of 19 September 2012, members of the Voice for Baloch Missing Persons later wrote to the UN and the Supreme Court of Pakistan about the death threats they had received from the Tehrik Nefaz Aman (TNA), one of the death squads supported by the intelligence agencies, after they appeared before the delegation, cited in Frederic Grare, 'Balochistan: The State Versus the Nation', Washinton DC: Carnegie Endowment for International Peace, April 2013, p. 22, http://carnegieendowment.org/2013/04/11/balochistan-state-versus-nation-pub-51488, (accessed on 27 February 2018).

31.   'Balochs Welcome U.S. Human Rights Intervention at UNHCR', *Tamil Guardian*, 28 March 2012, cited in Frederic Grare, 'Balochistan: The State Versus the Nation'.

32.   Amnesty International, 'Denying the Undeniable'.

33.   The Constitution of Pakistan, cited in International Crisis Group (ICG), 'Pakistan: The Forgotten Conflict in Balochistan', *Asia Report*, 22 October 2007, pp. 3–4, https://www.crisisgroup.org/asia/south-asia/pakistan/pakistan-forgotten-conflict-balochistan, (accessed on 2 March 2018).

34.   Malik Siraj Akbar, 'Munir Mengal not released despite court order', *Daily Times*, 14 September 2007, cited in ICG Report 2007, p. 5.

35.   'West "will fail" without Pakistan', BBC News, 30 September 2006, http://news.bbc.co.uk/1/hi/world/south_asia/5394278.stm, (accessed on 27 February 2018).

36. Inamullah Khattak, 'Jihadi groups blamed for disappearances', *Dawn*, 28 March 2007, http://www.dawn.com/2007/03/28/top2.htm, (accessed on 27 February 2018).

37. Ibid.

38. Human Rights Watch, 'We Can Torture, Kill, or Keep You for Years: Enforced Disappearances by Pakistan Security Forces in Balochistan', 2011, https://www.hrw.org/sites/default/files/reports/pakistan0711WebInside.pdf, (accessed on 2 March 2018).

39. HRCP Report, 2009, p. 14.

40. Ahmar Mustikhan, 'How Pakistan is abducting, torturing and killing Baloch journalists', *Daily O*, 21 January 2015, http://www.dailyo.in/politics/balochistan-the-world-capital-of-enforced-disappearances/story/1/1598.html, (accessed on 27 February 2018).

41. Tushar Ranjan Mohanty, 'Balochistan: Shooting the Messenger', *South Asia Intelligence Review*, Vol. 13, No. 44, 4 May 2015, http://www.satp.org/satporgtp/sair/Archives/sair13/13_44.htm], (accessed on 27 February 2018).

42. Declan Walsh, 'Pakistan's Secret Dirty War'.

43. Kalbe Ali, 'Malik Admits Failure On Missing Persons', 13 December 2015, http://www.dawn.com/news/1226082, (accessed on 27 February 2018).

44. Jon Boone and Kiyya Baloch, 'A new Shenzhen? Poor Pakistan fishing town's horror at Chinese plans', *The Guardian*, 4 February 2016, http://www.theguardian.com/world/2016/feb/04/pakistan-new-shenzhen-poor-gwadar-fishing-town-china-plans, (accessed on 27 February 2018).

45. Amnesty International, 'Pakistan: Mass graves a stark reminder of violations implicating the state in Balochistan', Public Statement, AI Index: ASA 33/001/2014, 5 February 2014, https://www.amnesty.org/download/Documents/8000/asa330012014en.pdf, (accessed on 2 March 2018).

46. Selig S. Harrison, 'Pakistan's Baluch insurgency', *Le Monde diplomatique*, October 2006, https://mondediplo.com/2006/10/05baluchistan, (accessed on 27 February 2018).

47. Nosheen Ali, 'The terribly sad state of Balochistan', *The Express Tribune*, 23 May 2011, https://tribune.com.pk/story/174433/the-terribly-sad-state-of-balochistan/, (accessed on 27 February 2018).

48. Declan Walsh, 'Pakistan's Secret Dirty War'.

49. Nasir Jamal, 'Settlers caught in crossfire', *Dawn*, 28 June 2011, https://www.dawn.com/news/640059, (accessed on 27 February 2018).

50. Tushar Ranjan Mohanty, 'Balochistan: Festering Wound', *South Asia Intelligence Review*, Vol. 17, No. 19, 5 November 2018, https://www.satp.org/south-asia-intelligence-review-Volume-17-No-19, (accessed 8 November 2018); Saleem Shahid, 'Six labourers gunned down in Kharan', *Dawn*, 5 May 2018, https://www.dawn.com/news/1405713/six-labourers-gunned-down-in-kharan, (accessed on 10 May 2018).

51. Nasir Jamal, 'Settlers caught in crossfire'.

52. ICG, Crisis Group interviews, Karachi and Quetta, May–July 2007, ICG Report 2007, p. 8.

53. Ibid.

54. Declan Walsh, 'Pakistan's Secret Dirty War'.

55. Ibid.

56. Ibid.

57. Amnesty International, Pakistan, 'Mass graves a stark reminder of violations implicating the state in Balochistan'.

58. Carlotta Gall, 'In Remote Pakistan Province, A Civil War Festers', *The New York Times*, 2 April 2006, http://www.nytimes.com/2006/04/02/world/asia/02pakistan.html?_r=0&pagewanted=all, (accessed on 27 February 2018).

59. Zoya Anwer, 'Balochistan has no say in national policy making', *The News*, 12 February 2018, https://www.thenews.com.pk/print/279759-balochistan-has-no-say-in-national-policy-making, (accessed on 27 February 2018).

60. UNICEF, 'Assessment of the Nutritional Status of Children and Women among Temporary Migrant Population in the Districts Naseerabad, Jaffarabad and Quetta', July-August 2006, cited in ICG Report 2007.

61. Carlotta Gall, 'In Remote Pakistan Province, A Civil War Festers'.

14. The Judiciary

1. International Crisis Group (ICG), 'Pakistan: The Forgotten Conflict in Balochistan', *Asia Report*, 22 October 2007, p. 4, https://www.crisisgroup.org/asia/south-asia/pakistan/pakistan-forgotten-conflict-balochistan, (accessed on 2 March 2018).

2. Human Rights Commission of Pakistan (HRCP), 'Pushed to the Wall', Report of the HRCP Fact-Finding Mission to Balochistan, October 2009, p. 14, http://hrcp-web.org/hrcpweb/wp-content/pdf/ff/14.pdf, (accessed on 3 March 2018).

3. Maqbool Ahmed, 'CPEC: Hopes and fears as China comes to Gwadar', 14 March 2017, https://herald.dawn.com/news/1153685, (accessed on 2 Marh 2018).

4. 'HRCP questions official figures of forcibly disappeared in Balochistan', *Dawn*, 25 December 2018, https://www.dawn.com/news/1453426/hrcp-questions-official-figures-of-forcibly-disappeared-in-balochistan, (accessed 3 January 2019).

5. Zia Ur Rehman, 'Long Way', *The Friday Times*, 29 Nov 2013, http://www.thefridaytimes.com/tft/long-way/, (accessed on 27 February 2018).

6. 'No Respite in Balochistan: Pakistan on the offensive', *The Citizen*, 8 February 2016, http://www.thecitizen.in/index.php/en/newsdetail/index/2/6777/no-respite-in-balochistan-pakistan-on-the-offensive-report, (accessed on 27 February 2018).

7. Human Rights Commission of Pakistan (HRCP), 'Blinkered Slide into Chaos', Report of the HRCP Fact-Finding Mission, June 2011, p. 12, http://hrcp-web.org/hrcpweb/wp-content/pdf/ff/6.pdf, p. 45, (accessed on 3 March 2018).

8. Human Rights Watch, 'We Can Torture, Kill, or Keep You for Years: Enforced Disappearances by Pakistan Security Forces in Balochistan', 2011, https://

www.hrw.org/sites/default/files/reports/pakistan0711WebInside.pdf, (accessed on 2 March 2018).
9.   HRCP Report, 2009, p. 15.
10. HRCP Report, 2011, p. 12.
11. Human Rights Commission of Pakistan (HRCP), 'Balochistan: Giving the People a chance', Report of a Fact-Finding Mission, June 2013, p. 34, http://www.hrcp-web.org/hrcpweb/wp-content/pdf/Balochistan%20Report%20New%20Final.pdf, (accessed on 3 March 2018).
12. Azam Khan, 'Missing Persons case: Fiery SC lays down the law for spy agencies', *The Express Tribune*, 2 March 2012, https://tribune.com.pk/story/344312/missing-persons-fiery-sc-lays-down-the-law-for-spy-agencies/, (accessed on 27 February 2018).
13. Pakistan Institute of Legislative Development and Transparency (PILDAT), 'Balochistan: Civil–Military Relations', Islamabad, March 2012, p. 25, https://pildat.org/civil-military-relations1/balochistan, (accessed on 3 March 2018).
14. Shezad Baloch, 'Balochistan Unrest: Apex Court Issues Ominous Warning', *The Express Tribune*, 24 May 2012, https://Tribune.Com.Pk/Story/383495/Balochistan-Unrest-Apex-Court-Issues-Ominous-Warning/, (accessed 3 March 2018).
15. Human Rights Commission of Pakistan (HRCP), 'Conflict in Balochistan', Report of the HRCP Fact-Finding Mission, August 2006, p. 16, http://hrcp-web.org/hrcpweb/wp-content/pdf/ff/20.pdf, (accessed on 3 March 2018).
16. Frederic Grare, 'Balochistan: The State Versus the Nation', Washington DC: Carnegie Endowment for International Peace, April 2013, p. 20, http://carnegieendowment.org/2013/04/11/balochistan-state-versus-nation-pub-51488, (accessed on 3 March 2018).
17. Mohammad Zafar, 'Balochistan Conundrum: Hearings Spotlight "Crumbling" Khuzdar Situation', *The Express Tribune*, 11 October 2012, https://tribune.com.pk/story/449940/balochistan-conundrum-hearing-spotlights-crumbling-khuzdar-situation/, (accessed 27 February 2018).
18. Frederic Grare, 'Balochistan: The State Versus the Nation', p. 21.

15: The Media

1.   Raza Rumi, 'Not Being Dead Is A Victory For Balochistan's Journalists', *Dawn*, 12 September 2014, http://www.dawn.com/news/1131535, (accessed on 27 February 2018).
2.   Malik Siraj Akbar, 'Why Pakistan Is Embarrassed to Talk About Balochistan', Huffington Post, 13 March, 2014, http://www.huffingtonpost.com/malik-siraj-akbar/why-pakistan-is-embarrass_b_4937159.html, (accessed on 27 February 2018).
3.   Ibid.
4.   Ather Naqvi, 'The windows of opportunities for peace were squandered through arrogance', *The News on Sunday*, 23 August 2015, http://tns.thenews.com.pk/balochistan-mir-ali-talpur-windows-opportunities-peace-squandered-arrogance/#.WsDZXa2B10s, (accessed on 27 February 2018).

5. '22 Balochistan journalists killed in four years', *Dawn*, 9 July 2012 https://www.dawn.com/news/732853, (accessed on 27 February 2018).
6. Shah Meer Baloch, 'Journalists in Balochistan: Caught Between the Devil and Deep Blue Sea', *The Diplomat*, 22 November 2017, https://thediplomat.co.m/2017/11/journalists-in-balochistan-caught-between-the-devil-and-deep-blue-sea/, (accessed on 27 February 2018).
7. Committee to Protect Journalists, 'Abdul Haq Baloch Killed', 29 September 2012, https://cpj.org/data/people/abdul-haq-baloch/, (accessed on 27 February 2018).
8. Committee to Protect Journalists, 'Equipment stolen, burned in raid on pro-Baluch paper', 8 April 2013, https://cpj.org/2013/04/equipment-stolen-burned-in-raid-on-pro-baluch-pape.php, (accessed on 27 February 2018).
9. Ahmar Mustikhan, 'How Pakistan is abducting, torturing and killing Baloch journalists', 21 January 2015, http://www.dailyo.in/politics/balochistan-the-world-capital-of-enforced-disappearances/story/1/1598.html, (accessed on 27 February 2018).
10. Muhammad Akbar Notezai, 'The Dangers of Being a Journalist in Balochistan', *The Diplomat*, 4 November 2014, http://thediplomat.com/2014/11/the-danger-of-being-a-journalist-in-balochistan/, (accessed on 27 February 2018).
11. Karlos Zurutuza, 'A black hole for media in Balochistan', Al Jazeera, 5 February 2014, http://www.aljazeera.com/indepth/features/2014/02/black-hole-media-balochistan-2014238128156825.html, (accessed on 27 February 2018).
12. Ibid.
13. Ibid.
14. 'The tragedy of journalists in Balochistan', *The News*, 2 October 2012, http://www.thenews.com.pk/Todays-News-13-17846-The-tragedy-of-journalists-in-Balochistan, (accessed on 27 February 2018).
15. Karlos Zurutuza, 'A black hole for media in Balochistan'.
16. Human Rights Commission of Pakistan (HRCP), 'Conflict in Balochistan', Report of the HRCP Fact-Finding Mission, August 2006, p. 13, http://hrcp-web.org/hrcpweb/wp-content/pdf/ff/20.pdf, (accessed on 3 March 2018).
17. Human Rights Commission of Pakistan (HRCP), 'Pushed to the Wall', Report of the HRCP Fact-Finding Mission to Balochistan October 2009, p. 7, http://hrcp-web.org/hrcpweb/wp-content/pdf/ff/14.pdf, (accessed on 3 March 2018).
18. 'Threat to journalists', editorial in *Dawn*, 27 October 2017, https://www.dawn.com/news/1366483/threat-to-journalists, (accessed on 27 February 2018).
19. Shah Meer Baloch, 'Journalists in Balochistan: Caught Between the Devil and Deep Blue Sea'.
20. Ibid.
21. Nasir Jamal, 'Settlers caught in crossfire', *Dawn*, 28 June 2011, https://www.dawn.com/news/640059, (accessed on 27 February 2018).
22. 'Muzzling the media', editorial in *Dawn*, 28 January 2018, www.dawn.com/news/1381478/muzzling-the-media, (accessed on 27 February 2018).

VI: ENDURING INSURRECTION

16. The Separatist Challenge

1.   Mir Ghaus Bakhsh Bizenjo's speech to the Kalat State Assembly on 12 December 1947, cited in Martin Axmann, *Back to the Future: The Khanate of Kalat and the Genesis of Baloch Nationalism 1915–1955*, Karachi: OUP, 2008, p. 230.
2.   Malik Siraj Akbar, 'The Days to Fight Political Battles Are Over: Mengal', 22 November 2006, cited in Frederic Grare, 'Balochistan: The State Versus the Nation', Washington DC: Carnegie Endowment for International Peace, April 2013, p. 10, http://carnegieendowment.org/2013/04/11/balochistan-state-versus-nation-pub-51488, (accessed on 3 March 2018).
3.   Syeda Abida Hussain, *Power Failure: The Political Odyssey of a Pakistani Woman*, Karachi: OUP, 2015, p. 631.
4.   Zahid Hussain, 'It's war now: A major rebellion puts President Musharraf's policies to test', *Newsweek*, 16 January 2006, cited in International Crisis Group (ICG), 'Pakistan: The Worsening Conflict in Balochistan', *Asia Report* No. 119, 14 September 2006, p. 13, https://d2071andvip0wj.cloudfront.net/119-pakistan-the-worsening-conflict-in-balochistan.pdf, (accessed on 2 March 2018).
5.   ICG, Crisis Group interview, BNP President Sardar Akhtar Mengal, Quetta, March 2006, ICG Report, 2006, p. 13.
6.   Human Rights Commission of Pakistan (HRCP), 'Blinkered Slide into Chaos', Report of the HRCP Fact-Finding Mission, Lahore, June 2011, p. 8, http://hrcp-web.org/hrcpweb/wp-content/pdf/ff/6.pdf, (accessed on 3 March 2018).
7.   Human Rights Commission of Pakistan (HRCP), 'Pushed to the Wall', Report of the HRCP Fact-Finding Mission to Balochistan, October 2009, p. 11, http://hrcp-web.org/hrcpweb/wp-content/pdf/ff/14.pdf, (accessed on 3 March 2018).
8.   ICG, Crisis Group interview, National Party (NP) President Dr Abdul Hayee Baloch, Islamabad, January 2006, ICG Report, 2006, p. 1.
9.   HRCP Report, 2009, p. 12.
10. HRCP Report, 2011, p. 9.
11. Pakistan Institute of Legislative Development and Transparency (PILDAT), 'Balochistan: Civil–Military Relations', Islamabad, March 2012, http://www.pildat.org/publications/ublication/cmr/issuepaperbalochistanconflictcmr.pdf, pp. 7, and 17, (accessed on 3 March 2018).
12. ICG, Crisis Group interview, Quetta, March 2006, ICG Report, 2006, p. 12.
13. International Crisis Group (ICG), 'Pakistan: The Forgotten Conflict in Balochistan', *Asia Report*, 22 October 2007, p. 3, https://www.crisisgroup.org/asia/south-asia/pakistan/pakistan-forgotten-conflict-balochistan, (accessed on 2 March 2018).
14. Naseer Dashti, *The Baloch Conflict with Iran and Pakistan*, Bloomington: Trafford Publishing, 2007, p. 218.

15. 'BNP-M pledges support to Imran Khan after inking deal with PTI', *The News*, 09 August 2018, https://www.thenews.com.pk/print/352512-bnp-m-pledges-support-to-imran-khan-after-inking-deal-with-pti, (accessed on 4 January 2019).

16. ICG Report, 2006, p.10.

17. Ibid.

18. Ibid., p. 11.

19. Ibid.

20. HRCP Report, 2009, p. 12; HRCP Report, 2011, p. 8.

21. Robert D. Kaplan, 'Pakistan's Fatal Shore', *The Atlantic*, May 2009 Issue, http://www.theatlantic.com/magazine/archive/2009/05/pakistans-fatal-shore/307385/, (accessed on 27 February 2018).

22. Carlotta Gall, 'Pakistan's Bitter, Little-Known Ethnic Rebellion', *The New York Times*, 23 August 2011, https://www.nytimes.com/2011/08/24/world/asia/24baluch.html, (accessed on 27 February 2018).

23. Mir Mohammad Ali Talpur, 'Seeds and soil', *The News on Sunday (TNS)*, 12 November 2017, http://tns.thenews.com.pk/seeds-soil/#.WgfgaYhx3IU, (accessed on 27 February 2018).

24. Human Rights Watch, 'Their Futures Are at Stake', December 2010, p. 10, https://www.hrw.org/report/2010/12/13/their-future-stake/attacks-teachers-and-schools-pakistans-balochistan-province, (accessed on 2 March 2018).

25. Jawad R. Awan, 'Cut in funds, surgical ops curtail Baloch militancy', *The Nation*, 24 February 2016, http://nation.com.pk/national/24-Feb-2016/cut-in-funds-surgical-ops-curtail-baloch-militancy, (accessed on 27 February 2018).

26. Naseer Dashti, *The Baloch Conflict with Iran and Pakistan*, pp. 221–22.

27. Zahid Hussain, 'Musharraf's other war', *Newsline*, January 2006, http://newslinemagazine.com/magazine/musharrafs-other-war/, (accessed on 27 February 2018).

28. Syed Irfan Raza, 'BLA declared terrorist organisation, Banned', *Dawn*, 10 April 2006, https://www.dawn.com/news/187183, (accessed on 27 February 2018).

29. ICG Report, 2006, p.12.

30. The responsibility for many of the attacks was claimed by a BLA spokesperson, Azad (Free) Baloch.

31. Haroon Rashid, 'Interview: Akbar Khan Bugti', *Newsline*, February 2005, http://newslinemagazine.com/magazine/interview-akbar-khan-bugti/, (accessed on 27 February 2018).

32. ICG, Crisis Group interview, Quetta, March 2006, ICG Report, 2006, p. 12.

33. Ibid.

34. Frederic Grare, 'Balochistan: The State Versus the Nation', p. 9.

35. Naziha Syed Ali, 'Situationer: Who's who of Baloch insurgency', *Dawn*, 1 June 2015, https://www.dawn.com/news/1185401, (accessed 27 February 2018).

36. Naseer Dashti, *The Baloch Conflict with Iran and Pakistan*, p. 223.

37. Naziha Syed Ali, 'Situationer: Who's who of Baloch insurgency'.

38. Ibid.
39. Naseer Dashti, *The Baloch Conflict with Iran and Pakistan*, p. 224.
40. Ibid.
41. Naziha Syed Ali, 'Situationer: Who's who of Baloch insurgency'.
42. Naziha Syed Ali, 'Situationer: Who's who of Baloch Insurgency'; Naseer Dashti, *The Baloch Conflict with Iran and Pakistan*, pp. 222–23.
43. Naseer Dashti, *The Baloch Conflict with Iran and Pakistan*, pp. 224–25.
44. 'Head money announced for 99 militants', *Dawn*, 18 March 2016, http://www.dawn.com/news/1246411/head-money-announced-for-99-militants], (accessed on 27 February 2018).
45. Naseer Dashti, 'Resolving the Baloch National Question: aspects of a negotiated settlement', https://www.thebaluch.com/050708_article.php, (accessed on 3 March 2018).
46. For example, the army tried to physically eliminate Nawab Bugti at the very first opportunity, even before the negotiations between the latter and the Mushahid Hussain-led delegation started. See Frederic Grare, 'Balochistan: The State Versus the Nation', p. 10.
47. Frederic Grare, 'Balochistan: The State Versus the Nation', p. 9.
48. Declan Walsh, 'Pakistan's Secret Dirty War', *The Guardian*, 29 March 2011, https://www.theguardian.com/world/2011/mar/29/balochistan-pakistans-secret-dirty-war, (accessed on 27 February 2018).
49. 'Balochistan schools abandon National Anthem, Senate told', *The News*, 30 April 2009, https://www.thenews.com.pk/archive/ print/664146-balochistan-schools-abandon-national-anthem, (accessed on 27 February 2018).
50. Saeed Minhas, 'Balochistan Diary: Army schools: too little, a bit too late', *Daily Times*, 4 July 2010, cited in Sushant Sareen, 'Balochistan: Forgotten War, Forsaken People', Vivekananda International Foundation, September 2017, https://www.vifindia.org/monograph/2017/december/07/balochistan-forgotten-war-forsaken-people, (accessed on 3 March 2018).
51. Taj Mohammad Breseeg, 'Baloch and the right of self-determination', http://bolanvoice.com/2012/08/17/baloch-and-the-right-of-self-determination/, (accessed on 3 March 2018).
52. ICG, Crisis Group interview, Karachi, May 2007, ICG Report, 2007, p.13.
53. Ibid.
54. ICG, Crisis Group interview, BNP national parliamentarian Abdul Rauf Mengal, Islamabad, February 2006, ICG Report, 2006, p. 10.
55. Mahvish Ahmad, 'Balochistan: Middle-Class Rebellion', *Dawn*, 5 June 2012, https://www.dawn.com/news/723987, (accessed on 27 February 2018).
56. Sasuie Abbas Leghari, 'The Balochistan Crisis', *The News*, 25 August 2012, www.thenews.com.pk/Todays-News-9-128196-The-Balochistan-crisis, (accessed on 27 February 2018).
57. Mahvish Ahmad, 'The changing face of Balochistan's separatist insurgency', *The Caravan*, 1 July 2014, http://www.caravanmagazine.in/reportage/home-front-changing-insurgency-balochistan, (accessed on 27 February 2018).
58. Shahzada Zulfiqar, 'Rage Revisited', *The Herald*, October 2006, p. 79.

59. Justin S. Dunne, 'Crisis in Baluchistan: A Historical Analysis of the Baluch Nationalist Movement in Pakistan', *Naval Postgraduate School*, Monterey, California, June 2006, p. 46, https://calhoun.nps.edu/bitstream/handle/10945/2755/06Jun_Dunne.pdf?sequence=1&isAllowed=y, (accessed 3 March 2018).

60. Shahzada Zulfiqar, 'The Baloch people consider the nationalist fighters as their saviours: Nawab Akbar Bugti', *Herald*, March 2006, reprinted 23 September 2017, https://herald.dawn.com/news/1153865, (accessed on 2 March 2018).

61. *Dawn*, 15 January 2006, cited in John C.K. Daly, 'The Baloch Insurgency and its Threat to Pakistan's Energy Sector', *The Jamestown Foundation Publication: Terrorism Focus*, Vol. 3, Issue: 11, 21 March 2006, http://www.jamestown.org/single/?no_cache=1&tx_ttnews%5Btt_news%5D=709#.VmglHYSGWfQ, (accessed on 3 March 2018).

62. Editor's Note, *Newsline*, September 2006, https://newslinemagazine.com/magazine/editors-note-september-2006/, (accessed on 27 February 2018).

63. Syeda Abida Hussain, *Power Failure*, p. 626.

64. 'Political Prisoners of Pakistan: Akbar Khan Bugti', http://politicalprisonersofpakistan.blogspot.co.uk/2011/09/akbar-khan-bugti.html (22-03-2013), (accessed on 27 February 2018).

65. HRCP Report, 2011, p. 9.

66. ICG, Crisis Group telephone interview with Abdul Hayee Baloch, 31 August 2006. ICG Report, 2006, p. 26.

67. ICG, Crisis Group interview, Karachi, May 2007, ICG Report, 2007, p. 13.

68. Saleem Shahid, 'Grand Jirga in Kalat decides to move ICJ', *Dawn*, 22 September 2006, https://www.dawn.com/news/211514/grand-jirga-in-kalat-decides-to-move-icj, (accessed on 27 February 2018).

69. ICG, Crisis Group interview, Quetta, July 2007, ICG Report, 2007, p. 12.

70. ICG, Crisis Group interview, Karachi, May 2007, ICG Report, 2007, p. 12.

71. Muhammad Ijaz Laif and Muhammad Amir Hamza, 'Ethnic Nationalism in Pakistan: A Case Study of Baloch Nationalism during Musharraf Regime', *Pakistan Vision*, Vol. 10, No. 1, p. 70, http://pu.edu.pk/images/journal/studies/PDF-FILES/Artical%20-%204.pdf, (accessed 3 March 2018)]

72. Kanchan Lakshman, 'The Neglected Insurgency', *Outlook*, 7 June 2007, https://www.outlookindia.com/website/story/the-neglected-insurgency/234811, (accessed on 27 February 2018).

73. 'Seven dead, 27 hurt as 3 bomb blasts rock Quetta', *Dawn*, 23 July 2000, cited in Sushant Sareen, 'Balochistan: Forgotten War, Forsaken People'.

74. 'Quetta Staff College under rocket attack', *Frontier Post*, 27 December 2000, cited in ibid.

75. Naseer Dashti, *The Baloch Conflict with Iran and Pakistan*, p.199.

76. Munawar Hasan, '24 rocket attacks in two years', *The Nation*, 23 February 2003, and 'Gas station blown up rupturing pipelines', *The News*, 22 January 2003, cited in ibid.

77. The Foreign Policy Centre, 'The Balochis of Pakistan: On the Margins of History', *The Foreign Policy Centre*, London, November 2006, p. 42, https://fpc.org.uk/publications/balochis-of-pakistan-on-the-margins-of-history/, (accessed on 3 March 2018).

78. Cited in Sushant Sareen, 'Balochistan: Forgotten War, Forsaken People', p. 50.

79. Zahid Hussain, 'Gathering Storm', *Newsline*, February 2005, cited in ICG Report 2006, p. 24.

80. BBC, 18 January 2005, cited in John C. K. Daly, 'The Baloch Insurgency and its Threat to Pakistan's Energy Sector'.

81. Sarfaraz Ahmed, 'Sardars face rebellious tribesmen', *The Friday Times*, 6–12 January 2006, cited in ICG Report, 2006, p. 9.

82. Justin S. Dunne, 'Crisis in Baluchistan: A Historical Analysis of the Baluch Nationalist Movement in Pakistan'.

83. Carlotta Gall, 'In Remote Pakistan Province, a Civil War Festers', *The New York Times*, 2 April 2006, http://www.nytimes.com/2006/04/02/world/asia/02pakistan.html?_r=0&pagewanted=all, (accessed on 27 February 2018).

84. Pakistan Institute of Legislative Development and Transparency (PILDAT), 'Balochistan: Civil-Military Relations', Islamabad, March 2012, p. 15, http://www.pildat.org/publications/publication/cmr/issuepaperbalochistan conflictcmr.pdf, (accessed on 3 March 2018).

85. Cited in ICG Report, 2006, fn 210, p. 25.

86. Madiha Tahir, 'From rallies to armed resistance in Balochistan', Al Jazeera, 6 May 2014, http://www.aljazeera.com/indepth/opinion/2014/05/from-rallies-armed-resistance-ba-20145665338680350.htm, (accessed on 27 February 2018).

87. Kaswar Klasra, 'Capital Fruit Market Blast Kills 24', *The Nation*, 10 April 2014, https://nation.com.pk/10-Apr-2014/capital-fruit-market-blast-kills-24, (accessed on 27 February 2018).

88. Madiha Tahir, 'From rallies to armed resistance in Balochistan'.

89. ICG Report, 2006, p. 17.

90. South Asia Terrorism Portal, *Institute of Conflict Management*, data updated till 24 March 2019.

91. Human Rights Commission of Pakistan (HRCP), 'Conflict in Balochistan', Report of the HRCP Fact-Finding Mission, August 2006, p. 43, http://hrcp-web.org/hrcpweb/wp-content/pdf/ff/20.pdf, (accessed on 3 March 2018).

92. Human Rights Commission of Pakistan (HRCP), 'Balochistan: Giving the People a chance', Report of the HRCP Fact-Finding Mission, June 2013, p. 34, http://www.hrcp-web.org/hrcpweb/wp-content/pdf/Balochistan%20Report%20New%20Final.pdf, p. 34, (accessed on 3 March 2018).

93. Human Rights Commission of Pakistan (HRCP), 'Hopes, Fears and Alienation in Balochistan', Report of the HRCP Fact-Finding Mission, May 2012, p. 46, http://hrcp-web.org/hrcpweb/wp-content/pdf/ff/12.pdf, (accessed on 3 March 2018).

94. Shahzada Zulfiqar, 'Rage Revisited'.

95. Salman Zaidi, 'Policy Brief: Making Sense of Violence in Balochistan 2010', Islamabad: *Jinnah Institute*, January 2010, http://jinnah-institute.org/policy-brief-making-sense-of-violence-in-balochistan-2010-2/, (accessed on 3 March 2018).

96. 'The Real Deal', editorial in *The Nation*, 27 September 2016, http://nation.com.pk/editorials/27-Sep-2016/the-real-deal, (accessed on 27 February 2018).

97. 'Brahumdagh Bugti's appeal to India: a political ploy?' editorial in *Daily Times*, 21 September 2016, http://dailytimes.com.pk/editorial/21-Sep-16/brahumdagh-bugtis-appeal-to-india-a-political-ploy, (accessed on 27 February 2018).

98. Malik Siraj Akbar, 'Balochistan—Point of no Return?', *The Express Tribune*, 12 January 2012, https://tribune.com.pk/story/319975/balochistan--point-of-no-return/, (accessed on 27 February 2018).

99. Inayatullah Baloch, *The Problem of Greater Baluchistan: A Study of Baluch Nationalism*, Stuttgart: Steiner Verlag Wiesbaden Gmbh, 1987, p. 28.

100. Saleem Shahid, '265 militants in Balochistan surrender arms', *Dawn*, 19 September 2018, https://www.dawn.com/news/1433819/265-militants-in-balochistan-surrender-arms, (accessed 30 September 2018).

101. Saleem Shahid, 'Led by top Baloch "commander", 70 militants surrender', *Dawn*, 21 November 2018, https://www.dawn.com/news/1446953/led-by-top-baloch-commander-70-militants-surrender, (accessed 28 November 2018).

102. '560 militants surrender arms in Nasirabad', *The Nation*, 3 January 2019, https://nation.com.pk/03-Jan-2019/560-militants-surrender-arms-in-nasirabad, (accessed 6 January 2019).

103. Shezad Baloch, 'Blaming India every time for the problems in Balochistan is really not the solution', *The Express Tribune blogs*, 28 March 2017, http://blogs.tribune.com.pk/story/48004/blaming-india-everytime-for-the-problems-in-balochistan-is-really-not-the-solution-pakistan/, (accessed on 27 February 2018).

104. Ather Naqvi, 'The windows of opportunities for peace were squandered through arrogance', *The News on Sunday*, 23 August 2015, http://tns.thenews.com.pk/balochistan-mir-ali-talpur-windows-opportunities-peace-squandered-arrogance/#.WsDZXa2B10s, (accessed on 27 February 2018).

105. 'Baloch surrenders—suspect timing?' editorial in *Daily Times*, 30 June 2017, http://dailytimes.com.pk/editorial/30-Jun-17/baloch-surrenders-suspect-timing, (accessed on 27 February 2018).

106. 'Wavering Baloch Resistance?' editorial in *The Nation*, 29 June 2017, https://nation.com.pk/29-Jun-2017/wavering-baloch-resistance, (accessed on 27 February 2018).

107. 'Who is surrendering in Balochistan? editorial in *Daily Times*, 30 January 2018, https://dailytimes.com.pk/191521/who-is-surrendering-in-balochistan/, (accessed on 27 February 2018).

17. The Response of the Government

1. Pakistan Institute of Legislative Development and Transparency (PILDAT), 'Balochistan: Civil–Military Relations', p. 7, http://www.pildat.org/

publications/publication/cmr/issuepaperbalochistanconflictcmr.pdf,
(accessed on 3 March 2018).

2.   International Crisis Group (ICG), Crisis Group interview, National
      Party leader, Dr Abdul Hayee Baloch, Karachi, April 2006, 'Pakistan, The
      Worsening Conflict in Balochistan', *Asia Report* No. 119—14 September
      2006, p. 13, https://d2071andvip0wj.cloudfront.net/119-pakistan-the-
      worsening-conflict-in-balochistan.pdf, (accessed on 2 March 2018).

3.   Ibid.

4.   Discussed in the chapter on Human Rights Violations.

5.   Human Rights Commission of Pakistan (HRCP), 'Balochistan: Giving the
      People a chance', Report of the HRCP Fact-Finding Mission, June 2013,
      p. 37, http://www.hrcp-web.org/hrcpweb/wp-content/pdf/Balochistan%20
      Report%20New%20Final.pdf, (accessed on 3 March 2018).

6.   Sairah Irshad Khan, 'Interview: Jamil Bugti', *Newsline*, September 2006,
      http://newslinemagazine.com/magazine/the-end-game/, (accessed on 3
      March 2018).

7.   International Crisis Group (ICG), Crisis Group interview, Shahzada Zulfikar,
      July 2007, 'Pakistan: The Forgotten Conflict in Balochistan', *Asia Report*, 22
      October 2007, p. 9, https://www.crisisgroup.org/asia/south-asia/pakistan/
      pakistan-forgotten-conflict-balochistan, (accessed on 2 March 2018).

8.   Zahid Hussain, 'Gathering Storm', *Newsline*, February 2005, p. 24, http://
      newslinemagazine.com/magazine/gathering-storm/, (accessed on 3 March
      2018).

9.   Asghar Soomro, 'Illusion of democracy in Balochistan', *The Express Tribune*,
      16   January   2018,   https://tribune.com.pk/story/1609445/6-illusion-
      democracy-balochistan/, (accessed on 27 February 2018).

10.   Taj Mohammad Breseeg, *Baloch Nationalism, its origin and development*,
      Karachi: Royal Book Company, 2004, p. 374.

11.   Human Rights Commission of Pakistan (HRCP), 'Blinkered Slide into Chaos',
      Report of the HRCP Fact-Finding Mission, June 2011, pp. 7–8, http://hrcp-
      web.org/hrcpweb/wp-content/pdf/ff/6.pdf, (accessed on 3 March 2018).

12.   Tariq Khosa, 'The Balochistan saga', *Dawn*, 21 December 2015, https://
      www.dawn.com/news/1227719, (accessed on 27 February 2018).

13.   Amir Mateen, 'Balochistan will stay if people stop leaving', *The News*, 29 May
      2012, https://www.thenews.com.pk/archive/print/622680-balochistan-will-
      stay- if-people-stop-leaving, (accessed on 27 February 2018).

14.   Monis Ali, 'The education crisis in Balochistan', *Daily Times*, 26 October 2016.
      https://dailytimes.com.pk/49812/the-education-crisis-in-balochistan/,
      (accessed on 27 February 2018).

15.   Abdullah Alam, 'Balochistan education budget—one step backwards',
      The Express Tribune, 10 July 2016, http://tribune.com.pk/story/1138481/
      balochistan-education-budget-one-step-backwards/, (accessed on 27
      February 2018).

16.   Adnan Aamir, 'The Balochistan budget', *The News*, 9 July 2016, https://
      www.thenews.com.pk/print/133513-The-Balochistan-budget, (accessed on
      27 February 2018); Mushtaq Rajpar, 'The political economy of Balochistan',

The News, 24 June 2017, https://www.thenews.com.pk/print/212514-The-political-economy-of-Balochistan, (accessed on 27 February 2018).

17.   HRCP Report, 2013, p. 32.

18.   Ibid., p.14.

19.   'Dance Macabre in Balochistan', editorial in *The Nation*, 17 November 2017, http://nation.com.pk/17-Nov-2017/danse-macabre-in-balochistan, (accessed on 27 February 2018).

20.   'Gen. Pervez Musharraf's Address to the Nation', http://www.ipripak.org/wp-content/uploads/2015/05/docs2006.pdf, (accessed on 27 February 2018).

21.   ICG, Crisis Group interview with National Party leader Hasil Bizenjo, *Dawn*, 12 February 2006, ICG Report, 2006, p. 14.

22.   'Saboteurs can't deter progress', *The Nation*, 15 December 2005, cited in ICG Report, 2006, p. 14.

23.   ICG Report, 2006, p. 14.

24.   Human Rights Commission of Pakistan (HRCP), 'Pushed to the Wall', Report of the HRCP Fact-Finding Mission to Balochistan, October 2009, p. 12, http://hrcp-web.org/hrcpweb/wp-content/pdf/ff/14.pdf, (accessed on 3 March 2018).

25.   ICG, Crisis Group interview of BNP Senator Sanaullah Baloch, Quetta, March 2006. ICG Report, 2006, p. 23.

26.   ICG, Crisis Group interview, JWP Secretary-General Senator Agha Shahid Bugti, Quetta, March 2006, ICG Report, 2006, p. 23.

27.   Sanaullah Baloch, 'The Balochistan Conflict: Towards a Lasting Peace', Pakistan Security Research Unit (PSRU) Brief Number 7, Department of Peace Studies at the *University of Bradford*, UK, 1 March 2007.

28.   ICG, Crisis Group interview, National Party leader, Dr Abdul Hayee Baloch, Karachi, April 2006, ICG Report, 2006, p. 21.

29.   Munir Ahmad, 'The Battle for Pakistan: Militancy and Conflict in Balochistan', *New America Foundation*, September 201, p. 4, https://static.newamerica.org/attachments/4342-the-battle-for-pakistan/Munir_Ahmad_Balochistan.c3f358a0fd9843679dedd6327454f08c.pdf, (accessed on 27 February 2018).

30.   HRCP Report, 2011, p. 9.

31.   'Balochistan's woes', editorial in *Daily Times*, 17 October 2017, https://dailytimes.com.pk/126203/balochistans-woes/, (accessed on 27 February 2018).

32.   Ather Naqvi, 'The windows of opportunities for peace were squandered through arrogance', *The News on Sunday*, 23 August 2015, http://tns.thenews.com.pk/balochistan-mir-ali-talpur-windows-opportunities-peace-squandered-arrogance/#.WsDZXa2B10s, (accessed on 27 February 2018).

33.   Peter Jacob, 'A Serial Transformation', *The Friday Times*, 26 February 2014, http://www.thefridaytimes.com/tft/a-serial-transformation/, (accessed on 27 February 2018).

34.   Adnan Aamir, 'What Nawaz Sharif did for Balochistan', *The Daily Times*, 5 August 2017, http://dailytimes.com.pk/opinion/05-Aug-17/what-nawaz-sharif-did-for-balochistan, (accessed on 27 February 2018).

35. Ather Naqvi, 'The windows of opportunities for peace were squandered through arrogance'.

36. Tushar Ranjan Mohanty, 'Balochistan: Unending Misery', *South Asia Intelligence Review (SAIR)*, Vol. 14, No. 32, 8 February 2016, https://www.satp.org/satporgtp/sair/Archives/sair14/14_32.htm#assessment1, (accessed on 27 February 2018).

37. Saleem Shahid, 'PM unveils 10-year uplift package for Balochistan', *Dawn*, 15 November 2017, https://www.dawn.com/news/1370584/pm-unveils-10-year-uplift-package-for-balochistan, (accessed on 27 February 2018).

38. 'Flashy Headlines', editorial in *The Nation*, 16 November 2017, http://nation.com.pk/16-Nov-2017/flashy-headlines, (accessed on 27 February 2018).

39. 'Balochistan package', editorial in *The News*, 16 November 2017, http://thenews.com.pk/print/244699-Balochistan-package, (accessed on 27 February 2018).

40. Raashid Wali Janjua, 'Human security and Balochistan', *The News*, 17 January 2016, http://www.thenews.com.pk/print/91686-Human-security-and-Balochistan, (accessed on 27 February 2018).

41. Lal Khan, 'Balochistan's deliverance?' *Daily Times*, 15 January 2018, https://dailytimes.com.pk/180983/balochistans-deliverance/, (accessed on 27 February 2018).

42. Adnan Aamir, 'Politics in Balochistan', *The News*, 15 March 2017, https://www.thenews.com.pk/print/192312-Politics-in-Balochistan, (accessed on 27 February 2018).

43. Mushahid Hussain, 'Has the Rubicon Been Crossed?' *Newsline*, June 2009, http://newslinemagazine.com/magazine/has-the-rubicon-been-crossed/, (accessed on 3 March 2018).

44. Ibid.

18. Response of the Army

1. Adeel Khan, 'Renewed Ethno-nationalist Insurgency in Balochistan: The Militarized State and Continuing Economic Deprivation', *Asian Survey*, Vol. 49, No. 6, November/December 2009, pp. 1071–91, University of California Press, Oakland, California.

2. 'The path to peace in Balochistan', editorial in *Dawn*, 28 September 2017, https://www.dawn.com/news/1360519/the-path-to-peace-in-balochistan, (accessed on 27 February 2018).

3. Shakil Sheikh, 'Musharraf warns India against blame game', *The News*, 3 August 2006; 'No Compromise with Baloch nationalists', *Daily Times*, 15 July 2006, cited in International Crisis Group, Pakistan (ICG), 'The Worsening Conflict in Balochistan', *Asia Report* No. 119, 14 September 2006, p. 24, https://d2071andvip0wj.cloudfront.net/119-pakistan-the-worsening-conflict-in-balochistan.pdf, (accessed on 2 March 2018).

4. Selig S. Harrison, *In Afghanistan's Shadow: Baluch Nationalism and Soviet Temptations*, Washington DC: Carnegie Endowment for International Peace, 1981, p. 3.

5. ICG Report, 2006, p. 9.
6. The issue is discussed in greater detail in the chapter on Human Rights Violations.
7. HARDtalk: 'Balochistan is not the most sensitive spot for the Pakistan Army —Life there is normal'—Major General Shaukat Sultan, 15 September 2004, http://archives.dailytimes.com.pk/editorial/15-Sep-2004/hardtalk-balochistan-is-not-the-most-sensitive-spot-for-the-pakistan-army-life-there-is, (accessed on 27 February 2018).
8. 'Insurgency has ended in Balochistan, says Lt Gen. Aamer Riaz', *The Express Tribune*, 6 November 2015, http://tribune.com.pk/story/986111/balochistan-situation-insurgency-has-ended-says-lt-gen-aamer-riaz/], (accessed on 27 February 2018).
9. Pakistan Institute of Legislative Development and Transparency (PILDAT), 'Balochistan: Civil–Military Relations', Islamabad, March 2012, p. 23, http://www.pildat.org/publications/ublication/cmr/issuepaperbalochistan conflictcmr.pdf, (accessed on 3 March 2018)
10. 'JuD on front line of earthquake aid', *Dawn*, 30 October 2015, https://www.dawn.com/news/1216385/jud-on-front-line-of-earthquake-aid, (accessed on 27 February 2018).
11. Abbas Nasir, 'Grateful for small mercies', *Dawn*, 24 December 2016, http://www.dawn.com/news/1304071/grateful-for-small-mercies, (accessed on 27 February 2018).
12. 'Pakistan: Army Creates an Organization to Kill Intellectuals and Activists in Balochistan, in the Name of Peace', *Asian Human Rights Commission*, 6 January 2012, http://www.humanrights.asia/news/ahrc-news/AHRC-STM-005-2012, (accessed on 27 February 2018).
13. Waqar Ahmed, 'Tackling Daesh threat assuming urgency', *The News*, 17 July 2018, https://www.thenews.com.pk/print/342578-tackling-daesh-threat-assuming-urgency, (accessed on 3 January 2019).
14. Human Rights Commission of Pakistan (HRCP), 'Blinkered Slide into Chaos', Report of the HRCP Fact-Finding Mission, June 2011, http://hrcp-web.org/hrcpweb/wp-content/pdf/ff/6.pdf, p. 11, (accessed on 3 March 2018).
15. Muhammad Akram, 'Baloch Leaders Made Their Points Well. Is Anyone Listening?' *Dawn*, 28 September 2012, cited in Frederic Grare, 'Balochistan: The State Versus the Nation', Washington DC: *Carnegie Endowment for International Peace*, April 2013, p. 14, http://carnegieendowment.org/2013/04/11/balochistan-state-versus-nation-pub-51488, (accessed on 3 March 2018).
16. Human Rights Commission of Pakistan (HRCP), 'Balochistan: Giving the People a chance', Report of the HRCP Fact-Finding Mission, June 2013, p. 18, http://www.hrcp-web.org/hrcpweb/wp-content/pdf/Balochistan%20Report%20New%20Final.pdf, (accessed on 3 March 2018).
17. Human Rights Commission of Pakistan (HRCP), 'Pushed to the Wall', Report of the HRCP Fact-Finding Mission to Balochistan', October 2009, p. 10, http://hrcp-web.org/hrcpweb/wp-content/pdf/ff/14.pdf, (accessed on 3 March 2018).

18. HRCP Report, 2013, p. 19.
19. Maqbool Ahmed, 'CPEC: Hopes and fears as China comes to Gwadar', *Herald*, 14 March 2017, https://herald.dawn.com/news/1153685, (accessed on 2 March 2018).
20. 'Political failure in Balochistan and FATA', editorial in *Daily Times*, 25 June 2017, http://dailytimes.com.pk/editorial/25-Jun-17/political-failure-in-balochistan-and-fata, (accessed on 27 February 2018).
21. Cited in Frederic Grare, 'Balochistan: The State Versus the Nation', Washington DC: Carnegie Endowment for International Peace, April 2013, *fn* 77, p. 29, http://carnegieendowment.org/2013/04/11/balochistan-state-versus-nation-pub-51488, (accessed on 3 March 2018).
22. Ather Naqvi, 'The windows of opportunities for peace were squandered through arrogance', *The News on Sunday*, 23 August 2015, http://tns.thenews.com.pk/balochistan-mir-ali-talpur-windows-opportunities-peace-squandered-arrogance/#.WsDZXa2B10s, (accessed on 27 February 2018).
23. 'RAW camps in Balochistan', *Dawn*, 31 August 2004; *The Herald* (Karachi), September 2004, https://www.dawn.com/news/369075, (accessed on 2 March 2018).
24. HARDtalk: 'Balochistan is not the most sensitive spot for the Pakistan Army'.
25. 'Afghans, India, fuelling Balochistan insurgency, says Owais Ghani', *Daily Times*, 7 February 2006, cited in ICG Report, 2006, p. 25.
26. Mariana Baabar, 'How India is Fomenting Trouble in Pakistan via Afghanistan', *News International*, 16 April 2006, https://www.thenews.com.pk/archive/print/642835-how-india-is-fomenting-trouble-in-pakistan-via-afghanistan, (accessed on 23 February 2018).
27. Ibid.
28. Farzana Shah, 'India backing Balochistan Liberation Army: Rehman Malik', *Asian Tribune*, 23 April 2009, http://www.asiantribune.com/node/16986, (accessed on 23 February).
29. Frederic Grare, 'Balochistan: The State Versus the Nation', fn 77, p. 29.
30. Kamran Yousaf, 'Balochistan now a hotbed of regional, global proxy war: army chief', *The Express Tribune*, 3 February 2016, http://tribune.com.pk/story/1038830/general-raheel-sharif-in-quetta-to-attend-peace-moot/, (accessed on 27 February 2018).
31. ICG, Crisis Group interview, Senator Sanaullah Baloch, March 2006, ICG Report, 2006, p. 26.
32. Selig S. Harrison, 'Will Pakistan Break Up?' Washington DC: Carnegie Endowment for International Peace, 9 June 2009.
33. Frederic Grare, 'Balochistan: The State Versus the Nation', p. 20.
34. Maqbool Ahmed, 'CPEC: Hopes and fears as China comes to Gwadar', *Herald*, 14 March 2017, https://herald.dawn.com/news/1153685, (accessed on 27 February 2018).
35. 'Baloch activist backs Indian narrative on Jadhav', *The Express Tribune*, 19 January 2018, https://tribune.com.pk/story/1612438/1-baloch-activists-backs-indian-narrative-jadhav/, (accessed on 27 February 2018).
36. ICG, Crisis Group interview, Sher Ali Mazari, Islamabad, February 2006, ICG Report, 2006, p. 26.

37.   Cyril Almeida, 'A security prism, not a human one', *Dawn* 30 June 2011, https://www.dawn.com/news/640593/a-security-prism-not-a-human-one, (accessed on 27 February 2018).
38.   'Bugti's son backs "resistance"', *Dawn*, 30 October 2006, cited in International Crisis Group (ICG), 'Pakistan: The Forgotten Conflict in Balochistan', *Asia Report*, 22 October 2007, p. 2, https://www.crisisgroup.org/asia/south-asia/pakistan/pakistan-forgotten-conflict-balochistan, (accessed on 2 March 2018).
39.   ICG Report, 2006, p. 23.
40.   Noshad Ali, 'Bank accounts of Bugti's kin frozen', *Daily Times*, 21 November 2006, cited in ICG Report, 2007, p. 2.
41.   'Graphic details: Killing of Brahumdagh Bugti's sister and niece in Karachi on 31st January', *Baluch Sarmachar*, 5 February 2012, https://baluchsarmachar.wordpress.com/2012/02/05/graphic-details-killing-of-brahumdagh-bugtis-sister-and-niece-in-karachi-on-31st-january/, (accessed on 27 February 2018).
42.   Mohammad Zafar, 'Awaran operation: BLF chief's brother, nephew among 13 killed', *The Express Tribune*, 1 July 2015, https://tribune.com.pk/story/912709/awaran-operation-blf-chiefs-brother-nephew-among-13-killed/, (accessed on 27 February 2018).
43.   HRCP Report, 2006, p. 41.
44.   Ibid.
45.   HRCP Report, 2009, p. 5.
46.   ICG Report, 2006, p. 18.
47.   PILDAT, 'Balochistan: Civil–Military Relations', p. 23.
48.   ICG, Crisis Group interview, July 2007, ICG Report, 2007, p. 8.
49.   'Balochistan at point of no return, Mengal tells Nawaz', *Dawn*, 20 December 2011, https://www.dawn.com/news/681889, (accessed on 27 February 2018).

Conclusion

1.   International Crisis Group, (ICG), 'Pakistan: The Worsening Conflict in Balochistan', *Asia Report*, 14 September 2006, p. 119, https://d2071andvip0wj.cloudfront.net/119-pakistan-the-worsening-conflict-in-balochistan.pdf, (accessed on 3 March 2018).
2.   Kaiser Bengali, *A Cry for Justice: Empirical Insights From Balochistan*, Karachi: OUP, 2018, p. 133.
3.   Naseer Dashti, 'Resolving the Baloch National Question: Aspects of a negotiated settlement', https://www.thebaluch.com/050708_article.php, (accessed on 2 March 2018).
4.   Naseer Dashti, *The Baloch Conflict with Iran and Pakistan*, Bloomington, Indiana, USA: Trafford Publishing, 2012, p. 229.
5.   Hashim bin Rashid, 'Why Punjab doesn't talk about Balochistan', *The Friday Times*, 17 April 2015, http://www.thefridaytimes.com/tft/why-punjab-

doesnt-talk-about-balochistan/#sthash.scfDSWvS.dpuf, (accessed on 27 February 2018).

6. International Crisis Group (ICG), Crisis Group interview, Karachi, May 2007, 'Pakistan: The Forgotten Conflict in Balochistan', *Asia Briefing* No. 69, 22 October 2007, p. 13, https://d2071andvip0wj.cloudfront.net/b69-pakistan-the-forgotten-conflict-in-balochistan.pdf, (accessed 3 March 2018).

7. Mohammad Zafar, 'Balochistan Conundrum: Hearings Spotlight "Crumbling" Khuzdar Situation', *The Express Tribune*, 11 October 2012, https://tribune.com.pk/story/449940/balochistan-conundrum-hearing-spotlights-crumbling-khuzdar-situation/, (accessed 27 February 2018).

8. Declan Walsh, 'Pakistan's Secret Dirty War', *The Guardian* 29 March 2011, https://www.theguardian.com/world/2011/mar/29/balochistan-pakistans-secret-dirty-war, (accessed on 27 February 2018).

9. Feroz Ahmad, *Ethnicity and Politics in Pakistan*, Karachi: OUP, 1998, p. 15.

10. Human Rights Commission of Pakistan (HRCP), 'Balochistan: Giving the People a chance', Report of the HRCP Fact-Finding Mission, June 2013, p. 13, http://www.hrcp-web.org/hrcpweb/wp-content/pdf/Balochistan%20Report%20New%20Final.pdf, (accessed on 3 March 2018).

11. Ather Naqvi, 'The windows of opportunities for peace were squandered through arrogance', *The News on Sunday*, 23 August 2015, http://tns.thenews.com.pk/balochistan-mir-ali-talpur-windows-opportunities-peace-squandered-arrogance/#.WsHEKa2B06g, (accessed on 27 February 2018).

12. Human Rights Commission of Pakistan (HRCP), 'Pushed to the Wall', Report of the HRCP Fact-Finding Mission to Balochistan, October 2009, p. 5, http://hrcp-web.org/hrcpweb/wp-content/pdf/ff/14.pdf, (accessed on 3 March 2018).

13. Stephen Cohen, *The idea of Pakistan*, Brookings Institution, 2004, New Delhi: OUP, pp. 221–22.

14. Selig S. Harrison, 'Will Pakistan Break Up?', Carnegie Endowment for International Peace, 9 June 2009, https://carnegieendowment.org/files/0609_Remarks_Harrison.pdf, (accessed on 3 March 2018).

15. ICG Report, 2007, p. 13.

16. Naseer Dashti, *The Baloch Conflict with Iran and Pakistan*, Bloomington: Trafford Publishing, 2007, p. 236.

17. Zoya Anwer, 'Balochistan has no say in national policy making', *The News*, 12 February 2018, https://www.thenews.com.pk/print/279759-balochistan-has-no-say-in-national-policy-making, (accessed on 27 February 2018).

18. Selig S. Harrison, 'Ethnicity and Politics in Pakistan', in John Hutchinson and Anthony Smith, (eds), *Ethnicity*, Oxford: OUP 1996, p. 298, cited in Justin S. Dunne: *Crisis In Baluchistan: A Historical Analysis of the Baluch Nationalist Movement in Pakistan*, Monterey, California: Naval Postgraduate School, June 2006, p. 76.

19. Ibid.

20. The Foreign Policy Centre, 'Balochis on the Margins of History', London: *The Foreign Policy Centre*, November 2006, p. 6, https://fpc.org.uk/publications/balochis-of-pakistan-on-the-margins-of-history/, (accessed on 3 March 2018).

Index

About the Author

TILAK DEVASHER HAS TAKEN TO writing after he retired from the cabinet secretariat, Government of India, as special secretary in 2014. He is the author of two widely acclaimed books on Pakistan—*Pakistan: Courting the Abyss* (2016) and *Pakistan: At the Helm* (2018).

During his professional career with the cabinet secretariat, he specialized in security issues pertaining to India's neighbourhood. Post-retirement, he has continued to take a keen interest in India's neighbourhood, with special focus on Pakistan and Afghanistan. He has written articles for various national newspapers and magazines and has also appeared on TV shows on leading news channels like India Today, Times Now, CNN News18 and Rajya Sabha TV.

Devasher did his schooling from Mayo College, Ajmer, and studied history at St Stephen's College, Delhi, at the undergraduate level and at the University of Delhi at the postgraduate level.

He is currently a member of the National Security Advisory Board (NSAB) and a consultant with the Vivekananda International Foundation (VIF).